The Feast of the Sorcerer

The Feast

Practices of Consciousness and Power

Suniyam demon (baliya).

of the Sorcerer

Bruce Kapferer

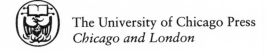
The University of Chicago Press
Chicago and London

BRUCE KAPFERER is head of the Department of Anthropology and
Archaeology at James Cook University of North Queensland, Australia.
He also maintains a post as professor of anthropology at University
College London.

The University of Chicago Press, Chicago 60637
The University of Chicago Press, Ltd., London
© 1997 by The University of Chicago
All rights reserved. Published 1997
Printed in the United States of America
06 05 04 03 02 01 00 99 98 97   1 2 3 4 5
ISBN: 0-226-42411-1 (cloth)
ISBN: 0-226-42413-8 (paper)

Library of Congress Cataloging-in-Publication Data

Kapferer, Bruce.
    The feast of the sorcerer : practices of consciousness and power /
Bruce Kapferer.
        p.   cm.
    Includes bibliographical references and index.
        ISBN 0-226-42411-1 (alk. paper). — ISBN 0-226-42413-8 (pbk. :
alk. paper)
        1. Magic, Sinhalese—Psychological aspects.   2. Magic, Sin-
halese—Social aspects.   3. Sri Lanka—Social life and customs.
I. Title.
BF1714.S55K36   1997
133.4′3′095493 — dc21
                                                            96-40337
                                                                 CIP

This book is printed on acid-free paper.

FOR CHANDRA VITARANA

Contents

Preface   xi

1   Introduction: Sorcery in Anthropology   1

    Definitions and Perspectives   8

    Issues in the Study of Sorcery   12

    Central Themes and Chapter Outline   21

2   Gods of Protection, Demons of Destruction: Sorcery
    and Modernity   27

    Mirrors to Power: Suniyam and the Demon-Deities   30

    Sorcery and Its Practices   36

    Domains of Sorcery   47

    *The Transmutations of Suniyam: Difference and
    Repetition*   55

3   Victim and Sorcerer: Tales of the City, the State, and
    Their Nemesis   61

    The Myths in Sociohistorical Context   62

*Myth 1: The Origin of the World (Loka Uppattiya or
Maha Badra Kalpa Uppattiya): A Story of the First
Victim of Sorcery and of the First Antisorcery Rite*   67

*Myth 2: Ambiguous Potencies: The Origin of Oddisa,
Master Ritualist and Sorcerer*   74

Conclusion: The Unity of Myth and Rite   81

4   The Suniyama: The Conquest of Sorcery and the Power
of Consciousness   83

PART I

*Suniyama Traditions and the Contemporary
Sociopolitical Context*   87

Knowledge and Power   89

The Decision for Performance   93

*Ritual Preparations and the Order of
Ritual Events*   96

5   The Suniyama: The Conquest of Sorcery and the Power
of Consciousness   105

PART II

A Suniyama Performance   106

The Rites of the Evening Watch   108

*Suniyam Kapakirima: The Gathering of Destructive and
Regenerative Power*   111

*The Consecration of the Patient: Seating, Anointment
(Nanumura), and Placing of Manikpala's Shawl*   113

*The Dances of Invitation to the Guardian Gods
(Deva Aradanava)*   125

The Rites of the Hatadiya   131

The Preparation of the Ritual Space   132

*Snakes, Fire, and Lotuses: The Setting Out of the
Seven Steps*   139

The Movement of the Seven Steps: The Path of Intentional Consciousness 149

The Events of the Morning and Midday Watches 156

A Farce of Brahmins: The Vadiga Patuna and the Celebration of Consciousness 158

Comedy, Consciousness, and Sociality 160

From Victim to World Maker 167

Valvalalu Tinduva: The Cutting of Sorcery's Bonds 167

The Final Judgment: The Impotence and Destruction of the Sorcerer 171

Ritual Practice: Virtuality and Actuality 176

Conclusion: The Suniyama and the Enormity of Sorcery 182

6 Sorcery and Sacrifice: Victims, Gifts, and Violence   185

Sacrifice as the Total Act 187

Sacrifice and the Violence of the Total Act 189

Victim, Violence, and Intentionality 191

Sacrifice, the Gift, and the Dynamic of Totality 199

The Agony of the Gift: Beyond Reciprocity 203

Sacrifice and the Paradox of Violence 206

Other Approaches to the Violence of Sacrifice: A Note 210

Sacrificial Violence and Contemporary Politics 213

From Rite to Shrine 219

7 Sorcery's Passions: Fear, Loathing, and Anger in the World   221

A Case of Sorcery's Fear 226

Fear and the Play of the Imagination 229

Anxiety, Fear, and Sociality 235

*The Contexts of the Shrines: Spaces of Death and Re-
birth*   238

The Qualities of the Shrines   240

The Pragmatics of the Shrines   243

Boiling Anger and the Cursing of Despair   247

Passions of Order and Resistance   253

Discourses of Dominance and Resistance   255

Sorcery, Culture, and the Passions   257

8   Faces of Power: Sorcery, Society, and the State   261

Sorcery as a Discourse of Power   263

Modalities of Power: War Machine, State, and Sorcery   274

*Power and Sorcery as the Dynamics of Exteriority and
Interiority*   275

Sorcery and Its Powers of Capture   282

The Dynamics of War Machine and State   283

The Sorcery of Power   287

The Terrorism of Order and Resistance   287

9   Thus, Man Is Always a Wizard to Man   298

Notes   305

References   335

Glossary   351

Index   361

Illustrations follow pages 12, 82, and 220.

Preface

THIS BOOK CONCENTRATES on practices of sorcery among Sinhalese Buddhists in Sri Lanka. I have chosen sorcery because it is one major practice found in different forms worldwide that seems to me to open out into broader issues of fundamental import in the understanding of human action and society. Not least among these are such enduring matters of scholarly and scientific concern as the nature of human consciousness and how human beings both make and conceive the construction of their existential realities. In my view, sorcery highlights that truly extraordinary capacity of human beings to create and destroy the circumstances of their existence. One of the most central features of sorcery's creative and destructive dynamic focuses on human beings as social beings, or as beings whose individual life courses are inextricably enmeshed with those of others. Sorcery practices address this fundamental aspect of human existential processes and expose some of the dynamics of human psychosocial formation. Here I extend the work of other scholars—anthropologists especially. But I aim to investigate sorcery as much more than an expression of inner psychological conflicts or a reflection of social and political forces. These are common ways of accounting for sorcery. While they are by no means a false analytical route, they tend to force sorcery practices into terms that are often distant from those of sorcery itself. Sorcery practices are denied their own rationality and, most important, the potential value of the understanding embedded in their practical knowledge. My aim is to show how sorcery practices expose some of the vital dynamics engaged in the way human beings construct their psychological and social realities.

The sorcery practices I explore are normal and routine activities in everyday life in which human beings address the crises of daily life and attempt to reorient themselves within it. In Sri Lanka, when people engage in sorcery, they seek to act directly on their life's circumstances insofar as they are affected by others who share their world. Their sorcery is concerned with a recentering of themselves in the world and frequently with a radical reassertion and recreation of their personal and social universe. Sorcery is both cosmogenic (as is expressly evident in its symbolism) and ontogenetic. It is engaged with the fundamental processes by which human beings construct and transform their life situations.

This is at the root of my fascination with sorcery practice. I am not concerned with the exotica of sorcery, with sorcery as a mystical and strange practice. These interests, in my view, often diminish the humanity that engages such practice and most of all refuse the insight that such practice produces into the human condition in general. Rather, I am interested in how sorcery reveals aspects vital to the way human beings constitute themselves and their realities, whether this be in Sri Lanka or elsewhere. Buddhist and other civilizational ideas as well as historical, cultural, and social factors specific to Sri Lanka obviously are fundamental in the accounts I give. However, I consider the practices I discuss to have relevance and authority for an understanding of the dynamics of human action beyond Sri Lanka's shores.

Through Sinhalese sorcery I address some issues at the heart of the contemporary discipline of anthropology and moreover attempt to demonstrate the significance of sorcery practices in the exploration of larger questions relating to the nature of human consciousness, the embodied character of human mental activities, the constitutive force of the human imaginary, the power of the passions, the dynamics of violence, and so forth. The very concept of sorcery is problematic. It is indicative of evil, of the supernormal, and is often used as a demeaning synonym for wrongheaded irrationality. But sorcery is too rarely investigated for the insights it harbors regarding the humancentric forces of humanly created realities. This is my aim, and furthermore, I try to show how sorcery practice suggests orientations to the study of human action that might be pertinent to those who would ordinarily deride sorcery practices.

This book stands on its own. However, it is part of my long-term ethnographic concern with Sinhalese Buddhist ritual, especially ritual dramas of healing or demon exorcism (*yak tovil*). This interest began with my first study, *A Celebration of Demons* (1983). In that work, based on fieldwork carried out in southern Sri Lanka in the seventies, I sought to interpret the structural process of Sinhalese exorcism by focusing on one of the more popular rites, the ceremony for the extraordinarily aggressive and violent Mahasona (the great cemetery demon). Although sorcery is an important feature of this rite and of other similar exorcism dramas, I did not explore it at any length. However, there was one major rite that I did briefly mention in the context of the general ethnography. This, known as the Suniyama (for the demon-deity of sorcery called Suniyam), had many features that did not fit with the Mahasona rite, and I noted this. There were structural complexities that seemed to be highly relevant to this rite alone which demanded more intensive fieldwork in the future.

Nonetheless, by sidelining this rite, I went against the advice of the Sinhalese ritual specialists who introduced me to their work and whose knowledge and ritual performances continue to fill me with admiration and wonder. They insisted that the Suniyama was the key to their work. They marked it out as the creation of the very first exorcist, the grand wizard and sacrificer Oddisa, whose practice contemporary exorcists regard as being at the root of their own. The Suniyama occupies a central role in this book, and thus some of the objections raised by exorcists over its earlier relative exclusion are redressed.

I referred to some of the results of subsequent work on the Suniyama in a later essay, *Legends of People, Myths of State* (1988a), on Sinhala Buddhist nationalism surrounding the 1983 anti-Tamil riots. The ethnography presented there was preliminary. One point of my essay was that the dynamic of the Suniyama sorcery rite, one that centers on sacrifice and reorigination, shares aspects of its process with the force of nationalism. I did not argue that contemporary nationalism followed the model of traditional exorcism rites, as some critics appear to have misconstrued my discussion. I made no statement to the effect that there was a causal connection between rite and riot, as a few scholars interpreted my argument. I referred to the former as in some ways a metaphor of the latter. My claim was that the ontogeny of nationalism—whose rhetoric drew on the mythic imaginaries of Sinhala history which are also integral to exorcisms such as the Suniyama—engaged similar dynamics in a highly inventive way which could in no way be reduced to the rite or to the vision of history presented in such ceremony. I was interested in the insight that the Suniyama, for example, yielded concerning the dynamics of power and the processes of personal and social regeneration and reordering. If there was a connection between rite and riot, this was in their highly different formation of a dynamics integral to both of them and thoroughly distinct in manifestation. I expand this point in this book.

However, it should be hardly surprising that there are shifts in perspective, as well as in issue and material, in this volume, written as it is over ten years later and in a very different climate of anthropological and general critical discourse. I make here some short comments with specific reference to *A Celebration of Demons,* the ethnography whose orientation influenced *Legends of People, Myths of State.*

Although this book is a self-contained ethnography, nonetheless, it assumes and builds on some of the argument of the earlier book. This is so particularly regarding the aesthetics of exorcism, specifically, the music, dance, and drama. I do not explore these aesthetic forms in the same depth in this study. One recent scholar (Scott 1994) argues that they have less importance than I give them. I am in total disagreement with him. This is especially so following my more recent research on the Suniyama, where the aesthetic of rite reveals its critical role in the formations of perception and the reconstitution of consciousness. Thus, this new book presents material that expands earlier discussion as it introduces a diversity of ethnography relevant not just to sorcery but to a wider complex of ritual practices in Sri Lanka.

In *A Celebration of Demons,* I described the dynamic of exorcism as following a hierarchical logic, the demonic becoming progressively tamed and subordinated within encompassing and unifying totalizing orders commanded by the Buddha and the major Sinhalese deities. The materials presented here do not contradict this perspective. However, they demonstrate what can be seen as the overordered and totalizing orientation of the earlier argument (see Taussig 1987, whose criticism is to this effect). The ultimate impossibility of such totalization is one of the key messages of sorcery. Sorcery, as I suggest in this book, simultaneously makes hierarchies and destroys them, at once crushing and fragmenting the dynamics of encompassing order. Sorcery is a force that springs against the enclosing and protective orders of hierarchy. It is a combination of foundational and primordial potencies from which hierarchy and order emerge and into whose void they collapse. The tension of sorcery as simultaneously the unresolvable dynamic of structure and antistructure, with neither ultimately dominant, constitutes the tension of the overall discussion.

Methodologically, I remain committed to certain features of situational analysis and the extended-case method developed by my teachers and colleagues at Manchester, especially Gluckman, Turner, and Mitchell. This perspective is directed to the logic of practices or the chaotic structures formed in everyday routine and not-so-routine activity. The approach is distinctive in its aversion to using practices merely to illustrate abstract theoretical or cultural ideas. Rather, it attends to practice in all its lived messiness and as the ground from which human beings continuously form and re-form their realities. My approach to Sinhalese sorcery practice expands within this potential of the situational perspective of Gluckman's Manchester School. Furthermore, I attempt to enter into the discursive terms of Sinhala sorcery practice and to give it wider authority than a situational approach might have permitted. Here I go in a different direction from that in *A Celebration of Demons*. In that study I was concerned to demonstrate the value of certain orientations then being developed in symbolic anthropology and related interpretivist orientations. The argument of exorcist practice was relatively subdued. In this ethnography I give far greater primacy to the discourse of practice, though not so much to abstract reflections on practice—which is rare for the exorcist specialists among whom I worked—as to the discourse which is embedded in practical activity itself.

In line with this emphasis, I develop further a phenomenological approach, one that, I should insist, is at a distance from those applications of phenomenology that consider human activity capable of being read as some kind of text—as in hermeneutics or the interpretivist approach sharpened in the work of Geertz (see Kersenboom 1995 for a critique of Ricoeur and others and their text-driven analyses). The redirection is attendant on a move away from human activity as performance, a central concept in *A Celebration,* to a stress on practice.

Some readers of this book are likely to complain that my engagement of phenomenology to understanding the import of Sinhalese sorcery practices constrains their work within a Eurocentric and Eurodominant frame. My doing so contradicts my intention to give exorcists and sorcerers voice through their practice, because it is confined to the authority of discourses developed in Western history and is ultimately validated with reference to commanding ideas of Western thought. This kind of criticism of anthropological ethnography, of course, has been well recognized by anthropologists well before current postmodern debates, which often appear to intensify the relativism of much earlier argument in anthropology. I believe that no ethnography can escape such or similar charges, and this inability is part of the eventually impossible character of anthropological understanding and perhaps all investigations of the forces at work in human creation. But I do not make this observation by way of excuse so as to proceed unaffected by important recent criticism in anthropology.

I should say at once that the phenomenological concepts and orientations of this study are intended to bring about wider consideration in anthropology and elsewhere of the possibilities of practice in a Buddhist world that already has much in common with certain directions in Western phenomenology. As others have noted, Buddhist and Hindu reflections in practice on the problematics of human existence have a high degree of resonance with many phenomenological notions. Western phenomenology is very much a Johnny-come-lately.

This comment is not made to legitimate my stance; phenomenology is all right because it is "culture-near." Rather, what I claim is that it is an orientation directed to bringing out or disclosing the import of the phenomena of human existence as these are manifested through human activity and practice. It is a method whereby the human processes involved in the formations of human construction comprising the realities of the life worlds of human being are revealed. A phenomenology has no authority or truth value either in itself as a theory or as a form of knowledge superordinate to those whose knowledge is disclosed or takes form through its method. In this sense, phenomenology is unlike many kinds of anthropological or general social science theory which are concerned to prove their worth by demonstrating that the empirical world conforms to the fundamental postulates and predictions of their systems of explanation or understanding. This is the way of a variety of anthropological functionalisms, of applications of Marxist materialism, and Weberian idealism, as well as theories of deep structure such as Freudian psychoanalysis and structuralism. The phenomenological approach I use and develop through the Sinhalese sorcery materials holds out no ultimate truth in itself. Here it has some affinity with recent approaches in deconstructionism, which often grow, sometimes reactively, in the context of phenomenological traditions. Both deconstruction and phenomenology are directed neither to dominate nor to loom over the materials at hand, dictating the import of human practices and denying them their own voice. The various phenomenological perspectives I use are concerned to open up space for the human phenomena in question, to disclose their dynamics of existential formation. Through such phenomenological (and deconstructionist) orientation, I aim to show what Sinhalese sorcery may disclose about general issues of debate centering on how human beings form themselves and their realities into existence. I attempt this in a way that does not remove from sorcery practices the full force of their own authority.

I collected the material for the book at various times over the past twenty-five years. Much of it is based on intensive fieldwork between 1984 and 1991 in the Weligama, Akuressa, and Morawaka areas of south Sri Lanka and also in the capital of Colombo. Throughout this period I worked closely with Mr. Chandra Vitarana, whose ideas on his own culture were continually instructive. Many of the preliminary arguments founded on the ethnography were worked out in constant discussion with

Chandra. Chandra died tragically in 1996 and this book is dedicated to his memory. I have lost a companion whose thirst for knowledge and marvelous humor will be greatly missed.

The idea of the book took shape when I was a fellow of the Netherlands Institute for Advanced Studies in 1991–1992. Saskia Kersenboom invited me to participate in her orality seminar organized at the Institute throughout the period of my fellowship. This enabled me to develop my thoughts with all the best facilities at hand and in the midst of a beautiful and relaxing setting. My thanks must go to all the Institute's staff for making the stay so enjoyable. Saskia's enthusiastic interest in the Sinhalese sorcery materials and her great knowledge and passion for her own South Indian experience were inspirational. Her own approach to South Indian dance has been enormously helpful, especially her focus on the centrality of practice. The term *knowledge-practice* that I occasionally use is her notion. Professor Rene Devisch, also a fellow of the Institute, contributed profoundly in discussion. Rene's insistence on the ritualist recognition of the reoriginating potency of chaotic forces seemed to me to give new direction to arguments present in Victor Turner's work (based, interestingly, on similar ethnography) and to expand the possibilities of a more general perspective.

My colleagues and students in the Department of Anthropology, University College London, provided the most important intellectual base for the development of the various arguments. The Anthropology Department is a rich and stimulating environment which encompasses a broad spectrum of discussion in anthropology, and its influence is reflected in this book. In particular, Allen Abramson, Fred Brett, Phil Burnham, John Gledhill, Danny Miller, Nanneke Redclift, and Mike Rowlands contributed in a variety of direct and indirect ways. I am most grateful to Buck Schieffelin, who was always patient with my disagreements and saw and encouraged many directions of thought. Some of the chapters were presented in preliminary form to the students in my Advanced Anthropology Seminar at University College. Their reactions were extremely challenging. I have tried to meet most of their questions, and I am in their debt.

The H. F. Guggenheim Foundation provided some support in the form of a small grant to explore aspects of the violent situation in Sri Lanka during 1990. Karen Colvard, Senior Program Officer for the Foundation, constantly showed enthusiasm for the theoretical implications of the sorcery materials. Upon my completion of the final draft, Karen organized a small group of scholars to criticize the result. Those gathered—Tom Csordas, Terry Evens, Jonathan Friedman, Don Handelman, Bruce Knauft, and Jos Platenkamp—caused me to try to sharpen the arguments.

Some of them are still offering useful reactions up to the moment of going to press.

I must single out my long-term friend and intellectual companion, Don Handelman, for particular mention. He made the effort to join the group even though he was experiencing the most intense personal anguish through the recent death of his deeply loved wife, Lea. Don has always been my hardest and most valued critic, and so he proved on this occasion and despite his loss. Don has thorough knowledge of my materials, and I have tried to answer at least some of his disagreements and to extend a little in the directions he suggested. He should know how much I respect his compassion and his thought.

Others have been most generous with their time and interest. Jorgen Anderson invited me for a short stay at the Institute for Cultural Studies at Aarhus University in 1991 to discuss our mutual interest in Sinhalese exorcism and sorcery. These discussions got me writing. Roland Kapferer has shown great interest in the development of the argument throughout the writing. His own research in philosophy has been immeasurably stimulating. He managed to resist my initial skepticism and convince me of the value of the work of Gilles Deleuze, which should be evident in this volume. Mahen Vaithianathan, my frequent host in Colombo, longtime friend, and confidant, has constantly contributed to a discussion of issues raised in this book. Desmond Mallikarachchi was not only a regular sounding board but was full of illuminating ideas on the possibilities of Sinhalese ritual practices. Professor Punchi Banda, then on secondment (temporary transfer) from Peradeniya to SOAS, was especially helpful. He was alive to a host of linguistic nuances, and his own knowledge of village ritual practice was highly instructive. Dianne Weir, Felix Von Schmidt, Peter Flugel, and Donnatella Bernstein commented on the drafts and caused me to clarify my analysis and shift analytical direction. Jadran Mimica, Rohan Bastin, Kirsten Alnaes, and Judith Kapferer always have reacted usefully to my arguments, as have the late Newton Gunasinghe and I. V. Edirisinghe. Niloo Abeyeratne has gone through the manuscript in detail and has made many corrections.

S. J. Tambiah, always supportive, Alfred Gell, Charles Hallisey, and Marshall Sahlins read the text and made highly pertinent suggestions. Marshall, even at a fairly late stage, identified tensions in the analysis which I am not certain need resolution but definitely need more discussion. His investigations into the generative structures of practice have been highly influential.

I am grateful to T. David Brent and Margaret Mahan of the University of Chicago Press for their guidance and encouragement throughout the publication process.

Overall, I am in the deepest debt to the Berava communities of southern Sri Lanka and especially the *gurunanse*s, or ritual masters, among them. They have always been generous with their hospitality and particularly with their deep and wide knowledge. The Berava community, in my view, is in possession of great knowledge that still perhaps does not receive the recognition that it should for an understanding of Sri Lanka's traditions. I am convinced that their knowledge has enormous importance for human beings everywhere. I hope this book—even with the inaccuracies that Beravas are certain to detect—will convey some sense of my awe and respect for their work. It is my hope that this book will communicate some of the reasons why they should be held in high regard and will encourage others in Sri Lanka and elsewhere to learn from them and to expand their practical knowledge. This book is my small gift to the Beravas and other ritualists in Sri Lanka in return not just for the knowledge they imparted but for the way they have sustained my continuing excitement with anthropology and its potential.

1

Introduction

Sorcery in Anthropology

> *Thus, man is always a wizard to man, and the social world is at first magical.*
>
> Jean-Paul Sartre, *The Emotions*, 1948, p. 84

SORCERY IS THROUGH AND THROUGH concerned with the forces of human action and with the responsibility that human beings must bear for their life situation as a result of such action. Above all, sorcery practices concentrate on the contingency of human existence and of human projects. Such contingency (including the fragility and uncertainty of life and its endeavors) is founded on the recognition in the ideas and practices of most sorcery worldwide that human beings act in the context of other human beings whose activities affect the life and projects of any particular human being. Sorcery in most descriptions asserts that human beings are embroiled with others, that they are often mutually oriented and share similar aims. Thus, they inhabit fields of intersecting human intentionalities that have existential consequence for them. In effect, the understandings of sorcery do not conceive of human beings as isolates but as engaged in a web of affective ties or relations. Widespread understandings of sorcery—whether they are European views of the witch's night journey or the African Azande's vision of the fiery spark of the attacking witch's consciousness traveling through the evening sky toward its victim—emphasize that human beings are at once individuals and beings who transcend and transgress the boundaries and space of their own and others' organic individuality. In other words, sociality is immanent in the fact of human existence. Sorcery practices concentrate on the paradox of the impetus to sociality, stressing the overcoming and possession of particular persons and their projects by the activities of others. Sorcery often takes the human body and its *primacy of perception* as foundational of sociality and of the paradoxes of social existence. Among Sinhalese, the senses through which human beings extend and realize their existence in the world—those of sound, smell, taste, touch, and sight—become, in the notions of sorcery, the processes whereby human beings are disrupted and inhabited by others to ill-effect.

These aspects of sorcery are elements of what Sartre referred to as the magicality of human existence. Human life is magical in the sense that human beings span the space that may otherwise individuate them or separate them from others. Their magical conjunction with other human beings in the world—imaginative, creative, and destructive—is at the heart of human existence. The magicality of human beings is in their embodied passionate extension toward others and in their construction of the shapes of those realities to which they are directed and in which they are transcended. Sorcery, as Sartre intimates, accentuates vital dimensions of the way human beings themselves explicitly or implicitly construct their realities as psychosocial agents, as well as the paradoxes and problematics of such construction. Sorcery as highlighting the magicality of human existence, and social existence in particular, is the central concern of this book.

Linked to this is sorcery as a practice that is quintessentially directed to the lived-in world and the crises of human beings within it. The ethnography of sorcery everywhere describes the presence of sorcery at vital junctures in human lives: at times of sickness and death, at periods of achievement or success, and in failure and acute abjection. It accompanies the personal and social upheavals of conflict and of war. The appeal to sorcery at such critical moments accents its importance for the exploration of how human beings make and break their life worlds.

Within the modern history of anthropology, the phenomenology of sorcery—how sorcery appears or is manifested in a great diversity of practices—has held a respectable position in the articulation and development of the anthropological project. The comprehension of sorcery, as I will explain at greater length, has been important in the representation of the realities of other peoples and in the demonstration of an anthropological expertise to reveal the rationality behind the apparently irrational. The concern with sorcery is at the root of the establishment of contemporary ethnographically based anthropology: that is, of an anthropology founded in firsthand, intimate (participant) observation of the everyday lives of peoples at the periphery of the history of those metropolitan centers, usually in the West, which gave rise to those attitudes and philosophies that have achieved particular shape in the modern physical, biological, and social sciences.

Two ethnographic studies at the start of fieldwork-based anthropology stand out. In both, the phenomenon of sorcery plays a critical role. I refer to Bronislaw Malinowski's *Argonauts of the Western Pacific* (1922) and Evans-Pritchard's *Witchcraft, Oracles, and Magic among the Azande* (1937). These studies in many ways set the path not just for the anthropological exploration of sorcery, especially among British social anthropologists, but for the analytical direction that much anthropology was to take as a whole. This was especially true with regard to Malinowski's work. His description of the Trobriand Islanders and their involvement in the long-distance voyaging of the *kula* trade in the South Pacific became a classic for many of the issues raised by anthropologists concerning the principles underlying social formation. Marcel Mauss's famous essay *The Gift* and a constantly expanding body of work in anthropology on the *kula* and apparently related systems of sociosymbolic exchange have maintained the significance of the *kula* materials in ongoing conceptual and theoretical debates in anthropology.

But anthropological argument about the *kula* aside, Trobriand discourse surrounding the *kula* indicates a powerful ethno-ontology concerning the formation of human being and the creation by human beings of their own lived-in realities. The myths and practices of magic and sorcery announce the dynamic of this ontology or the vital processes engaged in the construction and destruction of human beings and their realities. Let me focus on the *kula* momentarily to underline the major directions in this book, which addresses the specifics of sorcery practice in an effort to investigate and reopen issues at the center of the anthropological understanding of how human beings form their worlds.

In *Argonauts of the Western Pacific,* Malinowski relates that the oldest myths of the Trobriand Islanders tell how their ancestors emerged from under the earth at a place called Boyowa, "in full decoration, equipped with magic, belonging to social divisions, and obeying definite laws and customs" (Malinowski 1922:304). Other stories, part of the same complex of myths, recount the origins of sorcery, of love myths, of the flying canoe, and of *kula,* the ceremonial system of perilous long-distance trade.

The *kula* is far more than trade in any narrow sense. The dangerous *kula* expeditions are cosmogenic (and ontogenetic). They involve activities which are conceived of by Trobrianders as generative of the orderings of life, as constitutive of a humancentric totality that is brought into existence through human action. Metaphors of seduction, sexuality, and procreation flood the *kula* and are vital in the formation of the temporality and spatiality of the life worlds which have human beings at their center. The *kula* is focused on the obsessive desire to possess and exchange shell armbands and necklaces, whose value is in a beauty and a history of ownership evocative of the principles at the heart of *kula*. In their *kula* activities, the voyagers both (re)generate the *kula* (the living metaphor for the totality of existence) and (re)create and expand themselves as human beings of fame and renown who are not only critical in a set of political and social relations but are constitutive of them (see Weiner 1976; Munn 1986).

Sorcery, which embraces an enormous variety of spells and other ritual acts, is vital in *kula*. Malinowski describes how through the learning of sorcery knowledge *kula* traders can induce the current owners of highly sought-after *kula* shells to relinquish their prized possessions and to enter into partnership and the reciprocities of exchange. The sorcery has the power to enter into the very consciousness of the other, to open up the other to the charms and seductions of the Trobriand argonaut, to create a mutuality of desire on the basis of which a relation can be formed, and from which bounteousness and social and political replenishment can flow. The power of the sorcery must overcome extreme dangers, of the sort memorized in legend.

Malinowski tells one story in which not only did the vital *kula* partnerships fail to take root but also the voyagers were killed and eaten. The intentionality at the heart of social formation did not germinate into the mutuality of social relations. As a consequence, the very being of the voyagers was destroyed, a significance of their cannibalization. Of course, the *kula* symbolizes (for the Trobrianders and for anthropology) the fundamental sociality of human beings; it symbolizes their capacity in their very constitution as human beings to form social relations and the immanence of society in the fact of human existence. This is a significance of the Trobriand origin myths and the Trobriand desire for *kula*.

The Trobriand orientation toward the *kula* and the generative potencies of their activities which give rise to and reinvigorate Trobriand worlds manifest features of what I explore throughout this book as the dynamics of intentionality. This is a concept that I develop from Edmund Husserl (among others)[1] and that is at the heart of the phenomenological direction I take in the analysis of sorcery practices. Broadly, by intentionality I merely mean that human beings are directed toward the ever-shifting horizons of their existence. The forces of human action are emergent in the directional thrust of human beings and simultaneously in the horizonal pull of that to which human beings are oriented. In other words, the intentionality of human beings is a dynamic force of their being-in-the-world, of their world-oriented action, the worlds in which they are projected having force upon their activities.

I must stress that in my use of the term *intentionality* there is no sense of an underlying reason, motive, or guiding value. Such meanings are implicit in the ordinary English word *intention,* which should not be confused with my application of the term *intentionality.* When I write of intentionality I am merely stating that human beings as a fact of their existence are directed into the world. This is all. I imply no essential or underlying interest or reason in this directedness.

As I argue, meaning and value (and also social and political relations) are immanent in the intentionality of human existence. They are materialized in the growth of the consciousness of human beings achieved in the course of their intentional activities; value arises from these activities and becomes part of the way human beings simultaneously constitute themselves as subjects and come to form and experience the objectified nature of their existential realities. Reality or the world of lived existence as it is constructed culturally and historically does not start with the subject, nor is it an object that springs from individually isolated subjective creation. Both subjectivity and its objects are simultaneous, neither one being prior to the other. I develop this point later in my discussion of the ethnography of this book. For the present I note that there is a correspondence to what I am saying here with the "argument" of the *kula.* The directionality of the *kula* adventurers toward the horizons of their existence gives rise to the formation or revitalization of social and political relations through the intense activation of energies embodied in human existence. Through the intentional activity of the *kula* voyagers, the Trobrianders recreate themselves and their realities which are the condition for their existential continuity.

The power of human intentionality is double-headed. As it may extend toward the formation of social relations, it can also be a force leading to their destruction or rejection. Human intentionality is enduringly ambiguous, and it is this feature that sorcery highlights (and which it may be directed to overcome) and that is demonstrated by the sorcery spells, songs, and rites that Malinowski records. In other words, sorcery deals with the forces of intentionality and its transmutations that are at the heart of the creation by human beings of their social and political worlds. This is implicit in Malinowski's choice of title for his *kula* ethnography.

Malinowski undoubtedly wished to stress the perils of the voyagers and to draw a parallel between the Trobriand seafarers and their journey through the island landscape of the South Pacific, on the one hand, and the heroes of ancient Greek myths, on the other hand: the quest of Jason and his heroic companions on the Argo for the Golden Fleece of the ram sacrificed to Zeus.[2] But, of course, the central theme of this quest involves Jason's love and rejection of the sorceress, the Princess Medea,[3] and her terrible revenge. Medea is the instrument of Jason's success in stealing the prize of the Golden Fleece from Medea's father, whom she betrays, an action which also involves her slaughter of her brother as she flees with her lover. Her powers are engaged to the restoration of Jason's heritage, but he spurns Medea in favor of a younger princess more appropriate to Jason's political ambitions. In Euripides' famous version of the story, Medea exacts the most terrible vengeance, killing the young princess, who dies an agonizing death when she wears Medea's gift of a poisonous cloak, and slaughtering her own and Jason's two children.

Medea expresses many of the agent powers and ambiguities of sorcery and the sorcerer that I pursue here. Medea is thoroughly amoral, at once the figure of devotion and loyalty and also the source of betrayal. She engages her sorcery to avenge and to protect. Medea has the capacity to invoke the life-giving and life-destroying possibilities of the gift which lies at the heart of social relations. She is the life-giving and life-taking sacrificer, the medium articulating and inverting different modalities of being, the force of conversion and the agency of transgression, transformation and reorigination.

The ethnography of the sorcery practices among Sinhalese Buddhists in Sri Lanka is a far cry from the worlds of the ancient Mediterranean or the modern Trobriand Islands, although there are similarities in their dynamic. One of the great Sinhala sorcery myths concerns a sorceress, Kuveni, who is rejected by her lover—an ambiguous character like Jason—whom she assists to power. Some of the main demon-gods of sorcery are traders or people closely associated with trade (or who build their character through a play on the metaphors of trade) whose potencies are active, like the sorcery of the *kula,* at moments of danger and risk, who facilitate transgression or guard against it, and who open up paths for the development of action and the establishment of a mutuality of interest and remove or subdue the obstacles that may bar the way. It is with these aspects of sorcery, among numerous others, that I am concerned.

I aim to explore the specificities of the dynamics of contemporary Sinhala sorcery practices but with a concern to consider more general questions concerning the crisis that is human being. Undoubtedly the history and culture of Sri Lanka give particular shape to Sinhalese sorcery practices. They are constituted within Buddhist discourses articulated within a historical region of diverse and changing religious orientation. Moreover, they bear the marks of the specific political and social forces affecting life in the island. Sinhalese sorcery practices yield insight into these processes. I suggest that the rites of sorcery, for example, indicate and expand possibilities not immediately evident in abstract Buddhist doctrinal statements; I also suggest that they yield insight into modes of class suffering and into political processes relevant to the ordering of state power and resistance to it.

I claim that the very particularities of sorcery in Sri Lanka constitute it as a practice especially sensitive to issues of a broader kind that transcend the specific case. Thus, the practices contribute toward a general understanding of the nature of mind and consciousness. Without doubt Buddhist cosmology and orientation account for the emphasis on these aspects in some of the practices that I explore. These operate conceptions of sorcery, for instance, as above all an attack on the body of consciousness and thus the capacity of sorcery victims to act. My contention is that such practices and the problems that they confront have implications for the understanding of human processes beyond the Sri Lankan Buddhist world of these sorcery practices. Furthermore, the very cultural and historical particularity which structures the dynamics and problematics of the practices I examine makes them especially important for the investigation of more general issues, such as the nature of human consciousness and the processes of its development and use.

Overall I intend this study as a journey, facilitated through the practices of sorcery, which is oriented to some of the questions that are at the root of modern anthropology and, like the *kula* for the Trobrianders, maintain its excitement and what I regard as its importance among those disciplines that seek to understand the way human beings weave the realities in which they condition themselves. Thus, the book addresses some of the conventional interests of anthropologists—the ambiguities of the gift, the genesis of person and the social through sacrifice and rite, the social energies of the passions, the alienating and constituting forces of power—as these are acutely problematized in sorcery. A major objective is to pursue the lead of the practices themselves and perhaps to expose new directions in an anthropological quest to unravel the ways human beings form themselves and their realities.

What I have to say about sorcery is framed by extensive discussion on the subject within anthropology which embeds a variety of assumptions and assertions about not only sorcery practices but also human activity and how it may be studied. These have influenced aspects of the arguments I develop here. I hope that the reader will achieve some understanding of anthropological approaches regarding sorcery and my position within them. This should help to explain why I take some of the descriptive and analytical tacks that I do.

Definitions and Perspectives

I should make it clear from the start that although I begin with the general category of sorcery, my objective is effectively to demolish the value of the descriptive and phenomenal category of sorcery as a thing in itself. In other words, I address a kind of human practice which anthropologists and other scholars can recognize and delineate as being of a distinct order, but which in the final analysis refuses the categorical or phenomenal confinement that is imposed on it. The practices of sorcery break such bonds and relate to a great range of routine human practices that might otherwise be held apart from them. This is evident in Malinowski's famous ethnographies, where what he describes as sorcery appears to infuse everything.

However, as a working beginning I use the word *sorcery* very broadly to cover those practices, often described as magical, that are concerned to harness and manipulate those energies and forces which are centered in human beings and which extend from them to intervene—heal, harm, or protect—in the action and circumstance of other human beings. I subsume in this general usage the distinctions which in some situations may exist between sorcery and witchcraft, as, for example, in the Trobriands (see especially Tambiah 1985; Munn 1986).[4] Conventionally in anthropology, sorcery is conceived as a highly conscious practice involving the manipulation of particular knowledge and skills, whereas witchcraft frequently works beneath the level of reflective action and is subconscious. Sorcery is the work of specialists, whereas witchcraft may be practiced by anyone and everyone.[5] Among Sinhalese, activities that might appear to be distinct in these terms are more fuzzy in practice. They are, in effect, different dimensions of the same propensities in the action of human beings.

There are at least two major difficulties in the definition and use of the term *sorcery* that must be addressed immediately. The first concerns its ideological use, especially in a discourse of dominance. The second relates to the implication of an essential uniformity underlying a diversity of practice present in the application of a singular definition.

The very term *sorcery* is suspect, like a great many other labels in anthropology, such as *magic,* with which sorcery is often classed. They are laden with the prejudices of nineteenth-century European debate, the context out of which modern anthropology formed (see Tambiah 1990). This is balanced by the present-day valorization of sorcery and magic in some high anthropological circles, particularly among adherents of postmodern trends (see Sardan 1992). Some profess to have great intimacy with the ways of the sorcerer and to have unfettered hidden secrets and unmasked the falsity of those rationalist agents and agencies of dominant political, scientific, and technological powers that rejected sorcery's wisdom. Such orientations, which, as Sardan explains, place great stress on the writing of sorcery and other things in the intense first person, are often the inverse fantasies of a metropolitan and bourgeois authority: one that is extensive with an earlier prejudiced rejection to which such positions declare their opposition. I distance myself and this work from either orientation.

Anthropological interest in sorcery and magic took root at a time of Western expansion and colonial domination. It arose in a scientific climate alive with the spirit of Darwinism and concerned with the application of evolutionist thought to cultural, social, and political matters. The investigation of sorcery and magic, indeed the labeling of practices as *sorcery* and *magic,* was part of a philosophical and growing anthropological enterprise with huge political undertones. Their study was integral to the more general engagement of knowledge in the legitimation of the imperial domination of the West (the site of reason) over the subordinated rest (the site of unreason).

Most anthropologists have sought to distance themselves from the colonial heritages of the nineteenth and early twentieth centuries. However, the rooting out of these demons of the past is still a major enterprise. The anthropology of sorcery has been an important area where anthropologists have attempted to overturn colonialist and other forms of dominant knowledge and practice. Sorcery unsettles complacency and is a disturber of systems of control and order. In the hands of many anthropologists it has sometimes performed this function well.

The broad point which anthropologists pursued, mainly in the British tradition of social anthropology, is the social nature of sorcery. Sorcery is first and foremost a practice which grasps all manner of experience as a social phenomenon. It is to be understood in its historical and cultural context. This position was announced most strongly in Evans-Pritchard's justly celebrated ethnography of the Azande. It follows conceptual lines developed by Durkheim and especially Mauss and is aimed expressly against what appeared to be the evolutionist, mentalist, and acontextual perspectives of earlier scholars such as Levy-Bruhl and Sir James Frazer. Evans-Pritchard and later generations of anthropologists strove to redress an imbalance. They tried not to impose what they interpreted as uniquely Western conceptions, heavily influenced by a culture of Christianity. Furthermore, some tried to separate sorcery from science or the powerful tendency to measure sorcery against scientific rationalist canons—an orientation still staunchly defended in some anthropological circles (e.g., Gellner 1974). The irrationalities of scientific practice were occasionally celebrated, and some anthropologists (as well as philosophers, e.g., Feyerabend 1978) enjoyed discovering definite affinities in the methodologies of science and sorcery. Sorcery was denied as a primitive precursor to either science or modern technology.

Also attacked was any notion that sorcery demonstrated a fundamental anxiety and fear in human existence of the kind that gave rise to and was overcome by religion. Earlier anthropologists (e.g., Frazer 1890; Tylor 1889) had seen sorcery as a manifestation of the primitive awe of human beings before the magnitude of the universe and as evidence of a terror of the unknown. This was the ground for the emergence of religion and for the final authority of rational science that eliminated such fear through the amassing of objective knowledge.

These orientations to sorcery still linger, sometimes behind the approaches of those who would disparage them. They are implicit in the sacred: profane distinctions of Durkheim and Mauss. The notion of primitive science and of sorcery beliefs and practices as exemplifying the stubborn irrationality of those who remain outside the scientific orders also remain current in modern anthropology.

One way around such problems has been the strategy of cultural and historical relativism. A relativist current, most strongly evident in American cultural anthropology and supported by postmodernist trends antagonistic to Western intellectual and political hegemony, is oriented toward abandoning terms like *sorcery* and *magic* altogether and using indigenous labels.

Methodologically, there is merit to this position. The term *sorcery* as a descriptive label can group together, even for one context, a highly diverse set of practices that may not be reducible into one term. What I class as sorcery among Sinhalese Buddhists is highly diverse and has some of this methodological difficulty. However, there are at least two popular indigenous terms frequently used interchangeably (*huniyam* and *kodivina;* see chapter 2) that are used by Sinhalese for most events that I have broadly defined as sorcery.

A second and far more powerful reason to adopt indigenous terms is to break with the prejudices concerning the anthropological exploration of sorcery which are deeply ingrained in the practice of the discipline. The move also establishes that the phenomenon explored must be primarily understood in terms of the historical and cultural circumstances of its production and use.

I have chosen to stay with the term *sorcery* and with other difficult terms in the anthropological battery (e.g. *magic, exorcism, sacrifice,* etc.) while acknowledging the general point.

The term *sorcery,* for all its deficiencies, is a general term that places particular ethnographic observations into a comparative context. Such comparison recognizes difference but not uniqueness. The aim is to arrive at broader understanding without destroying specificity. Moreover, the study of particular cases in their historical and cultural context—a relativizing—is intended to open up possibilities ignored or suppressed when assuming and asserting already authorized or established perspectives. The phenomenon in its specificity should be explored before declaring the relevance or not of already accepted understanding. Such a relativizing orientation does not involve adding another case of difference to an expanding ethnographic museum of the exotic.

This latter style of relativism, of which anthropologists are the supreme exponents, is content to declare that the world is a sea of difference and that is all there is to it. The approach has benefits, one being that it continually threatens, with the maddening exception, the analytical and theoretical hegemony of the opinions that spread from powerful centers. This anarchic spirit in anthropology is one with which I am personally in accord. Nonetheless, the claim of anthropologists to speak with or present the countervoices of the periphery is fraught with traps, as much of the debate surrounding postmodernism in anthropology reveals (see, e.g., Clifford and Marcus 1986; Clifford 1988; Rosaldo 1989; Comaroff and Comaroff 1991; Kapferer 1988b; Sangren 1988).

My interest, however, is not to remain in the dark cave of methodological relativism. Rather, my direction is to consider sorcery practices among Sinhalese Buddhists as disclosing dimensions of human action which may be more obscured in apparently different or similar practices elsewhere. Overall, then, I take the relativist (in fact antirelativist) tactic of Dumont, as demonstrated in his Indian and later European researches. He is concerned to reveal more general possibilities without denying the radical distinction or difference of the ideological or cultural practices he examines. Thus, Dumont exposes principles in Indian ideological forms (cultural thought and practice) which continue, although suppressed or transformed, in cultural/historical contexts that overtly eschew such practices (see Dumont 1980, 1986; Kapferer 1988a, 1989). In such a perspective, relativism is not opposed to a more general understanding.

Furthermore, the phenomenon, in this case sorcery, is not treated as uniform but is explored through its diversity.

Issues in the Study of Sorcery

Evans-Pritchard insisted that sorcery in non-Western enclaves had little to do with sorcery and magic as they had come to be defined and grasped in Western historical contexts. I think the point was overdrawn. Thus, Evans-Pritchard (1937: 22, 34) in his famous account presents the Azande view that witchcraft is a substance originating somewhere near the small intestine which at night can be seen as a tiny spark of light traveling toward its victim (in my terms, the flight of intentionality). The European folk traditions are not dissimilar with their accounts of night journeys and night battles. The traditions of other cultures abound with similar examples, not least the traditions of sorcery practice in Sri Lanka. However, Evans-Pritchard's distinction was a positive attempt to separate other systems from the glare of a post-Enlightenment prejudice against all things that smacked of superstition. It was also part of the liberalizing move in anthropology (integral in its relativism) to in fact discover the actual rationality of practices that to outsiders appeared nonsensical and mystical. In other words, the ethnographic other was just as much a site of rationality (or irrationality and absurdity) as any other group of human beings, but only once the beliefs and practices had been understood in their own terms. Both Evans-Pritchard (1937), and Malinowski (1922, 1935, 1948) earlier for Trobriand Islanders, insisted that sorcery and other magical practices are pragmatic and not alternatives to other down-to-earth practices. Sorcery and magic are integral to ordinary and grounded knowledge. Sorcery did not necessarily obscure, mystify, or minimize the importance of hard knowledge and indeed was in itself a form of hard knowledge when examined in context. In Malinowski's example, Trobriand gardening magic is critical to the successful outcome of the application of sound gardening technique. The emphasis is on the "materiality" of magic and sorcery, an orientation that I develop in different vein later.

The strategy of anthropologists, stemming largely from the work of Evans-Pritchard and Malinowski (1948), was to use exotic practices from the periphery to critically pursue metropolitan concerns. A major focus was the nature of science. It was a metadiscourse on the nature of anthropology's own practice. That is, sorcery played a role in the demonstration of anthropology as itself a science despite its subject matter (a program that Radcliffe-Brown laid out for British social anthropology). This was

Plate I. *Suniyam vidiya*, the Mahasammata Palace

Plate 2. The sorcerer's viper and the lotus path: the course of the *hatadiya*

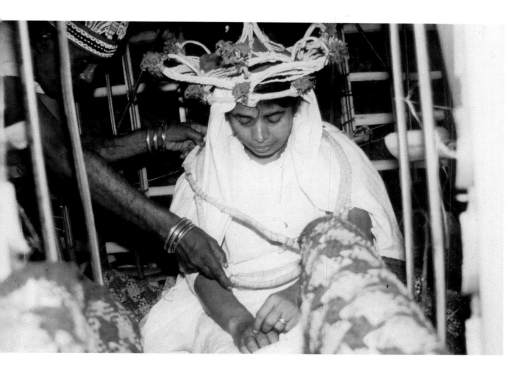

Plate 3. Within the Atamagala: the *valvalalu*. The patient, wearing Manikpala's crown, is shackled by sorcery's bonds.

Plate 4. The *vadiga patuna*, a farce of Brahmins

also a move in the politics of academia establishing anthropology as a serious and important discipline. The exploration of science and of rationality through sorcery was also part of the anxiety of anthropologists to demonstrate the practical utility of their enterprise in the context of colonial policies and in postcolonial development.

The strong focus in anthropology on the relation between science and sorcery has taken many turns. One was to discover the illogicality or irrationality of the latter in the former: science as sorcery. The discovery of irrationalities everywhere is one of the pastimes of anthropologists in which the familiar and presumed rational practices in dominant and technologically advanced societies are exoticized. These are made to appear as equivalent to or just as irrational as practices among peoples at the edge of the spread of science and modern technology. This practice could be seen as a forerunner of more recent arguments in anthropology that are aimed against the interpretation of sociocultural orders as rational systems. But this would be a mistake.

The liberal and humanizing concern of most of the anthropology of sorcery was committed to the rational and objectivist visions of science and was involved in developing these visions into a methodology for anthropology as a social science. The anthropology of sorcery was and is engaged in a discourse concerning the very aims and methodology of anthropology. Sorcery practices were not explored as part of an epistemological critique of a social science founded in a methodology of the biological and physical sciences. Rather, it was concerned, by and large, with applying the methodologies of natural science to the study of society.

There are some exceptions. Winch (1979) broached the issue in a critique of Evans-Pritchard's Azande study and the question of the entire validity of the sorcery-science debate. More recently, Taussig (1980, 1987) has vigorously questioned the validity of anthropological models and approaches that are not prepared to question their own epistemological grounds. He draws the subject of sorcery into a far more radical confrontation with established modes of understanding than was apparently the case in the early arguments surrounding sorcery and science and the debates over rationality.

The question of rationality, sometimes discussed as a logic or mode of reasoning independent of its context, leads uncomfortably back to mentalist and evolutionist notions current at the turn of the century. Winch, in my view, is completely correct to question the validity of sorcery-science comparisons. The contrast invites an overhomogenization of practices classed as sorcery or science. Indeed, like much comparison in the social sciences, there is often an underlying logic to the comparison in the first place which influences the way the phenomena to be compared are constructed. For example, assumptions about the nature of science become engaged in the construction of the critical dimensions *for comparison* of sorcery with science regarding their differences and similarities.

The strongest point to emerge in the debate over science and sorcery, already explicit in Evans-Pritchard's Azande study, is that science, like sorcery, is a social practice. The violations of the canons of scientific practice, the clinging to empirically disproven theories, even the absurdity of many of the theories, relate powerfully to the fact that scientists are enmeshed in social and political processes. The same processes, of course, are also positively involved in the creativity and imagination of scientific work. Social and political realities are the conditions or circumstances of scientific practice, and they play a powerful role in directing this practice and its results despite scientific ideologies of empirical objectivity and the attempts of some scientists to isolate themselves.

The logic of science and sorcery as systems of abstract explanation, a major deviation in anthropological discussion (see Wilson 1984), is of far less significance than the fact that they are both social practices. This is the single most important fact that links the two modes of knowledge. If there are connections between the practices of science and sorcery, as some scholars claim, then they are grounded in the psychosocial existence of their practitioners. Both sorcery and science are the constructions of human beings, and the conundrums that may consume their practitioners are partly (in the case of science) and totally (in the case of sorcery) born of psychological, social, and political realities.

Sorcerers make no attempt to separate themselves from the world or to construct abstract models of lived realities. The models that sorcerers make are not analogies to the world but materializations of its dimensions and processes, and they are conceived of as being fully vital in the reality of human experience. The success and efficacy of sorcery comes from this fact, and for the human beings who engage in it, sorcery works. It works because it is intimate with the processes of psychological and social existence and to the personal and particularistic projections of human beings into the actualities of their lives.

Once sorcery is seen as grounded in the worlds of human action and construction, we can see the supposed irrationalities of sorcery as integral to the circumstances of existence that produce it. If sorcery is irrational, then this is not the property of sorcery as part of a system of abstract knowledge but rather the property of the very concreteness of its foundation in the world of psychological, social, and political actualities. Furthermore, the force or power of sorcery's beliefs is not in the beliefs as such but in the processes of these actualities. This last observation is crucial.

Let me put the point another way. The definition of sorcery as irrational (in the sense of being a wrongheaded and mistaken view of reality) is in large measure irrelevant to understanding sorcery practice. Sorcery is above all directed to the contradictions, discordancies, and incompatibilities of life worlds as these are brought together in the immediacy of personal experience. In other words, sorcery is a form whose apparently irrational structure manifests the irrationalities and absurdities of the world as these conjoin in the life experiences of individuals. Its distortions are the distortions of the actualities of existence as these appear in experience. Sorcery is a practice that both expresses the enormities of the world of human action in experience and attempts to grapple with that world in terms of the enormities sorcery identifies. The discordancies and incompatibilities that sorcery refracts are produced in the world. They are modes of practice that will likely be continually reproduced or reinvented. This is because the irrationality of practice and belief is as much a refraction as a cause of the absurdities and incongruencies of the realities that human beings create.

Sorcery can realize the irrationality of the rational, the terrible absurdities and uncertainties in experience of worlds commanded by the most rational and technically efficient values and systems of organization. Part of the symbolic power of sorcery is its capacity to simultaneously express and act on the tragedies in experience flowing within worlds overridingly committed to forms of contemporary rationalism: economic, political, and technological. This is the *Zen* of sorcery, in Sri Lanka and elsewhere.

Students of sorcery have examined mainly its social implications. This is strongest, as is to be expected, within those branches of anthropology and history that are sociologically oriented, usually those influenced by Durkheimian or Marxist traditions. But psychoanalytic influences have also been of considerable importance (e.g., Devereux 1967; Spiro 1967; Obeyesekere 1981).

Anthropologists with functionalist orientations have described sorcery as representing a breakdown in social and political orders. They view sorcery as simply an index of the malfunctioning of the system, of its objective disorder, or as symptomatic of the chaos of transition. They argue that these become apparent on the psychological plane in the form of often monstrous fantasies, common in sorcery, expressing the atomization of integrated social and institutional structures, the increasing pattern of disordering and destructive social conflict, and coincidentally, the

collapse of psychological structures. A well-known and famously contested example of this perspective is that presented by Redfield (1941).
He accounted for the prevalence of sorcery in the Mexican city of Mérida
on the Yucatan peninsula on the basis that this was a place where the
well-integrated values and social order of village community life had finally completely broken down. A counterargument might be that sorcery
in Mérida was not the result of the dissolution of village life but of the
very order of Mérida itself, the contradictions of its capitalist context,
the structure of political processes within the city, and so forth. As Oscar
Lewis (1960) demonstrated, Redfield's small-scale "harmonious" villages
were also riven by conflict and sorcery but presumably in distinct structural circumstances.

Structural functionalist and psychoanalytic perspectives stressed far
more the normality of sorcery on both the social and psychological
planes. The symbolism and social patterning of sorcery were integral to
the motion of the organism: the social organism or the individual human
being. Sorcery revealed the conflicts and contradictions in these systems,
operated to overcome them, or expressed their repressive processes.

Empirical studies in anthropology and history exemplify either a mixture of these approaches or a development of one or another of them.
Gluckman and his colleagues and students at Manchester in the fifties
and sixties concentrated on sorcery as expressing social conflicts engendered by contradictions in the social and moral order (e.g., Gluckman
1956; Mitchell 1956; Marwick 1965; Turner 1957). Knauft (1985), in
a recent study of the Gebusi in New Guinea, makes a very similar argument. Gluckman and his students also stressed the instrumental use of
sorcery accusations in individuals' pursuit of their personal and collective
interests, interests which were both defined in social processes and definitive of these same processes. They were concerned with the political and
economic foundations of sorcery practice. Gluckman in particular saw
the role of sorcery in the larger structure of political processes, for example, in the dynamics of power surrounding Swazi and Zulu kings. However, he and others in his tradition tended to see sorcery (and witchcraft)
as a relatively conservative force, having more to do with the preservation
of the status quo than anything else. Thus sorcery functioned to reproduce social and political systems or was a dimension of their oppressive
force.

Other anthropologists and historians stressed more the connection between sorcery and witchcraft, on the one hand, and the dynamics of state
power, patterns of social resistance, forms of political transition, and so

forth, on the other hand. Sorcery and witchcraft in Europe, particularly the events of the witchcraft craze and the spate of witch trials that gathered momentum from the fifteenth to the eighteenth century, have been set against the changing social and political climate of the times. Thus, they expressed the shift from feudal structures to the formation of urban mass society founded in capitalism and the modern bureaucratic state, and crises in church and state power (e.g., Cohn 1961, 1975; Harris 1974). The emergence of the modern state with its firmly established legal systems of control has been linked to the decline of the witch craze (Douglas 1991). Some emphasis is given to the manipulation of sorcery and witchcraft accusations by authorities to attack outsiders or threatening populations.

Cohn (1975) and recently Ginzburg (1991) have shown the link between sorcery scares and attacks or pogroms on minority populations, especially Jews. There are indications of parallels between these processes and later state and popular support for human destruction and discrimination. The examples are Nazi Germany and the events in other European countries both before and after the Second World War. The point is not that sorcery and witchcraft beliefs are implicated in later human catastrophes but that aspects of the social and political dynamic that appears around them are similar. The processes of sorcery yield an insight into apparently unrelated events. The connection of sorcery with such events, in fact, in the historical past lends support to an understanding of larger processes through an investigation of the symbolism and other features of sorcery practice. This is an argument that I develop in subsequent chapters (see Chapters 6, 7, 8).

The dynamics apparent for Europe are comparable in certain respects to the witch-cleansing cults described for Africa and Melanesia (e.g., Marwick 1950; Willis 1968; Williams 1976). These movements occurred at moments of political and economic transformation and were connected with realignments in the boundaries and structures of power. As in Europe, they gained legitimacy both within traditional sorcery beliefs and practices and within other ideological forces such as Christianity, which provided a bulwark for colonial power and sometimes the basis of resistance to it and also to later organizations of state control. The powerlessness of internal cultural and political and economic institutions of practice in the face of external forces, of Christian missionizing, colonial conquest, and the establishment of capitalist enterprise, sometimes had the effect that subordinated populations turned against their own cultural and social institutions and destroyed them. Sorcery in some contexts in

Africa and New Guinea was identified as a source of weakness. Attacks on sorcerers or rooting them out was part of a process of social and political change and of reempowerment and regeneration.

In Sri Lanka, before more recent nationalist reevaluations, traditional practices such as exorcism were disregarded by elements within Sinhalese bourgeois elites. To these elites they exemplified the decline of Buddhist values and institutions. In many respects exorcisms and other folk practices were viewed by these elites much as the Dutch and later British colonial rulers viewed them: as demonic and primitive practices in a Western Christian and rationalist sense (see Kapferer 1983, 1988a, 1991). The attack on exorcism and other "superstitious" practices by Sinhalese, often English-educated members of local and national elites, was ideologically connected with the Sinhala Buddhist reformation (which aimed to purify Buddhism of its alien influences but at the same time was highly rationalist) and resistance to colonial rule (see Gombrich and Obeyesekere 1988).

Exorcism, especially episodes of its drama, and other elements of the folk tradition have been positively revalued in recent times. This is related to the acute cultural reaffirmations among Sinhalese in the circumstances of the Tamil-Sinhala ethnic war (which developed after the anti-Tamil riots of 1983). The reevaluation of exorcism and other practices is also related to changes in structures of class power. Over approximately the last fifteen years members of business and other entrepreneurial groups have played a role in this reevaluation. Many of them came to social and political prominence in the years following the opening of the island economy after 1977, with the accession to power of the United National Party, which has since been displaced by the People's Alliance, led by President Chandrika Kumaratunga. These entrepreneurs had social backgrounds different from those who came to wield influence and power in the colonial period. They are Sinhala educated and not English speaking and maintain strong connections with the peasantry and urban poor.

The perspectives discussed tend to subordinate cosmological considerations to economic and political processes. Crick (1976), building on Ardener's (1971) semantic approach, is critical of the undervaluation of cosmology. With reference to British social anthropologists, the "oversociologization" of the ethnography of sorcery obscures key distinctions between societies. For example, it masks very different constructions of the person. This obscures even such general sociological concerns as the relation of sorcery or witchcraft accusations to social structure. While such criticism is important, there is a tendency here to return to the closure of anthropological relativism. Parkin (1985), who makes observations similar to those of Crick, asserts more strongly the location and transformation of cosmologies in history and changing economic and political conditions.

The above reactions of some scholars expose the narrowness of many anthropological approaches to sorcery: for example, its treatment as a discrete phenomenon to be analyzed separately from its embeddedness in other cultural conceptions and orientations.

Sorcery is integral to a wider complex of practices and is not merely about interpersonal conflict or the explanation of personal misfortune.

Sorcery practices articulate cosmological and ontological assumptions. But so do those social science and philosophical epistemologies within which sorcery is comprehended. They contain assumptions concerning the orientation of human beings toward power, the forces motivating individual action, and so forth. The study of sorcery without sensitivity to the cosmological or ontological assumptions in generalist modes of understanding may therefore merely connect sorcery to the affirmation of these assumptions. This is a feature of much of the debate surrounding the rationality and illogicality of sorcery belief and practice.

The exploration of practices without attention to their cosmological embeddedness or their taken-for-granted assumptions is out of place in contemporary anthropology. Although it is undervalued in the approaches that Crick, for example, criticizes, it is not excluded. What some insist is that cosmological or cultural assumptions cannot be explored independently of practices, a notion developed from Evans-Pritchard. This is the central position of Gluckman and his colleagues at Manchester. To them, the cosmologies relevant to everyday realities do not constitute coherent systems. The appearance of cosmologies and social structures as integrated systems is true only if they are abstracted from practice and regarded as coherent wholes, as scholars do but not human beings in routine life. It follows that the conundrums that intellectuals and scholars find in beliefs and practices such as sorcery are often entirely of their own construction.

The view of Gluckman, which has been extended by anthropologists such as Victor Turner (who developed its implications into a criticism of Levi-Straussian structuralism), has a contemporary resonance. Gluckman and his colleagues were suspicious of notions of bounded and internally consistent systems and developed concepts such as *social field* to address the complexity and diversity of social practices. They believed that practices and the ideas relevant to them were not rigidly contained in either institutional or specific cultural arrangements, that they crossed the boundaries and flowed into other areas of action that certain kinds of analysis might otherwise keep separate (e.g., those which explored the economy separately from the polity). This approach drew on the work of the social psychologist Kurt Lewin, who used metaphors from physics to indicate fields of human action as fields of force. The idea has relevance to my discussion of sorcery in both its cultural conception and its practice.

One argument of Gluckman and his students was that practices, especially in the problems they addressed, opened dimensions of cosmological and cultural realities. If the structures of practice, for example, were directed in accordance with customary principles, then the nature of these principles and their potential contradictions was exposed in practice. This is a key rationale behind Gluckman's interest in conflict and sorcery. That is, such events bring to the surface of life the problematics of social relations and their underlying cosmological and ontological assumptions. Sorcery as conflict was a way into the study of complex cultural processes and not a mere sociological retreat from them.[6] However, the degree to which practices were either seen as sites for the production of cosmological or cultural meaning or regarded as in themselves a kind of indigenous critique of life's circumstances was reduced. But these aspects of sorcery practice were only reduced and could have taken the path of later approaches to the study of practice. Both Sahlins (1981) and Bourdieu (1977), coming from different traditions, have demonstrated the importance of a focus on practice as both critique and the site for the production or creation of innovative cultural and political and social directions.

Sorcery and the play of its symbolism manifest the problematics within cosmologies or systems of belief, or cultures. This is the case not as these are conceived through the frames of abstraction created by intellectuals or scholars, indigenous or foreign, but as they are lived in day-to-day existences. Put another way, sorcery addresses the problematics of existence as the paramount reality, and it is in this process that cosmologies continually take form. They take form not as coherent, integrated wholes springing up fully formed, things in themselves. Rather they appear as fragments of a larger whole, a whole that is more immanent than actual, and they derive their import and meaning from the contexts of practice in which they are both constituted and used. Their meaning is always in the dynamics of their situational production. Insofar as cosmologies and values are integral to the pursuit of daily concerns, sorcery practices manifest and recreate them as integral to the situated problematics of everyday life.

The symbolism of sorcery is frequently that of an internally unstable form. This instability is a feature of its characteristic of not fitting into any particular category of thought or scheme of expectation. It is inherently transgressive, problematic in itself. Sorcery is dangerous, as Mary Douglas (1966, 1973) has remarked, precisely because of these aspects. It is potent with possibility and uncertainty. Thus, it grasps and flows from the actualities of human experience in the world, giving them expression as it deals directly and immediately with them. Moreover, the symbolism of sorcery is of fusion, of the unity of incompatibles, and of the potencies of human beings to change the circumstances of their lives. This alchemy of sorcery, explicit in ancient and medieval European thought and practice and basic in Goethe's *Faust,* is evident in very different cultural senses elsewhere. The alchemy of sorcery is a vital aspect of its labile and volatile character, its capacity to metamorphose and maintain a relevance to any situation and to the changing circumstances of situations. In its changing form, sorcery can gather up and express something of the dimensions of the vast transforming forces which impinge on the experience of human beings caught in their vertices. Sorcery can, in its symbolism and practice, give shape to the nature of the contradictions of capitalism, as Nash (1972) and Taussig (1980, 1987) have shown for South American materials, or to the forces and transformations of the power of the state as these enter into the depth and ground of personal experience.

Central Themes and Chapter Outline

I essay an orientation to sorcery practice away from some of the more common approaches. For example, I refer to those arguments, some already alluded to, which concentrate on sorcery as a system of explanation, as a practice concerning the understanding of misfortune or of unusual events that otherwise defy rational comprehension, as a representation of particular kinds of social order, as something to be contrasted to science, as a particular kind of reasoning, as concerned with the problem of evil, or as a discourse on the depredations of capitalism, and so on. Although sorcery practices certainly address such aspects, a concentration on them can deflect attention away from the manifold other existential concerns that people address through their sorcery practices. Academic debates lose touch with everyday worlds that after all are the fundamental ground of such stratospheric concerns, for instance, as evil and the forces of capitalism that this book in no way ignores but which have frequently dominated discussion.

I try to steer a middle course, placing Sinhala sorcery practices within their social and political contexts and showing that the often grand themes that the practices display find their force in a capacity to gather up the deep psychosocial problematics that ordinary people confont in their daily lives.

Although my principal aim is to understand particular aspects of the phenomenon of sorcery as it is practiced, I focus on the practices as potentially yielding in themselves general insight into the processes of human action. Sorcery practices, like any other practice of human beings, need to be explained and understood. But they also are acute observations on human action, and I attempt to take some advantage of them. Although the techniques of sorcery may not appear rational or useful to those convinced that other means are more efficacious, sorcery is often founded in a profound grasp of the dynamics involved in the practices of human beings. In other words, the arguments of sorcery practice may be no less significant as a way to a general comprehension of the processes of human action than many of those social science theories constructed independently of the close observation of human action, yet applied to it. Such theories, for all their claims to be scientific and objective, are no less human constructions, than is the work of sorcerers, and in many ways are farther from the concrete problems of human existence and struggle.

My analysis proceeds through an application of a variety of social science perspectives and is especially informed by approaches in phenomenology. But my aim is also to interrogate these perspectives through the practices of Sinhalese sorcery and to give these practices authority in their own right for exploring the nature of the dynamic actualities of human existence.

Chapter 2 is a broad introduction to the complex of practices that I call sorcery. I focus on the Sinhala terms and practices of sorcery and attempt to give some indication of their diversity as well as the historical, social, and political contexts of which they are a part. I give particular attention to the shrines of the sorcery demon-deities and the divided character of these beings. Their powers are simultaneously constitutive and destructive; the one aspect is an immediate function of the other and is copresent with it. The duality of the sorcery gods is a dimension of their pragmatism and condenses a variety of other aspects of the everyday worlds of their potency. Sorcery gods may be distinguished from other gods of the Sinhala pantheon that are more hierarchical in form and process. The sorcery demon-gods manifest none of the potential of these other more central gods in the pantheon for transcendental resolution or unity. Rather, in keeping with their often violent origin, the sorcery demon-deities are the forces of the conflicts and divisions of daily social and political life.

Chapter 3 presents a discussion of two myths. One centers on the origin of sorcery and the attack on the first victim. The other is essentially concerned with the origin of the sorcerer, a totalizing figure who heals, protects, and destroys. The stories are significant primarily as frames (rather than paradigms) for the ritual action of the major antisorcery rite, the Suniyama. Through a preliminary analysis of these stories I lay out some of their mainly Buddhist themes that are relevant to understanding some of the cultural features of sorcery practice in Sri Lanka, especially the Suniyama. Within the context of these myths, I illustrate further some of the phenomenologically based concepts that I use in the exploration of sorcery practice: for example, such notions as intentionality, intentional consciousness, and sociality.

Chapters 4 and 5 should be taken together. Chapter 4 presents background materials central to the ethnography of the Suniyama antisorcery rite described in Chapter 5. These two chapters are at the fulcrum of the book and are critical (Chapter 5 especially) to the arguments in the chapters to follow.

The Suniyama is the most comprehensive antisorcery ritual in the exorcism traditions of the south of the island. It gives expression to heterodox ideological currents involved in the formation of Buddhist practices in Sri Lanka and turns them to pragmatic use. The rite incorporates many of the different kinds of sorcery that can be practiced, counteracts their force, and reconstitutes both the victim of sorcery and the sets of relations centering upon the victim. The rite sets the victim along the path of the striking snake of sorcery, the thrust of transgression that breaks down all barriers and crosses all boundaries. This is also the fundamental intentional thrust of Being, the opening out of time and space, the quest to the far horizons of existence. It is the motion of the microcosm in the macrocosm and in my terms is the transformation of human intentionality, a dimension of the destructiveness of sorcery, into the force of social formation. The rite manifests all the existential potentiality of sorcery and also expresses the full creative and regenerative powers of human being, which simultaneously makes itself and constructs its realities of existence.

The ritual is a practice of human and social regeneration and reformation par excellence. Moreover, it is an exercise in the constructive action of being human. I focus particularly on the rite as involving a victim of sorcery in the activities vital to social construction and the formation of those social boundaries, controls, and limitations which have been thrown down by the act of the sorcerer. In this quite astonishing rite—and I attempt to give the reader some sense of this—the existential forces integral to the unity of action and being are played out in such a way as to challenge and, in my view, to demand a rethinking of some of the fundamental categories of conventional anthropological analyses of rites and social practice. My descriptive analysis suggests some directions.

I do not reduce the world of human experience to the Suniyama. The Suniyama is an ideological practice which, although grounded in human beings' experiences of their existence, is a construction within historical and cultural processes. All attempts to grasp the processes whereby human beings form their realities, whether they are the articulations of rite or the doctrines and dogmas of social scientists, are ideological and in some way cosmologically founded. Thus they both lead to an understanding of human action and limit and obscure understanding. I concentrate on the Suniyama because it is certainly an ideological practice and therefore limiting but also one that leads to ways of exploring aspects of human action. More specifically, the rite provides a set of metaphors through which social and political events in Sri Lanka may be examined.

Let me make this last point absolutely clear. In no way can the social and political events of contemporary Sri Lanka be subordinated to the argument of the Suniyama. The dynamic processes of the Suniyama achieve particular import and meaning within the structure of the rite and cannot be applied to processes outside it. Even within the rite they can be grasped in numerous ways; its acts potentially receive a different import every time they are performed. What I do suggest is that the dynamics of the rite qua its dynamics opens up possibilities for the analysis of human action in Sri Lanka and elsewhere. This is not to say that such action can be reduced to the meanings and their logic as these are unified within the structure of the ritual practice. My application of metaphors relevant to the Suniyama (and other sorcery practices) extends well beyond their ritual use: I suggest possibilities for the general analysis of social and political processes. In some respects I use the dynamics of the Suniyama in the way some anthropologists might use theory.

Chapter 6 further elaborates the analysis of the ethnography of the Suniyama. In particular, I address the rite as a sacrifice, which is how it is described by the ritual practitioners. It bears strong resemblances to Vedic sacrifice, but of course it is a particular transformation or variation within a Buddhist context. I return to some of the issues raised in the famous study of sacrifice by Hubert and Mauss (1964), which was vital in the development of theories about the nature of ritual. This is a key study in Mauss's body of work and has considerable relevance for his seminal study, *The Gift,* central in much anthropological discussion concerning the nature of human sociality and the principles underlying social formation. Using the Suniyama materials, I explore sacrifice as a fundamental constitutive act of both human being and society. I also offer a critique of the concept of reciprocity and the gift as developed by Mauss and others.

The question of violence is central in discussions of sacrifice and sorcery. It is a focal problematic of the Suniyama as a Buddhist practice that attempts to overcome sorcery without repeating the cycle of violence through an act of vengeance. At least one anthropologist (Bloch 1992) has identified a structural and functional association of the sacrificial structure of rite with general social and political violence. This is not supported by the evidence from the Suniyama. However, the Suniyama's elaboration of the violent dynamics of sorcery expands our understanding of some of the processes of political destruction and suffering in contemporary Sri Lanka.

In Chapter 7 I turn to a consideration of the actual experience of sorcery and the expressions of sorcery as related to the situations of terrible abjection in which human beings can find themselves. I do not use the word *misfortune,* common in discussions of sorcery and witchcraft, because it weakens a sense of the intense distress that attaches to sorcery experiences.

The discussion focuses on the dynamics of consciousness. My general point is that sorcery practices do not evidence a particular kind of consciousness. A view that there is a consciousness that is specific to sorcery beliefs and practice is implicit and often quite explicit in anthropological discussion. Thus, sorcery is described as representing a particular style of rationality or reasoning (e.g., Horton 1967). I do not agree with this position. I adopt a phenomenological stance. Consciousness is always a consciousness of something, and it cannot be explored as a thing in itself, either apart from the life worlds of its production or as divorced from the body and contained in abstract categories of thought removed from concrete practices.

A key point in the discussion is that the processes of consciousness are passionate processes, intimately connected to the extension of the body into the world and simultaneously transcending the boundaries of the body. Sorcery practices make this abundantly evident. I concentrate on the emotions of sorcery and the way sorcery articulates the anguish of human beings in a social and political world.

Chapter 8, the final substantive chapter, returns to a theme that I begin in Chapter 2 and that is central to the book. This is sorcery as a dynamic of power and its paradoxes, or power as bearing the dynamics and paradoxes of sorcery. Deleuze and Guattari's (1988) metaphors of the state and the war machine—metaphors very relevant to the sorcery dynamics

I discuss and profoundly influenced by Asian materials—are of particular value to the discussion. My analysis develops with specific attention to the dynamics of organized bureaucratic power and its transformations in the context of political resistance and terrorism in Sri Lanka and elsewhere.

The overall aim of this book is not only to produce an ethnography of sorcery in Sri Lanka but also to treat sorcery practices as involving acute expressions and understanding of the processes of human action. One concern is to give to sorcery practice, and especially to the specialists in sorcery who deal routinely with human anguish, an authority in the exploration of the human condition. Sorcerers may not be interested in the questions that social scientists or philosophers ask of themselves and their worlds, but they are nonetheless acute observers and practitioners in human situations. Indeed, they are in many ways more intimately engaged on a regular basis with the problematics of human circumstance than those who claim a greater competence. In many cases they also share the same circumstances of existence as their clients.

This book takes sorcery seriously. When I say this, however, I distance myself from mystics and occultists in anthropology and elsewhere, those "merchants of the strange," to use Geertz's felicitous phrase, who see in sorcerers a profundity of another reality. They deprive sorcery practice and many other practices among human beings of much of their significance and their capacity for contributing to a rigorous understanding of humankind—certainly the promise of anthropology and of its ethnography.

2

Gods of Protection, Demons of Destruction
Sorcery and Modernity

SUNIYAM IS THE MAIN BEING of sorcery among Sinhalese Buddhists in Sri Lanka. At his urban shrines, he is often represented astride a blue horse, a mare (*velamba*), the potency of his *sakti*. In his left hand he carries a broken pot (*kabala*) of fire, a symbol of his fragmenting power and destructive heat. His right arm is raised, his hand holding the sword of his judgment and punishment. Suniyam's body is covered in snakes, representations of the world-destroying, body-enveloping poisons of sorcery that Suniyam both sends and controls. He bites the viper of his sudden strike and the messenger of his venomous destruction.

Such a representation of Suniyam in the solid form of an image, housed in a shrine, and made the focus of supplication and worship began mainly in this century, as Gombrich and Obeyesekere (1988; see also Obeyesekere 1981) explain.[1] He is in many ways a transmutation of the destructive force of human agency that Sinhalese have long recognized as *huniyam* and of the rites subduing its force. The form he takes refracts his world, the turbulence of contemporary urban social and economic realities, and possibly new modalities of political power connected with the development of the modern state out of the conditions of colonial rule. The shrines to Suniyam started to appear in Colombo, the capital city of the island, at the turn of the century and have since proliferated to other urban centers and rural areas. The growth in the popularity of these shrines corresponds with urban expansion in the pre– and post–World War II years.

It is conceivable that his enshrinement and the solidification of the potencies attaching to his image as an object for supplication and worship express a specific apotheosis of power achieved in the condition of colonialism and the further transitions to the postcolonial state. The Suniyam shrines first began to proliferate in the later period of British colonial rule. The British established themselves as the sole rulers of the land with the conquest of the hill capital of Kandy in 1815; Kandy was the seat of the last kings of independent Sinhalese. This British power, of course, was an alien and transcendent power. That is, the controlling and reordering force of British power was constituted outside and above the internal social and political relations of Sri Lanka.

With British colonial rule, power became centralized, comparatively stable, absolute, and all-encompassing. This rule, like the Portuguese and Dutch colonialism preceding the British, was radically alien. It transformed the political order of the island. Although the British drew upon social and political arrangements indigenous to the island's population, a bureaucratic order was established ideologically grounded in the technorational principles emergent in the contexts of political and economic transformations taking place mainly in northern Europe at least from the sixteenth century. In other words, a secular power was established that was guaranteed or warranted by its own principles of organization, which were not, at least initially, those of the people it controlled. Most important, it was backed by alien military force. British colonial rule belonged to a cosmological and moral universe that was external to Sri Lanka but which also internalized itself through the hegemonizing force of power and the restructuring of the social and political relations of the world that British colonial rule commanded.

A marked dualism of power attended the British conquest, a cleavage between the ruled and the rulers relatively unmediated by intimate social ties. This duality of power became entrenched in the formation of the class society instituted through colonialism and expanded and intensified in the global context of the postcolonial nation-state. Power became concentrated in the hands of mainly urban-based, often large-land-owning, English-speaking elites, who maintained and expanded the apparatus of rule of the colonial state which, of course, was instrumental to their own dominance and social mobility.

A context for the emergence of Suniyam that extends an understanding of some of the conditions and significance of his emergence, but not a causal explanation, relates to the expansion and intensification of patronal power and the development of charismatic political party leadership, sometimes verging on the dictatorial, in the postindependence period, from 1948 to the present day.

The spectacular careers of Prime Minister S. W. R. D. Bandaranaike in the fifties and those of Presidents J. R. Jayawardene and R. Premadasa from the late seventies to the early nineties condense some of these processes. These leaders pursued a Sinhala Buddhist populist chauvinism which had tragic results for both Bandaranaike and Premadasa, who were assassinated. A feature of their styles of leadership was a virtual sacralizing or divinizing of their persons by themselves and their followers.

For a brief period following his death, Bandaranaike achieved an almost godlike status. In one poor neighborhood in the southern city of Galle, for example, a statue was erected to him. This was more than a commemorative act, for Bandaranaike's image started to be worshiped and offerings were laid at its base, as if he had indeed assumed the potency of a god and continued to act in the pragmatic interests of his supplicants.[2] With the decline in the fortunes and popularity of the political party that Bandaranaike had led, however, his divine ascendancy came to a halt and the statue fell into disrepair. Far less popular, Presidents Jayawardena and Premadasa (whose dictatorial rule, especially, far exceeded the rule of law) claimed a direct lineage from ancient cosmic kings whose chronicled exploits became integral to the rhetoric of contemporary Sinhala Buddhist nationalism and populism (see Kapferer 1988a). Rumor has it that President Premadasa seated himself on a replica of the throne of the last king of Kandy, deposed by the British in 1815, when attending some official meetings.

The power of such leaders, especially Jayawardene and Premadasa, was augmented by constitutional changes producing a greater bureaucratic centralization of government power. The shift to a presidential system, a reorganization of provincial government centered more closely on the president and political clients, and a regular subversion of democratic processes through declarations of states of emergency, further entrenched a system of patronal power that affected most areas of social life. Such a power expanded and radiated through numerous points of the bureaucratic-political order, extending to minor politicians and petty bureaucratic officers.

The violent face of government and patronal power also intensified, often eclipsing the power of citizens with whom government agents or political patrons clashed. Ethnic tensions have escalated since Independence, leading to the extreme violence of the 1983 Sinhala-Tamil riots (which some sources suggest were facilitated by members of the government; see Obeyesekere 1984b; Wilson 1988), and these contributed to the development of an enduring war between the state and the Tamil Tigers, who are claiming independent control over the northern and eastern regions of the island. Two major rebellions by Sinhala youth, organized by the Janatha Vimukthi Peramuna (JVP: People's Liberation Front;

see Chandraprema 1991; Kapferer 1994a, 1996a; Moore 1993) and coordinated by charismatic leaders in 1971 and especially in 1989, resulted
in a massive loss of civilian life, often as a result of the extremely arbitrary
and frequently vengeful action of state agents. Official estimates of the
number of Sinhalese deaths during the last rebellion are around sixty
thousand.[3] In other words, in a few short months the lives of as many
human beings were extinguished as have been lost in over twelve years
of military conflict between the Sri Lankan government and the Tamil
Tigers.

The foregoing events were conditioned within global processes and the
long-term and continuing transformations of Sri Lanka: the dislocation
and migration of peasant populations attendant on economic development programs, industrialization, the expansion of social and welfare
schemes, and in recent years, their dissolution following the institution
of privatization programs (encouraged by International Monetary Fund
and World Bank directives). There is rising unemployment, especially
among rural youth, and others educated largely in the Sinhala language
medium (those who were educated in English still have advantage in employment) have difficulty finding well-paid work and achieving social mobility. Since 1977, when the United National Party came to power (a rule
that lasted until August 1994, when the Peoples Alliance led by President
Chandrika Kumaratunga came to office), the economy has been opened,
free trade zones have been established north of Colombo and in the south
of the island, and there has been a radical expansion of a commodity
market trading in imported luxury items. A widening gap between rich
and poor has opened. Much of the turmoil in the island relates to such
class forces, which are also apparent in ethnic violence and in the closely
connected discourses of culture and history appropriated to the expression of nationalist sentiment.

The processes I have outlined feed the formation of a being such as
Suniyam. The historical actualities of his context contribute to the construction of his symbolism and provide the metaphors for Suniyam's mien
both at the shrines and in rites such as the Suniyama. His representation
as a figure of furious destruction and judgment, as a force both alienating
and incorporating, and above all, as a magnification of mundane and
secular human action and power draws its concreteness, its metaphors,
and its meanings from the world of everyday experience.

Mirrors to Power: Suniyam and the Demon-Deities

Suniyam manifests power as the simultaneous appearance of the force of
authority and its ordering potency, on the one hand, and its threat of

dispossession and exclusion, on the other. Suniyam can also express power as not merely alienating but in itself alienated: in other words, power and its indices—status, wealth, political command—as opposing human beings and separating them from those with whom their fortunes are nonetheless embroiled.

I stress Suniyam as an image, an imagination, of the forces bearing on experience emergent in the ruptures and turbulence of recent history. Although he is the invention of what might be recognized as the circumstances of both modernity and postmodernity, however, Suniyam in his enshrined form is also a reinvention, both continuous and discontinuous, with notions of power and its problematics that have been long recognized in different registers and ways in myth, ritual, and religious discourse throughout much of Sri Lanka's history.

Thus, kingship is the major metaphor of power. The power of kings is both alienating and alienated. Vijaya, the legendary founder of the Sinhala line of kings and the conquering hero of the ancient chronicles of the *Dipavamsa* and *Mahavamsa,* is an alienating and alienated figure of power. He was thrown out of his father's kingdom in India for offences against the people. Vijaya and his followers landed on Lanka's shores and dispossessed the aboriginal inhabitants (the Yakas). Vijaya received the help of Kuveni, a princess of the people he dispossessed.

The Vijaya story, particularly the events surrounding Kuveni's curse of Vijaya (for he renounces her), is a major narrative in the textual, oral, and ritual traditions of sorcery in Sri Lanka. It is vital in one of the more magnificent antisorcery rites, the Suniyama, and a central theme of the ritual drama of the Kohomba Kankariya, a rite which cleanses people from the afflictions of sorcery and is performed in the villages of the central highland regions of the island (see Godakumbura 1963; Sarachchandra 1966). The Suniyama is said to follow procedures laid down in the Kabala (or Vadiga) Patuna, the book of the rite said to have been created by Oddisa to cure the first victim of sorcery attack. Oddisa is a grand sorcerer and a great healer. The story of his birth as Oddisa Kumara (also Oddi Raja) is sometimes incorporated into contemporary retellings of the powers of Suniyam, who inhabits the shrines. Oddisa furiously deserts the order of his father's city, draws the powers of destruction from the earth, the poisons of manifold snakes, and threatens destruction with his external, alienated, and alienating powers. Absorbing the poisons into his own body, however, Oddi becomes an embodiment of forces that he can control both to heal and to destroy (see Chapter 3).

The image of Suniyam is quintessentially the image of power wielded by human beings and present in the institutions and relations that they create and live among. This dominant feature of Suniyam is evident in other enshrined beings who share key characteristics with him (e.g., Gale Bandara, Devol Deviyo, Tanivale Bandara, Rajjaruvo Bandara, and Devata Bandara). Like Suniyam, these are connected with what Sinhalese generally call sorcery. A few, such as Tanivale and Rajjaruvo, appear to be growing in popularity.[4] They are divided beings who have two sides: a furious half and a judgmental, ordering half (sometimes joined as one, like the enshrined image of Suniyam, and occasionally as independent images).[5] Their double aspects exist simultaneously, each as an equal part of the function of the other. This kind of representation tends to distinguish them from other gods in Sri Lanka, who are not usually represented in this way (although, for example, the goddess Pattini sometimes appears in destructive-reconstitutive dual form).

The gods generally have their destructive aspects subdued in their singular representation. When they have demonic aspects, these tend to be expressed as a different and subordinate dimension of their coherent and ordering form. The demonic is transformed into an ordered whole and is not constantly present as the alternative polarity of the being concerned. This is especially evident in village rites (see Kapferer 1983). The capacity of the gods to transform into an ordered form, largely because of their orientation to Buddhist value, makes them beings of the center. They are often presented as clustering around the Buddha and supporting him. This is not so clear with the *devata*s or *bandara*s, who are broadly viewed by Sinhalase as low on the cosmic scale. They are often mediating beings, who mix categories and in village rites are often presented as beings of some absurdity.

The demon-deities, especially the *bandara*s, like Suniyam, are regarded as having once been human beings or the children of a divine-human union (Obeyesekere 1984a). A few are described as having been human beings with extraordinary magical power (*irdi*). In their birth stories they are usually the progeny of kings and queens who are located in "real" history, in real time: that is, they were actors in events that are directly continuous with the historical world in which their supplicants are involved. Tanivale Bandara, for example, whose main shrine is located at Madampe, north of Colombo, was a prince renowned for his furious battles with invading Muslim pirates. Unlike other supramundane forces in the everyday worlds of Sinhalese Buddhists, such as gods (*deva*) who visit the worlds of human beings from their higher abodes (*deva loka*), Suniyam and the other demon-deities are firmly in the world of human beings. It is significant, in my view, that some of the stories of the arrival of the demon-deities in Sri Lanka have them coming or invading from the historical world of India. They are not Indian gods (with some obvious exceptions, e.g., Bhadrakali) coming into Sri Lanka but human beings. Undoubtedly they reflect the history of Sri Lanka and its region: numerous invasions, the migrations of peoples into Sri Lanka over the centuries, the exploits of actual historical figures, and the violent turmoil of events (see Gombrich 1971; Obeyesekere 1984b; Holt 1991).[6]

The significance of the representation of the demon-deities as beings in "real time" and in "real history" is that their dynamic energy is thus declared as nothing less than a potency capable of intervening in the pragmatic affairs of human beings; furthermore, it is the very power of human constitutive agency. There is a tension to continually reinvent Suniyam and the other demon-deities as historical beings (particularly noticeable in the recounting of their stories), because they are figurations of the force of human being-in-the-world: their historicization is the constructive trope for the affirmation of such beings as the power of human being.

The supplicants to the shrines of Suniyam and the other demon-deities unite with the forces of magnified, transcendent, godlike human action. They join with the capacity of this action as a force in the destruction and re-creation of human realities, as a dynamic in the energies of exclusion and inclusion in the orders and relations of the life world, and as the expressive force of alienated and alienating power. When people visit the shrines to Suniyam and the other demon-deities or sorcery gods (usually to ask for assistance for some immediate practical matter concerning their everyday lives), they enter into the vertices of the turbulent power of human being. There they draw upon the magicality of human being and extend themselves into its magicality.[7] This extraordinary potency of human beings is as apparent in lack and dispossession as in possession, to which Suniyam and the other demon-deities give marvelous expression. I refer to the capacity of human beings to direct their consciousness actively and transformationally into the world, to make and unmake the realities of themselves and of their fellows, to become intimate and influential in the actions of others, and even, as it were, to become consubstantial with the very bodily being of others. This is the potency of sorcery.

Suniyam, as he is enshrined, is irreducibly a construction that manifests recent historical forces. He might be seen to reflect them: His enlargement expresses the apotheosis of secular power and the growth of the import of the modern state. In many ways he refracts the violence of the state, which often flows from the regulative function of its bureaucratic apparatus. Suniyam and the other demon-deities image the constitutive force of power, especially the force of the agents of state power, not only in the mediation of social, economic, and political processes but also in their constitution or generation (and destruction) of the circumstances on which social relations depend and are formed. State power defines the boundaries of inclusive/exclusive sociopolitical entities and to a considerable extent the lines of social demarcation within the orders that the state controls and forms.

The power of the state is most apparent simultaneously at its borders and at the lines of internal division or striation it constructs or protects. The policing and regulation of boundaries of all manner and kind (in the contemporary context not just the boundaries of its sovereign territory) is the means by which the agents and agencies (bureaucratic, legal, educational, military, ceremonial, ritual) constantly regenerate the order of the state, which is also the source of their own authority. It is at the borders of the state, at the lines of the definition and construction of the order of the state, that its power as a force of exclusion and inclusion is most apparent, and just as significantly, is continually rendered problematic and is frequently contested.

Suniyam and the demon-deities express such power; its dynamic is one of social and political creation and maintenance through acts of bounding, categorizing, and defining. This dynamic is one of continual exclusion and inclusion and furthermore one which is simultaneously generative of contestation and resistance.

The dual form of Suniyam and the demon-deities is the symbolic shaping of their particular power. The shrines to Suniyam and the other demon-deities are often located at boundary points of social and political communities and at key sites of social and political contestation (see Chapter 7). They express the powers of the margins, especially the energy of transition from outer to inner (from exteriority to interiority) and vice versa. The supplicants who come to the shrines of these demon-deities draw on such force.

I have concentrated these opening comments on the shrines to Suniyam to underline the fact that these and other sorcery shrines emerge and discover their symbolic form in the conditions of the political forces of recent history. But they do not merely reflect the turn of historical processes and the social and political world of contemporary forces. The shrines reveal most acutely what is central in sorcery practice, whether this is expressed at the shrines or in other rites.[8]

Sorcery concerns the dynamics of power and the potency of sociality, which I generally define as that constitutive action of human beings whereby they form their relations in their life worlds and affect the lives of others. The metaphors of the political—of violence, authority, command, control, containment, division, and transgression—are the metaphors of sorcery, at least in Sri Lanka. Such metaphors concentrate in the figures and exploits of the wielders or symbolic types of state power. Princes that guarded borders, bodyguards of the king (or state), royal treasurers, other beings of transgression and conversion who may range against the state: These are the symbolic forms of the dynamics of sorcery. I stress their association with lines of social and political demarcation, with bureaucratic processes, and often with trade and its conversions. It matters not that these symbols of sorcery's power are drawn in the form of officers of the state in Sri Lanka's precolonial and mythologized past. They manifest the dynamics of power in modern contexts just as well as they did in times long gone. To assert this is not to reduce the present to the past but to recognize sorcery as exploring the dynamic of power and social formation in all contexts of human experience. In other words, the symbolic types of power can endure as types or maintain their relevance through a great diversity of historical contexts (see Handelman and Kapferer 1980; Handelman 1990).[9] This should not obscure the fact that their meaning, the kind of power, potency, and force of human agency that the symbolic types represent, is formed through and reproduced in the social and political contexts of their use. The power the types manifest and organize through their symbolic form cannot be grasped independently of their contexts.

The tropes of power and sorcery that draw on the myths and legends of history discover original import in their events or constitute the meaning of the present as their significance. The legendary and mythological Prince Vijaya and Princess Kuveni are figures of alienating and of alienated power. Kuveni manifests the fury of alienation, and her curse (*dividos*) on Vijaya prevents him from generating direct descendants. It is a curse that brings suffering to his successors, alienating them, as in the case of Vijaya, from their own potency or capacity for (re)generative continuity. The parameters of this story are as relevant to the anxieties, suffering, and anger born of contemporary class processes in Sri Lanka as they were to the circumstances of some despotic cosmic king.

The issues and perspectives that I have broached largely with reference to the shrines of sorcery recur as themes in much of the ethnography and argument of the rest of the book. The shrines are contemporaneous with a great variety of other practices relevant to a discussion of sorcery. What follows now is an overview of the diverse practices and their social contexts that have a bearing on the anxiety and suffering addressed as sorcery or in the context of the beings normally associated with the pragmatic potencies of sorcery.

Sorcery and Its Practices

The most common Sinhala words used for sorcery are *huniyam* and *kodi-vina* (or simply *vina*). They are used interchangeably. There is a tendency, however, to apply the word *huniyam* to the situation of being in an ensorcelled condition. *Kodivina* typically refers to the action (*vina*), conscious or unconscious, of bringing disaster or some kind of suffering to another. It is the activity or the actual dynamic or motion of destructive or hurting or obstructing action.

The term *huniyam* often applies to the objectified or materialized form of sorcery, the action concretized. People who are ensorcelled cut (*kapanava, kapilla*) the *huniyam*, as they objectify it, that has been made against them. They also cut or tie *huniyam,* or the objectified form of the anguish, destruction, or hurt they intend to cause their victim. There are numerous kinds of *huniyam* objects that can be made and that in their destruction or placement in the environment or way of victims bring the appropriate disaster. People experiencing sorcery hunt, usually in their houses or the land around it, for evidence of *huniyam* objects. These can take a great variety of forms—wax images, things over which destructive incantations have been made, destructive designs inscribed on metal, and so forth—and they are continually being invented. The objects of sorcery are fashioned to fit with the matter at hand, with the particular kind of damage that people want to cause.

The representation of sorcery in the objectified form of the god or demon-deity of Suniyam fits with the use of the word *huniyam* to refer to sorcery objects. In Sinhala *h* and *s* are interchangeable, and the reference to the being of sorcery as Suniyam is indicative, according to Gombrich and Obeyesekere (1988: 123), of the modern elevation of what was a demonic and lowly energy into a higher and godlike status. I certainly agree that Suniyam as a demon-deity is a recent innovation, especially in his current enshrined form. But the objectification of sorcery in the form of an ambiguous, dual, and extremely dangerous being has historical depth, on the basis of manuscript and ritual evidence (see Nevill 1954), stretching back to precolonial times.

The derivation of *huniyam/suniyam* (either word can be used in reference to sorcery) is unclear. *Adura*s (exorcists) and some shrine priests (*kapurala*s) indicate that it is borrowed from the Tamil *cuniyam*.[10] The lexical definition of this word, and its derivative compounds, carries many of the meanings of Sinhalese ritual and everyday usage: for example, such senses as barrenness, defilement, ruin.[11] Some exorcists tell me that the word comes from the Sanskrit *sunya,* "void," and this has similar meaning in Tamil, as, for example, "nonexistence, vacuum, nonentity, defilement." The notion of *sunya* has much resonance with the existential nature of sorcery elaborated in sorcery and antisorcery rites and in the experiences of sorcery victims.

The ultimate effect of sorcery is the radical extinction or obliteration of the victim or the whole circumstance of the victim's existence, the social relations and the means whereby victims sustain their life world. The fear that people have of sorcery is that it strikes at both the victim and the ground of the victim's being. The major myths and rites of sorcery express themes of cosmic destruction and renewal. They indicate the condition of sorcery as being a virtual return to the void from which existence springs. Sorcery projects death, actual physical extinction, which is also the chief metaphor for the anguish of sorcery as a kind of death in the midst of life, a living death. The extinction threatened by sorcery is not a release from existence, the source of suffering, as in the achievement of *nibbana* (nirvana), but an obliteration in the continuity of existence. Again in the myths and major antisorcery rites, the force of the sorcerer and of sorcery is ranged against the Buddha teaching and the ultimate release from existence and suffering. The figure with whom sorcery and the destructive powers of Suniyam are often popularly associated is Devadatta, a kinsman and follower of Gautama Buddha who broke with his teaching. Devadatta is regarded as a form of Vasavat or Mara (Death), the great adversaries of the Buddhist order and of the Buddha himself and his teaching.

Kodivina is the term most frequently used for all kinds of malevolent human action (although *huniyam/suniyam* may also be used). Those who are specialists in sorcery work indicate that the prefix *kodi-* is borrowed from Tamil. This is plausible, and certainly the Tamil noun *koti*, which indicates a creeping plant, string, or umbilicus, has connotations of sorcery practice among Sinhalese. In some sorcery, poisonous creepers are buried in the path of intended victims. One sorcery specialist who discussed the etymology of *kodivina* likened the effect of his work to the strangulation of the child by the umbilical cord. Some victims of sorcery, indeed, describe their experience as a kind of asphyxiation. The Tamil verb *koti* carries much of the experiential sense that victims and sorcerers give to the practice: senses of burning and boiling energy, anger, rage, and desire.[12] Other sorcerers have suggested that *kodi* is a Sinhala corruption of the Tamil *kudi* (family), indicating some of the major effects of sorcery, which are the attack and ruination of household members and their kindred.

Kodivina can cover any action by human beings that results in harm or misfortune and need not be a purposive, motivated act explicitly designed to bring another human being suffering. Normally, a *kodivina* is regarded as a highly motivated act, but human beings can bring others harmful effects simply through the way they are directed or oriented toward others, without actually meaning to cause them harm. Thus Sinhalese recognize the dangers of envious or malicious talk (*kata vaha*, mouth poison), thought (*hovaha*, ear poison), or sight (*asvaha*, eye poison).[13] People may not be aware of the dangers of their talk or realize the envy in their thoughts, but such action can nonetheless cause harm and in effect is sorcery. It can have all the risk of a highly motivated act of sorcery and can be addressed as if it were an explicit purposive act and can therefore be dealt with through the same rites of antisorcery.

Sorcery experts (*huniyan karayo, vina karayo*)[14] recognize a profusion of different kinds of destructive action that they consider sorcery. Among the most powerful is the action known as *anavina*, the destruction that is wrought by sound or verbal action; the commanding and ordering power of the sounds and words themselves are both the instrument and the effect.[15] *Mantras* (potent prescribed organizations of sound and word) or *mantra/yantra*s (powerful sounds and words inscribed into powerful diagrams) are typical means of *anavina*. The notion of the destructive power of sound, word, and utterance contained in the concept of *anavina* is of course a critical dimension of all ritual action and is specifically central to both sorcery and antisorcery work.

Some sorcery specialists regard *anavina* not as a subclass of *kodivina* but as a form of sorcery action that should be distinguished from *kodivina*. They say that *kodivina* is a term that should be restricted to sorcery action that is achieved through the power of objects rather than through sound and inscription. The principles of *anavina* and *kodivina* thus distinguished are inseparably part of most sorcery and antisorcery work. The curses (*vas kavi, des, avalada*) at the temples before the main demon-deities of sorcery are understood by sorcerers and the shrine priests (*kapuralas*) as actions that have the potency of *anavina*.

Other more specific kinds of sorcery techniques include *pilluva*, which generally involves sending an animal (e.g., a snake or dog) or some other small creature as an instrument of destruction;[16] *iri* or *val-pannum*, the drawing of lines (e.g., with funerary ash) or the planting of poisonous creepers[17] in the way of victims so as to kill them or block or impede them in some way in their daily activities; *katugasima*, making wax effigies and sticking them with thorns at the five vital parts of the body; *patali giniam*, the burning of copper foil shaped like a human figure, causing furious and maddening fever;[18] the introduction of poisons into food or through the medium of tiny drops of oil onto the victim's skin;[19] *bumipalu*, the throwing of the ash of a burned corpse (*mini alu*), or the earth from a black ants' nest (*geri pas*) into the house or onto the land of victims.

The notion of binding or tying (*bandana,* vb. *bandinava*) is basic to sorcery action. Sorcerers tie their charms to their victims or bind their victims to their destructive work. The idea of binding and tying has strong connotations of union with the sorcerer and of constraint to the terms of a relation dictated by the sorcerer. The term *hira bandana* (tight or marriage bond) is a sorcery trope that indicates the controlling intimacy of the destructive sorcerer and his victim.[20] Sorcery is infused with the metaphors of sexuality, and these express the intense intimacy of sorcery's relations as well as its capacity to strike at the core of generative being. A *hira bandana* is suspected in the case of disputes between close kin and in the difficulties between husbands and wives. The expression *muka bandana* is sometimes used with reference to sorcery that is explicitly meant to control the speech of another or to strike another dumb. I was told that it is appropriate in instances where there is an interest in controlling court judgments, especially in criminal cases or decisions in litigation over land. A *preta bandana* is especially feared. Through this action the ghost of a dead relative becomes bound to the house of the victim, causing a train of misfortunes to afflict householders.

The bond of sorcery limits and denies life. In effect, it is an antirelation, and in the rites to overcome sorcery, the aim is to cut (*kapanava*) such bonds. This is the meaning of the term *kapuma* (*kapilla*) used for antisorcery ritual.[21] The main antisorcery rite that I discuss in detail in later chapters is an all-embracing *kapuma.* The ultimate object of such rites is to tie or bind victims back into the life-regenerate aspects of their life world and to break the life-threatening bond that sorcerers and their demonic agents have established with them. Indeed, the bonds of the sorcerer must be broken, and sorcerers must themselves be bound and contained. Several ritual experts in antisorcery have described to me how they capture the essence of the agents of sorcery in bottles and throw them into the sea. At Kabalava, a major shrine to Suniyam, his destructive potency is understood to be constrained in a book (Kabala Patuna) bound by nine threads (*nul*).

Broadly, the kinds of *huniyam* or *kodivina* that I have outlined are inversions and subversions of routine aspects of the relations and practices of everyday life. They take the form of the relations and processes integral to the life worlds of human beings but in actuality are their negation. In other words, sorcery practices are constructed on the basis of how people imagine their social and political worlds and their dynamics and achieve their force through an insinuation into such dynamics. Their force is connected with a capacity to unify in appearance with the very relations and processes sorcery aims to subvert. The main myths of sorcery make this point plain. The beings of sorcery are often violent sons, and in the case of the overarching manifestation of sorcery (Vasavarti Maraya, often represented as synonymous with the absolute destruction of sorcery) assume the outer appearance of the world ruler (*cakravarti*), King Mahasammata, the central constituting figure of social and political order (see Chapter 3).

The fear (*baya*) of sorcery is premised on the fact that it lives in the intimacies of ordinary everyday relations as well as being an energy present in forces external to them. It is in many senses the internality that externalizes. Antisorcery rites (*kapuma*) give explicit recognition to such notions and are directed to the internal (*atul*) and external (*pita*) forces of sorcery (a further dimension of the symbolic dualism of sorcery).

I am not saying that Sinhalese are in constant fear of sorcery but rather that when the suspicion of sorcery arises, it can provoke not only intense fear but also great anger, because victims suspect that its agents are close and intimately part of a person's life world. Sorcery is widely described by anthropologists as a phenomenon that is normal, a routine expectation of existence. And so it is for many in Sri Lanka. It is common sense that ordinary precautions should be taken. Thus, specialists in sorcery (exorcists, shrine priests) ply a good trade in providing protective charms and mantra/yantras. Those who are highly dependent on the development and extension of social relations and on the safeguarding of contacts, and are constantly entering into social intercourse of a fragile, fleeting, and transgressive nature (politicians, business people, traders) demand not only protective charms but charms that will assist them in developing their enterprise, both drawing persons to them and unblocking barriers to their activities. They especially work on that duality of power which sorcery intensely symbolizes, particularly at the shrines, simultaneously to extend into the world and to defend against it.

The practices of sorcery refract the dynamics of the life world and the subversive forces that are vital in its continual formation. The routine of sorcery is located in this fact and so is its enormity. People can express through sorcery the realization that the entire basis and structure of life is arranged against them. This may be evident as a disorder of their person, often as extreme nausea or some other physical frailty; but it is a disorder caused by the forces and structures of the world in which their life would normally be sustained and in which victims would ordinarily make their way unimpeded.

The expectation of sorcery and the fear that might build in its context are tied to notions that human beings are the agents of the realities of their lives. Furthermore, the actions and experiences of individuals are inextricably tied to others. Human beings live in webs of causation intricately linked to the actions of others in the present and the past. This is exacerbated in a cultural context of Sinhala Buddhist ideas and practice, which give a heightened value to the potentially disastrous effects not only of present action but of the accumulated effects of past action. This is expressed in doctrinal and popular notions of karma (action). The story of Prince Vijaya's rejection of Kuveni carries the karmic theme. Vijaya's wrongful action brings forth Kuveni's reaction, and the results of these events reverberate down the generations. He has no legitimate sons who can succeed (save those that Kuveni takes into her exile), and Kuveni's scourge attaches to Vijaya's kin and successors.

The force of sorcery can go on and on. There are many aspects of sorcery that bear comparison, in anthropological discussions, of the feud and feuding. Feuds never end. They rankle beneath the surface of outwardly harmonious relations, an enduring and underlying conflict within the formation of social relations that occasionally breaks into the surface. The story of Kuveni's revenge expresses the entering of the forces of conflict and the feud into the ongoing fabric of social relations: indeed, the close connection of conflict and enmity with the very formation of sociality and its orders.

Sorcery does not merely afflict individuals but ramifies through their relations, attacking other members of their households and other kin. It discovers its cause and its index in the history of the feuding between deceased kin whose enmities continue as the source for suspicion and accusation of sorcery among the living. In a commonsense way, almost Freudian, the consciousness which may be revealed in sorcery accusation and suspicion is often regarded as the true motivation underlying routine social and political activity. There is a powerful historicity in sorcery that parallels a deep sense that present social relations build out of past histories of relations whose dynamic is vital in the present and augurs a future. People who experience themselves as being in the situation of sorcery explore their sociohistorical world or construct it in a historical vein, the presence of sorcery being manifested in a cycle of conflicts, disasters, and impediments afflicting them and others close to them.

In June 1984, Simon, a hospital orderly in the southern town of Matara, complained to his wife that all the strength had drained from his body. She suggested that he see the doctors at the hospital, as he worked there, but Simon insisted that he had already done this and that things had become worse. Simon and his wife went to a local soothsayer (*sastra karaya*), who indicated that a neighbor had made a *kodivina,* a *val pannum.* Simon's wife immediately suggested the culprits were relatives who were currently involved in litigation over a land title. This dispute had started some thirty years ago and had involved his father, since dead, and others, also deceased. The son of one of the deceased had recently taken up the case. He was suspected of planting the *huniyam.* But the ghost of the suspect's father was also understood to be attacking Simon. A small *kapuma* rite was held to cut the *vina* set by the son and the malevolence of his father's spirit. The illness abated but was soon to break out with renewed energy. Simon collapsed, vomiting blood, which was diagnosed a sign of the blood demon's (Riri Yaka) involvement. At an ensuing exorcism to overcome the growing crisis and to break the blood demon's grip, Simon became entranced. As is quite common at these times, the presiding exorcist interrogated Simon about the cause of the attack. Simon went through the history of the land dispute, declaring that it started when two sisters of his great grandfather had married out of the village. They and their relatives had not been granted proper title. In effect, the fury of the blood demon, his life-threatening grip, was the monstrous forming of the accumulated anger growing within a body of kin through the generations. Simon felt that this fury born in the struggles of land and kinship were responsible for many of his work problems and for the fact that he had been forced to move from job to job for many years.

Land claims along with other matters were at the center of the next example of sorcery attack, on a young unmarried woman aged twenty-three who lived outside of the town of Galle, on the southwestern coast. Her father was a wealthy landowner and farmer. Her elder brother owned many properties in the area but had just been dismissed as the manager of a government cooperative, in revenge by government officials, the family thought, for supporting the candidates of a rival political party in recent elections.

Kumudu's sorcery first became apparent during what was later diagnosed in the hospital as a serious asthma attack. Although she was under treatment, her condition did not improve. Her speech became hoarse and high-pitched "like that of an old woman." At one time Kumudu fell unconscious. Her body felt heavy, and she could hardly raise her head. An exorcist was called in, and he declared that a *preta bandana* had been tied. A divination was held, and after much questioning it emerged that the patient's elder brother had recently bought the house. The exorcist asserted that the person who had sold the house had himself been frightened, because protective sorcery had been planted in the house surrounds, and the ghost of the original owner (Karonchie) was clinging to the place. Karonchie was possessing Kumudu and was also bringing difficulties to other household members.

The brother's dismissal from his job was one instance. The situation was further complicated by the presence of envy and jealousy in those living around them, their malicious talk, thoughts, and looks adding to the distress of Kumudu and her brother.

The following case is of a young woman in her midtwenties who had recently married, only to be widowed. Her husband had been killed in a bomb blast, set off by Tamil Tigers, in central Colombo. She believed that this was only the last in a long line of personal disasters dating from the time of her puberty and involving her father's sexual abuse of her. She had come to a Suniyam shrine in the city to attack her tormentors with sorcery.

Premawathie said that her troubles began at puberty; she had *malvara dosa* (puberty illness). Her puberty had come when she was under the dangerous planetary effect of Mars. Shortly after her ritual of first menstruation she had been raped by her father. Her father continued to abuse her, and she still fears his presence, although he has been dead for two years. Her father stopped her from going to school, and she says she began to sleep with many men. Eventually she married and gave birth to a son. But the son died shortly before the explosion that killed her husband. Premawathie expressed a certain relief at his death, for he was a drunkard, beat her, spent all their money, and sold her jewelry. Driven by poverty, she was now working as a prostitute. Premawathie attributed her suffering to her father's abuse, and she wanted to cut what she felt continued as his relation with her. She was angry at the pimp who was taking all her money. Premawathie wanted a new life, and she asked the Suniyam priest to perform a small *kapuma* rite for her, one that would cut the connection with her father, bring suffering to her tormentors, and also assist her in finding a new life. Premawathie declared that her nights were full of nightmares. She felt Suniyam's vipers crawling over her body, a sensation that she associated with her abusive and burdensome sexual experiences.

The events of sorcery I have described clearly mark the experience of it as the intrusive and destructive force of the malign action/consciousness of others within the victim's field of everyday action. It is overtly expressed as such. The point should be underlined. Anthropologists (e.g., Obeyesekere 1981) commonly rationalize sorcery as a folk idiom for the expression of psychological and social tension. Such a social science translation adds nothing to what is self-evident to victims and can trivialize the events of sorcery as they are experienced. I stress the sense of sorcery as a destructive force that is consubstantial with the being of the victim. This is the malignant possibility that is taken for granted and considered natural among Sinhalese—a possibility that is given explicit assertion in doctrinal and popular Buddhism and in the work of *aduras* and sorcerers—that a person's existential being is inseparable from the world which is the conditionality of such being. Furthermore, the action/consciousness of others are integral and part of the materiality of a person's being. The notions of eye, mouth, and ear poison or evil carry their force in this fact. That is, the consciousness of others enters into one's own body through the victim's organs of perceptual awareness, which are vital in the formation of a person's consciousness in the world and in the very materiality of being. The fear of sorcery and the outrage that people express through sorcery action builds within the ground of the kinds of understanding I have outlined.

Sinhalese who engage in sorcery practices often expect to kill their victims, and as Obeyesekere (1975) explains, it is a viable alternative to direct murderous physical attack. Clearly, in such sorcery, supramundane agents are engaged. However, this does not allow for an easy contrast between physical and mystical means. The supramundane agents of sorcery augment the potent consciousness of the attacker, which is a material energy virtually equivalent in its materiality to the force of being struck by a bullet or a knife. Much of the appeal of sorcery, I suggest, is because of the very materiality of its force; it is a manifestation of the substantial potency of intentional consciousness on the basis of which human beings conjoin and constitute their realities.

I note here what I will later develop as a profundity in sorcery practices concerning the nature of human consciousness (see Chapter 7; Kapferer 1995a). Sorcery works with the notion that consciousness is based in the activities of the body, but that it is simultaneously a force transcendent of the body and centered on objects in the world. In effect, consciousness is always directed and body seeking; it cannot be disembodied. Intentional consciousness is inherently intrusive and transgressive of the body, mind, and lives of others. Sorcery activities highlight the dangerous and destructive possibilities of such material consciousness. Although Sinhalese notions of sorcery are in many ways culturally specific, they express what I suggest are aspects of a human ontological universal: what may be described as consciousness is the force of directed human activity in-the-world. The cultural construction of the agency of consciousness in sorcery beliefs, for all their invention, is nonetheless founded in the factuality of human being in existence.

Obviously, in the desire to inflict injury, sorcery is the preferable material means because it does not involve the same legal dangers or the risk of exposing one's malevolence as do other kinds of material action. The supramundane agents also bear the major burden of the immorality and pollution of the hurting or murderous action. Moreover, as the accounts of sorcery practice should have made clear, sorcery is not limited merely to a focal victim. Its energies spread through the life context of the victim. In this sense, sorcery is more efficient than a singular individually directed physical attack.

Sorcery is widely condemned among Sinhalese, especially that which is premeditated. To make a *huniyam* or to tie (*bandinava*) sorcery is immoral action and Sinhalese avow that it is against Buddhist ideals. The major rites to overcome sorcery (e.g., the Suniyama; see Chapter 5) locate much of their force in the reiteration of the Buddha's virtues. The main beings of sorcery are not seen as the epitome of Buddhist morality. They are violent gods, and Suniyam, for example, although he appears to be gaining place in the Sinhala Buddhist pantheon (see Gombrich and Obeyesekere 1988) is seen by many who supplicate him, including some of the priests who serve him, as being a low, loathsome (*pilikul*) being, a god of the outside (*pita pantiya*) rather than an inside (*atul pantiya*) god. The latter category includes the main guardian gods (Hataravaran Deviyo) of Buddhism and of Sinhalese (e.g., Vishnu, Kataragama, Pattini, Saman, Natha). There is a sense among those who appeal to the sorcery gods to bring disaster on their enemies that they are contravening Buddhist morality. But it is this fact which is vital in the fragmenting force of the sorcery gods and which attracts supplicants to them.

Despite the widespread moral abhorrence of sorcery, people routinely practice it. The specialist sorcerers that I have discussed it with say that they are frequently asked to tie *huniyam*, although they are not always keen to admit to such acts. One sorcerer freely declared his involvement in the tying of sorcery, adding that he had no fear, as he had the protection of his brother, a local police officer. The ambivalence of power and of punishing authority that sorcery expresses is apparent in this comment. The police in Sri Lanka are widely seen as being as much, perhaps more, the transgressors as the enforcers of justice, law, and order. Their favor and power can be bought under the cloak of secrecy, and by means of their intervention, matters of interpersonal dispute are converted into offences against the state but are frequently dealt with outside the rules of the state (by beating and threat). The practice is not uncommon of pursuing personal vendettas by implicating erstwhile friends and neighbors in offences against state-sanctioned laws and regulations. This has become particularly noticeable in the last ten to twenty years of political and ethnic turmoil. Civil liberties have been radically curtailed, and the police have had their powers increased, becoming at times a law unto themselves, judges and executioners.

There is no necessary contradiction between engaging in sorcery and moral injunctions against it. Indeed, the assertion of morality within the context of sorcery, as I have already intimated, can have all the power of sorcery. The major rites of antisorcery, such as the Suniyama, are described as *santiya* or *santi-karma*,[22] or actions that both assert the Buddha's morality and seek the blessing of the gods protective of Buddhism. This kind of antisorcery rite is opposed to the immoral sorcery action or *vina-kirima*. The force of the moral action of antisorcery has the effect of reestablishing protective boundaries resulting in the death of the sorcerer. To put it another way, morality has destructive power.

People do engage in sorcery action without any concern for the morality or otherwise of their action. They do so in secret, traveling to powerful centers of sorcery far away from their neighborhood or hiring a specialist well outside of their everyday circle of acquaintances and activity. This is for technical reasons rather than to hide the shame or guilt that might attach to participating in such action. Sorcery is understood to be most effective when victims are unaware of it and are not alerted to counteractive measures.

There is a widespread view that innovative or foreign sorcery practice is more likely to achieve desired results. This is because antidotes to its poison (*vasa*)[23] are not developed. There is a great tension to innovation and borrowing in sorcery practice: it is the space of the bricoleur par excellence. Mantras from the Maldives are prized, and sorcerers and their clients are on the lookout for new methods, especially those practiced by Malayali Hindus or Muslims. Malay magic is valued, and the Hambantota area in southeastern Sri Lanka, an area of Malay settlement, is renowned as a center for sorcery. The culture of sorcery is alive to borrowing and invention, and the more foreign or strange the practice, the greater its potency for death and destruction. *The foreign* and *foreigners* (*parangi,* a word originating from the Portuguese presence in the region starting in 1505)[24] are metaphors for annihilating and destructive power, and this is conveyed in some of the mythic narratives of the main demondeities of sorcery, specifically Suniyam.

Relatively few people will admit to engaging in sorcery that does not have a basis in morality. Premawathie, in the above example, declared that she was engaging in *kodivina* but that it was a reaction against the illegitimate and immoral offenses of others. This is the feature of much of the action in the contexts of sorcery. Victims declare that they are acting in response to the action of others and that their action has moral impetus, although few are as forthright as Premawathie in admitting their actions are sorcery. The main view is that one's own action drives against immorality and the alienating and harmful action of others.

According to Sinhalese and numerous other peoples, sorcery is absolutely amoral, hidden, and death dealing. Counteracting it is in effect moral action or can give rise to it. Indeed, the major rites of antisorcery are assertions of morality. The action at the sorcery shrines is more blatantly pragmatic and less hedged with moral assertions. But the outrage expressed has moral resonances. Sorcery and its principal sites are in many ways places for the resurgence of morality even in the midst of the human destruction that is the aim of so much of the action.

Domains of Sorcery

The fields of sorcery and sorcery counteraction mainly center around, (1) male traditional specialists or *adura*s, who normally belong to a lineage of such experts who have inherited and been trained in the several arts of sorcery and antisorcery practice. Many caste communities have their *adura,* but most are drawn from the Berava community (see Chapter 4; also Kapferer 1983). (2) There are *sastra karaya*s, or soothsayers, usually women but also men, who operate shrines at their houses. These often divine the source of suffering and validate suspicion. They also organize and perform rites, usually of their own invention. I distinguish them from astrologers (*nakatsastra karaya*), learned men of the book. *Sastras* ground their knowledge in direct experience. They have an intimate association with demons and gods linked to sorcery, and when they are consulted by clients often they become the agent through which the demon or god speaks. (3) There are *kapurala*s, or male priestly intermediaries at shrines to sorcery gods (and to other gods) within Buddhist temple grounds and especially at shrines that are apart from or outside of the space of Buddhist temples. At some of the more powerful sorcery shrines, the Buddhist temple is more a symbolic adjunct than a central focus. The sorcery *kapurala*s usually come from the higher castes (Goyigama, Karava, Salagama, Durava). Many do not have family traditions of such practice and have been drawn to the work by a history of suffering. Their experiences are similar to those of *sastra karaya*s, who cannot work as *kapurala*s, which is a male preserve. I should add that the *kapurala*s for the other gods tend to have inherited their positions. The burgeoning of sorcery shrines since the turn of the century and the recency of their emergence may account for a tendency of sorcery *kapurala*s not to inherit their positions or knowledge.

These specialists are not the only people involved in sorcery work. Astrologers, *vedarala*s (village physicians in the ayurvedic tradition), fortune-tellers (*pena, anjanan*), and Buddhist priests also become involved. Indeed, some individual Buddhist priests are famous for their sorcery and antisorcery work and have been the prime movers in setting up well-known sorcery shrines. *Pirit* rites are a common practice in contemporary Sri Lanka for protection against sorcery. Monks are invited into the house of a victim and chant Buddhist texts through the night in an effort to overpower sorcery and rid a household of its effects. Almost anyone can get some of the knowledge that might be used for malevolent or protective purposes. The knowledge and practice of most authority and appeal, however, is controlled by the specialists I have discussed.

I stress the different location and source of their authority. *Adura*s command a knowledge and a practice that is not produced out of highly personal experience but is vested in a diversity of named ritual practices that have been passed from teacher (guru) to teacher down the generations. The skills of their practice are not necessarily the property of one person, and in major antisorcery rites, such as the Suniyama, several *adura*s must pool their knowledge skills, although these will be coordinated under the authority of a generally acknowledged master (*gurunanse*). The vital and distinctive aspect of the work of *adura*s is that the efficacy of their practice is in the practice itself; in the mantras, the yantras, the songs, and numerous other features of their action that they organize into a particular ritual form. Their knowledge and practice has authority and potency primarily because it is learned and is an extension of tradition rather than a knowledge that is experientially based and embodied as the result of a succession of significant personal biographical events.

*Sastra karaya*s, by way of contrast, have their authority grounded in personal experience. Most of the women *sastra kari*s (often referred to as *maniyo* or *amma,* "mother") I have encountered come from poverty-stricken families and are often from low castes. They recount personal histories of suffering and of attack and possession by ghosts and demons who are finally controlled by the relationship they establish with a particular deity, sometimes Pattini, Bhadrakali, Kataragama, and in some cases, Suniyam.

Lillian is a *maniyo* who attends supplicants at a Bhadrakali shrine at a Hindu temple in Colombo. Lillian claims that she was the first *maniyo* at the temple and started her work there in 1935. She also has her own shrine at her house in a shantytown where she is visited by clients. Lillian is in her early seventies and lives in the part of the city known as Slave Island, notorious as a place of crime and poverty. Her father, a rickshaw man, had come to Slave Island from an equally notorious part of the southern provincial city of Galle. Lillian and her parents lived among a group of Tamil drummers, members of an outcaste community. As Lillian tells it, she would dance at their ritual occasions, and at eleven she experienced her first encounter with the goddess Bhadrakali, who possessed her. Three years later she married Liyanage, who sold tea to the dockworkers. By then her father had died, but his ghost (*preta*) maintained an attachment to her. When she became entranced by her father and danced possessed, her husband was infuriated and beat her. Her husband continued beating her as Lillian had other possession experiences. The ones she recalls in particular are her entrancements by the goddess Pattini, whose violent and punishing form she connects with Bhadrakali. In 1935, after bearing five children, she left her husband and journeyed to the main shrine of Kataragama in the southeastern corner of the island. While she was at Kataragama, her husband, who was still fighting with her, met with an accident and was killed. Lillian felt that he had been punished by the god Kataragama and by Bhadrakali for beating her and her ill-treatment. Lillian possesses the violent and punishing powers of Bhadrakali and Pattini. She has her warrant (*varam*) from the main Bhadrakali shrine at the Hindu temple of Munnesvaram (outside Chilaw, north of Colombo). Lillian also has a warrant from god Vishnu, which she achieved at the time when she first began to manifest and use her violent powers. As she describes it, she would visit the shrine to Vishnu at a local Buddhist temple and declare before the god that she had achieved knowledge, or realized the truth (*satyakriya*), and that she was pure, refusing sexual contact with her husband and having no intention to be married again. On one occasion, the eyes of Vishnu's image closed and then opened. Lillian took this as a sign that Vishnu had granted her his powers through which she could control the violent forces that she manifests. Lillian constantly renews her relationships with the gods by visiting their key shrines. She claims that she got the idea of being a *maniyo* at the Bhadrakali shrine from her involvement in the annual festival at Kataragama, where the god is attended in procession by the six mothers (*kartikeya*) who took care of him at his birth.

Lillian expresses in her own life a personal suffering and a violence present in close ties. She also embraces in herself wider forces of violence as well as difference. She freely admits a connection with criminal elements in the city, and this is vital in her own power. Lillian represents herself as a totalization of diversity and claims a knowledge of eighteen languages (eighteen being a symbolic number of the totality of human existence). She lists among her languages Malay, Gujarati, Urdu, Hindi, Tamil, Kannada, and Telugu.[25] Lillian, I note, is an embodiment of fragmenting force but also a potency for the control and mastery of such force. This is one significance of her warrant from Vishnu, the guardian of Buddhism on the island and a major ordering power. Lillian is pleased with her own success in business. She has controlling interest in three taxis.

Lillian's clients invoke the powers that reside in her body. Some address her directly as Bhadrakali *maniyo*. Lillian says that she has cut thousands of *huniyam*s, and has used her powers in the making and breaking of marriages, the settlement of court cases, and the killing of personal enemies.

The particularities of Lillian's biography and practice find parallels with other *sastra karayas*. The *sastra karaya*s are the mouthpieces of the deities whose bodies of experience are the sites and the testimony of the destructive and ordering power of the beings with whom they have achieved a close relation. Some *sastra karaya*s ecstatically re-present in condensed form the dimensions of their struggle when approached by clients. Thus Alice Nona, a *sastra kari* near the south coast town of Koggala, the daughter of an impoverished bullock-cart driver, becomes gripped by the violent demon Mahasona and also by the demon of sexual obsession Kalu Kumara. These are ultimately subdued by Pattini and Kataragama. Alice Nona is almost blind, but she has a divine sight whereby she can tell the underlying reason of clients' distress and the presence of hidden sorcery. I give one abbreviated example of her performance.

The client presents an offering of betel to the *sastra*.
Sastra kari, in a gruff and altered voice: Shall I begin at the start or at the end?
Client: *Amma,* start at the beginning.
Sastra: You came to ask about land?
Client: About land and the house.
Sastra: I see a house with six rooms, a kitchen . . . Two people from outside the village have been coming. One is known to you. Has there been a fire?
Client: No, no . . . nothing has been burned.
Sastra: No (she insists). There has been some fire very recently. Someone called Ariyadasa . . . and another . . . Sedawathie . . . have made a *kodivina*, a *bumipalu!* Has your business been failing?
Client: Yes.
Sastra: I see others making *kodivina*. Do you want more?
Client: What about my son?
Sastra: I see someone . . . his name starts with W.
Client: Wije
Sastra: Yes that's right. He has something in his stomach . . . a lump of meat. The *kodivina* must be cut. There is Sannikalukumara *pilluva*

(a sorcery with the potency of the demon of erotic and lustful obsession in his disease form).

Alice Nona both divines problems and suggests ritual specialists appropriate to the complaint. Also, for an additional fee, she provides remedies of her own. A small cult had formed around Alice Nona, and she and her husband organize fire-walking ceremonies, innovative versions of the closing fire-walking rites at the Kataragama festival and the village community rites for Pattini (*gammaduva*). They had also taken to organizing on a fairly regular basis mass versions of the antisorcery Suniyama rite. For these consumer Suniyamas, Alice Nona contacts traditional *aduras* who perform, under her direction, events from the Suniyama for a group of clients afflicted by sorcery.

Deity priests (*kapuralas*) at the shrines for Suniyam and for other demon-deities, usually of the *bandara* class (e.g., Tanivale Bandara, Rajjaruvo or Devata Bandara, Gale Bandara, Devol Deviyo), control most sorcery. The shrines for the Hindu goddess Bhadrakali at Munnesvaram (near Chilaw) and in Colombo are also popular. Bhadrakali appears in the Sinhala exorcist ritual traditions, sometimes as a wife or female consort of Suniyam. Shrine priests in Colombo see her as the female counterpart of Suniyam, and like this demon-deity, she has a double aspect, destructive and ordering. Her popularity has grown since the 1960s and concomitantly with the emergence to dominance and spread of Suniyam shrines. The god Kataragama (a Buddhist Sinhalese transmutation of the Hindu god Murugan) is a major god in the Sinhala pantheon. He is associated with war and violent transformation and this century assumed greater import with the growth of Sinhala ethnic nationalism. He is often linked with the Sinhala hero Prince Dutthagamini of the ancient chronicle of the Sinhala kings, the *Mahavamsa*. His main shrine is located in a jungle area in southeastern Sri Lanka in territory marginal between Sinhala and Tamil-speaking populations. It is close to the ancient site of Magama, whence Dutthagamini is said to have set out in his war against the control of the Tamil overlord King Elara. Kataragama is a god who expresses in his mythological and historical formation clear dimensions of transgression and of transition at the boundaries (religious, cultural, ethnic), and in these senses has much in common with other beings prominent in sorcery practice. Supplicants at his shrines engage the priests (*kapuralas*) to curse (*avalada, vas kavi*) and to win Kataragama's aid in the destruction of their enemies or those who have wronged them in some way. These practices are within the broad spectrum of action that may be seen as connected with sorcery. But Kataragama is not himself a sorcerer, as is Suniyam, and he is not understood to be as closely associated with sorcery or sorcerers or as peripheral to the Buddhist Sinhalese moral order as Bhadrakali. In practice, the distinctions are often slight. Broadly, however, the demon-deities of sorcery and the destruction that they bring are more an extension of the destructive and ordering potency of human being than a power of a god whose potency is bestowed on human beings.[26] This point is elaborated in later sections (see also Chapter 7).

The priests (*kapuralas*) for the major gods in the Sinhala pantheon and for some of the lesser *bandara* deities whose shrines are long established have succeeded a previous incumbent and occasionally come from a family line of deity priests. They are generally from high or dominant castes (mostly Goyigama but also, especially along the coast, Karava, Durava, and Salagama). These priests usually profess a knowledge of the appropriate plaints for the gods they serve and make reference to the textual traditions.

Some shifts in both social background and styles of practice are evident at the newer shrines for Suniyam, most of which have sprung up in Colombo and other major urban centers during the last fifty years. Although most of the priests are still from dominant castes, a number are from low castes but disguise the fact. At the main Bhadrakali shrine in Colombo, seven *maniyo* are in regular attendance. This is certainly a break with established practice at the shrines normally attended by Sinhalese, where the priests are invariably male. There is a tendency for the priests at the Suniyam shrines to be from backgrounds with no tradition of service to the deities at the shrines. Two Suniyam *kapuralas* that I met were former civil servants who had gained their knowledge from reading texts. Another had practiced as an astrologer before becoming a Suniyam priest, and another had come from a line of high-caste (Goyigama) *aduras*.

As Gombrich and Obeyesekere (1988: 106) record, there is a growth of what can be called ecstatic priests (often referred to as *sami*), who like many *sastra karayas*, become inhabited by Suniyam's energy and are his mouthpiece. They *directly* and immediately manifest Suniyam's force rather than intercede between clients and the power of the demon-deity. Thus Shelton, who operates a small shrine on the outskirts of Colombo, becomes possessed by Mulu[27] Suniyam (the entire, all-encompassing, originating Suniyam). Clients address him directly as this manifestation. Mulu Suniyam reveals further aspects of their troubles and declares that he will punish the offenders. All the *kapuralas* recognize a specific shrine from which they derive their warrant (*varam*). Shelton gets his power from Kabalava (the shrine for Mulu Suniyam), and he goes there regularly, asserting that at each visit his power grows. Kabalava is the main warranting shrine for many other Suniyam priests, but some also name the main shrines for Vishnu and Kataragama.

Overall, there is a tendency for the three main domains of ritual practice relevant to sorcery to articulate and ground their authority in different kinds of knowledge, although I do not wish to overemphasize this. *Aduras* have their authority by virtue of both generations of such practice in their families and extensive training in the several arts of their ritual work (see Kapferer 1983). They apply ritual knowledge rather than create it. This conservatism does not mean, of course, that their practices are unchanging. But they are conscious of innovation, occasionally referring to it disparagingly as *arumosan,* "modern moves." *Aduras* are entrepreneurially minded and are willing to introduce new performance ploys in order to attract a clientele. But the efficacy and potency of their rites are dependent on the rites being representations of "original" ritual forms.

Traditional exorcists become afflicted by demonic and destructive forces. They too are attacked by sorcery. When this happens, they have rites performed that are the same as those they perform for clients. *Aduras*, like anyone else, may have recourse to Buddhist temples and the shrines to the deities. However, although I admit the possibility, I have not come across *aduras* using their personal experience or an enduring intimate relation with demons or gods as the basis of their power. Their authority resides in the rite and their skill.

Those specialists in sorcery work who operate outside the context of established shrines usually connected to Buddhist temples (*vihara*)— those I have referred to as *sastra karaya,* some *samis*, and *maniyos*— derive their authority, their knowledge, their powers, and their manipulative skill from their enduring and embodied intimate relations with demons and deities. Much of their potency also relates to their personal history of suffering and to their articulation and control of dangerous and destructive forces in their own lives. These are also aspects of the practice of some of the *kapuralas* at the more established shrines associated with sorcery and other problems which are in the grounds of Buddhist temples. Generally, the priests and priestesses of sorcery embody the crisis that the anxiety of sorcery expresses and demonstrate a personal power in overcoming the rupturing forces in the personal, social, and political world so much at the root of sorcery.

The organization of the practice of *aduras* is distinct from that of other specialists in sorcery work. *Aduras* work mostly in village communities and not in the larger urban complexes. They visit the households of their clients and work on a diversity of problems, from minor ailments and other complaints to those considered to be far more serious. Not all of these involve sorcery as the key problem, although it must be stressed that exorcists usually believe sorcery is involved (see Kapferer 1983). In other words, they always regard human action of some kind as being implicated in the crises of their clients. *Aduras* attend to a wide variety of physical and other problems of persons and households brought about by the malevolent attention of ghosts and demons. *Aduras* tend to have long-term associations with, and knowledge of, their clients. They often work in cooperation with other *aduras*, calling them in should this be demanded by the ritual needs of the client's problem.

Sastra karayas and the *kapuralas* for the demon-deities draw their clientele from an extensive geographical and social range. People travel all around the island to visit particular *sastra karayas* and shrines that have built reputations for their powers. Rural and urban bourgeoisie (civil servants, teachers, business people) are very much in evidence, along with the urban and rural poor. The relative anonymity of *sastra karayas* and their shrines is valued by some clients. In their contexts, they can deal with problems away from the eyes of neighbors who may be implicated. It is not easy to conceal the visit of an *adura*. Moreover, *sastra karayas* and *kapuralas* can be addressed more easily as the need arises, and a visit to them is more an individual decision. Other family members need not be consulted, and the required work can be done there and then. The calling of an *adura* often involves agreement from other household members and frequently their commitment to further ritual action that may take weeks.

But appeal to specialists is not mutually exclusive. They are regularly approached in combination, each expanding the potentiality of the other or overcoming the other's failures or insufficiencies. Supplicants before *sastra karayas* and at the shrines assume greater individual agency in addressing and overcoming their plight than when they are clients of *aduras*. With the latter, clients are more acted upon; they are the relatively passive recipients of expert knowledge rather than themselves immediately active in addressing their own problems. Moreover, in the contexts of shrines and *sastra karayas*, supplicants come into the immediate presence of living embodiments of destructive and restitutive force: human beings like the supplicants but in whom the dynamics of humanly fragmenting and ordering action are magnified. Thus, supplicants expand, extend, and recapture their own agency through the heightened capacity of another who expresses most completely aspects of their own situation and the ultimate direction of the resolution that the client intends. At the shrines especially, supplicants destroy and punish, shattering the persons and relations that have caused them anguish. Such action is inextricably tied to the recreation and regeneration of themselves and their life world.

A distinction can be drawn between *adura*s and the other specialists in sorcery work: The former *intervene* between patients and destructive agents, whereas the latter *mediate* or link supplicants to destructive and ordering forces. *Adura*s break the connection between their clients and sorcerers. They interpose themselves between the sorcerer and their clients and carry out the bulk of the destructive work. Clients therefore are relatively separated from destructive acts that offend Buddhist virtue and may encourage vengeance. By way of contrast, *sastra karaya*s and *kapuralas* articulate and facilitate the direct contact of supplicants with destructive and ordering powers. Victims are drawn to their sites because *sastra karaya*s and *kapuralas* contain and control forces of destructive and recreative power. Their appeal is closely linked to the fact that the sites of their shrines as well as their bodies are concentrations of destructive and regenerative force. Supplicants are oriented to come within the context of this power and to engage directly with it for destruction and personal generation. They augment or regain their own potency through their own mediated interaction with Suniyam or the other demon-deities. The clients themselves turn the ambivalent power of the sorcerer to their concern and interest.

I do not wish to force too clear a distinction between *adura*s and the other specialists in sorcery. Clear continuities and similarities are apparent in spite of the differences of practice. Thus, in the major antisorcery rite of the Suniyama, patients come to assume some of the functions of the *adura,* though they operate the potency of his skill rather than the force he may contain or embody. The actions at the sorcery shrines can be seen as a kind of do-it-yourself innovation that parallels the culminating acts of sorcery and antisorcery rites practiced by *adura*s.

Overall the specialists and the practices of sorcery that I have discussed are part of a complex and diverse field of practices. They are mutually influential; the practices of shrine *kapuralas* borrow freely from the practices of village *adura*s and vice versa. Some of the latter act as assistants to shrine priests at urban shrines, and many of the priests trace their knowledge to information imparted to them by *adura*s.

The Transmutations of Suniyam: Difference and Repetition

The practices of sorcery that I have outlined are common in contemporary Sri Lanka. They are not atavistic and do not hark back to some bygone age. Historical processes vital in the formation of the diverse modern realities of Sri Lanka are integral to the continuity and change of sorcery. Sorcery practice is not the mere habit of tradition, a passive continuation of the past into the present, but always a practice made relevant to the present through historical action. As such, sorcery refracts the processes involved in the diverse shaping of modern life and is continually being adapted, created, or reinvented to address everyday exigencies. The sorcery shrines—those to Suniyam with which I opened this chapter— are a particularly clear instance of the formation of sorcery practice in the context of modern political and economic urban circumstances. The shrines are addressed by persons from all walks of life and from remote villages as well as those living in bustling commercial centers. They can be conceived of as powerful centers whose shape, as well as their apparently growing importance in everyday life, is that of the dynamic forces of order and destruction born of Sri Lanka's particular incorporation within global political and economic processes. Emergent mainly in the cities, especially Colombo, the shrines are situated in the spaces that concentrate these processes.

The shrines are new forms, relatively original to modern realities. However, they manifest in their difference, in their distinction, a dynamics integral to much sorcery practice in Sri Lanka. This dynamics is vitally directed to reorienting and shifting the relation of human beings to their lived realities, of moving them from a position of frequently impotent abjection external and subject to the determining force of other human beings and agencies to a position in which they possess active constitutive potency. Supplicants at the shrines are made internal to world-ordering and life-giving and protective forces as they come to internalize these powers. Thus, the action at the shrines, although it is frequently destructive, revengeful, spiteful, and filled with the agony of human anguish (see Chapter 7), is also regenerative—the sorcery activities at the shrines engage a dynamic of human action whereby people muster energies that reconstitute them and their life worlds.

The shrines and their activities actualize in a contracted and intense way aspects of the dynamics and the potentiality of other sorcery rites (see Chapter 7). This is not to say that they are the same as other rites of sorcery or the same as those that belong to specialist, usually village, practice organized independently of the shrines (see Chapters 4 and 5). There are great differences. Most obvious among them is the relatively unrepressed anger and the frequently open intent to cause others damage, often death. As I will demonstrate, the great Suniyama rite to overcome the effects of sorcery actively suppresses vengeance on the part of the victim at the center of the ritual action and distances the victim from other violence of the rite. It might be said that the shrines manifest as central what is hidden and marginalized in rites such as the Suniyama. Shrine and village rites are not the same but are different actualizations of what is immanent in the dynamics of action culturally considered sorcery or closely associated with it.

Deleuze ([1968] 1994), following Nietzsche and also Marx of *The Eighteenth Brumaire of Louis Napoleon*,[28] argues for the identity of repetition and difference: what is repeated is never the same, but the difference of the repetition is immanent in what appears to be repeated. In other words, every repetition of acts that appear to be the same is what Deleuze calls a process of *différenciation* and is potentially an invention of something completely new. What is immanent in a dynamic is realized through historical action. That is, the potentiality of a dynamic is not prior to its historical manifestation but is created in the historical practice itself. The connection between the present and the past is made in the present, which originates or makes existent aspects of processes previously unrealized.

This is the case with the Suniyam of the shrines. As manifested, he is a relatively original form. His originality derives from his particular materialization of an aspect that is immanent or differently organized in long-established village rites. Gombrich and Obeyesekere (1988) see Suniyam as illustrating what they see as a widespread process over historical time in Sri Lanka whereby once lowly supramundane beings achieve god status, eventually to fall from grace into disuse. In effect, they state that the Suniyam of the shrines was once an unambiguous village demon whose elevation is reflected in his current ambiguous god-demon character. But this view obscures vital aspects of Suniyam's transmutation—in fact of his originality—and of why his shrines and others for similar beings may be expected to increase in popularity. Suniyam's ambiguity, and that of similar demon-deities, is not a function of general god-creating processes apparent in different historical conditions, as Obeyesekere (1984a) argues. Suniyam and the other demon-deities describe a specific dynamic manifest in their appearance and location as switchers and boundary crossers, as beings of passage and transition, whose identity condenses the forces of human self-creation and self-destruction.[29]

Huniyam/Suniyam in the ritual practices of village *adura*s is a highly ambiguous figure, not the unambiguous demon of Gombrich and Obeyesekere's interpretation of textual materials. In the rites, Huniyam/Suniyam manifests a double aspect, protective and destructive, and the process of the rites is one that involves a passage between these two moments of his single being. The representation of Suniyam in the shrines describes such a transition along an axis of destruction and protection. Supplicants in effect travel such a line, being transposed from a point of impotency to potency, and themselves often embody such transition (see Chapter 7).

The urban incarnation of Suniyam is probably a conflation of Oddisa Kumara, the master sorcerer and legendary inventor of the sorcery-antisorcery rites of village tradition, with the energies he ritually engenders and comes to embody. The shrine at Kabalava, held to be the original shrine for Suniyam, is stated by the priests there to be the place where Mulu Suniyam (a form of Oddisa Kumara or Oddi Raja) located himself when he arrived in Sri Lanka. Oddisa Kumara is described by exorcists and priests in southern Sri Lankan traditions (which have been most influential on the urban construction of Suniyam) as a *devata* (demon-deity), and even more interestingly, as being one of the *tunbage bandara*s ("officials" of the three divisions, sometimes described as the three brothers).

The *bandara*s, as described earlier, are divided or split beings who are often understood as having been human beings who were local lords in precolonial states, remarkable for their violent-ordering power, who reincarnated as demon-deities after death. The *tunbage* seem to comprise a subcategory. They are specifically significant as beings with magical, ritualist, and shamanlike powers. The three most commonly named are conceived of as being very closely associated (to work in partnership) and form a hierarchy: Dadimunda (Vahala); Devol Deviyo (Irugal Bandara, Gange Bandara), and Oddi Raja Bandara (Oddisa Bandara, Suniyam Bandara, Mala Raja Bandara).[30] In village rites, Oddisa Kumara or Oddi Raja has the capacity to become the shape of sorcery, of the malevolent projection of human action, and to enter into immediate confrontation with the killing sorcerer. He overcomes his rival with his knowledge and skill and reappears as the protective and guardian ritualist. Oddisa Kumara, the ritualist, the human being, merges with the very forces of destruction, turning them back against themselves (see especially Chapters 3, 4, and 5).

The urban Suniyam reissues, condenses, and materializes (concretizes) dimensions of village sorcery traditions. Thus, the power of the village sorcery rites to convert and revert the attack of sorcery and the mastery of the ritualist (who operates the knowledge of Oddi Raja or Oddisa) is achieved in the frame of the ordering potencies of the Buddha and of the Guardian Gods. This is repeated at the urban shrines as Suniyam is placed in proximity to Buddha and the other dominant gods in the pantheon. He is usually placed at their perimeter or they at his. This also manifests a distinction whereby the Buddha and the Guardian Gods are beings of the center whereas Suniyam is a being of the conversional/transitional.

Suniyam is a being very much like the *bandara*s with whom he is associated. His image underlines and expands the distinctive nature of their power and his own, a potency that also repeats aspects of the conversional dynamics of the sorcery-antisorcery rites. Suniyam is the mirror of power as an inseparable unity of ordering and destructive potency; they are not only inevitably joined, but the one is fundamental to the function of the other. This is a basic theme addressed in the antisorcery rites of the village tradition. It is a central paradox of Buddhist doctrine, which the village antisorcery rites attempt to overcome. They cannot avoid it, but the ritualist (*adura*s as the manipulators of Oddisa Kumara's skill) takes the burden of the immorality, as does Suniyam at the shrines. The god Suniyam expresses the paradox in his dual form and also the dynamics of the paradox. The paradox is at the heart of his power and his appeal.

I must stress that the transmutation of Suniyam—a contraction of processes apparent in village rites and a realization or accentuation of elements that may only be immanent or may be suppressed in them—is related to contemporary processes. The emergence of Suniyam shrines, especially in the cities (and the revaluation and growth in popularity of other demon-deities such as the *bandara* gods), is connected with structural forces born of the contradictions of class, the growing gaps between the haves and the have-nots, and the divisions wrought in nationalism with which I began this chapter. Suniyam refracts such forces and assumes an even stronger version of the dynamics of village traditions. He is a reinvention or remaking of them into a bricolage, a new cultural form that bears in a different register or transmogrified shape the dynamic apparent in village traditions. The village traditions do not continue into the shrines and their activities as a survival of tradition or as the stubborn persistence of outworn beliefs but are an original recreation out of the processes of modernity. Suniyam reappears as a being of transition and conversion who crosses boundaries, who transgresses and breaks down orders, and who restores and reforms.

Suniyam's shrines are located in the cities, at the centers of commerce, the points of the entry and egress, and places where the forces of economic and political transformation, ordering and disordering, extend through Sri Lanka. In Colombo his more potent shrines are at the political and economic boundaries of urban space. They mark points of social and cultural crossover and fusion within the shifting orderings of the city. In certain aspects he can be interpreted as the speed of the city, an image of the labile energies of its forms of life, of alternating and crisscrossing currents, of the flow of experience always being restructured, of life in its changing circumstance and uncertain fortune as human beings pass through different contexts, engage in particular activities, and assume diverse identities. The emergence of this urban god, a god perhaps of postmodernity, is at once the radiating potency that consumes and disrupts the lives of human beings, their relations and the grounds of their sustenance, and also the dynamic of their reconstitution. This is a clear feature of the daily practices that center upon him (see Chapter 7).

Above all, the apotheosis of Suniyam, as a difference in repetition, reveals sorcery as concerned with the capacity of human beings to make and to break their realities. In the rites before Suniyam, human beings address each other, intrude into the intimacies and relations of others' lives, seek to rebuild or to sustain their own, and bring each other to account. As the being of sorcery, Suniyam manifests as his radical difference the deified condensation of the fundamental paradoxical forces of the potency of human being-in-the-world.

The dual and divided form of Suniyam highlights the ambiguities and paradoxes of power, its capacities to alienate, exclude, and include. These dimensions are also integral to the forces of human sociality and to the processes of social formation. The intentional orientation of human beings toward one another has the potential for both the creation of social relations and their destruction and also the possibility of exclusion. Suniyam enshrined gives focus and expression to such dynamics. His pivoting form is not merely the Janus-like character of sorcery so widely described in ethnography. He is also a manifestation of the fundamental paradoxes that are integral to the fact that human beings must create the social and political realities on which their existence depends. Such dimensions of sorcery are elaborated in the main myths and rites of sorcery still performed in village traditions. It is to these that I now turn.

3

Victim and Sorcerer
Tales of the City, the State, and Their Nemesis

THIS CHAPTER PRESENTS two myths of sorcery. The first relates events surrounding the first victim of sorcery, Queen Manikpala, the wife of the first World Ruler, King Mahasammata. The second myth tells of the birth and exploits of Prince Oddi (or Oddisa), the sorcerer and healer supreme, who creates the ritual that restores Queen Manikpala from her attack of sorcery. These two myths are at the center of the great anti-sorcery rite the Suniyama, and this is one major reason for concentrating on them.

The myths open up immense cosmological themes. They are stories of the origin of human being and of the world order, of kingship and the institution of the cosmic city, of hierarchy, society, and state, of their destruction by forces externalized in their formation, and of their restoration. The discourses of the myths undoubtedly bear the manifold traces of the heterodox cultural and historical realities of the subcontinent and are infused with Buddhist themes born of the complex and changing universe of Sri Lanka. The stories concentrate on the inescapability of suffering in existence, the paradoxes of power and social existence, the failure of human-created orders and totalities in the midst of more embracing totalizing forces, the limits of reason and the dangers of ignorance, and the destruction wrought by desire and all-consuming greed. The myths make it evident that sorcery concerns foundational forces and nothing less than the world-making and world-shattering potencies of human being.

The events and cosmic themes of the myths indicate what is potentially at stake in the apparently most minor occurrences of sorcery, and people utter the names of the central figures, Manikpala, Vasavarti, Oddi (Oddisa), and Suniyam to communicate a sense of the depth of their distress. The vast cosmic scheme of the stories and the dynamics signed by their chief characters provide a ground against which experiences grasped as sorcery may approach the dimensionality of the enormity and outrage that such references have for their victims. I outline a few of the significances in the stories which provide a frame for the organization of sorcery experiences. What I have to say about the myths at this stage must be preliminary, however, and it must await a discussion of the major rites for which they are relevant and which are their context.

The myths are open to innumerable interpretations, and I make no claim to provide a comprehensive understanding. The myths exhaust interpretation. They open out to meaning rather than circumscribe or contain it. That is, the myths have broad thematic structures through which the experiential possibilities and the import or the meaning of particular contexts of action can be constructed. The myths are not so much structures of meaning in themselves as instruments through which dimensions of human actualities are enframed and grasped. In this sense, the myths I discuss are not representations of lived realities but rather thematic schemes which can gather an immense diversity of concrete experience into the organization of their events. They do not constitute a closed circle of interpretational possibility but are continually open to new meaning and import derived in the contexts in which they are reiterated. This openness to meaning of the myths that I recount is, I suggest, critical in their resilience and their capacity to maintain a continuing relevance to diverse contexts of experience constituted in historically distinct social and political circumstances.

The originary and primordial character of the events in the myths that I present facilitates their opening out to meaning. It is, I suggest, a basic dimension of primordial themes to be so open, to be directed toward the diverse contexts of experience and meaning in the world, and indeed, to discover the full sense of their primordiality in the diversity of experience. The human action and experience that are drawn within their dynamic is made to share the momentous significance of the foundational or refoundational character of originating acts.

The Myths in Sociohistorical Context

These observations are not meant to obscure the historical forces that have been influential in the constructions of these myths and which continue to influence their formation in their retelling. I have one version of the myth of world origin and of the first victim that relates how Maha-sammata established the hierarchical standing of each of the Sinhala castes prominent along the coastal belt of the island. The telling of the myth was used in the legitimation of one perspective on the ranking of various communities in the local area. Undoubtedly, the violence of the main myth of the sorcerer, Oddisa Kumara, is patterned to some extent on events in folk memory and on texts concerning a long history of tumul-tuous invasions and warfare affecting Lanka and its region. There is evi-dence in both stories that Buddhist rites and ritualists are valued more highly than Brahmanic practice. The story of Oddisa Kumara's furious journey to Lanka can be interpreted as a metaphoric rejection of Hindu-ism or Brahmanism and an acceptance of Buddhist authority.

It is entirely possible that the prominence of the two myths I recount in the sorcery traditions of southern Sri Lanka is a consequence of recent historical processes that may have displaced other significant stories of sorcery from a master or framing position in the major rites of sorcery. I refer in particular to the legend of Prince Vijaya and Kuveni, princess of the indigenous Yaka population (see Chapter 2). Very briefly, after Kuveni betrays her own people and assists Vijaya in slaughtering them, Vijaya, in his turn, rejects her, breaking his marriage vows to Kuveni and banishing her and their two children to the jungle fastness. Vijaya does this when he establishes the political order of his Sinhala kingdom and takes his queen from the south Indian city of Madurai. Kuveni curses Vijaya and wishes affliction on Vijaya and the line of his successors. This is a story prominent in the ancient chronicles of kingship, and there is a rich poetic tradition (see Godakumbura 1955, 1963; AmaraSingham 1973; Obeyesekere 1982) with numerous folk variations of the key events, especially evident in the exorcism traditions I studied.

The first rite of sorcery is occasionally said to have been performed for Vijaya himself, but most usually for Vijaya's successor, King Pandu-vas, who suffers the full effects of Kuveni's curse in response to Vijaya's rejection of her. This story and the summoning of Malsara (Mala) Raja to perform the first rite to heal the king of Kuveni's curse is central to the Kandyan and Sabaragamuva traditions of the central highland regions of the island. They are vital in the ritual-drama of the Kohomba Kan-kariya, which is still performed in these areas (see Godakumbura 1963). Kuveni's curse is significant in the use of the *punava* pot (the cursing or "leopard" pot, the leopard being one transform of Kuveni)[1] at Devol Deviyo's shrine and in some healing rites (see Obeyesekere 1982). Sym-bolic articles said to have been used to protect Panduvas in the rite to overcome Kuveni's curse are placed before the patient in all major healing exorcisms of the southern traditions, including performances of the anti-sorcery Suniyama rite (Nevill 1954: 2, 64; Kapferer 1983: 256 n. 19).

Such evidence might support the contention of a minority of *adura*s in the south that the Vijaya-Kuveni legend, although still highly significant, has been removed from a master position by the Mahasammata-Manikpala and Oddisa Kumara stories. This might gather further credence in the context of contemporary political discourse. The Mahasammata-Manikpala story is filled with explicit Buddhist values: it is a story of ideal kingship and society centered around Buddhist principles. The Vijaya-Kuveni legend has as a major theme the pragmatics of power (Kuveni can be interpreted as a victim to political necessity). Its events are located in "real" time (an orientation that might influence the significance of the story in modern Sinhala nationalism; see Kapferer 1988a) and in a period before the establishment of Buddhism in Lanka.

In many ways, the Vijaya-Kuveni-Panduvas myths may be more relevant to precolonial orders and to those groups that ideologically maintain a close affinity with "tradition" in the modern political environment. There are indications that the stories have a stronger presence in village life in the Kandyan and other up-country areas, the center of the last independent Sinhala kingdom and a major zone of resistance to colonial intrusions. The traditionalism of this region was sustained in the administrative arrangements of British rule and has relevance in political and social discourse that sometimes expresses an opposition between up-country and low-country (the western and southern littoral) interests.

There are reasons to suspect that the Mahasammata-Manikpala story may have risen to ritual significance, especially in the southern sorcery traditions, as a consequence of the rise of new class fractions to dominance, particularly among caste communities hitherto regarded by high-ranked castes as low in the order. Members of these new class fractions were interested in eschewing the traditional orders which contradicted their social and economic power. These orders were defined in accordance with the *rajakariya* system or services, often linked to caste, performed for the king (see De Silva 1981: 36, 212–216). The notion of *rajakariya* has very broad use these days and is part of a discourse, frequently inventive, whereby people assert or deny the status legitimacy of caste identity (see Roberts 1982, 1994:xxi, 111, 115; Holt 1991).

The Vijaya-Kuveni myths support traditional hierarchies, whereas the Mahasammata-Manikpala myths can be seen as relevant to emergent class structures. I encountered a poignant example of this on one occasion of the narration of the myth. The storyteller (a *kapurala* at one of the shrines), not content with listing the four main caste divisions instituted by King Mahasammata (see below) and repeated in every version I have, also listed each of the castes in his village area, giving precedence to caste communities otherwise conceived as subordinate within the *rajakariya* system.

A revitalization of Buddhist value and practice (often described as the Buddhist Revival) was and is associated with processes of embourgoisement and gave renewed stress to doctrinal features indicative of rationalism and individualism. The explicit Buddhist themes of the Mahasammata-Manikpala myths fit with such developments.

I do not discount the possibility that processes like these may account for the present importance of the Mahasammata-Manikpala myth. (They certainly give it renewed and modern value; see Chapter 4). This is the case in addition to the fact that the southern sorcery traditions have clear differences from up-country traditions, which I think reach well into pre-colonial times. There is textual evidence, however, that the Mahasammata story had primary significance in the south well before the changes I have mentioned. Casual information that I have on up-country sorcery traditions indicates that the Mahasammata myth is also important and that it is not a recent southern import.

The Mahasammata-Manikpala myth can be interpreted as being in a relation of complementarity to the Kuveni-Vijaya story and its event of key significance in sorcery traditions—Kuveni's curse on Vijaya and the effect of this curse on his successor, Panduvas, and the latter's cure. As I have said, the former myth composes the ideal values of kingship and the order of society. Mahasammata as the incarnation of the Buddha embodies the direction to which kingship and society should be oriented. The Vijaya-Kuveni story is about "real" space and time and pragmatic actualities. In popular conception, the myth concerns the beginning of Sinhala history in the territory of Sri Lanka. The curse that Kuveni casts on Vijaya is popularly understood as the source of the suffering of Sinhala people.

Furthermore, the ideal of the Mahasammata-Manikpala myth may be understood as standing in an encompassing and transformational relation to the "real" of the Vijaya-Kuveni legend. The former myth embodies the projected ideal principles involved in social and personal reformation and restitution that effect the transformations (the recovery from the sorcerer's curse) in real space and time which the Vijaya-Kuveni story signifies.

The transformational complementarity of the two myths (the transformation of the real within the encompassing projection of the ideal) is a dimension of the major Suniyama rite and a feature of other major exorcism rites.

Thus, the patient throughout the Suniyama has the main objects used in the cure of Kuveni's curse on Panduvas (Vijaya's successor) placed at the feet. The objects are chiefly protective but have ambiguous connotations—they indicate both the destruction of sorcery and protection against it. The movement from illness to cure in the patient is effected (see Chapter 5) in the victim's orientation and projection toward a ritual building, the palace of Mahasammata or the Suniyam Vidiya, which symbolizes the ideal order. In other words, the transformation in the real is effected by means of the active relation to the ideal. Toward the end of the Suniyama performance, the victim of sorcery enters the Mahasammata palace—inhabits the ideal. The principles and process of the ideal encompass the real. The victim is reconstituted, and the objects of Panduvas's cure become highly potent in protection.

The dynamic relation of one kind of myth to another (of the ideal to the real) is a feature that becomes evident in the context of rite. It is a pattern that is repeated in other myth relations. Indeed, the main myth of the sorcerer Oddisa Kumara can be seen as standing in a relation of the real to the ideal similar to that of the Vijaya-Kuveni story to the Mahasammata-Manikpala myth.

This analysis of the connection between different kinds of myths should not ignore actual historical processes affecting their relation and significance. Clearly, social and political forces alter the position of myths in ritual practice and must give them new import. There are grounds for considering this with regard to the current prominence of the Mahasammata-Manikpala legend, as already noted. However, I emphasize ritual practice as influencing the relation and significance of myths. It seems to me that historical forces have their greatest effect on mythic relations and traditions when they alter or disrupt the ritual systems in which the myths and legends are located. Moreover, I stress the obvious fact that the kinds of myths and legends that I deal with here—universal, or archetypal, myths—do not reflect actual social and political relations. Rather they indicate a dynamic that achieves a distinct import in the separate contexts of their repetition.

The myths I retell here have historical durability (versions of the events I relate are present in manuscript form from precolonial times) in their broad form, but there is considerable variation in the significant events that they contain. The stories are frequently altered in their details by their narrators, who freely include events from other stories in the vast Sinhala folk traditions and like storytellers anywhere, introduce innovations of their own. However, the intermixing of events from what seem to be different stories is not simply the way of the storyteller or necessarily a confusion of knowledge. It is a practice connected with rite, where it is common for a diversity of events from various myths to be drawn together, for example, into a single song sequence (see Chapter 5).

The versions of the two myths that I present here were told by an *adura* in the south coastal town of Weligama. They are very similar in general outline to other versions of the myths I have collected from exorcists and shrine priests. But it should be noted that the myths retold here are rarely uttered outside the context of incantation or rite, where they are abbreviated or elaborated in accordance with their performative or presentational mode (i.e., poetic or song form) and specific function (e.g., as a praise designed to attract the attention of a powerful being or, as a rhetorical prolegomenon to a specific ritual event, etc.; see Chapter 5). In other words, the narrative form of my presentation of the two major myths is not their usual manifestation, and is a construction by the exorcist concerned in the situation of my enquiry.

Myth 1: The Origin of the World (Loka Uppattiya or Maha Badra Kalpa Uppattiya): A Story of the First Victim of Sorcery and of the First Antisorcery Rite

The following myth is a village version of events some of which are also recorded in Buddhist canonical texts (e.g., Agganna Sutta of the *Digha Nikaya;* Mahavastu).[2] The Manikpala events of the story are an addition from the village sorcery traditions.

A. Before the present age (*kalpa*) the billions of worlds (*sakvala*) were consumed in the fire of the sun. By the power of the merit (*pin*) of earlier living beings, a deluge of rain fell. There were seven deluges, each of different size. The first rainfall was in droplets of needle-like size, growing in size until the final deluge, when the raindrops were the size of eight *yodun*. The whole world was flooded, and the waters reached to the Heaven of Maha Brahma (Brahma Loka). He felt the water around his bed and rose up and planted a lotus seed in the middle of the ocean. The lotus was called Ananda, and it was saffron in color. Seeing this, Maha Brahma knew that a new age was about to begin, and he was pleased.

B. At the start of this age, two Brahmins descended the lotus stalk to the human world. The world was in darkness, and they walked with the light that shone from their bodies. They stopped eating sacred food. One drank up the floodwaters, and they receded, and the earth appeared. At first they ate mud which tasted as sweet as the honeycomb, and then mushrooms, other small plants, and eventually creepers. The Brahmins changed physically into human beings, developing anuses and sexual organs. The human population was propagated from these Brahmins and proliferated. Paddy appeared and human beings cultivated it. They began to divide and separate their lands. They started to quarrel and steal. Now they were also in darkness, for human beings had lost their divine (*irdi*) powers both of flight and of the light that glowed from their bodies.[3]

C. The people gathered together and prayed, and the sun appeared. But there was still darkness at night, so once more they prayed and the moon appeared. Then the names of the days were created, and the weeks and the months. The nine planets appeared, and the twelve signs of the zodiac, and the twenty-seven houses of the horoscope.

D. Then the world was divided into the four quarters. The mountains, oceans, ponds, and rivers appeared. The trees, fish, snakes, birds, insects, and animals were created.

E. The people realized their great suffering. Looking around them they saw that the other creatures of the water, land, and air did not appear to be suffering. Human beings noticed that these creatures had kings and orders of their own. Because of the stealing and quarreling, the people decided that they must choose a king. They assembled and elected a person, the most handsome of them all, who had been born from the womb of Sriyakantava as a result of her union with the Sun. He was called Suriyakumara (Sun Prince), otherwise known as Mahasammata, the Great Elect. The people also chose from their midst four of the most learned among them to be the Four World Guardians. With the election of Mahasammata, human beings were divided into four castes. First among them were the kings (*raja*), then the Brahmins (*bamunu*), followed by traders (*velanda*), and finally the cultivators (*govi*).

F. Mahasammata was sorrowful in his loneliness and chose as his queen Manikpala, the sister of Vishnu. When Manikpala reached the marriageable age of sixteen, she was wed to Mahasammata. She came to the royal bed wearing golden jewels. Manikpala was as beautiful as the full moon, and she loved her life. Her breasts were like golden pots. The gods dwelled at her hips. She was as rare as the most precious stone, and thus she was known as Manikpala.

G. Mahasammata and Manikpala enjoyed their love. But Mahasammata had to leave his palace to take part in the war between the Sura and the Asura. He journeyed to the city of the Asuras to wage war against them. This war was a war of words, not of weapons. The news of Mahasammata's departure was carried to the ears of Vasavarti Maraya (also called Devadatta). Vasavarti was jealous of Mahasammata and lusted after his queen. He desired to have sexual intercourse with the tender Manikpala.

H. Vasavarti Maraya flew to Mahasammata's palace, and as he approached, he changed his voice and his form so as to take on the appearance of King Mahasammata. But he could not change his smell. Mahasammata had the sweet smell of the lotus bloom and sandalwood, but Vasavarti had the stench of the viper (*pangiri*). The queen's servant smelled the stench and looking through the keyhole of the palace gate saw that the visitor was indeed Vasavarti Maraya. The servant shouted to Manikpala to warn her, and the queen barred her bedchamber and cursed Vasavarti to make him leave.

I. Vasavarti was furious. Vasavarti took water into his hand, drawing it from the fiery hell (*aviciya*). From this was born the fire/water viper (*gini-jala polanga*), and Vasavarti cast it at the queen's bedchamber. The viper entered into the queen's womb and Manikpala fell unconscious. Thus was the first *anavina* created.

J. Manikpala's servant cradled the queen's head in her lap and lamented. The god Sakra's throne grew hot, and Sakra came to Manikpala and helped her to regain consciousness. But the sickness of the queen grew, and her body was covered in sores.

K. Mahasammata returned and was told of Manikpala's illness. Mahasammata assembled his ministers and the palace astrologers. The astrologers said that only Oddisa Rsi could heal the queen. But no one wished to ask Oddisa's help. All were afraid of his dreadful powers. His dwelling place was Ajakuta rock, a place so hot that a person's body would be consumed in its heat.

L. Sakra prevailed on Vishnu to ask Oddisa's help. Vishnu changed himself into a beetle (*kuruminiya*) and brought Oddisa to the palace. Oddisa then performed the first ritual to cure the queen's illness.

The basic thematic structure of the myth—what I usually refer to as the myth of Mahasammata-Manikpala—associates the most powerful form of sorcery with the formation of the political constitution of the social order symbolized by Mahasammata's cosmic city-state. Vasavarti Maraya is a figure of radical destruction and evil, who is not just against the moral and ordering force of society, constituted by Mahasammata, but attacks the regenerative center of life, Manikpala. Vasavarti is a manifestation of the Buddha's great adversary, Mara, or Death, the Evil One, who in Buddhist texts and popular traditions opposes the Buddha Teaching and Path. It is Mara who attempts to sway the Buddha from his course toward Enlightenment. However, Vasavarti Maraya, as the most intense manifestation of the energy of sorcery, reveals the nature of its evil as through and through connected with the constitution by human being of society and as a dimension of the energies which bring human beings into relations and are integral to the generation of their relationships.

Sorcery, the Mahasammata-Manikpala myth reveals, is intimately part of both the existential circumstances and the material wants integral to the formation of human being, and the forces underlying and productive of the sociality of human being; or the capacity and orientation of human being to constitute a social and political order and to generate and protect its life within the boundaries of the society it creates. The myth identifies society as the creation of human being, and furthermore, as an act which involves the self-recognition of human being. I note that in this myth of Sinhala sorcery traditions, human beings choose Mahasammata when they realize their difference from other animals, which express a hierarchy and social order that human beings lack. Although society is increasingly immanent in the formation of human being, it is constituted as an act of fully reflective consciousness. Mahasammata, as the Great Elect, is the manifestation of the collective consciousness of human being and of its active will for the constitution of society. In effect, although society may be conceived of as natural for animals, it must be actively created or generated by human beings.

The immediate impetus for the self-creation of society by human being is the suffering integral to existence and its continual development as the differentiating entropy of existence. This is of course a central Buddhist theme. Suffering is at the root of existence. In other myths of the sorcery traditions that I have collected, at the moment of the great rains at the dawn of the new age, Rahu, the Dragon's Head, a cosmological force associated with intense disaster and misfortune, appears as a beetle and hides in a ball of dung in the primeval sludge. The force of suffering is there at the beginning and becomes more and more powerful in the formation and development of human being. In the myth I have recounted, the original beings who take progressive shape as human beings do so as a consequence of their dependence on the materiality of existence and in their consumption of the primeval mud. Their attachment to existence is vital in their development and proliferation as human beings and is vital to an expanding suffering. The natural light-giving luster of original Being is lost, as well as its capacity to fly. The emergence of the gender distinction between male and female is the force underlying the generative multiplication of human beings, relevant to the expansion of their suffering and metaphoric of the process of differentiation. Envy and greed grow apace in the continual growth and proliferation of human beings. Human beings create society to overcome their suffering.

Sorcery assumes its most intense manifestation, in the shape of Vasavarti Maraya, on the constitution of society by Mahasammata. The formation of society reveals sorcery, or the energies that Vasavarti Maraya expresses, to be that which threatens society at its very (re)generative core. This can hardly have a more potent image than Vasavarti's attack on Manikpala and the lodging of his essence within her womb. His attack is nothing less than an extraordinary cosmic rape that drives through and transgresses all social and moral barriers. Commentaries on this event by exorcists and by laypersons consider Vasavarti's act an expression of the rape of sorcery, often colloquially referred to as *hadi huniyam,* a phrase which people apply to their own sorcery experience. The conception of sorcery as a rape condenses the full shocking and violating potential of what is often expressed as the experience of sorcery.

In the myth, the attack takes place at the moment when Mahasammata, the principal constitutive force of society, is absent. In my interpretation, society is weakened while Mahasammata is involved in his war against the Asuras. The servant woman's warning to Manikpala is an expression to the queen of the extreme danger of delusion. It may also be seen as a warning from a symbolic representative of the hierarchy of order, a servant woman, of the impending breach of the protective boundaries of society and of the body. I might add that the servant woman, as a subordinate, could be understood as expressing the weakness of hierarchy in the absence of Mahasammata.

Vasavarti's assault on Manikpala not only strikes through the order of society that Mahasammata institutes, it strikes at the regenerative root of human being, at its life source, the female, Queen Manikpala. The formation of society establishes the condition for a unity of difference. Mahasammata's hierarchical ordering of the different estates or castes of human beings enables them to reconstitute a unity in Being that was lost in the formation of human beings. Thus, after the constitution of society, Mahasammata chooses his queen, and the female principle is brought into conjunction with the male principle. The balanced harmony that Mahasammata and Manikpala express is the energy of life and regeneration.

It might be added that in the myth recounted here and in all other versions I have collected, the potency and unity of human being is in the conjunction of the male and female principles. Manikpala separated from Mahasammata and exposed to Vasavarti's attack becomes a vessel of disease, fragmentation, and death—symbolized by the boils that spread over her skin and the fact that she falls lifeless. Similarly, Mahasammata is impotent before the plight of his queen. Her sickness, a destruction of the life-giving generative female principle balances Mahasammata's own incapacity to act, a loss in the power of the constitutive male principle. Their mutual plight is born of their disunity in separation.

A major theme of the myth is that human beings incorporated within society are nonetheless vulnerable. This is the case as a consequence of the very formation of society. Although the order of society reduces suffering, its creation is also constitutive or productive of an intensification of the energies that can destroy society. This is because the formation of society constitutes a division in existence, a separation between that which is interior to society and that which is exterior to it. In other words, the society of Mahasammata arises against the natural entropy of existence (in which it is nonetheless conditioned). It is an ordered totality within an encompassing totalization. In a sense, Vasavarti is the energy of such totalization and ultimately is a greater force than Mahasammata. Although Mahasammata strives to bring all of existence under his sway (his war against the Asuras) in the narrative of this myth, he must fall back to his queen, whose illness manifests the destruction of the totality he has instituted. What I stress is that Vasavarti, the quintessence of sorcery, reveals it not only as the energy of totalization which forces against structure and the boundaries and orderings of society and of human beings within society, but also sorcery as the violence of externality made in the formation of society.

Vasavarti manifests sorcery as part of the formation of human beings and as integral to the dynamics wherein human beings strive to create their orders and relations in existence. Sorcery has an identity with the processes to which it is opposed, which is expressed by Vasavarti assuming Mahasammata's shape in his confrontation with Manikpala. That he is not what he appears to be exemplifies the dangers of delusion to which the queen is subject and her lapse from conscious alertness. She expresses the import of the Buddhist insistence on mental alertness which is so much a part of doctrinal teaching. Thus, a verse of the great Buddhist text *The Dhammapada* reads, "Knowing that this body is fragile like a jar, and making his thought firm like a fortress, one should attack Mara, the tempter, with the weapon of knowledge, one should watch him when conquered, and should never rest." However, I emphasize Vasavarti and sorcery as the energy of destruction which is the force of consciousness and of its intentionality (i.e., consciousness as inseparably part of the directedness of human beings toward existence).

Sorcery as epitomized by Vasavarti is the annihilating force of self-directed individual consciousness. Indeed, the ultimate individual closure of such action is antagonistic to a vital openness, and the mutuality of such openness is critical to the creative formation of social relations and the order of society.[4] (The mutuality of such openness is expressed, I suggest, in the love of Manikpala and Mahasammata for each other.) Vasavarti, expressing the furious power of self-interested individuality and desire, can only generate the sterility and fragmentation that is intrinsic to his force. Moreover, not only does the intentional consciousness of

Vasavarti—which is ultimately self-directed and enclosed—destroy the consciousness of others but also the intentionality on which their consciousness, and ultimately their very being, is dependent.

I emphasize that Vasavarti manifests that dimension of intentionality which, although it is integral to sociality, must be transformed for sociality to take root and for the creation of social relations and their order to be established. The choice of human beings for Mahasammata is the expression of such a transformation, a decision that moves human being from closure to openness. Mahasammata is a symbolic condensation of this move, the collective agreement of human beings, which shifts them away from self-destructive action to action that is generative and beneficial and life-giving.

To expand my interpretation of the myth, it explores the paradox of what I refer to as the sociality of human being, which is founded in the emergence toward consciousness. Society is immanent in human being, that is, in the fact—evident in the Mahasammata-Manikpala story—that human beings live in a world inhabited by other human beings who are enmeshed in a field of potentially destructive intentionalities that are integral to human action and activities. Society is achieved through the recognition by human beings that their destructive activities and suffering are not necessary. This realization is one they arrive at through a recognition of themselves (they see themselves as human beings) in relation to other forms of life. In their recognition of their difference, which expresses the emergence to consciousness, human beings agree to the hierarchy of society and its life-sustaining external and internal boundaries.

I remark further on the themes of sexuality in the myth. The metaphors of sexuality, as elsewhere among human cultures and particularly in the context of Sinhala myths, constitute a commentary on the potentialities of human action for destruction and generation. The sexual themes also point up the paradox of human action that is simultaneously self-interested and other-directed, of action that is both individual and social. Vasavarti's action is all excess and transgressive individuality. His metaphors are of lust, rape, and extreme violation. His fiery leap toward Manikpala is the thrust of intentionality, which in this instance kills, but (see Chapters 5 and 6) is also the action of human beings, which is a foundation of consciousness and sociality from which social relations and society are formed. Although Vasavarti displays the forces that are destructive of the social and of individual being, he nevertheless reveals aspects that are a dimension of their growth and sustenance. In contrast, Mahasammata is restraint; he subdues the transgressive dimension of his intentional consciousness. A few exorcists who have commented on the myth

suggest that Mahasammata and Manikpala do not engage in sexual intercourse. The consciousness of one does not override that of the other,
and they manifest a harmony of mutuality. Mahasammata expresses the
virtues of Buddhist compassion and love, which do not involve the extinction of the other in an assertion of self and which are other- rather than
self-directed.[5]

Myth 2: Ambiguous Potencies: The Origin of Oddisa, Master Ritualist and Sorcerer

The myth of the sorcerer that I now recount is also the myth of origin
of Oddisa, the first exorcist,[6] the archritualist who is brought by the gods
to cure Queen Manikpala of her sorcery. In the exorcism traditions of
southern Sri Lanka, it is the skills of Oddisa that *adura*s regard themselves
as continuing in most areas of their healing practice (see Chapter 4). Oddisa is in many senses the originator of rite, and as the following story
indicates, the grand sacrificer, whose function is to mediate the reconstitution of the orders of existence that protect human beings and within
which they can develop their lives once more. Oddisa is a figure of profound ambiguities, which are vital to his ritual powers, and the formation
of these is a central theme of his story.

I present the myth of Oddisa's ruling form (Oddisa Kumara or Raja;
he has other births; see Wirz 1954; Gombrich and Obeyesekere 1988,
for similar stories). Oddisa is usually conflated with the demon Suniyam,
but I think the two are better understood as distinct. That is, Oddisa is
the sorcerer and Suniyam is the energy of sorcery that he controls and
embodies. Oddisa is a shaman-sorcerer. At some shrines he is maintained
as a small turbaned figure apart from the main image of Suniyam, the
objectification of sorcery. The *adura*s see themselves as the exponents of
Oddisa's art.

This version of the main Oddisa myth is similar to most accounts I
have collected. Certain events that are incorporated into this myth, as
with so many other myths in Sri Lanka, have been drawn from other
stories connected with different figures. The mythopoesis of story construction in Sri Lanka, forever dynamic and changing, is one that constantly draws on the materials at hand in diverse traditions.

THE BIRTH OF ODDISA KUMARA

A. The king of Vadiga (the father of Oddisa Kumara) ruled the country
of Oddivadiga in the land of the Kalingas in Dambadiva. Vadiga Patuna,
the city of Oddisa, was protected by three walls, one of crystal, the second

of stone, and the third of metal. Three ditches also surrounded the city: the first a dry ditch, the second of mud, and the third of water. The people of Vadiga were divided into four castes: The first was the royal (*raja*) caste, the second was Brahmin, the third were traders (*velanda*), and the fourth cultivators (*govi*). Likewise, the king's army had four divisions: the elephant and horse divisions, and the chariot and infantry divisions. The country of Vadiga was rich in gold, silver, pearls, and gems. The king of Vadiga was married to the daughter of the Kalinga king.

B. One day when the Queen Yawudagiri[7] was walking in the royal park, she wanted to bathe in the pond. This pond had seven different water lilies growing in it, among them the blue water lily (*manel*). While she was bathing, she was seen by one of the great deities (*mahesakya*), who was passing overhead (Mara, Vasavarti). Desiring to possess (*avesa*) her body, the god had sexual intercourse with the queen, and she fell unconscious.

C. The king found his queen unconscious and brought her back to his palace. The king sought the advice of rsis. They said that a ritual (*yaga/* sacrifice) called a *garbha mangalaya* (womb ceremony) should be performed, for the rsis knew that the queen was pregnant.

D. The queen's face became lifeless, her body pale, her breasts enlarged, and her nipples dark. The queen had two pregnancy cravings (*dola duka*). First, she had a longing to eat food that had a burned/roasted taste (*dumbul*), a sour (*ambul*) taste, and a milk (*kiri*) taste. The second longing caused her great embarrassment, and she went to the king with her desire.

E. The queen told the king that she was afraid to tell him of her craving. She longed to coil her body with cobras and vipers and to walk naked around Vadiga city. The king exclaimed that he had never before heard of such a craving. He was overtaken by fear, and he commanded the royal executioner to kill the queen. But the queen pleaded with the king for mercy and he relented.

F. Ten months later, the queen gave birth to a son. The king summoned learned Brahmins from throughout the land and feasted them from golden plates. He told the Brahmins the prince's birth time and allowed the Brahmins to examine the prince's body. The king wished to know what the future held.

G. The Brahmins announced that the prince was extraordinarily powerful and that when he achieved adulthood he would kill the king and take command of his kingdom. They foretold further that he would make an alliance with the kingdoms of the Kalingas and of Danta. With this alliance, the prince would invade Lanka and eat all the human beings who lived there.

H. At first the king thought of killing the prince. Instead he gave the prince into the care of nursing mothers (*kiri amma*). When the prince reached the age of seven months, he was given his first rice to eat (*kiri bhat*) and given his name, Vadiga Kumara. When the prince reached the age of sixteen, he left the palace and went out into the jungle (Hirandara jungle).

I. In the jungle he found an anthill (a golden anthill), and he reached into it, pulling out many cobras. He broke their fangs and absorbed their poison into his body. He coiled his body with all kinds of serpents: the *mapila* (a bloodsucking snake), the *polong telissa* (jumping viper), the *kara-vala* (black-and-white ringed snake). He collected the bones of vipers and the thorns of poisonous creepers: *timbol* (a tree with toxic fruit and thorns) and *ukkuressa* (the fruit parches the throat). The prince garlanded his head and shoulders with foul-smelling flowers. He captured the Maha Kala Naga (the great snake at the beginning of time) and extracted his four venomous fangs on which dwelled the demonesses Takari, Makari, Yami, and Yama-duti.[8]

J. The prince now returned to Vadiga city. He killed his father, the king, and he ate all the people of the Vadiga country. He then attacked the kings of Kalinga and Dantapura, killing them and eating all the inhabitants of these kingdoms. The prince gathered around him the eight demonesses of these two countries (Ailakkandi, Mailakkandi, Vatakkandi, Totakandi, Asanikandi, Visanikandi, Kalaraksi, and Kaksadevi). He also gathered terrible gods around him like Riratta, Maratta, Goratta, Mara (Harbinger of Death), and Gora (a kind of terror).

K. The prince now journeyed to Visalamahanuvara (the mythic city of the Licchavis in Nepal), where he gathered about him the eighteen Sanni demons. Prince Vadiga ate uncooked human flesh. He then journeyed (now assuming the form of Oddi Sanni Yaka) to the abode of the Asuras and threatened to destroy them. Eventually he came to the city of the lord of the demons, Vessamuni, at Kuverapura. Vessamuni gave Oddi authority to be a demon. Oddi then returned to Visalamahanuvara, with his eighty-four thousand followers, and he started to eat all the people of that city.

L. The Reverend Ananda commanded Oddi to stop eating human beings and ordered Oddi to accept performances (*keli*) and offerings (*puda*). Ananda then recited a *gatha* and repelled Oddi from Visalamahanuvara. But Oddi returned at midnight and screamed three times at the north gate. The screams were so loud that Buddha heard them.

M. Buddha preached a *gatha*. Oddi Yaka prostrated himself in worship before the Buddha and declared that he had come to gain the Buddha's authority so that he could kill and eat human beings for as long as the Buddha's teaching lasts. The Buddha forbade Oddi to kill and commanded Oddi to receive offerings (*dola pideni*) and sacrifice (*degata billa,* "animal with two legs"). Suniyam Yaka responded with furious anger and threatened to kill everyone in Lanka if the Buddha did not grant him this authority.

N. So fearlessly did the demon speak that Buddha knew that Suniyam was of high birth. Buddha asked Suniyam who his parents were. Suniyam replied: "I am the son of King Oddi Vadiga, and I was born from the womb of Queen Yawudagiri. I am called Surandara, Purandara Vadiga Oddi Kumara. I am the demon who killed three kings and have eaten the human beings of three countries. I am called Sri Oddi Madana (lust, form of Vishnu), Kadiranga (horn of the buffalo killed by Mangara deviyo),[9] Kama Rakshya Devatava."

O. "What kind of authority can I give you," replied the Buddha? "I command you to stop eating people and to accept *dola pideni* (offerings)." Buddha intoned a *gatha* to bind Oddi to his command. Buddha summoned the god of rain (Harahara, Vishnu) and ordered this god to take Oddi Kumara to the Aviciya hell and to bind Oddi to an iron pillar.

P. But the Buddha relented. He considered it inappropriate for such a powerful prince to be so bound. He ordered Oddi to be brought back. Buddha greeted Oddi: "O Sri Vadiga Oddikumara Surandara Purandara Kadiranga Kamarakshya Oddikumara . . . you must obey my commands." Oddi replied that he would bow to the commands (*ana*) of the Buddha. "I will honor your name (*namo*), and I will heal all illnesses and protect against diseases."

Many of the themes of the Mahasammata-Manikpala myth are expanded in this story or made even more apparent. Oddisa embodies the chthonic energies deep in the ground of existence. He is the dreadful force of externality, conceived beyond the boundaries and defenses of the city-state-society, and assumes his most powerful and destructive force in the wild jungle regions outside. However, this apparently external force is also interior, dynamic within the relations and orders that it comes to destroy. Oddisa manifests the totalizing force of sorcery and also the ambiguous potencies of the sorcerer, who works with the energies and materials at once integral to the ways human beings constitute themselves and their realities and to their destruction.

In the version of the story I have retold, Queen Yawudagiri is impregnated by Vasavarti, but in other versions she is impregnated by Suniyam.[10] As with Manikpala the force of destruction enters into the center of the city-state and grows within its borders and within the very womb of city and society. The failure of the ritualists, the *rsi*s, to cure the illness of her womb looks forward, I suggest, to the greater powers to be harnessed to rite, those of Oddisa Kumara, which in fact are growing in the queen's womb.[11] An interpretation that could be placed on the queen's pregnancy cravings is that they are an expression of her embodied awareness of her defilement by sorcery, of the destructive energies of the outside that are rooted in her body—an experience of sorcery that is expressed in contemporary contexts of rite and shrine. The queen's outrageous and shaming desires are indexes of her possession or inhabitation by another consciousness. The king's refusal to grant her desires effectively prevents the queen from externalizing her defilement. This refusal is an unreasoned act of confining and repressive power fueled by anger (and of disunion between king and queen and of further development in the breaking of the life-giving conjunction of the male and female principles eventually brought to fruition in the birth of their monstrous son). These actions and others—for example, the king's rejection of knowledge, his ignoring of the Brahmins' warnings that Oddisa Kumara will bring great disaster—are actions that are instrumental in the formation of Oddisa and that he manifests in the most totalizing form.

Oddisa chooses the way of the sorcerer. He is not just born to destruction but actively gathers the ingredients of sorcery. Unlike Yawudagiri, he is fully aware, and makes himself into the agent of sorcery when he becomes mature and attains independent consciousness (sixteen in most Sinhala myths). Oddisa becomes the most feared kind of sorcerer, certainly in the Sinhala context, one who is purposefully oriented to the course of destruction and extinction.

Oddisa assumes the form of absolute annihilation. Moreover, he is the figuration of the complete destructive capacity of action and intentional consciousness. This, I suggest, is carried most strongly in the symbolism of princes rather than kings. The obvious Oedipal dynamics of the Oddisa story aside, the prince in this and numerous other Sinhala myths (e.g., the myths of Prince Vijaya and the conquest of Lanka) is a figure of becoming, and of action directed toward a potentiality, a being of the process of intentionality par excellence. In contrast, the symbolism of the king is more one of completion, a center around which action swirls and toward whom it is directed. Kings control, maintain, and react; princes express the dynamics of action, the processes of becoming, and the building of power. But Oddisa—at this moment in his formation—manifests that energy of intentional consciousness that can reproduce itself only as destruction. It achieves no objective beyond itself.

Remorselessly directed toward the city-state-society, Oddisa levels all in his progress. He destroys his father, the king of Vadiga, the ordering principle and the center of political and social hierarchy. City after city and country after country are exterminated, and Oddisa eats their human populations, continually moving toward horizons that constantly recede before his all-consuming thrust. His is the full transgressive force of intentionality that breaks through boundaries and the lines of defense and order of body, society, and state, and courses along the relations of alliance, dissolving them in his passage. Oddisa is the voracious insatiability of intentional action, a ravenous consumption of Being in existence, a monstrous formation of Being annihilating itself.

His thoroughly amoral consciousness is more than the opponent of the consciousness motivated in the morality of reason and order; it is the greater force not only overcoming them but, in effect, causing reason and the principles of order to subvert themselves. Oddisa's story may be seen as conveying a deeper Buddhist message: that consciousness and the knowledge of consciousness are processes of existence and therefore cannot escape the suffering of existence. Thus, Ananda, the great follower of the Buddha's path, cannot control Oddisa—nonreason overcomes reason. In the myth, the powers of reason appear to fail even the Buddha himself, and he must resort to having Oddisa bound by Vishnu, the protector of Buddhism. Oddisa and sorcery are aspects of the double bind of the action and consciousness of human beings. Only with the extinction of consciousness—the ultimate nonexistence of the Buddha teaching—can suffering and the possibility of sorcery and the sorcerer be avoided. Oddisa expresses the incontrovertible paradox of Being and consciousness, that they are the seeds of their own suffering and destruction. The ambiguity of sorcery and of the sorcerer, indeed the rebounding danger of the action of sorcery and the sorcerer, has its dynamic in the fundamental paradox of intentionality and consciousness.

The totalizing powers of Oddisa are such that he incorporates all existence. All other manners of totality, bounded entity, or finitude are consumed within Oddisa's great maw. In other myths and songs, Oddisa is described as having an enormous mouth. Nevill (1954: 2, 232) collected a text at least a century old that records Oddisa's mouth as fifty *yoduns* wide.[12] Everything is drawn within him; his ever-voracious movement is a traversal of all possibility and potentiality. As bounded and ordered totalities of city and society appear before him, Oddisa becomes something like the war machine that Deleuze and Guattari (1988) describe, flattening and "deterritorializing" them, overcoming their spatial boundaries and the internal divisions and striations of order. Deleuze and Guattari develop their notion of war machine and also of state through a consideration of sorcery and the sorcerer (see also Chapter 8).

I underline the consuming dynamic of Oddisa's masticatory totalizing progress in which he fuses diverse political and social forms and their human populations by breaking them down and merging them together. It extends the implication of such totalization: What is reduced into Oddisa's form is also immanent within him.

Oddisa, the myth relates, travels back to Maha Kala Naga, the great snake of the beginning (and end) of time, and extracts his teeth. He may be understood as drawing the roots of temporality, which of course contain death's poison. In other myths collected, Suniyam and Sanni Yaka (Kola Sanniya) are born through the left and right nostrils, respectively, of the great snake of time. I suggest that this may be interpreted as establishing a powerful association between the force of destructive intentional consciousness, on the one hand, and the annihilation of social relations, society and human being, on the other. Sanni Yaka is a collective representation of communicable disease, the destructive force acting against communities and within them. In the myth I have related, Oddisa travels to Visalamahanuvara City, which Sanni's most annihilating form, Maha Kola Sanniya, reduces to a putrid stinking ruin of death (see Barnett 1916: 94; Wirz 1954: 42–47; Obeyesekere 1969; Kapferer 1983). He becomes the form of Sanni Yaka (Oddi Sanni Yaka).

Confronted by the Buddha, Oddisa reveals the names of the destructive powers with which he identifies, but he also manifests the hierarchializing forces immanent within him, powers that are reconstitutive of body, society, and state. Not only does the Buddha recognize the ordering potency of Oddisa but he causes, by virtue of his confrontation, Oddisa's transformation into a being of protection and of the restoration of the orders of human beings. In other words, the infinitude of the Buddha, whose path projects beyond consciousness and intentionality, encompasses the finitude of Oddisa and converts his destructive consciousness and intentionality into a healing force regenerative of body and of society. These are dimensions of Oddisa's powers that perhaps become clearer in his major rite, the Suniyama. But Oddisa, in this story and other versions, appropriates the poisons of destruction and by doing so becomes their antidote.

Oddisa Kumara is a liminal being. He assumes the monstrous form of totalizing forces. He becomes a being capable of entering into their swirling vortex of destructive and generative energies—potencies that fill his symbolism. The ambiguous, originary, creative, destructive, overpowering, transgressive, and conjunctive imagery of sexuality and birth floods his representations. Oddisa dwells at Mount Ajakuta, Goat Mountain,[13] a place so hot that no other being save Vishnu can approach it. Vishnu himself is a figure of sexuality and is usually closely associated with Oddisa, who is described as taking one of Vishnu's forms, Madana Yaka—the demon of sexual obsession, of lust. Oddisa is a being of mediation, a "betwixt and between" figure, a property apparent in his very pattern of movement. Engaging with totalizing forces, he makes himself into an instrument of their dynamic, a being who can articulate and direct their force.

Oddisa Kumara is the full dimensionality of the powers of the sorcerer, an amoral figure who can embody and manipulate the forces of human action, turning them to destruction or recreation. He is the arch-ritualist/ magician and the sacrificer whose stories record the magnitude of the knowledge and skill which are engaged to the service of human beings for the making and the unmaking of their existential realities.

Conclusion: The Unity of Myth and Rite

My purpose in this discussion of the main sorcery myths has been to give some sense of the profound Buddhist themes (and others in the subcontinent) that organize their events. In other words, the dynamics of sorcery and the sorcerer are not processes that should be grasped initially as part of general categories often constituted through the frames of Western thought that are strongly influenced by Jewish and Christian tradition. Nonetheless, the stories indicate some parallels with this tradition. Sri Lankan Buddhists have been described as having a far less radical notion of evil and the demonic than those of Christian traditions.[14] Perhaps the oppositions are less absolute and the contradictions between good and evil are less clearly drawn. It is not my interest, however, to participate in an abstract debate of a comparative theological nature but to emphasize that despite many undoubtedly irreducible differences, these myths recognize sorcery as nothing less than the capacity of human beings to make or break the circumstances of their lives. Furthermore, the myths indicate the dimensions of these human capacities.

The sorcery myths describe the most potent destructive form of sorcery as part of the efflorescence of human consciousness. It is integral to human action and choice and develops in proportion to the orientation of human being to overcome its suffering, which is grounded in the conditions of existence. The forces of sorcery reach their apotheosis in the formation and context of the social and political orders constituted by human beings. The manifestation of one produces the extreme of the other. Sorcery is connected with the dynamics of human action whereby human beings form their relations and constitute the fabric of a social existence in which their lives progress and are sustained. The forces of sorcery grow within the very orders that human beings form around themselves and express a fury against the externalizing processes of social formation. Sorcery is simultaneously the outrage and transgression of conscious action against the very body of Being and of the consciousness at the center of created orders. There can be few more powerful images of the annihilating force of sorcery than Vasavarti's rape of Manikpala.

The myths not only present a scheme but also indicate the fundamental processes at work in the construction and deconstruction of human-centered worlds. The myths are only suggestions of what these processes are, however, bare traces of what is revealed and developed in rite. The stories are regarded by ritual specialists as projecting the aim of a practice that will restore their clients to action and a capacity to participate in the construction of their realities. The myths are less paradigms for rites than their residue, which, when separated from their ritual context, assume the character of stories, the tales that people tell. In some ways, the narrative elaboration of the myths outside the context of rite may be regarded as an impossible effort to recapture the force of the rites of which they form a part. I question a dialectical approach to myth and rite which sees the one as being a function of the other, as is the case in many structuralist and antistructuralist perspectives (e.g., Lévi-Strauss vis-à-vis Victor Turner). These often seem to be nothing more than different sides of the same argument: in the one, the logos of myth is favored over praxis and in the other praxis over logos. In my analysis neither is prior to the other, but both discover their full force in an indivisible conjunction.

Within the process of the major sorcery rites, myth becomes a lived reality in which its existential force is discovered as a property of the unfolding dynamic of the complex of ritual practices of which it is a part. The myths have immanent within them the reconstitutive forces underlying the capacity of human beings to act and to form their being-in-the-world. The denial or inhibition of this capacity is a central import of the assertion of sorcery's malevolence. The myths suggest what might be called a practical anthropology, a dynamics of human construction and therefore of reconstruction. Reconfigured into the structure of rite, the myths become elements in a process of human (re)formation which unfolds the complexity of human sociality and of the ways human beings must constantly create and recreate themselves and the orders of their worlds.

1. A priest curses at the "original" *Suniyam* shrine at Kabalava, north of Colombo, near Chilaw

2. A *Bhadrakali maniyo*

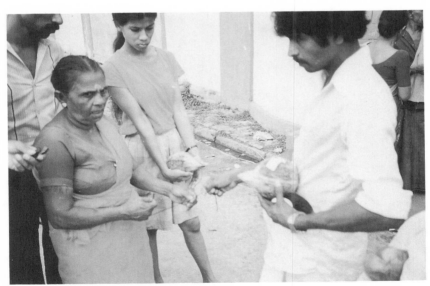

3. A *punavva* at a shrine to Devol Deviyo

4. A leopard pot at the private shrine of a *sastra*

5. A small antisorcery cutting rite, or *kapuma*

6. *Above:* A gathering of victims at a *Bhadrakali* shrine. *Below:* A woman curses before *Suniyam*.

4

The Suniyama

The Conquest of Sorcery and the Power of Consciousness

PART I

THERE IS NO GAINSAYING the phantasmagoria of a Suniyama performance and the sheer enchantment of its entertainment. I think both the foreign anthropologist and locals can share in its marvelous spectacle, in the splendid artistry of ritual building and decoration, in the aesthetics of its music and dance, in its earthy and scurrilous comic theater, and also in its perilous moments of anxious tension and violence. There is little in my experience that compares with the occasion of a Suniyama.

I recall one instance, early in my fieldwork, when I arrived late, after dark, and the ceremony was well under way. I heard late in the afternoon that a Suniyama was to start that evening in a distant village tucked away in the southern foothills of the island, some forty miles away from the small coastal town where I was living. Traveling at night on a scooter along Sri Lanka's more remote and often hazardous roads is a pleasing experience. The cinnamon-sweet night air is warm, and I always feel both free and protected in its embrace. Climbing through lowland rubber and tea plantations, I found the darkness was broken by glints of light revealing clusters of houses and small villages stretching into the distance on either side of the road. The larger pools of light, I fancied, betrayed an exorcism of demons or quite possibly a village deity rite for Pattini or Devol Deviyo (a *gammaduva* or *devol maduva*). There had been a number of these rituals recently, and I expected that this night would be given to the struggle of gods and demons. The time came to leave the road. The exorcism house (*tovil gedera*) was about half a mile away across a stretch of irrigated paddy and amid a group of houses circling a hill which rose above the fields.

Leaving the scooter in the safe care of a roadside stallholder, I and a couple of Sinhalese friends, one an *adura,* began to walk along a narrow pathway between the fields. As we drew near, we could hear the shrill call of the demon pipe (*vasdanda*) and, at that distance, the confused rattling staccato of the demon drums. At first the ritual noises were alternately faint, then loud, then faint again, and finally louder, increasing in intensity until the full exciting heavy rhythmic beat of a number of drums palpably shocked our bodies. Rising and threading through the sound, the high-pitched nasal resonance of an exorcist singing and the choruslike refrains of his companions could be heard. Clambering up a sudden steep and muddy slide and then around a corner, we burst into a throng of spectators at the fringe of the performance arena. We found ourselves within a large open-sided hut (*maduva*) roofed with corrugated iron and specially built for the occasion. Its supports were hung with a variety of young fruits and the flowers of different palms. At the far end of the hut was the most beautiful Suniyam Vidiya, the palace of King Mahasammata and his queen, Manikpala. It stood some twelve feet high and modeled eighteen pinnacled roofs, the most I had seen, and its splendor indicated the high status of victim and household.

The entire palace was wonderfully decorated and festooned with colored lights (the rays of the Buddha). The highest point of the palace, the center pinnacle or tower, was painted with a figure of Suniyam, with his sword of judgment raised, in protective and punishing stance. On the lower pinnacles at either side were paintings of the Sun (right) and the Moon (left). The victim (*aturaya,* patient), with his back toward us, was seated in a chair and covered by a white shawl. He faced a tiny doorway on the ground floor of the palace, the entrance to a structure known as the *atamagala,* and more popularly, among the onlookers, as the bedchamber of Queen Manikpala. The victim was soon to enter the *atamagala,* and an exorcist was clearing and purifying the way. The exorcist threw *dummala* (a powdered tree resin) onto a flaming torch. Huge gusts of orange flame enveloped the palace. The burning *dummala* filled the air with its acrid fumes. The whole scene was tense; people in the gathering, which must have numbered well over two hundred, were craning forward, though when they noticed us, some shoved their companions to make way for the unexpected visitors.

My own wonderment was broken by a householder tugging at my arm to greet me and my companions and to invite us inside. This is typical of the warm hospitality of exorcism households and indeed a vital part of the performance of *tovil*s. I could not help noticing, however, that at this Suniyama, as at many other similar performances I was to witness, there was not such a separation of women and children from the male spectators as is evident at exorcisms for other demons. And at these latter ceremonies, the women tend to huddle closer to the house and often remain within its safer confines (see Kapferer 1983). On the occasion of this Suniyama, many of the women of the household sat near the victim. A small girl in her finest dress stood beside the victim holding his hand. She was his granddaughter, I discovered later.

Although there are many tense moments in Suniyamas, their atmosphere is relatively relaxed. The easier and freer ambience of a Suniyama has much to do with the heightened stress on Buddhist values in the rite and the fact that in many respects it is an act of worship of the household and the community to Buddhist ideas. The other demon exorcisms place the victim and the household in a more dangerous and precarious relation to demon attack.

This, no doubt to some, overromanticized impression of a Suniyama is intended both to convey a sense of my own continuing enchantment with the rite (a fact which I cannot expunge from my understanding) and to present some overall picture of the magnificence and general character of the action in the ceremony.

The aesthetic pleasure and spectacle of the Suniyama are vital to the various objectives which the patient, the members of the patient's household, and the wider network of kin might plan for the occasion. Overall, the rite is a gift. It has many similarities with what Mauss classically describes as a "total prestation." As such, the rite is an organization of the gift that gives rise to the hierarchical order of the cosmic totality. The complex interweaving of numerous supramundane beings—gods, demons, ghosts—and the presence of the forces that they embody is achieved through the dynamics of the gift, which is also the medium for recentering human beings within the cosmic complex. The ritual as a whole is a gift to the Buddha idea and to the totality the Buddha encompasses. Moreover, and of no less significance, a Suniyama is a gift to the community of the rite—to the kin, friends, and neighbors who are invited into the domain of the household to witness the proceedings. The magnificence and spectacle of the Suniyama is a gift in the brilliance of its aesthetic display, the beauty (*laksana*) of the occasion having constitutive force: it draws and presences gods, demons, and human beings. In this and other respects, the aesthetics of the rite are central for overcoming the sorcery attack and restoring harmony.

The Suniyama is a magnificent rite of conspicuous consumption. In the view of the ritual specialists who perform the rite and their clients, the Suniyama is a cornucopia, overwhelmingly directed to the presentation of bounteous fruitfulness and wealth.

The Suniyama has much in common with a potlatch,[1] a sacrificial destruction and exhaustion of wealth. The powerful conclusion of the ceremony, when the marvelous edifice of Mahasammata's palace is destroyed, supports a comparison with the potlatch. The Mahasammata palace is also a supreme materialization of desire, of the bounteousness, harmony, and wealth that are the objects of the envy, jealousy, and appetite of the sorcerer. The destruction of the palace is a destruction of the gift. It destroys the wealth of the gift, or that paradox of the gift which in its generative dynamic can create the wealth, power, and harmony that motivates sorcery.

The Suniyama grasps sorcery as an event that strikes at the heart of human existence: an action that annihilates both human beings and the worlds of which they are at the constitutive and generative center. The Suniyama deals with sorcery in its fullest sense as no more and no less than the radical creative and destructive, world-unmaking and world-remaking, action of human beings. A Suniyama addresses that multiplicity of experience that is culturally objectified and totalized *as sorcery* in the breadth and depth of its import for both the victim and the community that are at the vortex of the forces considered sorcery. Overall, the Suniyama is directed toward recentering victims in their worlds of action and making them once again active agents in the reproduction and sustaining of their own lives and the lives of those around them.

Anthropologists in their traditional work of demystifying the cultural worlds of others have insisted on sorcery as a routine, ordinary, everyday event. This is indeed the case for many in Sri Lanka. But the ordinariness or routine of sorcery in no way reduces its extremely offensive, shocking, and terrible nature. Sorcery denies the agency or capacity for action in the world that is vital to human beings. The Suniyama reveals these aspects as fundamental in sorcery. It reveals that the ordinariness of sorcery is related to the problematics at the heart of human existence.

The Suniyama is a rite that exposes the existential potentiality of a diversity of other sorcery practices. It is the most complex and elaborate of Sinhala sorcery practices and is regarded by *adura*s and their clients as the ultimate rite of protection against sorcery and for the restoration of the social harmony broken by the sorcerer's attack. The Suniyama is the consummation of all the sorcerer's skills in one master ritual form which can counteract all attacking techniques of the sorcerer. It is a totalizing ritual form that organizes a diversity of rites, many of which can be used on their own to attack or protect victims. Because of this totalizing aspect of the Suniyama, it brings together a great deal of knowledge and practice relating to sorcery as it is widely practiced in Sri Lanka.

New sorcery practices are constantly being devised in Sri Lanka, and those who construct them often have had direct experience as victims or patients in key ritual events included in the Suniyama. They use such knowledge born of experience. I do not claim that the meaning of the practice that I will present for the Suniyama is directly applicable to other sorcery events or practice. However, the Suniyama is contemporaneous with these other practices and works with similar cultural materials and references. I regard the Suniyama as a paradigm of the practices of the sorcerer, a culturally based framework through which a variety of sorcery practices can be seen in both their symbolic and experiential potential. The Suniyama is a highly elaborate culturally and historically grounded articulation of the practice of sorcery.

Suniyama Traditions and the Contemporary Sociopolitical Context

What is called the Suniyama in the southern coastal sorcery traditions that I studied incorporates ritual events that have a long history of practice, reaching well back into precolonial times. Some of the descriptions of central ritual events (e.g., the rites of the *hatadiya*, or seven steps), many of the mantras and songs, and the key elements of myth around which the action of the Suniyama are organized, constitute a major part of Hugh Nevill's (1954, 1955) *ola* palm manuscript collection which he gathered together in the latter part of the nineteenth century. Nevill estimates that some of the documents were two or three centuries old at the time of collection. Suggestions are that many episodes of the Suniyama date from medieval times in Sri Lanka, and possibly earlier.

However, it is far from certain how long the Suniyama has been in operation in the way I routinely saw it performed. The picture is complicated by the fact that there are different ritual traditions in Sri Lanka, and Nevill's manuscripts, for example, come from a variety of such traditions. These often are quite distinct ritual practices, although they may involve similar songs, mantras, and so forth. Nonetheless, many of the songs recorded by Nevill can be regarded as manuals for actual practices, and Nevill's texts certainly record events that were crucial in the Suniyama performances I witnessed.

The Suniyama rite with which I am concerned is limited to the southwestern and, especially, the south coast (in the Galle-Akuressa-Matara sorcery and healing-exorcism traditions) of Sri Lanka. Although some events similar to those performed in the Suniyama occur elsewhere (e.g., in the Sabaragamuva and Central Province), it is only along the western and southern littoral that such a complex rite as I describe is enacted. Moreover, it is only in this area that the name Suniyama, or more accurately Suniyam *yagaya,* is applied to the largest, most encompassing anti-sorcery rites to be held in domestic space.

Other traditions inland and toward the central highlands refer to a similar rite as a *dehi kapuma,* or lime cutting. These performances do not involve the building of the Mahasammata palace, the architectural hallmark of the performance traditions of the south where I did field-work. Nonetheless, the action of these rites is centered around the *hatadiya* (seven steps) sequence and is oriented to a ritual enclosure or shrine (*atamagala*). In the southern traditions, this is also regarded as the bridal chamber of Manikpala and is the space (in all traditions) that the victim of sorcery must enter, a high point in the rite.

The main exponents of the Suniyama (colloquially and respectfully known as *suniyam karaya*) are drawn from the castes (primarily the Berava and to a lesser extent the Oli)[2] whose traditional role was to provide ritual services to other castes, often as healers and soothsayers. Berava ritualists, who command great knowledge concerning ritual traditions among Sinhalese as a whole and are vital to their continuity (see Kapferer 1983), regard the Suniyama as the most complete manifestation of the exorcist's practice. They see it as the masterwork, in Berava traditions, of the first *adura,* Oddisa himself.[3]

The most respected *adura*s are those who command the necessary knowledge to preside over the performance of the Suniyama. It is evidence of an *adura*'s ritual authority and power and of his being a person able to command the cosmic forces integral to the pragmatic affairs of human beings. The height of an *adura*'s career is achieved when he can preside at a Suniyama performance. Berava exorcists usually only do so after they have mastered the several arts appropriate to its performance, sometimes by their late twenties or well into middle age. In the past, members of particular Berava lineages (*parampara*) provided the main *suniyam karaya*s. Such lineages were highly ranked, and these lineages also provided the ritual experts in the rites for the planetary gods and demons (*bali tovil*). These latter rites are considered by Berava ritualists to be closely connected with the Suniyama. Both kinds of rites are at the apex of a hierarchy of healing rites commonly held in domestic space and generally referred to as *tovil,* a term which includes several other large-scale ritual performances held under the presidency of the major demons in the Sinhala pantheon (see Kapferer 1983). However, Berava exorcists often distinguish Suniyama and *bali* performances as *yaga(ya)* (and also as *santiya*), and refer to them explicitly as such rather than using the more colloquial term *tovil*. By doing so, exorcists emphasize the auspicious and regenerative sacrificial dynamic of the Suniyama. This sacrificial dynamic of the Suniyama becomes a major theme of later discussion.

I should note here that some variations in the performance of Suniyamas by Berava ritualists relate to the lineage tradition in which the *suniyam karaya* learned his art. But the most important variations in southern Berava traditions are connected to divisions of political territory under the suzerainty of Sinhala lords in precolonial times. This is further support for the claims of Berava to long-term authority for the performance of such rites.

Although the information I present in this chapter relies on Berava knowledge, Suniyamas are performed by exorcists from other castes. Those from traditionally high castes in the Sinhalese caste ranking often make a point of claiming specialist knowledge of the Suniyama. This is rarely, from my information, knowledge that has passed down through the generations (*parampara*). Rather it has usually been picked up through apprenticeship to a Berava exorcist. Likewise, priests to Suniyam at his modern shrines have often gained much of their knowledge of the relevant chants and songs from Beravas. These priests are usually from the higher-ranked and politically and economically powerful castes in Sri Lanka. Beravas as a traditionally low-ranked caste (and in the recent past, subject to considerable social restriction and discrimination; see Kapferer 1983) are still effectively proscribed from officiating at temple shrines. This is legitimated in the teleology of popular discourse, which describes the low rank and the pollution of the Berava (derived from their ritual work dealing with demons) as inappropriate to rites directed chiefly to the pure deities.

Knowledge and Power

The equation of social and political power with knowledge is given particular emphasis in Sri Lanka. The acceptance of or acquiescence to another's authority on ritual and cultural matters in contemporary Sri Lanka often has to do with a person's caste rank, political and economic group, or class membership, regardless of whether the person actually has that knowledge. This is integral to the hegemony of present-day class and political processes. I have encountered numerous instances where highly skilled and knowledgeable Berava ritualists defer in public to the ritual and cultural authority of persons who are in positions of social and political superiority, even though in private Beravas freely denounce these persons' claims.

The distribution of ritual knowledge and the control over ritual practices among Sinhalese refracts the hierarchies of social and political relations. Those persons and groups that define themselves and are defined by others as socially and politically powerful manifest such power both in their command of the ritual services of others and in an interest in professing an expertise in what are regarded as the higher reaches of ritual or religious knowledge. As Obeyesekere has demonstrated, ritual and religious knowledge among Sinhalese Buddhists is extraordinarily dynamic and constantly inventive. This dynamism has much to do with the important place of ritual knowledge and practice in the definition of social and political power. Caste and lineage relations were and continue to be defined with reference to ritual knowledge and practice. If anything, contemporary class forces have intensified the centrality of ritual knowledge and practice in the definition and redefinition of social and political relations. Developments in modern Buddhist doctrine and practice expressing such processes have been well documented, particularly with reference to the so-called Buddhist Revival (e.g., Ames 1963; Malalgoda 1976; Roberts 1979, 1982; Gombrich and Obeyesekere 1988; Bond 1988).

The Suniyama is a knowledge-practice that has had particular significance in the definition of social and political relations in a contemporary class society. Buddhist value is especially marked in the rite, and this permits it to become a significant class practice, especially in contemporary Sri Lanka, where class power and social standing are expressed in displays of devotion to Buddhist ideals and practices. The Suniyama is a practice that can be seen as having a role in the moralization of dominance and power.

The highly explicit Buddhist orientation of the rite and the particular position of the major deities of the Sinhala pantheon in the ritual distinguish it from the other demon exorcisms (*yaktovil*) with which it is often classed. The central ritual structure of the Suniyama, the *atamagala* set within Mahasammata's palace, is, in all understandings, the space of the Buddha encompassing the Guardian Deities of the Sinhala pantheon and the divine originator, Maha Brahma. It is a site of repose, release, and regeneration that the sorcery victim *must* enter. In the other major demon exorcisms, the main building of ritual orientation (the *yakvidiya*) *must not* be entered if it is possible to avoid it. To enter the building signals absolute demonic control and not freedom or protection from demonic malevolence, which is a major meaning of the entry into the *atamagala* of the Suniyama.

The Buddhist orientation of the Suniyama is one reason Berava *aduras* and others give for the high regard in which the rite is held and for why those who can master all aspects of its performance should have high status among ritual exponents. The Suniyama, in fact, is a marginal rite and within the hierarchy of ritual practices and knowledge is located between demon exorcisms, on the one hand, and larger communal rites to Pattini and Devol Deviyo (*gammaduva, devol maduva*), on the other hand. I should add that *aduras* themselves describe the Suniyama as a *madu tovile,* in fact classing it with such rites as the *gammaduva.*[4]

The Suniyama is a site of some contest for control between rival *aduras*. *Aduras* from castes higher than the Berava, Goyigama, and Karava see specialism in Suniyama performances as appropriate to them. Some householders also believe that because the rite is expressly oriented to the Buddha and to the deities, exorcists from the higher castes should perform it.

The Suniyama is caught up in the politics of class and caste and also in wider processes having to do with Sinhala ethnic identity and nationalism. These factors continually recreate the rite as a vital and quite common practice in villages and towns, one that is thoroughly contemporary and not a relic of a bygone age.[5]

Reasons for the significance of the Suniyama in class and nationalist dynamics, apart from the no less real exigencies of sorcery, are its rich unfolding of many Sinhala legends and myths in the context of assertions of Buddhist value. It is a rite tailor-made for use in contemporary political discourses of culture and Sinhala identity. One indication of this significance is the display in the National Museum of the special clothes worn for the Suniyama donated by Sauris Silva. Sauris Silva was a well-known expert in the Suniyama from the Karava community, a member of the urban bourgeoisie, and the author of a work published in Sinhala based on his knowledge and practice of the rite (Silva 1970). While the Suniyama finds renewed relevance in class and nationalist politics, these also have probably been dynamic in a heightening of the significance of certain legendary and Buddhist aspects of the rite and in developing new twists on their import.

The Suniyama is frequently performed at the houses of members of local elites or political patrons. Undoubtedly this manifests their fear and sense of vulnerability in a world of often furious class-driven hostilities. But I stress related aspects of the performance of Suniyamas whereby they can express their own nationalist sentiments and Buddhist morality, factors legitimating their community position. The Suniyama is highly appropriate to such motivation, because, among other things, it expresses a powerful Buddhist face of folk practice or, in the view of many, a relatively pure instance of the continuity of essentially Sinhala Buddhist practice from the past into the present. Sinhala nationalists, especially in the south, which is seen as a major center of Sinhala chauvinism, encouraged a return to cultural roots and a reassertion of their values held to have been demeaned in the rupture of colonial conquest and the long years of British rule. Other exorcism practice among Sinhala elites is often disparaged as Hinduized and as practice inappropriate to Buddhists. The Suniyama, from the position of some among local elites, can escape this charge, although it is more than likely that the attraction of local elites to the Suniyama is a factor in further expunging the Suniyama of its supposed foreign content and in elaborating Buddhist doctrinal references of contemporary value.

Recent Buddhist revitalization, starting in the late nineteenth century, often in direct reaction to British rule, and taking several directions, has been an influential force not only in Sinhala nationalism but also in framing modern Buddhist practice, especially among dominant class fractions. Certain features of modern practice have been referred to as "Protestant Buddhism" (see Gombrich 1988; Gombrich and Obeyesekere 1988). Of relevance here is an insistence by laypersons that World Renunciation is not vital to following the Buddha's Path. Indeed, it is by being a virtuous Buddhist in-the-world that its suffering can be overcome and success in everyday ventures achieved. This particular interpretation of Buddhist doctrine is popular among local professional and business elites and is an ideology appropriate to current class processes in a modern capitalist society. Thus, ideas and events in the Suniyama receive new import in the context of Buddhist revitalization and make the Suniyama additionally attractive for socially and politically powerful households.

The Buddhist concept of the *bodhisattva*,[6] of the person who has achieved Buddhahood returning selflessly and regeneratively to a suffering world and relinquishing the opportunity for Non-Existence, is one powerful organizing theme in the Suniyama. It is an aspect of the ritual sequence of the *hatadiya* (seven steps) in which the person at the center of the rite journeys toward a central space (*atamagala*) which, in the interpretation of many participants, is the direction of the Buddha's Path, the space of the Buddha's encompassing knowledge at the verge of Non-Existence, and the end of suffering. The journey toward the *atamagala* is accompanied by recitations of the Buddha's glorious deeds (*paramitas*, or spiritual reflections) and accounts (*jatakas*) of events in his former lives. The action of the Suniyama makes the patients or victims the center of acts of piety and puts them in the midst of their social and political community.

I might add that the Suniyama can function as a display of meritorious Buddhist action (*pin*), like other rites popularized as part of Buddhist revitalization. Thus Vesak (the celebration of the Buddha's Enlightenment) is a festival which has steadily grown as an occasion for the display of bourgeois power. Prominent businessmen organize the distribution of food to the public at specially erected almshouses (*dansalas*) or cause to have erected magnificently decorated and lit hoardings (*toran*) illustrating a *jataka* story or an event in the life of Gautama Buddha. Such public expression of Buddhist worthiness, however, is limited to particular seasonal moments. A Suniyama can be performed at virtually any time.

The contemporary religious significance of Suniyama performances, their import as a religious practice of dominant groups, though far from exclusively, does not necessarily corrupt their transformational objective to overcome sorcery. The experience of sorcery or the definition of experience as sorcery is constituted in the conflicts and tensions of processes relating to class, but to other dynamics as well. The transformations effected through the Suniyama can gain potency through its capacity to adapt to the meaning contexts historically developed around it.

But developments and changes in the Suniyama and aspects of contemporary Buddhist emphasis, insofar as they are the constructions of modern historical realities, obscure critical features of the rite that are central to its process. Because people value it as a Buddhist rite to be distinguished from other demon exorcisms, they overlook processes present in it that are thoroughly part of these other rites. The Buddhism of the Suniyama, like that of the other exorcisms, is grounded in a diversity of historical processes, not merely those of recent colonial and postcolonial times.

The Suniyama, along with the other demon exorcisms, can be conceived of as a bricolage of mythical and ritual influences emanating from different sources within the subcontinent. Within any modern performance of the Suniyama will be found traces of Brahmanic sacrifice, of tantra, and of many other religious and ritual traditions. The Suniyama is therefore not the product of a single continuous Sinhala Buddhist tradition. It organizes influences from diverse traditions and is continually open to changes that are part of the particular historical contexts of its performance.

The Decision for Performance

The Suniyama is the most elaborate rite to overcome sorcery. There are a host of smaller rites that can be performed. Among the more common

is the *kapuma* (or *krema kapuma*), which is explicitly oriented to destroying the sorcerer who is causing the victim's anguish. It is organized by
two or three exorcists (sometimes only one) and lasts through the night.
Usually only householders and a few other close kin attend. It is not a
public occasion, and its relative secrecy is said to increase its destructive
objective, for the sorcerer is caught unawares and cannot engage protective magic. But most people in a neighborhood know that such a *kapuma*
is being held. The noise of the rite, its drumming and singing, carries over
some distance. Indeed, a *kapuma* is seen by victims and those excluded
from the rite as a kind of accusation that places the victim and the household in a dangerous and threatening relation to the larger community.
This is reflected in the fact that if one household has a *kapuma* performed,
a number of further performances of similar rites will follow among
neighboring households. The initial performance sets off a rash of *kapuma*s. Destruction is in the air, and the rites express the conflicts that rive
localities and contribute to the expansion of such conflict.

The Suniyama, in the conceptions of exorcists and victims, is not such
a rite. It is the ultimate antisorcery rite, because it is not only the master
rite and a rite that incorporates and overcomes all the techniques of the
sorcerer but is also reconstitutive and harmonizing. The community (that
excluded in a *kapuma*) is drawn within the compass of the rite. The victim
of sorcery is cleansed of the destructive forces of sorcery which in certain
respects can be seen as simultaneously an expunging of the destructive
forces emanating from within the community and a relocation of these
potencies to the space beyond the boundaries of the community. The victim and the household are presented as the focus of desire, envy, and
jealousy which drain their power. The Suniyama converts the victim into
a willing giver of that which others may desire. In this process the victim
and the household are repotentiated, and as themselves the sacrificed (the
"sacrifiers") and eventually sacrificers, become reconstitutive of both
themselves and the community in which they are a particular center.
These are among the chief aspects that distinguish the Suniyama from
other antisorcery rites such as the *kapuma*s and give the rite its ultimate
appeal. The Suniyama overcomes the techniques of the sorcerer and much
more.

The rite addresses the very ground of sorcery and is oriented to overcoming the circumstances of its continuity or reproduction. *Kapuma*s and
numerous other rites attacking or protecting against sorcery contain powerful elements of revenge. They can provoke counter-rites and the revengeful response, what Girard (1977) refers to as "the reciprocity of
violence" (see Chapter 6). The Suniyama is directed to overcoming the

cycle of revenge (even though there are numerous acts of vengeance in its ritual process). It ends a relation of vengeance between a victim and other members of the community that may be constituted through anti-sorcery action.

The passage to the performance of a Suniyama is not necessarily from smaller more minor rites and then, when all else seems to fail, to the organization of a Suniyama. The Suniyama is an expensive occasion, stretching the resources of most households. Less elaborate rites are normally preferred. These other rites use many of the important mantras, spells, and other ritual acts that are used in a Suniyama and that exorcists regard as highly effective. But if the aim is to deal with sorcery in the most profound and radical way possible, if victims believe that their whole ground of existence and that of those who are closely connected to them is infused with the destructive work of the sorcerer, then they will press for a Suniyama. Other factors (aspects of class and local prominence) also influence an immediate choice of a Suniyama. The sheer cost of the ceremony is an element in the relatively disproportionate tendency of the wealthy to decide on a Suniyama, sometimes in immediate preference to other more modest and routine measures.

The performance of a Suniyama does not exclude other measures, and Suniyamas are not necessarily performed because other measures have failed. Victims continue to pursue their outrage at sorcery by other means: visits to the sorcery temples, the performance of other rites oriented to destruction, and so forth. I have encountered two or three occasions when a Suniyama was performed after a victim and a household believed that their other sorcery action had brought result. The Suniyamas, in effect, were intended to close off the violence of sorcery and to ensure that its suffering would not return. These performances of the Suniyama underlined the ability of this rite to overcome through its overriding assertions of Buddhist virtue the dilemma of sorcery action, especially in a Buddhist moral universe. Sorcery action, even that considered a justifiable response to the malevolence of another, must cause suffering and is directed to do so. The Suniyama to a degree separates the victim from direct responsibility for another's anguish and cloaks the victim and the victim's community in the protective order of Buddhist morality.

The Suniyama acts to prevent the possibility of sorcery. People who have suddenly come into wealth or some other good fortune or success may organize a Suniyama. A Suniyama works directly against the dangers of desire. Thus, I have witnessed the performance of a Suniyama for persons who returned from periods of employment overseas. The money and presents with which they returned had elevated their social and economic standing in their local neighborhoods. Their Suniyamas both signaled their changed status and were instrumental in restructuring their social and political position in their localities. The Suniyama is fundamentally a rite of reconstitutive power which not only places victims at the center of a set of social and political relations but invests victims, symbolically at least, with the potency of self re-creation and with the power to reform their social and political relations and the vectors of their force in relation to themselves (see Chapter 8).

Ritual Preparations and the Order of Ritual Events

The exorcists who present the rite are selected by the presiding exorcist, the master of ceremonies, or *gurunanse*.[7] Most often they are kin who have experience of performing together (see Kapferer 1983). Usually the *gurunanse* has been in consultation with the victim or organizing house-holders for days and often weeks before the event. Small thread-tying ceremonies (*apa nul*) have usually been executed before the event in order to protect the victim and the household from further misfortune and also as a promise to Suniyam that a rite in his honor is to be held. Such a promise is considered by some exorcists to reduce Suniyam's threat. The *gurunanse* who is responsible for the performance will also search the victim's house and the land around the house for sorcery objects that might have been buried or hidden by the sorcerer.

The typical size of a performance troupe for a Suniyama is around six exorcists. Apart from the master of ceremonies, who controls the mantras and songs and the pacing and sequencing of the ritual events, there are two or three drummers and the same number of dancer-actors. The Suni-yama, like all major demon ceremonies, has a special officiant, the ritual assistant (*madu puraya*). This person is sometimes not an exorcist at all and is frequently a kinsman of the ritual house. He has the lowest position among the performers and occasionally is treated with some jocular deri-sion. His role is to prepare the ritual food for the gods, demons, and spirits who are addressed in the course of the rite. Exorcists usually help the *madu puraya* in this work if he has no previous experience.

The exorcists generally arrive in the morning for the start of the Suni-yama in the late afternoon. The household has been given a list (some-times printed) of the materials needed for the ritual buildings and other objects to be used in the performance. The exorcists, of course, bring the ritual clothing that they will wear and their drums. The materials that the household must provide include those required for the offerings and clean white cloths to be worn by the patient and occasionally used by the exorcists. Of great importance are the building materials for the Mahasammata palace (also known as the *Suniyam vidiya*), the *atamagala,* the *suniyam purale* (or Suniyam's death space), the offering shrine for Buddha and the guardian deities (*pahan pala, buduge*), and the various offering baskets and other receptacles and instruments (e.g., the *vas danda,* or poison pipe, and the *igaha,* or commanding arrow of the exorcist's magical power).[8]

The preparations for the rite take most of the day. The most important work involves the construction of the ritual buildings. A ritual hut (*maduva*) is built in an area to the front of or to one side of the victim's house. This is roofed (with corrugated iron or canvas) and is open-sided. Ideally the *maduva* encloses the bounded area of the rite in which the Suniyama is performed. As in all major exorcisms, the ritual action occurs in a demarcated ritual space, the *sima midula.* In the case of the Suniyama, this space symbolically describes Mahasammata's city, the hierarchically structured and internally bounded ordering of political society that he institutes. The poles that bound the performance space and support the roof are hung with young fruits and leaves. The audience that gathers for a Suniyama usually sits or stands at the perimeter of the ritual hut/Mahasammata's cosmic city.[9]

Mahasammata's palace (*Suniyam vidiya*) is built at one end but within the *maduva.* It is a facade some twelve feet high made from flattened banana trunk. The outline of the palace usually forms five pinnacles or towers, a central tower, and two towers, each lower than the other at the sides. The palace is understood as having three levels, or floors, the highest for Isvara (Siva), the second for Vishnu, and the lowest or ground floor for Brahma. Other towers and doorways are set into the facade. At the apex of the central tower is a painting of Suniyam, holding his sword of authority and justice. At the apex of the second right-hand tower is an image of the Sun, and a representation of the Moon is at the apex of the second left-hand tower. The top of the towers on the ground floor of the palace frequently have cutout images of the *bahirava* demons, demonic forms of Isvara. Various other motifs decorate the palace, for example, lotus flowers, the lotus stalk, and the *hondala* creeper which is associated with sorcery. Red, black, yellow, and green are the dominant colors. The palace is often garlanded with light-reflective tinfoil and hung with brightly colored electric bulbs.

There is some variation, as might be expected, in the structure of the building, depending on the limitations of space and also money. Wealthy patrons of the Suniyama desire the most elaborate and magnificent of palaces. *Adura*s assert that in the past the design and structure of the building varied according to the caste and lineage rank of the household. A well-known story circulates in the south of the island concerning a family that had a palace built and a Suniyama performed that were inappropriate to their rank. As a result the family suffered ill fortune, a suffering that has continued down the generations to the present day.

The palace is replete with meaningful potential which emerges in the course of the rite. It represents the hierarchical ordered totality of human existence instituted by Mahasammata and the cosmic forces that condition it. The edifice is seen by some exorcists as a temple and by others as also a representation of Mount Ajakuta, the dwelling place of Oddisa-Suniyam, and therefore there is a representation of his figure at the top of the building. Certainly various motifs and other aspects of the design are indicative of the creative and violent destructive forces that the ritual performance will bring into play. The Mahasammata palace is frequently referred to as the *Suniyam vidiya,* indicating that it is bounded space under the protection of Suniyam and relatively safe from sorcery's destruction.

On the ground floor of the palace's central tower is a small doorway. This is the entrance into the *atamagala* (or, roughly translated, the place of eight auspicious things). The *atamagala* is the most vital structure of the Suniyama, the ultimate objective of the victim in the Suniyama. The events that occur within the space of the *atamagala* constitute a vital culminating moment in the rite during which the victim is freed from the grip of the sorcerer and is reempowered.

The *atamagala* is a framelike enclosure that extends behind the palace facade.[10] Like the palace, it has three levels: the ground level for Brahma, the middle for Vishnu, and the top for Isvara. At the three levels are offering troughs or plates (*aile*) made from banana trunk. Different offerings are placed at these three levels, usually betel offerings (*dalumura*) at the top, flower petals and rice (food for the gods, *murutan*) at the middle, and on the ground, young coconuts (two at each of the inside corners) and two pots (*punkalas*) with areca flowers at either side and before the entrance to each of the four doorways into the enclosure. These doorways (including the front entrance) mark the principal cardinal directions. The uprights for the doorways are made from young green sticks (*kopili, pangiri kotu*) from the lime tree. At their top points are impaled limes (a fruit whose juice is likened to the venom of the viper and of sorcery). Just below these is a decoration made from coconut leaves (*gokkola*) formed into testicular shape. These uprights (there are eight) are understood to be Siva lingas. These, like the entire *atamagala,* encode the destructive and recreative forces that are at work in the rite as a whole and embodied in the victim.

The victim in the Suniyama comes to sit on new rush mats placed on the ground of the *atamagala*. This space is one of regenerative potency. It is a place of force, a condensation of cosmic powers engendering the motion of life. In preparing this space, the *adura* marks out two magical designs, or yantras. The first is drawn in ash (*basma*) on the ground. Its major significance is death, projected at the instant of life's start, and in an exegesis on its import, some exorcists refer to an event in the life of Siva when the funerary ash demon (Basmasura) lusted after Uma, Siva's queen. This story has structural similarity to the Buddhist story of Mahasammata and Vasavarti's desire for Queen Manikpala. The yantra is covered by a rush mat (*hangala padura*)[11] occasionally described as the bed of Manikapala and Mahasammata. The same yantra is then drawn again, but this time rice flour and nine betel leaf offerings, together with nine coins, are put at the places for the nine planets on the design and covered by a further mat. This is the marriage mat of Mahasammata and Manikpala, the mat of regenerative and ordering life and in some exorcist interpretations, the mat of calm and meditative peacefulness. Effectively, the higher form encompasses the lower.

The yantra of the *atamagala* (fig. 1) is known as the *kaksaputa yantraya*.[12] Its central point is described as the locus of *Maha Kala Purusha*, the original human being from whose sacrifice is created the hierarchical divisions of human existence. This underlines the vital sacrificial theme of the Suniyama. Yantras do not have force in themselves. They must have life (*jiva*) breathed into them. This is the force of mantras that are uttered in relation to them. Yantras and mantras comprise an inseparable unity, the mantra giving the life which the yantra then holds and further materializes. In some respects, I surmise, the whole process or architectonic dynamic of the Suniyama rite can be conceived of as one gigantic yantra enlivening mantra. Furthermore, the victim can be seen as a moving and growing life force who brings energy and power to the yantra of the *atamagala* that, in turn, is further regenerative of the patient.

The *atamagala* as a whole is conceived of as a womb, or the germinal center (*garbha*) of the world totality represented by the palace. It is conceived of as the key *cakra* point at the vortex of world and human regeneration, a locus of the power of the nine planets, a place of knowledge and truth (*satta/satya*) commanded by the Buddha's teaching, and much else.

There are two other important buildings erected in preparation for the

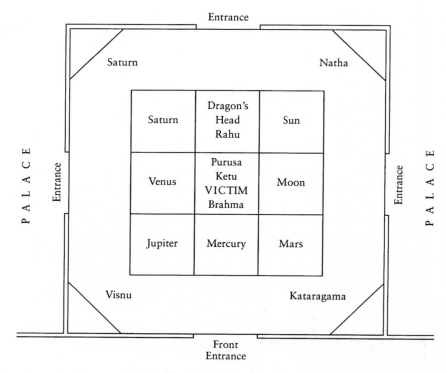

Floor Plan of Atamangala

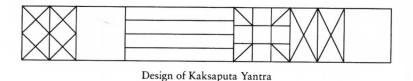

Design of Kaksaputa Yantra

Figure 1. The Atamagala

performance and necessary to it, though of lesser significance for the later account of the rite. A small shrine (*pahan pala*) is built from coconut leaves for the main guardian deities (Natha, Sakra, Kataragama, Pattini), and lamps to these deities are placed inside. More specific to the Suniyama (but also constructed at other exorcisms) is the *Suniyam purale* (or *Suniyam* death space); see figure 2. This is a large rectangular frame supported

Hina (Vayu)	Aries	Taurus	Gemini	Hina (Yama)
Pisces	Saturn	Ketu (Dragon's Tail)	Sun	Cancer
Aquarius	Venus	Rahu (Dragon's Head) Brahma Suniyam	Moon	Leo
Capricorn	Jupiter	Mercury	Mars	Virgo
Hina (Kala)	Sagitarius	Scorpio	Libra	Hina (Murtu)

VISI PAS GÄBA
Suniyam Purale
(The Death Space of Suniyam)

Figure 2. Purale Yantra or Visipas Gaba

on four poles. Essentially it is a giant offering tray divided into twenty-five places (*visipas gaba*) for offerings. In some structures I have seen, the central section is raised and contains offerings for the nine planets.

The distribution of these ritual buildings varies from performance to performance. The shrine to the deities and the offering bench for Suniyam (*purale*) are located to the perimeter of the performance arena. It should

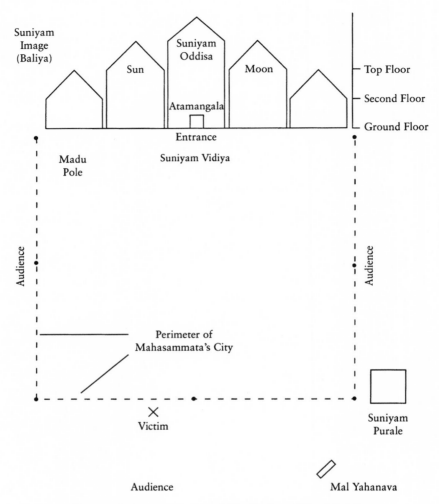

Figure 3. Performance Space and Distribution of Ritual Buildings

be noted that the *Suniyam purale* is normally located parallel to where the patient will be seated at the start of the rite and facing the Mahasam-mata palace or *Suniyam vidiya*. This location signs the patient as in a situation of destruction but also at the point of reorigination; see figure 3. In the course of the rite, the patient moves from the region of the *purale,* a death space, and journeys toward the site of release from suffering, regeneration, and bounded protection, the palace or *Suniyam vidiya*. A further sense of the *purale* is that it is itself a place of hot generation in which the human world and its cosmic forces are in a process of turbulent reemergence.

At some Suniyamas, a clay *baliya*, or image made from ant bed, is made and painted yellow, the color of Suniyam's sterility or infertility. This is placed on the ground away from the performance, in the darkness outside the audience's view.[13] Other preparations include the making of various offering baskets, including the *mal bulat tattuva*, in which are placed various objects used to cleanse and cool the patient, as well as offerings to be used by the victim as gifts. Baskets (*tattu-va*), beautifully decorated, are made to contain offerings to the demons. These are divided internally according to the yantra design of the relevant demon. The design has power to hold or trap the essence of the demon so that its relation to the patient can be cut. Other objects and offerings relevant to the main events of the *hatadiya* (lotus plates, rice packets, etc.) are also made. When all this is done, it is time for the rite to start.

The Suniyama starts at dusk and proceeds, with some short breaks, for a period of eighteen hours, until midday the following day. Its events cover the four main periods, or junctures (*sandistana*), of the day: the evening watch (*sandayama*), midnight watch (*mayama*), morning watch (*aluyama*), and the period of midday (*iramudun*). Broadly, the timing of the events proceeds from a moment of great vulnerability, when demonic forces are growing in strength, to a period when divine and ordering forces are at their height, the period of midday.

The main events start with rites of consecration which are focused on the patient (*aturaya*), seated at the edge of the ritual boundary (*sima*), or Mahasammata's city. The rites until the beginning of the midnight watch involve the building of the ordering forces of the cosmic totality and the hierarchy of gods and demons.

The vital regenerative actions of the rite, which involve the passage of the patient along the Buddha Path (and a reversal of the line or snake of the sorcerer) into the *atamagala*, take place over the period of the midnight watch and until midday. The actions center around the reconstitution of the victims as a body of consciousness capable of (re)constituting their social and political realities. The closing acts of the rite manifest a breaking out of the victim into the full flow of consciousness whereby the victim bursts free from the confines of sorcery.

In the Berava traditions of the Weligama and Morawaka divisions (*korale*), on which my understanding of the Suniyama is based, the rite is conceived as an organization of sixteen corrective acts, sentencings, or

judgments (*solos tinduva*).[14] The term *tinduva* has the sense of completion, a ritual action that finishes or brings a process to an end. It also
carries the notion, in this context of sorcery, of judgment, verdict, or
punishment having been carried out in the patient's favor (the completion
of an act of vengeance) and the cutting of the bonds of sorcery. *Adura*s
liken *tinduva*s to the punishing actions of the goddess Pattini when she
burned the city of Madurai following the wrongful execution of her husband (see Obeyesekere 1984a). Moreover, the notion of *tinduva* carries
the sense that all the impediments to the attainment of full consciousness
have been cut and the reconstitutive work of the Suniyama as a whole
completed. Exorcists say that there should be sixteen *tinduva*s in the Suniyama, one for each of the sixteen years of Manikpala's life until she
reached the age of maturity and marriage. That there are ideally sixteen
*tinduva*s emphasizes the Suniyama as fundamentally a rite for the (re)con-
stitution of consciousness (*hita, manasa*), after which patients become
active in the regeneration of their lives and their social and political order.
Thus, the Suniyama is a rite of (re)origination whereby the patient effectively repeats the primordial world-ordering action of Mahasammata,
who is the collective manifestation of the constitutive power of the consciousness of human being. In other words, the Suniyama reinstills within
the patient the potency of the first world-creating act whereby the patient
is reempowered with consciousness and once more becomes capable of
socially constitutive action in which the patient's life and that of others
can be developed and sustained.

5

The Suniyama
The Conquest of Sorcery and the Power of Consciousness

Part II

> *It is in this fathom-long body with its impressions and ideas
> that I declare lies the world and the course of the world and
> the causation of the world and the course of action that leads
> to the cessation of the world.*
>
> *Kindred Sayings,* Sutta Rohita, Samyutta Nikaya

In the dynamics and structures of their practices, human beings explore the nature of their realities as they may experience them and also bring their realities of experience and action into existence. The Suniyama is, in my view, a demonstration of the power of practice and may be regarded as a practice of practice. That is, the Suniyama is a ritual that takes its key participants into the practices of consciousness through which human beings may routinely constitute and reconstitute their lived realities. The Suniyama expresses through its practice both a theory of practice and a technical discipline or organization of the constructional dynamics, motional in consciousness, whereby human beings become constitutive agents of their worlds. This is one of my key interests in the Suniyama. It sets out, in the context of the sorcerer's radical deconstruction of reality, not just a cultural understanding of the nature and dimensionality of the experience of sorcery through practice but also a practice "theory" of how human realities shattered in the attack of the sorcerer are recreated.

A Suniyama Performance

I describe a Suniyama performed for a seventy-five-year-old man, a leading patron in his local community (composed largely of members of the Durava caste),[1] situated on the coast between Galle and Weligama. He had established a successful timber and trucking business with interests spread across the southern and southeastern regions of the island.

Things had not been going well in recent months. Sales of timber had slumped slightly, and worst of all, his sons, who now largely managed the business, had been involved in arguments with some of the employees. He suspected that one of his managers was engaging in fraud. The victim was involved in long-haulage trucking, and he was having operational troubles, especially with the drivers. Two grandchildren who lived in his house had been sick. To top things off, the old man felt ill and was feeling his age. He went to an astrologer to consult his horoscope and was informed that he had entered a dangerous planetary period (*apale*). His life and business were at risk. He was told that he was the focus of much jealousy, and that it might be advisable to hold a Suniyama. The idea appealed to him for other reasons as well. He believed in customary ways and usually consulted a local astrologer, herbalist, deity priest, or exorcist at times of trouble. These he regarded as being more effective than Western medicine and other alien imports. The old man was proud of Sinhala tradition. He believed that his sons were too given to foreign influences and were overly impressed by modernity. A Suniyama was the thing, and he pressed for the most magnificent of performances, which would impress his family and the wider community. And so the performance proved to be, the audience at times swelling to over three hundred.

The master exorcist was from a village outside Matara, a large center some twenty miles to the south. He brought with him two sons who performed regularly with him and four other skilled drummers and dancers with whom he often worked. Although he had never before organized an exorcism for the old man, in the course of the performance the two men developed a close relationship. The chief exorcist was three years older than the victim, and although extremely agile and fit, was nearing the end of his life. Indeed, he died two years later. Perhaps the two men recognized their own anxieties in each other. The *adura* ministered to his patient throughout the performance and with intimate concern. A warmth was revealed as the performance and the relationship between the two men progressed. So when the Suniyama was finally completed shortly after midday the following day, the old man invited the chief exorcist and his companions to have lunch with him at his table inside his house. He ate with the exorcists and displayed a friendly satisfaction with the ritual events.

Although Berava exorcists are shown hospitality by the households they serve, it is unusual for them to be seated at the same table as their hosts and to share the same food from the same plates. In fact the customary or conventional treatment of Berava exorcists is for them to eat separately and be seated on mats laid on the ground. The depth of understanding that developed between the old man and the exorcist, which was obvious to everyone, added to the considerable charm that this particular Suniyama performance had for me.

There is nothing especially exceptional or extraordinary about the events forming the background to the Suniyama I describe. Many Suniyama performances have more obviously dramatic events at their root: chronic and life-threatening illness, a concentration of disasters—a series of sudden deaths, major conflicts among closely related kin, sudden alterations to the social position of households, and so forth. I have chosen to describe this performance not just because it was particularly memorable for me but also because of the unexceptional quality of the events leading to its performance. As anthropologists have commented, sorcery for many peoples is vital in the very ordinariness of the ordinary world and is manifest as much in the routine as in the extraordinary. Moreover, anxiety and distress are as much part of everyday rhythms, with their apparently slight deviations or redirections, as in seemingly more momentous events. But the depth of personal anxiety or suffering has no necessary external or objective measure, and even the apparently most trivial complaints may be deeply disturbing to the person concerned.

I should stress that the patients or sorcery victims who are at the center of Suniyamas usually remain silent throughout the performance. Although the possibility cannot be ruled out, I have never witnessed a Suniyama where the patient has been interrogated by exorcists (a common feature of other exorcism rites) or has seemed other than calm. The victim usually shows great composure, and this is entirely in keeping with the aims and largely Buddhist objectives of the rite. The rite, I suggest, is not so much a symbolic organization for patient (or ritualist) abreaction or catharsis as a process that enables and insists on patient composure and quiescence, even against the forces of destruction that are integral to the realities of the rite. The Suniyama *is* a cooling rite, and much of its force and efficacy is located in its reconstitution of the victim as a person able to control and overcome those passionate energies of sorcery that are inseparable from the conditions of human existence. Such passions are vital in the organization and process of the Suniyama, but the trajectory of the victim is to overcome them. Generally, the ideological force of the Suniyama is to suppress an emotional or passionate expression on the part of the patient that is inconsistent with the progressive balancing-equilibrating dynamic of the rite. It is not appropriate to the performance or efficacy of the Suniyama that the patient should have any focus of thought other than those of the Buddha's life and teaching. Patients had little opportunity to talk with me about their experiences during performances, and I felt inhibited from asking them questions during the ritual events. What they had to say after a performance was very limited, other than that they now felt restored and protected. The following account, therefore, focuses on the performance that embraces the patient and is constructed largely from my own experiences and observations of this and other Suniyamas, and from detailed discussion with the exorcist-performers concerning their objectives both during and after ritual events.

The Rites of the Evening Watch

The master *adura* starts the performance at 5:30 P.M. He invokes the authority and power of the Buddha and the Guardian Deities at their small shrine (*mal yahanava, pahan*), uttering their praises and giving them incense (*suvanda dummala, sambrani*). He then shifts his attention to the *Suniyam purale,* on the top of which are kept the main offering baskets to be used at various points throughout the rite. Mantras are intoned, and songs (*kavi*) are sung summoning the deceased kin of the victim and household (*gnati preta* and also other spirits attached to the house (*gevala preta*), all of which are disturbing the victim and other householders. This is followed by further invocations to the major demons in the Sinhala pantheon.

The opening actions of the presiding exorcists proceed according to the conventional order of most such Sinhala rites. The invocations to the Buddha and to the Guardian Deities assert, in effect, the ordering power of the totality or the forces that command the hierarchical order of the whole within which human existence is framed and which controls other forms of existence. Acting through the power of the Buddha and the Guardian Deities, the master *adura* can bring the other beings affecting human lives into play and impel them to desist from their malevolence. These early actions condense themes that will be elaborated further throughout the rite, culminating in the full efflorescence of the harmony and order that spread from the Buddha and his virtue.

Ghosts and demons are in close contact with the mundane realities of human beings. They are attracted by such realities and are extreme manifestations of the attachments of human beings to existence and the force of such attachments in the everyday actions of human beings. Ghosts and demons are usually implicated in sorcery attacks. They are conceived of as being at the base of the cosmic hierarchy and are most dangerous and powerful when they are free of the ordering force of hierarchy. The summoning of the ghosts and demons is in itself an act of authority that is hierarchializing, a process of placing ghosts and demons within the structures of control that subdue their dangerous power.

Ghosts (*preta*) are the epitome of greed and desire. Insatiable, they are represented in paintings as emaciated, their forever-hungry condition driving their need. *Preta*s are human beings that hover between one birth and the next because of their overriding attachment to the material needs and wants of existence and to the emotional and social bonds of human life. They are forms of human existence in extreme suffering, and they bring suffering by their insistent demands on kin and householders. There are powerful moral aspects which Sinhala beliefs and a consciousness of ghosts enliven. The attention of ghosts, particularly those of recently dead close kin (specific kin are referred to, often a sibling, parent, or grandparent), raises issues of the relation of the living to the dead concerning the fulfillment of personal obligations, the nature of their relationships before death with their living relatives, and so forth (see Obeyesekere 1981).

The attention to ghosts at the start of the rite (and in all exorcisms) establishes the ground of the rite, that it is centered on a household that is part of a network of social relations whose forces, present and past, are driven in the material conditions of human social existence. These comprise the qualities of human social and political relations (many instances of troublesome ghosts manifest long-term conflicts over land deals and inheritance) as well as the needs of life (food, clothing, etc.). Ghosts as figures of consumption (of overconsumption) mark the victim and house as not only subject to the suffering resulting from their own attachments, desires, and needs but as affected by the sufferings of others.

The major demons invoked—Mahasona, the great cemetery demon, Riri Yaka, the blood demon, and Sanni Yaka (or Maha Kola Sanni Yaka), the disease-spreading demon (see Kapferer 1983; Obeyesekere 1969, 1984a; Wirz 1954; these give accounts of their characteristics and relevant myths of origin)—are among the most feared in the Sinhala pantheon and are routinely associated with sorcery. They expand the senses that are integral to the ghosts and are elaborations of destructive forces flowing through the relations of human action.

Above all, they are the consummate figures of ravenous consumption, of death as a function of anger and desire. The disease-spreading demon, or Sanni Yaka (closely associated with the female deity Pattini in her demonic and pox-spreading form) is symbolic not just of the fragmentation of the body (which diseases of the skin are understood to manifest) but also of social and political relations.[2] In exorcist theory, there are eighteen different forms of Sanni Yaka or Maha Kola Sanni Yaka. The number eighteen is a symbol of the totality of human society (conceived of as being made up of eighteen different tribes or divisions). The Sanni demons manifest the distortions and infirmities of the body and society.

The early ritual attention to the ghosts and to the demons is not merely a conventional stage in a progressive cosmic ordering and rehierarchialization but an active centering and recentering of the victim and the household in the pragmatic forces of everyday life. To put it another way, ghosts and demons are oriented toward human actualities, they live off human existence and indeed intrude into the bodies and worlds of human beings for their own sustenance.

The relation of human beings with demons and ghosts can be distinguished from the relations that human beings have with deities. Broadly, human beings are oriented to gods rather than vice versa. Gods have to be pleased and attracted into the domain of human beings. This is one import of the aesthetic and other entertainments of the ceremonies held in their honor.

However, demons and ghosts are already in the human world and meddling in its routine affairs. It is in their very condition of existence to be attracted to the worlds of human beings. No special treatment needs to be offered to ghosts and demons, in contrast with gods, to draw their attention. The performance of special rites for them feeds their self-delusion and works on their greed and lust. Rites for them (Kapferer 1983) are designed to trick and entrap them within the controlling hierarchically structured power of ritual performance.

By initially addressing ghosts and demons, the rite starts immediately with the forces that affect the victim and house directly, forces that are integral to the everyday world. Moreover, the ritual management of ghosts and demons is a process of changing the way victim and household are positioned in their social and political realities, the dangerous dynamics of which are expressed through the actions of ghosts and demons.

With the conclusion of the invocations before the *Suniyam purale,* the exorcist's assistant (*madu puraya*) takes the offering basket for the ghosts (*preta tattuva*) into the house and puts it in the victim's bedroom. A technical reason for this is to remove their greedy and transgressive attention from the other offerings and thus the risk that they might take what is inappropriate for them. Should their attention not be deflected, then, in the view of exorcists, the proper hierarchical order of the rite will be upset and the higher gods and demons will refuse to assist in the ritual work or (in the case of the demons) will refuse to withdraw their malign attention.

Two other baskets are taken from the *Suniyam purale* and placed on tables (*mesa*—chairs placed on their sides) just to the right of where the patient is to be seated. One is the *mal bulat tattuva,* in which are placed small oil lamps for the Buddha and Guardian Deities. It also contains important articles for the purificatory anointment (*nanumura*) of the victim. A shawl (*mottakkili*) which will cover the head and shoulders of the victim is also kept at the basket. The second basket (*hatadi vattiya*) contains the objects and offerings to be used in the events of the seven steps (*hatadiya*). A rooster, the main two-legged sacrificial offering (*degata billa*), lies with its feet bound near the patient's chair.

I should note that during these preliminaries, the patient is not yet on the scene. The patient is still in the house and will not make an appearance until the main invocations, which start the rite proper, are under way. These are known as the *Suniyam kapakirima,* and the mantras and songs presented by the master exorcist before the *Suniyam purale* command the gathering of powerful demons and demonic deities, concentrating and building their force. It is now a little after 5:35 P.M. I summarize some of the action and its import.

Suniyam Kapakirima: The Gathering of Destructive and Regenerative Power

Demons of violent power and destructive heat are summoned from the eight cardinal directions and from their mountain retreats, from the waterfalls, from the wild fastnesses at the fringes of the world of human beings. The beings called are the violent energies of cosmic forces in becoming, in formation. A mantra (*disti mantra*) commands them to cast their eyesight (*disti*) on the ritual scene. The turning of their gaze toward the ritual scene makes them present and vital within it. The mantra is a mixture of Sanskrit and Sinhala words. The angry and hot forms of Kali, Siva, and Indra (Sakra), among a host of others, are summoned.

> *Om hring satprava saruvakama rupa jala tala*
> *Indra harna vaddita karma yantra Kali disti Rudrapura*
> *Kali jiva jiva saruva mantra jiva jiva vara vara*
> *Bhadrakaliye namahsri vara vara*

The power of the mantra brings these beings to the rite and exposes them to the exorcist's control.

Toward the end of the *Suniyam kapakirima,* five lighted tapers (*vilakku*) are fixed in the *Suniyam purale.* Before this they have been energized with the vitalizing force of a mantra (called the *bili vilakku matirima,* "charming of the sacrificial torch") which builds their potency (*kirima*). The tapers are themselves offerings of light as well as fusions of regenerative sexual energy.

> *Om om hring hring*
> *Deva Bagavati³ yaksani yan sat denata*
> *Avulu evan bili vilakkuva ada ma situvanne*
>
> *Om om hring hring*
> It is the same sacrificial torch that was lit for seven Bagavati demonesses
> That I put here this day.

The mantra continues, commanding Siva to cast his look (*Siva distiya*), and the Lord of the Sun (*Suriya*) as well as the sixty million demonesses. All are invited to gaze upon the *Suniyam purale,* the Mahasammata palace, and the scene of the performance.

By the end of the *Suniyam kapakirima,* the performance area is hot with the cosmic forces of origination. The repeated naming of Siva and Kali and their manifestations (Bagavati, the demonesses, etc.) is constitutive of the dynamic creative and destructive powers of *sakti.* The fixing of the lighted tapers into the *Suniyam purale* signs the presence of such turbulent power. The tapers themselves are metaphoric materializations of sexual energy and potency.

The patient now enters into the heat of the ritual context. He is dressed in white clothes, specially washed and prepared for the occasion. For days before the performance he has been required to refrain from all action that might bring him into contact with the dangers of pollution, including sexual activity. The events surrounding the seating of the patient begin a process whereby the victim is cleansed of the impurities of sorcery which cover and invade the body like a disease. It is a crucial positioning which condenses a plethora of meanings whose significance is elaborated throughout the rite.

The victim is seated at the edge of the performance arena (figuratively, at the perimeter of Mahasammata's cosmic city) and oriented toward Mahasammata's palace, which is located some twenty feet away. Expressly exhorted by the master exorcist to focus his thoughts on the Buddha's life and teaching, the patient is already in motion and projecting along a line that will be generative of his transformation and release.

The victim is quite literally in the hot seat, simultaneously in the heat of destruction and of recreation. Much of the action surrounding the anointment of the patient is designed to cool and to balance the forces concentrating on the victim.

Of primary significance is the fact that the victim is situated in the position of Queen Manikpala, which all patients, regardless of gender, must assume. This is central to the objective of the ritual as a reperformance of the original Suniyama. Furthermore, in the position of Manikpala, the patient is simultaneously a body of transgression and a body poised on the brink of regeneration. That this body is female expresses, I suggest, the symbolic excess of sorcery—its cosmic enormity of experience and significance beyond any finite representation—and the immensity of the forces that the event of sorcery brings into play. In terms of the mythopraxis of the rite as a whole, Manikpala's body, the female body that is far more than a merely gendered body (a female body as distinct from a male body), is at once the plane of the totalizing forces of existence and of their dynamic metamorphosis and transformation. Manikpala is in some senses a locus of male and female energies and is progressively manifested as such in the rite, from which a new unity is generated and a separation from the condition of sorcery is achieved.

I summarize some of the key ritual actions performed at the patient's seating, which expand some of the themes to which I refer and indicate further the symbolic density of the events.

The Consecration of the Patient: Seating, Anointment (Nanumura), and Placing of Manikpala's Shawl

The master exorcist holds before the patient the *Suniyam vattiya* (or *hatadi vattiya*), which contains the diverse articles to be used in the later ritual sequence of the seven steps (*hatadiya*). He projects the later performance of this crucial series of events and invokes the powers of Oddisa Kumara, who created the *hatadiya* and whose ritual skill the master exorcist will replicate. Addressing Oddisa as *appochihami* (honored father), the *adura* invites Oddisa to watch over the rite and to assist in the patient's cure. The *adura* recites a list of the food offerings that will be given to the gods, to the demons, and to Prince Oddisa so that every part of the patient's body (the veins, the hairs, the bowels, the chest, the limbs, the joints, the head, etc.) will be rid of the sorcerer's attack.

The patient is seated facing toward the Mahasammata palace. Two prepubescent boys (in a state of purity) hold a white cloth (*kadaturava*)[4] before the patient, blocking his view. A short mantra is uttered and incense (*sandun*) is drawn across the cloth, which is removed suddenly as burning resin (*dummala*) is thrown at it. The master *adura* exhorts the patient to concentrate on the life and teaching of the Buddha. The Mahasammata palace and the *atamagala* within are made the singular focus of the patient, and this concentration and focusing is dynamic in the motion and transformation of the patient.

The consecration (*pe*) principally involves the anointment of the victim with *nanumura*. This includes other purifying and cooling acts (the sprinkling of turmeric water, *kahadiyara,* and the application of pressed young coconut oil to the forehead, *hisatel*), and the spreading of the white shawl, the *mottakkili,* over the patient's head and shoulders.

In the *nanumura* event the (antidote?) paste (*nanu*) of boiled limes is applied to the victim's forehead, after which other cleansing and purifying acts follow. *Nanumura* rites are performed in other ceremonies for the gods and demons and in festivals of the Buddhist New Year and, significantly in this context, in the rites of coronation and annual reempowering of the king, which are also reconstitutive of the order of which he is the center (see Seneviratne 1978: 57–62). The application of *nanu* at New Year and in the rites of the king cleanses the fragmenting and weakening evils (*vas-dos*), the poisons, misfortunes, and sicknesses arising from the actions of others and the person to whose body these destructive, polluting forces have attached. In the Suniyama, the songs (*nanumura kavi*) surrounding the application of *nanu* convey these senses. The patient and others in the ritual assembly listen intently to the tales of the renowned cleansing properties of *nanu*.

The first story sung, led by the presiding exorcist and in refrain by the other *adura*s, tells how Gautama Buddha cleansed the city of the Licchavis, Visalamahanuvara. This city is attacked by the furious demon of disease and pestilence, Maha Kola Sanniya, who avenges the wrongful execution of his mother by the Licchavi king. So furious is the vengeance that the population is reduced to a putrefying mass.[5] The fury is stopped only with Gautama's intervention. This song can be understood as demonstrating the ordering encompassing power of the Buddha and his potency in correcting the faults (*dosa*) generating misfortune of ordinary impassioned action not oriented to the terms of the Buddha's reason.

Exorcists describe their ritual practice as corrective action, and none so much as the Suniyama. Its ritual practice is preeminently directed to a readjustment of the total situation of the person, of the forces and relations that impinge upon and are also organismically embodied in the person. Their practice is strongly instructional. The songs are intended to instruct patients and those who come to watch the proceedings in the meaning and the potency of acts. Such instruction is integral to the rite as corrective and readjustive. Similar instructional purpose and associated correctional agency are also vital in the dances and the drama of later ritual episodes. All these elements of the performance, especially the songs, also carry a strong moral load, the morality of the rite being integral to its adjusting and correctional aims. The moral force of the songs is apparent in the songs about Prince Vijaya and his demon lover Kuveni that the *adura* now sings.

The song (*nanumura upata*) recounts the event of Vijaya's breaking of his marriage vow to Kuveni, the demoness who assisted him in conquering Lanka, and of Kuveni's terrible curse (*dividos*). This curse wrought a dreadful sickness and suffering on Vijaya and his successors (Vijaya's nephew Panduvas in particular) and is viewed as a force in the misfortunes of Sinhala people to this day. It is the energy of Kuveni's *dividos*, a furious rage against injustice, that is invoked at sorcery shrines such as that for Devol Deviyo at Sinigama (see Chapter 2).

> Kuveni born from the womb of Ivarama
> Kuveni bathes at a pond where the Nuga grows.[6]
> The Prince (Vijaya) dwelled with Kuveni by the pond.
> He swore (*divuru*) never to leave her.
> The Prince became sick because he broke his vow.
> A canopy of red and blue cloth (*ratnil piliyena*) was raised to heal him.

The song lists the offerings that were given to Kuveni to assuage her anger and to correct the wrong done to her. In the same way, says the presiding exorcist, Kuveni must be active in removing the pains that afflict the sorcery victim. These pains are described as being like thorns piercing the flesh. The reference is to the practice of the sorcerer, who pierces a wax image of his victim with thorns (*katugasima*).

The verses now extol the making of *nanu* from the boiling of limes given by the Naga king, their mixture into paste with rose water, and the use of *nanu* in dispelling Kuveni's curse.

> Vijaya's hair is like a peacock's plumes.
> His body shines like a golden statue.
> His head is anointed with *nanu*.
> All the *dividos* were dispelled (by the anointment of *nanu*).
> Since that time the power (*balaya*) continues (of *nanu*).
> In the same way *nanu* is applied to the patient.
> All the afflictions (*dosa, roga*) will be dispelled and the patient protected
> from this day.

During this song, *nanu* is applied to the patient, and the subject of the singing shifts to the event of Queen Manikpala's anointment. The exorcists sing of how only Oddisa had the power to bring the *nanu* limes, and how the *nanu* itself is brought to the ailing Manikpala, first by Rahu, who passes it to Vishnu, then to Saman, Skanda, Viskam, the divine architect (who constructed the ritual buildings for the first Suniyama), and finally to the right hand of Teda Pattini, Pattini in her hot (*tejas*) regenerating form.

> Queen Manikpala's hair falls loose.
> Her head and body grow hot with the fever of the *vina.*
> Oddisa cut the Suniyam *dosa.*
> Her head was anointed with *nanu.*

At the end of the *nanumura upata,* the master *adura* intones a mantra (listing the various names of the powerful deities) which empowers the cleansing force of the *nanu.* It is routine to use mantras in this way, to complete and thus effectively to engage the powerful properties of the actions and substances recounted in song. Brief verses about the history and properties of turmeric water (*kahadiyara*) and oil (*tel*) are now sung, followed by empowering mantras.

Singing of *kahadiyara,* the exorcists tell of a monk who travels to the sacred Lake Anotattavilla at Mount Meru in the Himalayas. The lake is guarded by the Naga (Cobra) king, who addresses the monk insultingly and refuses to let him take the water until the monk gives the king an animal sacrifice. The monk curses the Naga king and plants his foot on the cobra's head so it sinks beneath the waters of the lake. The monk then fills his pot, and like the swan king (*hansa raja*), flies from the scene. High above, the god of rain could see the snake king hissing clouds of angry smoke. The monk gave the pot of pure water to Oddisa to remove the *dosa.*[7] The verses concerning the oil tell how it was brought from a palm in Sakra's garden to counteract *vina* and brought by King Buwanindu to the human world.[8]

The events of consecration are completed with the placing of the *mottakkili* (also referred to more colloquially as a head cloth, *osariya*) over the patient. This cloth has major significance in the Suniyama and in the Pattini rites, where it is explicitly associated with this goddess (see Obeyesekere 1984a:538–539). The *mottakkili* is worn throughout most of the rite and is removed only after the conclusion of the events of the *valvalalu* (the bonding and release of the patient) that follow the events of the seven steps (*hatadiya*). It is a condensed symbol, at once the protective shawl of Pattini but also indicative of the countervailing forces that concentrate on the victim in the position of Manikpala.

Narada, the divine messenger and musician, so the master *adura* relates, went to plead with the goddess Pattini on her mountain dwelling place Mount Andungiri for her assistance in curing Manikpala. Pattini gave her own shawl, a symbol of her chaste power.[9] Obeyesekere (1984a: 538 — 539) notes that although the *mottakkili* is a shawl worn by Sinhala women (and typically found in nineteenth-century painting), in the context of the Pattini rites it is better described as a veil. He argues for the general importance of the Pattini cult (which has a long and ancient tradition) in uses of the veil among Sinhala and Hindu populations in Sri Lanka.[10] Among high-caste Tamils in Sri Lanka, the veil (*mottakku*) is used at weddings to indicate the chastity of the wife, but Obeyesekere (1984a:539) states that in South India a similar veil is associated with widowhood and is regarded as highly inauspicious—a sense that Obeyesekere implies is not associated with Pattini's veil.[11]

In the context of the Suniyama the *mottakkili* is indicative of chastity and purity, but also of death, of the unity of life in fragmentation, of purity defiled, of reformation, of encompassment in higher unity, and so forth. Before it is placed over the patient, the *mottakkili* cloth is held by the master *adura* specially folded, like the front decorative part of a turban, the *mundasana* of Oddisa's turban, in his form as the creator of the Suniyama and the master sacrificer. It is also in the shape of the *indra kila* cloth that is placed before the new statue of the Buddha during the eye-painting ceremony (*netra pinkama*), when the statute is finally completed and potentiated. The *indra kila* protects the Buddha statue from malevolence directed toward it while it is in a vulnerable condition before the eyes have been painted and its potency awakened.

The *mottakkili* is filled with the sense of the immanent dangers, transformation, conscious awakening, and repotentiation of the victim it protectively shrouds.

I emphasize the *mottakkili* as a refraction and a totalization of the changing and shifting meaning and senses of the ritual process. Thus, although the *mottakkili* is the protective veil of Pattini (herself an ambiguous being, chaste and vengeful), it is also worn by Manikpala, a virginal bride in the condition of the sorcerer's defilement following her vulnerability occasioned by Mahasammata's absence in his war against the *asura*s. The very orientation of the victim-Manikpala at this starting point in the rite is toward the *atamagala*, which is the bridal chamber of Mahasammata and Manikpala, the place of the marriage bed, the site of regeneration, and, therefore also a potential place of danger and pollution. Such danger indeed surrounds the space, as later events in the rite make clear. At moments in the rite (during the episodes of dance that follow the placing of the *mottakkili*), the exorcists joke and draw out the dangerous properties that are signed in the *mottakkili*.

In their wordplay, they pronounce *mottakkili* as *mottappili*. This term is used to refer to the marriage sheet, which demonstrates lost virginity and the consummation of the marital unity. But the blood is also indicative of defilement (*kili*) or pollution, and the fragmentation immanent in union. The *adura*s play on the meaning of the suffix *pili*. This is sorcery practice whereby an object, usually an animal (commonly a snake), is the bearer of the sorcerer's destructive energy. Vasavarti's flinging of the fire viper toward Manikpala and its lodging in her womb is an archetype of *pili* (*pilluva*) sorcery. The *mottakkili* projects the line of the sorcerer and the condition of the ensorcelled (of a person close to death in life) as it also indicates the orientation toward higher union and transcendence.

The *mottakkili* is a dominant symbol in the sense of Turner's (1957, 1967) now classic discussion of the Ndembu symbolism of the *mudyi* tree and the whiteness of its sap. I have concentrated on the *mottakkili* as a condensation of symbolic potentiality, a totalization. It can be reduced to particular meanings or to an article with specific properties, as I have indicated. However, any of these properties always implies, or has immanent, a great many other possibilities extending beyond any particular attribute. In other words, the *mottakkili* is an article of symbolic surplus or excess, a totalizing symbol. It gathers and carries a great fan of meaningful potential. Worn throughout much of the rite by the victim, it refracts the changing meaning of the ritual contexts through which the victim passes. The *mottakkili* achieves its ultimate senses of purity, of ideal unity, harmony, and transcendence, when worn by the patient inside the *atamagala*. Here it materializes the restoration of regenerative unity to which it points at the start of the rite and furthermore a separation from the dangerous and defiling forces which are aspects of its significance at the beginning. When the patient enters the *atamagala,* the victim usually changes into fresh clothes and dons a new *mottakkili*.

The acts of consecration and purificatory protection extend into actions that draw out the destructive and polluting forces that have entered the body of the patient and disrupted the victim's equanimity. The master exorcist engages in a series of actions generally referred to as *sirasapada* (head to foot). He instructs the victim to worship the Buddha and to focus his mind on events in the Buddha's life. A *sirasapada* mantra is uttered as he draws the *igaha*, the arrow of Siva that focuses the commanding energy of the mantra, down the body of the victim. The forces of malevolence are drawn out from the extremities of the victim's body. These head-to-foot actions are repeated at various times throughout the rite.

A set of songs (*kavi*) are sung mainly by the dancers who have been dressing in the performance arena and executing brief dances in association with the earlier consecrating acts. The songs extol actions and qualities (*buduguna*) displayed in events of the lives of the present Buddha, Gautama, and of previous Buddhas. Thus, the songs tell of Dipankara Buddha's encounter with Sumedha (a previous incarnation of Gautama) who spreads himself across a pool of mud so that Dipankara could walk on his body and not soil his feet; of the former birth of the Buddha as a rabbit (*sasa*) that offered to sacrifice himself to satisfy the demands of a *raksaya* demon (the god Sakra in disguise) for a meal of roasted flesh rather than cause the death of another animal; of Buddha's purification of Visalamahanuvara and taming of Kola Sanniya; and finally, the story of Prince Vessantara, who engages in extreme acts of generosity (giving away all his wealth and even his wife and children), which exemplify the highest Buddhist virtues of nonattachment. The events in these songs are repeated at other stages in the rite and expounded at far greater length relative to their more abbreviated presentation at this time. The songs have force. They are understood as having the property of *set kavi*, or songs and verses that protect and cool and that negate the power of the cursing verses of sorcerers (*vas kavi*).

Moreover, the songs are intended to focus the victim's attention on the virtues of the Buddha and by means of this attention produce a mental calm and overall cooling and equilibrating of the body. They also help the master exorcist remove the destructive energies of sorcery from various points along the patient's body. Thus, at the end of each of the songs on one of the Buddha's qualities, the presiding exorcist points the *igaha* at a particular part of the body, starting from the head and moving down, repeating "by the power of this action may the *dosa* be removed from the (and then the name of the body part)."

The Buddha manifests ultimate encompassing and ordering principles of cosmic forces that condition the equilibrium of the body. Specific planets, the gods, and the demons have force over particular parts of the body. They affect the balance of the three body humors (*tun dosa*), dimensions of the five elemental essences of all matter (*pancamahabuta*). The Buddha is the principal force by means of which patients can be positioned or recentered in the play of cosmic force and subject to its ordering rather than disordering possibilities. The actions and songs surrounding the *sirasapada* express such aspects.

Furthermore, these events indicate the importance of the conscious action of the patient directed to the qualities of the Buddha. Such directed consciousness restores the body, inseparably the seat of consciousness (*hita, manasa*). This is a dynamic that progressively regenerates consciousness as the controlling and ordering force of the body. Through such projection, the victim becomes self-active in his own restoration and recreation as an agent in the world—a process that is developed further and made a greater possibility of the action in later ritual events. This projection of consciousness by the patient is integral to the motion of the patient—a self-generated motion—away from the condition approaching death which the patient is in when the rite starts.

Other exorcisms insist on a similar practice on the part of the patient, but it is elaborated to a far greater extent in the Suniyama. The distinction is to be found in the very different relation of patients to the focal ritual building, or *yak vidiya,* in these other exorcisms compared to the victim's relation to the focal building (the Mahasammata palace) in the Suniyama. The *yak vidiya* is in effect a place of ignorance, confusion, and a loss of consciousness. Although patients start their progress in other exorcisms oriented toward the *yak vidiya,* they should not enter it. To do so can sign immanent death. The objective of the other demon exorcisms is to break the patient's orientation to the *yak vidiya* and to prevent the patient's entry. However, in the Suniyama, the major impetus of the rite is toward the focal building, for it is the place of the attainment of full consciousness (of Enlightenment, of release or *moksa*), and furthermore, the ordering center of the life worlds of human beings. When a patient moves toward the *yak vidiya* in other exorcisms, this is movement away from the life world. But in the Suniyama, a similar move is a motion to the vibrant heart of the life world, a motion to the highest development of the consciousness of human being.

The songs of the *sirasapada* are over by 9:30 P.M. The performance is now dominated by the dance of the four exorcist dancers. A brief comment on their dress is relevant to an understanding of the significance of both the dance and the work, in this instance, of the antisorcerer.

The dress of the dancers is regarded by all the *adura*s with whom I have spoken as specific to the Suniyama. Although exorcists wear the dress at other healing rites, it is inappropriate to do so. The dancers' attire is, in fact, the garb of the original exorcist-sorcerer, Oddisa, the creator of the Suniyama. Two distinguishing parts of the dress are a black vest embroidered with pearl shell in the shape of the *hondala* vine (*L. juncus*). It is used for binding and is associated with snakes. *Hondala* is used in sorcery, and among some exorcists, its use as a motif on the vests represents the snakes with which Oddisa garlanded his body. The dancers also wear the *kangul toppiya* headdress. This is somewhat like the jester's cap of European traditions. This should have five protuberances in the shape of a cockscomb, but is interpreted by *adura*s as snakes (*naga*) or the locks of Oddisa's hair and also the twists of his turban.[12]

Although in some popular traditions Oddisa is treated as synonymous with Suniyam, exorcists in the traditions I studied insisted that Oddisa is not to be confused with Suniyam. Oddisa's power and skill is that he can assume the shape of Suniyam. He can enter into the form of the demon of sorcery and partake of its energy. Oddisa, entering into the guise of the demon, can engage immediately with its force and turn its power against those who use it or else employ it himself in destruction. This is how *adura*s describe their own skill and work, which involves entering into the highly dangerous world of sorcery power and engaging closely and directly with its force. Some exorcists liken themselves to Oddisa in the sense that they become inhabited, or possessed (*avesa*), by sorcery. A closing event in the Suniyama, the *chedana vidiya*, manifests the exorcists as the angry destructive energy of Vasavarti Maraya/Suniyam. One *adura* becomes possessed with Suniyam's fury.

In effect, the dancers appearing in the guise of Oddisa present themselves as masters of his illusory skill and as about to enter into direct and intimate struggle with the forces of sorcery. Appearing in the dress of Oddisa, the dancers also present themselves as repeaters of Manikpala's rite and thus as re-presenting all the recreative potency of that original rite.

The dance of the *adura*s opens with the ceremonial drum rhythm known as the *magul bere,* played by three drummers on the long cylindrical *yak bere* (the main instrument in the southern ritual traditions). The dancers circle the perimeter of the arena (left to right, an auspicious motion) and in fact fully define the boundary (*sima*) of the ritual space. Each dancer carries two large cloth torches (*pandam*) which are aflame.

The orientation of the dance then shifts; the dancers move rapidly between where the patient is seated and toward the entrance into the *atamagala* in Mahasammata's palace. Powdered resin (*dummala*) is touched to the torches, and balls of orange flame burst in the night air. The dancers throw billowing clouds of fire toward the palace. A heat is generated; the audience can feel it gusting across their bodies. This sensation is indeed the meaning of the occasion, for the ritual space is now hot with cosmic energies in process and with the fire of sorcery. Throwing the fire toward the palace, the dancers mime Vasavarti's fiery viper's thrust toward Manikpala and define the dangerous line of the victim's relation, the destructive and invasive relation with the sorcerer that later ritual events will erase and transform.

The dancers pause before the entrance into the *atamagala*. Here a mantra is uttered (*disti matirima, atamagala disti karanava*) which summons the whole pantheon of gods and demons to cast their gaze upon the *atamagala* and the palace as a whole. The mantra names a multitude of demons and gods and concludes with the invocation of the powers of Vessamuni, the demon lord (otherwise known as Kuvera, the guardian of treasure and wealth), and the Guardian Gods (*hataravaram deviyo*). The palace comes alive with the forces of the cosmic totality, signed by the dancers' fixing of five lighted tapers (*vilakku*) at points on the palace facade.

The motion of the dance now presents and further manifests the expanding play of cosmic powers as well as their dynamic tension and uncertain balance. The dancers juggle their lighted torches in the air. Occasionally, they mistime their catches (usually intentionally), the dropped torches accenting the struggle, tension, and uncertainty of the forces in process.

The sexuality of the dance, its metaphors of sexuality, which are also present in the rhythms of the drums, and the multivalency of this sexuality should be noted. The drums have a male (right drumhead) and female (left drumhead) side which express a different timbre. Played simultaneously, male and female are brought into generative conjunction that instances in sound the engendering of cosmic force engulfing both patient and audience (see Kapferer 1983). Two dancers facing each other to the quickening tempo of the drums embrace and part, embrace and part repeatedly, the torches they hold meeting behind the other's back. Sexuality is made explicit as the metaphor of generation, which also has immanent within it the force of destruction.

Several times the dancers become hopelessly entangled. They cannot keep pace with the drumming and, in effect, boil over, an indication of the growth of cosmic energy. On one occasion they lock completely and cannot move. A dancer places his torch at the other's anus. "What's that in your arse?" the dancer asks. "A taillight for my *gu-lori* (shit truck)," retorts his partner. The audience explodes with enjoyment. This is a standard joke at most Suniyamas I have attended. Like most humor, the interchange reveals a plethora of meaningful possibility that is alive both at this moment and in the total context of the rite.

At a stroke, the dancers pointed to the torch as a penis, making explicit and literalizing one symbolic meaning of torches (both *pandam* and *vilakku*) as Siva lingas. Their action drew attention to the destructive forces integral to the creative process. Further, the obscenity underpinned the transgressive energy and violence fundamental in the situation of sorcery.

Obscenity (see also Kapferer 1983; Douglas 1975), unlike many other kinds of humor and joking, does not play with ambiguity and generate more embracing and unifying frames of meaning through ambiguities but rather breaks through category distinctions and attacks and dissolves ambiguity. Obscenity and the sorcerer share an identity in their destruction of categories, in their transgression, and in their reduction of difference into a decaying totality (as the dancer might have implied, into a truckload of shit). This is an argument that I will expand in later discussion of the major comic drama of the Suniyama, the *vadiga patuna*. Here, the torch at the anus highlighted the invasive and polluting quality of the sorcerer's attack. Like Vasavarti's fiery thrust toward and rape of Manikpala, it indicates the degenerative violence of sorcery at the regenerative core of the ordering of human existence.

As the dance of the *adura*s comes to a close, the *madu puraya* (exorcist's assistant) removes the offering basket for the ghosts (*preta tattuva*) from the patient's bedroom, where it had been placed earlier, and takes it away from the house area to the margins of the village (it was thrown into a roadside ditch). The ghosts have come for their offerings; their greed and the attractive power of the offerings and the basket in which they are contained holds and traps the ghosts. The removal of the basket takes the ghosts away from the house, freeing the victim and household of their defilement or pollution (*kili*). This purifying aspect of the event is vital in itself. But it is in addition significant as an action instrumental in the simultaneous reestablishment or redefinition of the sociopolitical boundaries and relations centered on the victim and the victim's household and the boundaries and relations of the cosmic hierarchy.

Thus, the removal of the offering basket (*preta tattuva*) separates beings who have transgressed the boundaries of house and household. The transgression effectively denied the existence of such boundaries and opened the household to disordering elements. Moreover, it is an externalizing action. The ghosts are the force of social relations (kin and nonkin). Although they emanate from the deceased, they are present in the situation of the living. The very notion of ghosts in this Sinhala context is one that recognizes the energy of past relations in the present. The action surrounding the *preta tattuva* addresses specifically the malevolence in social relations (past and present), what is understood as sorcery (*kodivina*) in a general sense.[13] Therefore, the removal of the basket reestablishes the boundaries of house and household and externalizes the malevolence of social relations (their death-dealing possibility), opening the way for their more positive redefinition.

Another equally instrumental and pragmatic aspect of the foregoing action is to deflect the attention of the ghosts from the other offerings. The view of exorcists and laity alike is that the ghosts are so greedy that there is a danger that they will take the gifts and other offerings to the demons and to the gods. In other words, the ghosts will break the rules of precedence and propriety which constitute the internal boundaries and separations of hierarchical order. Demons and the gods will be so infuriated by ghostly transgression, say exorcists, that the former will not agree to remove their destructive malevolence and the latter will not give their healing protection.

The deflection or removal of ghostly attention from the scene of the ritual performance is a stage in the ritual rebuilding of the cosmic hierarchy, an assertion of the boundaries between ghosts, demons, and gods and their appropriate ordering of relations. Such a ritual constitution of the cosmic hierarchy is productive of the force that will ultimately fling the energy of sorcery back upon itself, thoroughly externalize sorcery, and enable the repotentiation of victim and household in their world.

The dance of the *adura*s comes to an end. The exorcist-dancers stand before Mahasammata's palace and sing concluding verses asking the hosts of demons and gods to cast their gaze upon the ritual buildings. The palace is purified with gouts of flaming resin (*dummala*); the fire dispels impurities but also sign the life of the palace and the heat of recreation.

There is now a short pause. The dancers go behind the Mahasammata palace to change for the next event, when they will make their appearance in the guise of the Guardian Gods. They demonstrate their skill as exorcists to enter into the guise of the forces they invoke. They mime the gods and give dramatic illustration of that which they invite to and make present within the ritual context. Their mimesis is powerful in a further sense. It is a delighting and pleasing of the gods and as such draws their gaze to the performance.

Other themes already apparent in the rite are expanded, especially the dynamic interplay between the progressive and ever-elaborating building and growing of the cosmic hierarchy, on the one hand, and the definition and formation of social relations centered on the house and victim, on the other hand. Both are organized around the giving of food. Members of the household are almost constantly engaged in handing around refreshments of cups of tea, bananas, and oil cakes (*kavum*). During this pause, some members of the audience are called inside the house to be served a meal. Usually those regarded as of high status are invited first. The dance that is about to start expresses dimensions of the generative interconnection between the principles engaged in the hierarchy of the gods and those relating to the sociopolitical world of human beings.

The Dances of Invitation to the Guardian Gods (Deva Aradanava)

It is now 9:45 P.M. and the master *adura* goes before the Mahasammata palace and gives salutation (*namaskaraya*) to the Buddha and the Guardian Gods and requests their assistance in commanding the demons. The presiding *adura* then utters the mantra that commands and assembles the demonic and divine forces from the four and then the eight directions of the universe (*astakarma matirima:* mantra of the eight actions). The Guardian Gods who are celebrated and invited in the later episodes of the dance are the commanding forces at each one of the directional points: Vishnu (east), Saman (west), Kataragama (south), Natha (Maitri Buddha, north). The *astakarma* mantra which empowers the Mahasammata palace and especially the *atamagala* (which in the ritual events that now start is called the *astakarma mangala*) is repeated a number of times and its force and meaning elaborated in song.

The master exorcist commands the great horde of demons to come from the eight directions and invokes the authority of the demon lord Vessamuni (Sanskrit Vaisravana, or Kubera, the Guardian of Treasure), who governs from the northern quarter under the power of the next Buddha, god Natha. Vessamuni is a being of enormous violent power and controls great wealth, and numerous stories describe him as engaging his horde of malevolent beings to cause all manner of illness, misfortune, and pestilence among human beings. Vessamuni is the commanding and ordering totalization of all demonic energy (see Wirz 1954:23–24; Kapferer 1983: 112, 115). He has his authority (*varam*) to control the demons from the Buddha.

The dancers dressing behind the Mahasammata palace join the master exorcist in singing plaints (*kannalavva*) of Vessamuni's qualities. These describe him as wearing an enormous crown encrusted with blue sapphires and a blue cloak twelve *yoduns* in length. Vessamuni, the verses tell, needs sixty carts to carry his huge treasure of weapons, jewels, and other ornaments. "Vessamuni gathers around him a host that comes with the destructive force of the typhoon (*veramba vataya*)."

The closing verses of the songs recount an event that reveals the force of Vessamuni's power over the demons. They tell of a furious argument that broke out among the demon hordes assembled in Vessamuni's golden palace that was so terrible that the twenty-eight generals (*yaksa senadipati*) of the demon army gripped their swords in anger. But Vessamuni gave a gigantic sneeze (*nilocchumbaya*), and the golden mountain on which Vessamuni's palace is built rumbled with the sound of thunder. The demons scattered like waves in the sea. "When Vessamuni," sing the exorcists in praise, "casts his eye weapon (*nayanayudaya*), which has the power of Sakra's thousand eyes, at the demons, they are smashed into seven bits. All the demons worship Vessamuni." With this last verse, the master *adura* invokes the power of Vessamuni and demands that the demon hordes attend to the ritual scene and accept the five kinds of ritual offerings (*pancopacara:* flowers, food, incense, light, betel) that are to be presented.

"Come," cries the master exorcist, "come (demons) to the *hastakarna vidiya* (a reference that links the *atamagala* to the power of the mantra used). Take the offerings of incense (*suvanda-dum*), flowers and light (*mal-pahan*), foods (*dola-pideni, bali-bili*). Should you refuse I will call on Vessamuni to bring you suffering (*dukvindinava*). Take the offerings!"

The Four Guardian Gods who are at the apex of the cosmic hierarchy are now summoned individually. The presiding *adura* invites them to take the offerings (*pancopacara)* appropriate to their status and to cast the power of their gaze (the essence of their presence) upon the rite.

The dancers in the guise of each of the gods now appear in the performance arena, entering from behind the Mahasammata palace. Each wears a magnificent headdress in the color of the god concerned and richly embroidered with a flower design. They hold areca palm flowers that represent the cooling yak-tail whisk (*camara*). The gods enter the performance arena one by one to the accompaniment of an announcing drumming rhythm (*saudan*), their signature tune. The order of appearance is first Vishnu, then Kataragama, then Saman, and finally Natha.[14] The dances of Vishnu and Kataragama are the most elaborate and extensive of the individual dances. These deities are found in most temples and are the gods that Sinhalese approach in daily worship and to solve everyday problems. Saman (the god of Adam's Peak, where Buddha is understood to have left his footprint on one of his visits to Sri Lanka, and which is a major site for pilgrimage) and especially Natha are more remote from daily practice.

That Natha is the last of the gods to appear (and this is repeated at all the Suniyamas I have witnessed) is significant. Natha as the Buddha-to-be embodies aspects of the Buddha ideal which is the guiding force of the rite as a whole. Gautama Buddha, since he achieved nonexistence, cannot be represented as a living presence. However, Natha still exists and can be represented as a living force and materialization of Buddhist virtue. Moreover, Natha, as the final god to make an entrance in these episodes of dance—events that demonstrate the ultimate forces of ordering power in the cosmic hierarchy—signs the Buddha Path and the power of his Teaching as the ultimate orienting principles of cosmic order. In effect, the power of the Buddha opens and closes these major dance sequences. Natha locates the power of the Buddha ideal in existential realities and indicates the Path that the victim himself must come to travel (in the later events of the *hatadiya*).

The gods must be drawn to the rite, and the dancers present this process. Vishnu, the first to make his appearance, keeps the audience waiting for some twenty minutes. Poems describing and lauding his power and his beauty are sung. He is summoned by his various names: Upulvan and Krisnanarayana. And he is summoned by the articles of his power: his iron mace, the conch, the lotus weapon, and the *cakra*.

The foods and other gifts that he will be given are listed (*pancopacara,* the five offerings). The drummers beat magnificent rhythms as their offering of sound (*sabda puja*). Further songs implore Vishnu to grant his presence to the ritual gathering.

> Vishnu, who commands the East
> Come to this flower bed (*mal asna*).
> Forgive any omissions in the offerings.
> Break the demon bonds that tie the patient.
>
> Lord Vishnu, come on Gurula.
> Cool the walls of fires (*ginivata*) with the *camara*.
> Bring the divine cloth (*deva saluva*) with its golden threads.
> Cool the fire and come to the *chedana vidiya, kapum vidiya*
>   (fragmenting, sorcery-cutting *vidiya*, Mahasammata palace).

Vishnu must be enticed into the performance space. At last he starts to appear. He peers out at the audience from one side of the Mahasammata palace and then from the other—showing only his face. Some members of the audience call out to Vishnu and tell him to come and not be shy. Still going from one side of the palace to the other, Vishnu gradually shows more of his body, and then he suddenly darts into full view, only to quickly disappear again behind the palace. At last, apparently overcoming his bashfulness, to the huge enjoyment of the audience, Vishnu dances in his full splendor before the gathering. He displays his beauty and performs as if absorbed by his own shimmering magnificence. Slowly at first, drummer and dancer match rhythm to step and to gesture, building the tempo faster and faster. The drummer executes a drumroll (*su-*

rala), and Vishnu's whole body shudders in synchrony. Then, to another rhythm, the dancer leaps, cartwheels, and swirls around the arena, eventually coming to a stop before the patient. A short mantra and poem are uttered by the presiding exorcist requesting Vishnu to take his offerings. *Dalumura,* the betel-areca offering appropriate to the gods, is given by the patient to Vishnu, who then leaves the arena.

Kataragama follows, and like Vishnu, he must be enticed. His entry is at first hesitant until he dances, giving a full view of his magnificent splendor. Eventually he departs when he receives his *dalumura* offering, agreeing by his acceptance of it to use his powers to rid the patient of sorcery. He then returns, this time in the company of Vishnu, and the two dance together. They compete in demonstrating their skill. The one repeats and expands the dance gestures of the other until the two leap together around the arena. Saman and Natha then make their appearance, and the dances come to an end with all the dancers performing together. They leave giving salutations to the patient, the master exorcist, and generally to the audience. The dancers remove their divine guise and change into the apparel of Oddisa, donning once again the *kangul toppiya.*

The dances, with their spectacle and humor, are intended to please the audience and to cool the heat of the victim's sorcery. More specifically, the appearance of the gods and the way they act in relation to the audience is a demonstration of *dakum* (Skt. *darsana*). *Dakum,* or *darsana,* as Eck (1985: 3) describes it for Hindu India, is an auspicious gaze, a central act of worship in which human beings see and are seen by the deity. There is a reciprocity in the gaze. The gods in their appearance are in effect presenting a gift of their magnificent ordering power to those who see them. Alternatively, human beings by gazing upon the gods are honoring them with the gift of their admiration, which the gods are concerned to attract. This vanity of the gods provides much of the fun of the occasion.

The spectacle of the god's dance is more than mere entertainment, a demonstration of the totalizing power of the gods, or even a mimetic presencing of their divine energies. Through the mediation of the spectacle of the dance, human beings and the gods are brought into touch. Thus, human beings become integral with the cooling and protective force of the gods.

The values played out in the dance of the gods elaborate a symbolic context for the valuation or revaluation of social and political relations as these center on the victim and the household.

Obeyesekere (e.g., 1984a, 1990) has constantly stressed the close connection between religious and ritual symbolic orders and the everyday dynamics and practicalities of status and power in Sinhalese communities. He demonstrates this through a discussion of *dakum* in the context of a broader ethnography of the Pattini ceremony of the *gammaduva*. The *gammaduva*s in his observations, and in my own experience of these ceremonies, are community rites that give vital expression to local political hierarchies: a function of the rites that can be traced well into Sri Lanka's precolonial history. There are very many symbolic and organizational parallels between *gammadu* rites and the Suniyama—the Suniyama being classed by exorcists as a *madu tovil*, although it is centered on the house within the village rather than on the village or wider community of interconnected villages, as is the case with the *gammaduva*.

I cite Obeyesekere at length. He understands the Sinhala concept of *dakum* in the general setting of South Asian notions of power, including those of *pirisa* (following), *pirivara* (retinue), and *sima* (boundary), all concepts of relevance to the Suniyama and its social context. He states:

> In Sinhala culture there are standard occasions where a man's following pays him court or homage. The Sinhala New Year is an occasion for the tenant to pay *dakum* to his lord, the son to the father, the junior to the senior, the low in status to the high. In the realm of kingship, *dakum* is the occasion where the rulers of the provinces pay court to the king. The larger population also may pay homage to the king at annual processional events like the parade of the tooth relic, where the rulers of the divine as well as secular realm appear (*dakum*) before the public. (Obeyesekere 1986a:55)

I have noted that Suniyamas are occasions for the expression of the local political importance of victims and their households. This is all the more true because sorcery is often understood to arise out of the fact that the victim is wealthy and powerful, the Suniyama, of course, being equal to such a threat against wealth and power. At some Suniyamas that I have attended (including this one), the political following of the victim has been a strong presence, the clients of their patron (the victim) making a point to greet the patient and to have their support noticed.

The symbolism of royal power and feudal hierarchy of the dance of the gods emphasizes the potential political import of a Suniyama. Exorcists refer to the *dalumura* offering that the victim gives to the gods as *tevava,* a term describing the act of homage and service of subjects to rulers. This relation between victim and gods may also be seen as yielding the value of the relation between many of those in the ritual gathering and the victim and his household. These people are part of the following and retinue of the victim; they come to see and be seen in the midst of the magnificent splendor of the Suniyama. The Suniyama grasped through the trope of *dakum* is a gift of the seen to the seeing and vice versa. Such reciprocity expresses a total world of power and status, of dominant and encompassing cosmic forces that define and include the striations of power and status in the mundane realities of local communities.

The Suniyama is part of an extensive and vital Sinhalese religious and ritual field that can operate as symbolic capital in contemporary structuring processes of class, status, and power. The Suniyama is a particularly potent symbolic resource because of its focus on sorcery and a virtual obsession with the problematics and symbolism of wealth and power at the heart of sorcery, all of which are accented in events such as the dance of the Guardian Gods. But the Suniyama is potentially far more than a "capital" resource. It "generates" or "multiplies" more "capital" (even "launders" it, for the rite protects and purifies persons from the dangers inherent in success and possession; see Chapter 8). The dance of the gods is a building of power, a creation and a recreation of their dominant hierarchical energy. Within this dynamic, the human relations of power, those of victim and household, inextricably connected with wealth and status, are produced, defined, and redefined. That is, the building and manifestation of the power of the gods translates into a demonstration and revelation of the structures of power and status as these center around the victim and the household. The dynamic competitive growing of the power of the gods in dance is parallel to the growing of wealth and power in the ordinary world, especially that embedded in capitalist forces.

In other words, the competitive processes of everyday life on which success and failure are contingent are mirrored in this dance of the gods. Furthermore, the dance (and indeed the Suniyama as a whole) is an act of symbolic conversion whereby the wealth expended on the performance is transformed and manifested as the protective and ordering presence of the gods.

Some of these themes continue into the events that follow, the rites of the *hatadiya* (seven steps), which are the most crucial of the entire Suniyama. This is because the *hatadiya* rites are the repetition of those which Oddisa, the master sorcerer and sacrificer, instituted for the cure of Manikpala. The action now focuses on the patient alone. He becomes progressively a brilliant center in the metaphors of Buddhist kingship that are dominant in the rite, virtually a *cakravartin,* a pivot of world recreation. The victim, prepared as a being for sacrifice, becomes in the course of the rites both an agency and an agent of reconstitution, regeneration, and revitalization.

The Rites of the Hatadiya

These rites in this performance (and in all the other Suniyamas I have witnessed) start almost midway through the period of the midnight watch, indeed as the vital temporal juncture of midnight approaches. This is the moment when cosmic forces, particularly the energies of sorcery, are at their greatest potency. But it is also a major cosmic pivoting point: a moment when destructive processes at their height also begin to weaken and when the forces of life begin to come alive with the beginning of the ascent of the sun. The *hatadiya* is the longest sequence of events in the rite, and it continues almost unbroken over a period of three to four hours, until the start of the morning watch at 3 P.M.

The duration of the *hatadiya* has much to do with what I understand as its major thematic. This involves the victim in a cosmic passage that is nothing less than the recreative motion of the macrocosm in the microcosm. The seven steps that the victim takes (from where he is initially seated on the boundary, *sima*, of the performance arena to the *atamagala* in Mahasammata's palace) trace at once the emergence of humankind to consciousness culminating in the present age of Gautama Buddha; the first seven steps of the Buddha; the passage from death, to life, to the edge of nonexistence; from ignorance to knowledge and truth, and so forth. The patient as the microcosm, the progressive embodiment of macrocosmic processes, is himself taken from a condition near Death to a location within the *atamagala* (a point at the edge of Nothingness and absolute release from suffering). In this place, the patient is turned around and reoriented toward the life world as a force that is both regenerate and regenerating. In this motion of the microcosm in the macrocosm, the energies of sorcery are subdued and returned furiously to their source. Moreover, the victim is progressively imbued with the ordering qualities of the cosmos, his body and mind harmonized, and ultimately thoroughly reconstituted as a being of agent-consciousness.

These processes of the *hatadiya*, which incessantly reiterate the themes of birth, death, and life, of origination and reorigination, are contained in the focal metaphor of the rite, Vasavarti's attack on Manikpala. This emphasizes the event of sorcery as striking to the very core of the existence of human being, which the *hatadiya*, the rite that Oddisa performed to heal Manikpala, addresses in its full cosmic and existential enormity and outrage.

The *hatadiya* manifests the scale of its process in the long-drawn-out nature of the performance (it lasts around four hours, and sometimes longer) and also in the more complete elaboration of the myths that are integral with the dynamic of metamorphosis and transformation of the Suniyama as a whole. The *hatadiya* rites are a blossoming of knowledge, and the victim is at the focus of such practice-knowledge: he is a center for the exercise and practice of a knowledge that the poems and songs of the *hatadiya* unfold. Moreover, in the victim's practice of the knowledge of the *hatadiya,* the patient becomes reconstituted as an agent-consciousness or a being aware of his own consciousness, able once more to become in control of his action in the world, motional in its processes, and capable of participating in the institution of his own life possibilities.

The events of the *hatadiya* may be described as falling into three parts:
1. The preparation of the ritual space
2. The setting out of the seven steps (or lotuses)
3. The seven steps of the patient and the entrance into the *atamagala*

The Preparation of the Ritual Space

The events of the *hatadiya* open with a salutation (*namaskaraya*) by the master exorcist to Buddha and the Guardian Gods. The *adura,* speaking in everyday conversational Sinhala, announces to the victim and the ritual assembly that he has been given permission by Mihikata[15] (Polova Mahi Kantava, Bumi Devi: the earth goddess who protected Buddha from the forces of Mara) to recite the origin of the *vidiya* (*vidi-upata kavi*). He informs the audience how in ancient times the *rsi*s, Oddisa, and the other holy men who assisted him performed a sacrifice (*yagaya*) to heal Queen Manikpala. The *Perarajavaliya,* the ancient book of kings, the master exorcist says, records that Sakra commanded Visvakarma (the divine architect) to build the *vidiya* for Oddisa for the removal of Manikpala's illness (*dosa*).

The exorcist dancers gather in front of the palace while the presiding exorcist starts a cycle of songs. The dancers sing in refrain and elaborate on the themes introduced by the master *adura*. They circle the arena, punctuating their songs and dance with great gusts of burning *dummala* touched to the torches (*pandam*) that they carry. The opening songs describe the building of the *Suniyam vidiya,* the *atamagala,* and the decorations and fruits that are hung from the ritual hut (*maduva*), the shed that covers the space of Mahasammata's city. The events surrounding

Manikpala's illness and Vasavarti's attack are then sung at length followed by an account of the appearance of Oddisa, in the form of Suniyam, to perform the sacrifice (*yaga*) for Manikpala. The songs end with a repetition and elaboration of the songs that began the cycle and give varying accounts of the building of the *atamagala* and the construction of the Mahasammata palace (*maligava, Suniyam vidiya*).

The series of songs are collectively referred to as the *vidi upata* (origin of the *vidiya*) and as the *madusarasilla kavi* (songs of ritual adornment). The songs are praises (*kannalavva*) of the actions constituting the original rite and imbue the whole situation of the rite with healing force.

I present some of the verses from the central and key event recounted in the songs, that of Vasavarti's attack on Manikpala.

> THE ATTACK ON MANIKPALA (PART OF THE VIDI UPATA)
>
> Manikpala came to the royal bed wearing golden jewels, like those
>   of Laksmi.
> Manikpala and Mahasammata enjoyed their lovemaking.
> Manikpala was as beautiful as the full moon.
> She loved her life.
>
> Her breasts were like golden pots (*kumba*).
> The gods dwelled at her hips.
> She was as virtuous as the king.
> The queen was as rare as the most precious stone.
>
> Mahasammata and Manikpala made love as one.
> They could not live apart.
> They cooed like lovebirds in their marriage bed.
> Their luxury suited them as *cakravartin*.

The verses continue describing Vasavarti's lust for the young queen and the way he approached the door of her bedchamber, appearing in the shape of Mahasammata. The song tells how the queen sees through Vasavarti's disguise and curses (*desdenna*) him; how Vasavarti is furious at his discovery and rejection; and how he reaches into the hell of ignorance (*aviciya*) and draws out the burning flames (*ginijala*: poison? semen?) which Vasavarti flings toward the queen, becoming the fire viper (*ginijala polanga*) that lodges in Manikpala's womb, causing her to fall unconscious.

> Mahasammata with love took the hand of Manikpala.
> But Manikpala could not speak.
> Tears poured from her face, as beautiful as the full moon.
> Her body gleamed like a golden creeper covered in gems.

When the king saw the queen's great sorrow
He could not bear the pain.
His stomach burned like a fiery furnace.
When he fell asleep the king had a dream.

The king dreamed of a viper.
The viper was eating rocks and stones.
It spat flames into the city.
Then Mahasammata knew what had happened to his country and
     his queen

The demon of five colors, riding his horse
at night, brings fear.
His horse paws the ground, kicking gravel and stones.
His *mundasana* (turban) is red, and tied like a cobra's hood.

When he bites the blood viper, his body turns red.
When he mounts his horse, his body turns blue.
This is the demon, Suniyam.

The gods chose Vishnu to bring Oddisa.
He went to Mount Ajakuta.
Vishnu said, "Tie the *mundasana* like a beautiful flower.
Gird your *vadiga* sword at your belt hung with bells.
Come and heal the queen."

The god of the moon (*candra*) mandala at whose brow is a co-
     bra's hood.
Who has a *raksaya* at his chest.
Who drew the fire from *aviciya* and threw it toward the sky.
Who carries the Sun and Moon in his hands.

Oddisa, appearing like Suniyam, makes the sacrifice (*yagaya*) for
     the queen of Suriyavamsa.

The closing verses of the song cycle return to the ritual buildings and
their adornments: how they were built by Visvakarma appearing with
his matted hair (*sadapalu*); how Mihikata measured out the floor plan
of the palace and *atamagala,* purified and decorated the buildings, fixed
golden stars and flags to the palace's uppermost spires (*kota*), and hung
golden flower buds and honeycomb from the rafters. The final verses tell
of the painting of the palace with lime paste (*nanu*) and the hanging of
different-colored canopies (*viyana*) from each of the three floors: red for
Kataragama on the top floor, blue for Vishnu on the second floor, and
white for Brahma on the ground floor.

     The last preparatory event for the *hatadiya* is known as the *doratu
panima,* the crossing of the threshold into the palace and the *atamagala.*
In effect, it concludes the building and ensures that the space inside the

atamagala is free of destructive forces. The key action is the crossing of the threshold by the master exorcist. This act, in the context of the events immediately surrounding it, is extraordinarily potent and highly tense. The presiding *adura* essentially comes between the victim and the energies of destruction. He takes the place of the victim and enters into direct and intimate struggle with the attacking sorcerer. It is a crucial turning point in the rite as a whole when the forces of sorcery are not only deflected from the victim but also start to be turned back on themselves and returned to their source.

Furthermore, the *doratu panima* is a ritual moment when the victim begins to be separated, or disconnected, from a relationship with the sorcerer. Thus he is opened up to processes and action which remove the sorcery or its effects but which do not involve the victim directly in causing suffering to the sorcerer. This is because the victim is separated from a direct, intimate relation with the sorcerer. Rather, the destruction and other suffering that turns back to the sorcerer is caused by the *adura*, who now enters into a direct relation to the sorcerer and also must now bear the full risk.

The events of the *doratu panima* begin with the master *adura* throwing burning resin through the entrance into the *atamagala*. This is an ambiguous action, purificatory but also indicative of Vasavarti's fiery leap (his throwing of the fire viper) toward the place of Manikpala. As the *adura* performs this action, he utters a quick reference to Vasavarti's *vina* against Manikpala. The *adura* signs the aim of the events he now is performing, which is to secure the purity and safety of the *atamagala* and to disconnect the sorcerer from his victim. A short verse from a *sirasapada kavi* (head-to-foot poem used to draw illness from the patient's body) is uttered. The presiding exorcist invokes the power of the Buddha and then the gods Isvara, Saman, Boksal, Vibisana, and Kataragama, who he declares have given him the authority (*varam*) to cross the threshold.[16] The *adura* also declares that he has the authority from his teachers (gurus) to engage in the action of the *doratu panima* and to rid the patient of sickness.

During the invocations, the dancers go to each of the other three doors of the *atamagala* and throw burning resin across the thresholds. This action has the same ambiguity as that of the master exorcist at the main entrance. There is a parallel between these actions and earlier purifications of the house when the offering tray to the *preta* (ghosts) was removed. At that time an exorcist-dancer went through each room in the victim's house, burning great gusts of *dummala*. In other performances of the Suniyama that I have seen, an exorcist passes through the victim's house burning resin simultaneously with the purification of the *atama-gala*.

There is a crucial symbolic identity between the victim's house and the *atamagala*. The house is the central space in a set of social and political relations that extend around it. The *atamagala* is the vital center (*garba*) and the space of human being within the cosmic entirety (*sakvala*). On some ritual occasions an *atamagala* yantra is drawn inside the house (e.g., at a girl's first menstruation), and the drawing of an *atamagala yantra* is also made at marriage, the bridal bower (*poruva*) that is built bearing architectural comparison to the *atamagala*. The *atamagala* in the Suni-yama, of course, becomes a space inhabited by the victim. I suggest that the *atamagala* is or becomes the (re)generative habitus (habitus in the sense developed by Bourdieu 1977): the victim by inhabiting the space embodies the principles or *doxa* that organize the space or are substan-tially embedded in the space and integral to its architectural arrangement, and thus the victim is also made into an agent for the regeneration and development of the *doxa* vital in Being and its ordering.

Moreover, the *atamagala* can be described as the habitus of the habi-tus, a place where all dimensions of lived being (birth, death, sexuality, cooking, eating, sleeping) are symbolically concentrated and centered within encompassing cosmic ordering processes. The *atamagala* is the revitalizing habitus and in the Suniyama is realized as the life-generating hub of the house and the household, and by extension, of the social, economic, and political relations of the everyday world that center on the house and the household.

The acts of purification that surround the *atamagala* and which pro-ceed from events that effectively build the *atamagala* (the songs of the *vidi-upata* and the *madusarasilla* are a building of the *atamagala*) are similar to ritual actions that are performed when a new house is com-pleted.

The master *adura*'s dangerous and risky action of crossing the thresh-old is accompanied by invocations, mantras, and songs. These indicate the crisis of the moment and, the songs especially, assert the powers of former Buddhas and the great qualities (*guna*) evident in the actions of Gautama or in his former lives.

The longest song tells the popular story of the marvelous generosity of Prince Vessantara, who gives away his wealth and possessions, includ-ing his wife and two children, to the Brahmin Jujaka (see Gombrich and Cone 1977). The verses specifically elaborate the episode of Jujaka's de-mand that Vessantara give him his daughter and son to be enslaved. The audience, all absorbed, crane forward, especially the many children present who appear spellbound as they hear how Jujaka beat Vessantara's children and then, when he decided to sleep, tied them with creepers to a tree.

Other verses tell of Gautama Buddha's birth, how seven lotuses appeared in the place of each of his first seven steps, and of the moment of his enlightenment while he was seated on his diamond seat (*vidurasna*), when he was attacked by the demon hosts of Mara. Buddha, unswayed from his purpose by the attack, is protected by the intervention of Polova Mahi Kantava, the goddess of the earth.

When the *adura* completes these songs, he presents his left leg (the vulnerable female side of the body) to the doorway into the *atamagala*.

> I recite the qualities of the Buddha
> Bathed, anointed with oil and sandalwood, and dressed in clean clothes.
> By the power of Kakusanda Buddha
> Cross the threshold with the left leg first.
> (repeats inserting the names of Konagama, Kasyapa, and Gautama Buddha)
> Mindful of the virtues (*guna*) of Pattini
> I have permission from the fire-breathing Devol.
> I have permission from Upulvan (Vishnu), who gave rise to all living things.
> I cross the threshold.

The *doratu panima* ends with an invocation to Natha to protect the *adura* and a demand that the *adura* who has performed the sorcery have his own life taken as a sacrifice (*billa*).

I stress that the *adura* mimes what the patient will do later. It is a trick that deflects the sorcerer's attention from the victim to his own body. Moreover, the exorcist presents the weak left side of his body (while the patient will enter presenting his strong right side). He deliberately makes himself vulnerable so that he enters into direct and intimate struggle with the force of the sorcerer. In effect, the exorcist assumes the guise of the victim, and in such guise and engaging the powers that he invokes, he proceeds to destroy the sorcerer.

Furthermore, the master *adura* can do this because he possesses the skills of Oddisa and of the sorcerer. The vital feature of these skills is the ability to change or switch guise and to unify with or to enter into the identity of, or into direct and unmediated relation with, that which the *adura* must struggle with and destroy. This is simultaneous with the capacity to manifest other aspects of identity and relationship which control and destroy. Thus exorcists are masters of illusion, and they embody intense and profound ambiguities integral to the existential realities with which they are involved and which indeed are central to their ritual work.

The mimetic aspects of this work go beyond mere representation or *appearance*, a word I use but which routinely imparts a sense of superficiality that I do not wish to convey. Exorcists in their ritual work *are* and simultaneously *are not* what they appear to be, victim and exorcist, sorcerer and antisorcerer.

The thoroughgoing lived-in depth and intensity that is the potential of their guise, the fact that they can become what they might otherwise be seen to represent, is critically instrumental in their work. This is the significance of episodes of exorcist trance in the healing rites that they control. On specific occasions when exorcists become demons, they are indeed inhabited by demonic potency, and so inhabited, they enable themselves or, most usually, other exorcists to deal directly with the demonic.[17]

In the *doratu panima,* the exorcist becomes the victim, a sacrificial victim (*billa*). The metaphors of sacrifice are strong in the Suniyama and in sorcery generally. There is a dynamic in the *hatadiya* as a whole (see Chapter 6) to change what is forcefully taken by the sorcerer (the possessions, riches, well-being of the victim) into things freely given, unwilling sacrifice into willing sacrifice. In such a process, the victim is separated from the conditionality of the sorcerer and emerges as progressively the embodiment of morality, while the sorcerer becomes ever-increasingly the epitome of immoral baseness. In effect, the sorcerer is made to choke on his own obsessive greed. The Prince Vessantara story, which receives emphasis in the *doratu panima,* carries this theme, and I think the story achieves a heightened significance in the context of the Suniyama. Jujaka, the greed-driven Brahmin, ultimately chokes to death on food, while the generous Vessantara is fully restored to position, riches, and family. Jujaka's disastrous overconsumption is a direct result of Vessantara's return to equanimity.[18] The sorcerer's greed causes him to take the *adura* as his victim; the *adura* then becomes the agent, the food, of his destruction.

Short offerings of dance, referred to as *adavv,* close the *doratu panima.* The dances are presented to the gods on behalf of selected members of the audience, first the victim, then other members of the household, and finally various local notables gathered.[19] There is an air of amusement, for the audience knows that those for whom a dance is presented are expected to pay the dancers for the service. The payments, especially from the victim and others in the household, are not just for the individual items of dance performed specifically on their behalf but more generally and symbolically for the ritual services of the exorcists and for the dangers and risks that they must take upon themselves.

Many in the audience begin to drift away. It is after midnight, and most go home to sleep for a while and then return later in the morning. Some go into the house to eat and to gossip, and only about fifty or so remain (out of a crowd of well over two hundred). The exorcist-dancers also take a rest; a couple sleep on mats behind the palace. The others sing in refrain to the master exorcist, who now concentrates his attention completely on the victim and the matters involving the victim's passage into the *atamagala*. The audience, until the *hatadiya* ends, is of little relevance to the process.

Snakes, Fire, and Lotuses: The Setting Out of the Seven Steps

Before the patient can make his crossing into the *atamagala,* his path is drawn and the seven (lotus) steps laid out together with the offerings to be used. The series of actions, painstakingly conducted by the *adura,* establish the fundamental ground of what is to be achieved in the victim's progress. This ground, as I interpret it, is the very foundation of Being and consciousness. What are set out are the ingredients of existence, which are imbued with life-giving, rather than life-taking, force. The energies of sorcery are subordinated systematically to cosmic ordering powers, those of the gods and the qualities of the Buddha. These constitute the central themes of the songs, which are also about origination. The setting out of the lotuses and their offerings is a veritable creative and generative bursting.

Another facet of the songs is that they tell of the way certain items or instruments of the rite, as creations of cosmic forces and the gods, came to the hands and use of human beings. Thus, the cosmic and creative powers of the ritualists are stressed. But a further interpretative extension on these themes can be made, one which is consistent with the organization and orientation of the Suniyama as a whole and its context of sorcery. This is that the powers of creation and destruction are in the possession of human beings like the sorcerer and the antisorcerer, who are able to unmake and to remake their lived realities. Constitutive cosmic power is in the hands of human beings. The Suniyama and the events of the *hatadiya* resound with the understanding, which is shared in more learned discourse on Buddhism, that it is human beings who are at the controlling and constitutive vortex of existence.

The setting out of the steps starts with the master *adura* invoking the power of the Triple Gem (Buddha, Dharma, Sangha—the Buddha, the Teaching, the Monkhood) and uttering a short salutation.

> *Namo tassa bhagavato arahato samma sambudassa*
> *Sivamastu namo ramah*
> *Kandasena samagamah*
> *Vadiga-tantra mani kamtah*
> *Oddimangala namo namah*

> Salutation to the Buddha who awakens and enlightens.
> Prosperity! Salutation to Rama.
> Greetings to Skanda and his retinue assembled.
> Greetings to Siva (Mani Kanta)[20] of the *Vadiga-tantra.*
> Hail! Oddi the auspicious.

A verse follows relating how Manikpala fell unconscious (*sihimurcha una*) and her body became lifeless (*pana nati una*), and how the Guardian Gods came to the queen's bedside, bringing the golden *igaha* with which to draw the lines (*iri*) at which the lotus steps will be placed. The *adura* announces that he will tell of the origin of the *hatadiya.* A short verse from a song about the origin of the world (*loka upata*) describes how the lotus stem, like the world axis (*kapa*), grew to the roof of the sky. The song then shifts to how Queen Mahamaya delivered the infant Siddharta into the hands of Maha Brahma and of Prince Siddharta's first seven steps. The song relates how Siddharta, starting with his right foot (*dakunu paya*) walked in a northerly direction (*uturu diga*), and that as he took each step, the earth burst open and a lotus bloom appeared. The *adura* informs the victim and the audience that he will draw with his *igaha* seven lines (*iri*) where the lotus blooms grew.

The curving form of a snake is drawn in cow-dung ash;[21] its head is positioned where the victim is seated and its tail at the entrance into the *atamagala.* The snake is a condensed symbol alive with the struggle of the contradictory forces engaged in the transformational processes at the center of the rite. In itself, of course, the figure of the snake in this setting and in numerous other cultural worlds is the dynamic image of change, transition and transformation, and continuity. The snake can be described as a dominant or key symbol, a vital motif of the rite: its dominance or keyness a property of its capacity to exhaust meaning, to extend beyond, to encircle or encompass all meaning that may be fed into it. The snake is virtually the birth and the death of meaning in existence, a description quite in keeping with this Sinhala Buddhist context.

Exorcists describe the snake as the fire viper (*ginijala polanga*) that Vasavarti thrust toward Manikpala. They assert that its head must be located at the genitals of the victim, striking quite explicitly at the center of generation. In this position it manifests simultaneously the fiery heat of destruction and the heat at the source of (re)generation. The mo-

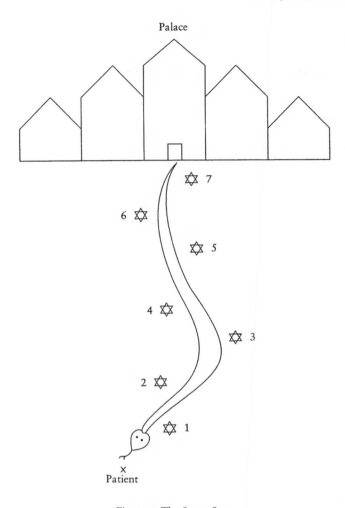

Figure 4. The Seven Steps

ment of death is also potentially the starting point of recreation. The orientation of the viper's head away from the palace and *atamagala* also indicates *the externalization of sorcery,* that it forces its victims outside the life world; see figure 4. Wirz (1954:77) describes the viper's head as pointing into the *atamagala.* This does not agree with any of my observations or statements from *adura*s. Indeed, to have the head oriented in the direction that Wirz states would be tantamount to a repetition of the act of sorcery and not of its correction, the whole aim of the rite.

Aduras also refer to the snake as the form of Maha Kala Naga, the great snake of time, the primordial snake located in the bowels of the earth, which is coiled around the base of Mount Meru, the great cosmic mountain at the center of the universe. The myths of Maha Kala Naga, the cobra king, some of them sung in this and other Suniyamas, tell of Suniyam's birth from one of his nostrils and tell that from Maha Kala's body grew the lime (*dehi*) cut at exorcism (Barnett 1916: 53; Nevill 1955: 330). The snake is also understood as the shadow cast by Muchalinda, whose great hood shades and protects the Buddha. In exorcist traditions, Muchalinda is kin to Maha Kala Naga and is sometimes regarded as the same being.[22]

The line of the snake—the course drawn by the snake rather than the representation of the snake—is referred to by *aduras* as the stalk of the lotus (*nelum danda*) which Maha Brahma climbed down in the primordial creation of the world-universe (*loka upata*). Indeed, thus conceived, the lotus stem is the stem of all the lotuses that are to be distributed along its path, and it connects ultimately with the lotus seat within the *atamagala* where the victim will finally come to rest. Moreover, in exorcist interpretation, the path of the snake also describes the body's spinal column (*kondu naratiya, susumna*). The base of the spine is where the patient is seated with the snake's head at his genitals. The apex of the spine is at the *atamagala,* the place of the head, the highest seat of awareness and consciousness.

The obvious tantric influences in the Suniyama are especially evident in the *hatadiya* and expand the import of the lotuses, but within the overall Sinhala Buddhist context of the rite.[23] An earlier song for Oddisa explicitly refers to him as a master of tantra. The line of the snake can be likened to the *kundalini* of South Indian tantric Hatha Yoga (see Kersenboom-Story 1987: 94–97; Zvelebil 1973), the spinal energy flow of the micro/macrocosm. (As noted above, exorcists conceive of the line of the snake as the spine of the body and refer to it also as the *kapa* or *Meru danda,* the axis or rod of the universe.) Exorcists see the lotuses as points of whirling energy (*cakra*) from which the elemental forces of existence rise up and become formative of body and consciousness. The places of the seven lotuses in the *hatadiya,* like those of the *cakras* in tantra, are aligned along the sympathetic plexuses of the body starting at the base of the spine and moving toward the head. *Aduras,* in accordance with tantras, state that at each *cakra* or lotus step a particular feature of body or consciousness is addressed and brought into equilibrium. This is not always clear in practice.

Kersenboom-Story (1987:96) shows how the snake and the *cakras* constitute an implicit design of orientation in South Indian temple grounds. In her description, the head of the snake is positioned at the temple entrance (the reverse is the case in the *hatadiya*). The progression along the snake is constitutive of a balancing of the body energies, which achieve their highest expression in the temple, the abode of the gods. This is the broad sense, of course, of the victim's progression in the *hatadiya*.[24]

Seven lines (*iri*) are drawn with the *igaha* by the presiding exorcist at intervals along the body of the snake. These seven lines are lines of destruction. They have a fiery energy, and the master exorcist refers to them as rays of the sun (*ira*), which in Sinhala mythology and folk belief have destructive and generative properties. In this sense the lines mark points of hot potentiality.

The symbolism of seven is heavy with the sense of life and death.[25] The seven lines are ostensibly barriers or obstacles that sorcerers place in the way of their victims, but they indicate an ambiguity, a force that will banish and destroy the sorcerer's power. The *adura* mimes the action of the attacking sorcerer; as he draws each line, he declares that it is like a line drawn in funerary ash across the path of the sorcery victim (*iripannum*) or in the sorcery where poisonous creepers are placed in the quarry's way (*valpannum*).[26] Drawing other lines, the exorcist commands that an effigy (*pambaya*) be made of the victim's assailant and that the name of this sorcerer (*vinakala adura*) be inscribed on it. The *adura* commands that the effigy be taken to the boundary of the village, where nails and thorns should be driven into it (a type of sorcery called *katugasima*). This last kind of sorcery is in fact carried out later in the *hatadiya* away from the performance arena, in the dark beside the *bali* image of Suniyam.

The drawing of the lines by the *adura* imitates the action of the sorcerer and in this action indicates what in actuality bars the life course of the victim and constitutes the real forces of destruction that the victim must cross. The lines are not mere representations even in the strong sense applied here. They sign great danger that is actually present. Furthermore, they are potent with their own force, in effect, the potency of antisorcery, or the ordering power of the Buddha and the gods that the *adura* mediates into play. At each line drawn, a quality of the Buddha or a former Buddha, as well as the power of a particular god, is invoked. This (see Chapter 6) begins a process of the reestablishment of boundaries, limitations, and the striations of personal and social order transgressively sundered and

Figure 5. Letters at the Seven Steps and their Principal Associations

Step	Letter	Sound	Humor	Day	Planet	Deity
1		*i* (or *ra*)	*pita*	Sunday	Ravi (Sun)	Kataragama Devol
2		*sa*	*sema*	Monday	Chandra (Moon)	Saman Natha
3		*ku*	*pita*	Tuesday	Kuja (Mars)	Kataragama
4		*bu*	*vayo*	Wednesday	Buda (Mercury)	Natha Pattini
5		*gu.* (or *bra*)	*sema*	Thursday	Guru (Jupiter)	Siva
6		*ki*	*pita*	Friday	Kivi (Venus)	Kataragama
7		*sa*	*pita*	Saturday	Sani (Saturn)	Visnu

blocked by the sorcerer. This process in the *hatadiya* bears comparison with Devol Deviyo's encounter with the goddess Pattini.[27]

At each of the seven lines cosmic signs and letters are drawn in ash. On this occasion, the sign drawn was that of the six-pointed star, the symbol of male-female union; it indicates the generative forces present in the ritual action. Seven Sinhala letters are inscribed on the ground, one at each line where a lotus will be placed.

The letters, which I set out in figure 5, are conceived of by exorcists as being life-giving letters (*pranaksara*), open sounds rather than closed sounds and letters (*gatraksara*). Ideally, healing and cooling mantras or songs (*set kavi*) should start with such life-giving letters or sounds. Each of the letters is linked with a particular planet, with a day of the week, and with the primary elements of existence (*va, pit, sem,* the threefold reduction of the *mahabuta*).[28]

Seven lotuses (lotus-shaped offering tables or alters (*aile*) are now placed on the letters. Five different offerings are set at each of the *aile* in turn. They are food, usually milk-rice cakes (*kiri bat*) and flower petals; areca-betel (*dalumura*); coins (*panduru*); limes (*dehi*); and lighted oil wicks (*pahantira, ginivata*). These offerings are explicitly associated by *adura*s, in this Buddhist context, with the five material aggregates of the internal and external world (*panca skanda*), which are derivatives of the fundamental elements of existence, the *panca mahabuta*. Thus, the offerings are substantializations of, or bear relation to, sight or visible form (*rupa*), sound (*sabda*), odor (*ganda*), taste (*rasa*), and touch or feeling (*sparsa*), which are inextricably linked with the five sense organs (eyes, ears, nose, tongue, body).

The offerings mediate between, on the one hand, the victim and the experiential processes of his body, and on the other hand, cosmic forces that are integral with the dynamic of the body. As each offering is set, it is first presented to the patient, sometimes moved down the patient's body (head to foot), and in the course of these actions and placement at each lotus, the object is empowered with invocations to the forces in the cosmic hierarchy, the Buddha, the gods, and the demons.

There are ambiguities in the presentation of the offerings. They are occasionally indicated as gifts to the demonic forces associated with sorcery attack. But this is a ruse. The energies of sorcery are lured to the gift referred to as *dola*, the kind of food that demons like. But the gift is not *dola* but a pure gift, inappropriate to demons and poisonous to them. The gifts are imbued with the ordering forces of the cosmos, which act to cut or remove the agonies of the sorcerer's attack. The types of sorcery that are cut and their suffering are referred to in the invocations and songs as the various items are set. Thus, as the exorcist sets out the offerings of rice:

The demons cannot stay in their houses because of the burning rays of the
    Buddha.
With this *dola* remove all the *piripata* (black magic, disastrous occurrences).
May the Buddha's power remove all the *dosa*.
I place the *kiri bat* at the first *aile*.

The body itches and shivers.
The body burns like fire.
Madness comes, the tongue is full of sores.
Demon come and take the offering at the first step.

With the mind attentive to the Buddha's qualities.
May the *anavina* cast by envious people return to them.
May the *vina* demon be punished by the Buddha's power.
With the giving of this golden rice may the *vina* be repelled.

Terrifying dreams of cobras coiling around the body.
Dreams of being eaten by poisonous vipers.
The *vina* demon who has done this will have his poison removed
    at the second step.
Take the *dola* and calm the mind.

Most of the themes that are sung as the offerings are set out are repetitions of those already presented. However, two stories, previously unheard in this performance of the rite, the origin of the betel vine (*nagavalli*) and of the lime tree, are sung at length. I recount their events as presented by the *adura*s and the other exorcists in refrain. They expand themes of sacrifice central in the rite and illustrate the instructional significance of song, which is vital in the healing process.

The song of the Origin of Betel (*Dalumura Upata*) is a version of the popular *Sasa Jataka*.[29]

God Sakra saw, with his Divine Eye, that the hare (the Buddha in a former life) observed the Buddhist precepts. He realized that the hare would become a Buddha, and so Sakra decided to put the hare's observances of the precepts to the test. Sakra disguised himself as Solos Gara Giri Raksaya, with his golden sword and shaggy matted locks of hair, and appeared where the hare was meditating. The *raksaya* was terrifying to behold. The hare asked why the *raksaya* had come, to which the *raksaya* answered that he wished a gift from the hare—a gift of roasted meat. He added that should the hare agree, the gift would help the hare on his path to Buddhahood. The hare replied that even though he was in the present lowly birth, he had done no harm and had taken no life. Moreover, the hare declared that he was frightened of sinning (*pavata bayai*), and that his fear made him even stronger in keeping the precepts. Because of the hare's diligence, he could not satisfy the *raksaya*'s demand. Indeed, insisted the hare, if things had been otherwise he would have been only too willing to give the *raksaya* the five tastes of cattle (*pasgorasa*). But, as it happened, the hare did not have even so much as fruit to give the *raksaya*. (In the singing of the story, the *raksaya*'s demand and the hare's response were repeated several times.)

There is nothing to give you, repeated the hare, other than my own head, my own eyes, my own body. The wicked *raksaya* pressed his demand for the hare's gift, saying that unless the hare agreed he would not achieve Buddhahood. The *raksaya* demanded his gift of roasted meat. The hare then brushed his own body against the *raksaya* and said that the *raksaya* could eat him. But the *raksaya* rejected this offer on the grounds that he refused to eat uncooked meat. The hare asked the *raksaya* how a fire could be built in the jungle so that he could cook his own body.

The *raksaya* said that he would help the hare reach Buddhahood and built a fire at the foot of a mountain three *gavva*s in height. The *raksaya* then demanded that the hare should climb to the mountain top and throw himself into the fire below. The hare agreed but first went to the sacred pond Anottattavilla in the Himalayas, where he cleansed (*pirisindu*) himself so as to be a pure offering. Then climbing to the mountain top, all the while declaring that he would never take the life of another animal and that he would make a gift of his own flesh, the hare flung himself toward the fire.

The *raksaya* now revealed himself to be Sakra and caught the hare as he fell. Sakra was so moved by the hare's action that he wept. He decided to honor the hare and painted his image with a golden brush on the moon so that no one should forget the hare's marvelous action.

However, when Sakra finished his painting, he dropped the paint-brush. It fell from the divine world down to the world of human beings. But the earth burst open and the brush fell deeper into the Naga world beneath. The Naga king, Maha Kala Naga, spotted the brush and quickly swallowed it. The Naga king died within seven days, and a creeper (*naga-valli*) grew from his head, which is how the betel leaf came to have its cobra shape.

This story, instructive and amusing in itself (both adults and children still present at the performance enjoyed the tale hugely, even though they had heard it many times before), gains force in the context of the pure offerings of the *hatadiya*). These, I have noted, are occasionally referred to as *dola* (offerings including roasted grains, *pulutu*, and sometimes meats, given to demonic beings). The disguising of what they actually are snares the demonic and intensifies the ordering power of the pure gift. Most of all, the story projects an import of the *hatadiya* as a sacrifice. The victim can be likened to the hare, for in certain respects he is a body of sacrifice, and furthermore, one that will escape his immediate corporeal death because of his fixity on virtuous Buddhist action.

The songs relating the origin of the lime (*dehi upata*) present two myths. The first narrates the skill of Oddisa, and the second identifies the healing lime, the antidote for sorcery's poison.

STORY 1

The *rsi*s who came to cure Queen Manikpala asked that seven limes be brought. The gods surrounding the queen's bed commanded that Oddisa journey to the abode of the Naga king. Disturbed by Oddisa's approach, the Naga king was furious, and flames and poisonous fumes shot from his fangs. Oddisa sprang to one side and then leaped into the Naga king's left nostril and so entered his stomach. Here he found the lime to cure Manik-pala, and Oddisa, leaving by the Naga king's right nostril, returned to the human world.

STORY 2

Sakra took a precious blue stone upon which he wiped his sweat and flung it toward the earth. The earth burst open, and the gem fell into the Naga world. The Naga king saw the gem enter his domain and went with his retinue to examine the stone. When he came close to it, the Naga king suddenly rushed upon it, as if it were prey, and swallowed it. The king became sick and died. The lime tree grew from his body, leaves from his hood, and thorns from the snake's venom. The Naga king's teeth became the seeds of the lime, and the Naga's venom, its juice. The poisonous spray of the cobra's venom is like that of the squeezed lime (*pangiri*).

The lime came through the seven seas until it reached Nanaya beach, and here, on the first day, it took root. By the sixth week it blossomed, and on the seventh week the tree bore fruit. The branches grew in eight directions.[30] The *rsis* declared that they needed limes to cure Manikpala. Sakra, with his all-seeing divine eye, saw the lime tree and said that the small green lime growing on the northeast branch should be brought in procession, wound in a cloth, and placed in a golden casket, shaded by an umbrella and cooled by the *camara* (yak-tail whisk). The *rsis* cut the lime and removed the *vina*.[31]

In the context of the ritual event, the first story indicates Oddisa's capacity to enter into the inner being of demonic and poisonous forces. He can intrude into the very stomach of sorcery, grapple with it, and then separate himself from its grip. The second story indicates the poison-destroying power of the lime. It is similar to what it defeats, but like the offerings in the *hatadiya*, it contains the potency of the gods, indeed of Sakra, the king of the gods. This ordering power is indicated by Sakra's demand that it be brought in royal procession. Moreover, as interpreted by the master exorcist, the lime from the northeast branch is chosen because this is the one direction from which Mara, the demon of death, does not come.[32] The lime's presentation in the story is as a totalizing object: that is, it unites poisonous and ordering forces and is part of a plant that spread in all cardinal directions. The cutting of the lime is a separation of the ordering from the poisonous and, I suggest, bears some similarity to other constitutive acts—such as Mahasammata's formation of political and social order—which involves a division out of the social order from within an embracing totality.

Once all the offerings and objects have been laid at the seven steps, the *adura* consecrates the lime cutter, or *gire* (an areca nut cutter), with incense, singing that he is repeating the action performed by the *rsis* for Manikpala.[33] The final act before the victim starts his journey to the *atamagala* is the *aravali kapima*. The *adura* takes three limes joined on a single stem and cuts them with the *gire* at the forehead, the waist, and last, the feet of the victim. With this action he opens the victim's path and removes any final obstacles.[34] He utters a curse as he does so.

> Place the skull of a human being in a tree fork.
> Write the sorcerer's name on the skull
> With the ash from a funeral pyre.

Maru Riri Suniyam, take the offering!
Make a human effigy with the *hondala* root.
Drive thorns into the head.
May the body of the sorcerer be covered in sores.
When the lime is cut, may the sorcery return to its maker.
May the victim's bonds of sorcery burst like a lightning strike.
The *vina* must return and the sorcerer die.[35]

The *aravali kapima* embodies the potency of the forces that have been progressively built in the preceding events. It marks the start of events that will actualize the radical separation of the forces of sorcery from their unity with the victim. It may be understood, given the imagery of the curse, as marking the start of a new birth from out of the circumstances of death. The moving of the victim across the seven steps is now to begin.

The Movement of the Seven Steps: The Path of Intentional Consciousness

This most critical series of events demands that the victim's mind be focused on the qualities of the Buddha's action. The victim, seated at the edge of the performance arena (at the perimeter of Mahasammata's city), is in a condition of heat (*tejo*), the heat of destruction and immanent rebirth. It is the place of desire (*tanha*), of utmost disorder (*akramavat*), and of ignorance (*avijja*). Alternatively, the Mahasammata palace, and specifically the *atamagala*, is conceived of as a place of calm, of order (*kramavat*), of contemplation (*samadi*), of knowledge and truth (*sat*), and also of regenerative fruition. It is the marriage house (*hirage*) of Manikpala and Mahasammata, and the victim is understood by some exorcists to be going toward a marriage. The patient wears, it will be recalled, the *mottakkili*, a bridal veil.

The orientation of the victim toward the *atamagala* is itself a motional action, an extending toward which engenders further and increasing movement. In other words, the act of projection toward the palace is dynamic and is the initiating force in developing further movement in the patient. Moreover, the orientation of the victim is a beginning act of consciousness (what I will explore in Chapter 6 as an aspect of intentionality integral to consciousness) that will develop progressively, as the victim moves along the seven lotuses, into the ordering (*pilivela*) of the patient's body and the full regeneration of his consciousness. Furthermore, this progression of the patient is impelled by the victim's concentration on the Buddha's deeds and qualities, which are the forces on which Mahasammata's world order (imaged by the palace) depends.

The concentration upon (*adhistana*) and the active wishing (*patima,* or less commonly, *prartana;* see Gombrich 1971: 217–226)[36] for the goals of Buddhist virtue are stressed by exorcists throughout the Suniyama, especially when the victim is about to take the seven steps. *Adura*s say, "the patient must concentrate his mind to achieve mental balance" (*aturaya sit ekanga karala adhistanekata samavadinava*).

To recapitulate, the motion of the victim toward the *atamagala* is a function of, or is empowered by, his mental projection toward the Mahasammata palace. As the victim crosses each of the steps, the victim's consciousness grows further, and achieves its height when the victim comes to be seated within the *atamagala*. The motion of the victim is both a growing of consciousness and a manifestation of the increasing power of consciousness. The victim remains seated throughout much of the progression from lotus to lotus. He does not so much walk as mentally effect his motion.[37]

Other actions are integral to the patient's movement from lotus to lotus. After invocations to the Buddha, the guardian gods, and specifically to Vishnu (referred to as the sacrificer, *yagapati*), the *adura* holds a lime (taken from the altar toward which the patient is in motion) in the areca cutter at the patient's forehead. As he does so, he sings of one of the Buddha's ten exemplary deeds (*paramita*). The *adura* draws the lime down the patient's body. He describes aspects of the patient's suffering, makes reference to further qualities of the Buddha, and repeats fragments of *jataka*s and other mythical events already referred to in the rite. Finally, he cuts the lime at the feet of the patient while uttering a mantra which commands the removal of the sorcery. The lime halves, having drawn the sorcerer's poison, are quickly disposed of in a hessian sack held by the exorcist's assistant. The patient places a small food-packet (*gotu,* made from jak, *kos,* tree leaves) offering in the lotus altar. This is for Suniyam and for other cosmic forces, and as elsewhere throughout the rite, is a nourishing constitution of them. It also defines and refracts differentiating and hierarchializing cosmic processes.[38]

After his food offering, the victim performs three times a face-wiping gesture (*muna-ata-pihadanava*), indicating the removal of the sorcery from his body. The victim then moves to the next lotus step and positions himself in his chair just before it. The previous lotus altar is disposed of, and the section of the snake, cosmic designs, and Sinhala letters along which he has passed are erased. This sequence of actions is repeated at each lotus until the patient enters into the *atamagala*.

I present, in abbreviated form, the utterances at the first lotus or step and at the seventh, last step.

STEP 1

With mind concentrated on the first day of the Buddha's Enlightenment
O Patient come to the first step.
May you be victorious (*jayamangala*).

Dipankara was the first of the twenty-eight Buddhas
Journeying to the city of Rambakan.
Dipankara had to cross a pool of mud.

The Brahmin, Sumedha, seeing this, lay down in his path so that the Buddha would not soil his feet.
By the action of the Buddha accept this offering of lime.

A wax image has been made and written with the patient's name.
May the thorns in the image be taken out. The letters of the nine planets (*navakuru*) have been inscribed at an inauspicious time.
The lime is cut to finish this *vina*.

When the Buddha was born he walked across seven lotuses and became the greatest power in the three worlds.
I cut a lime at the first *adiya* to end the *vina*.

(A mantra in demon speech is uttered. Many of the words are Tamil.)

The victim suffers headaches. He babbles nonsense and glares furiously. The victim loses his appetite. His chest burns and he vomits. I give *dola* to remove the *vasdos*.
(Patient gives offering packet to the exorcist to be placed in lotus *aile*).

When the Buddha was under the Bo tree, Vasavarti Maraya attacked him but was defeated. May the *dosa* leave from the head, from the forehead, from the eyes, from the nose, from the ears, and from the mouth.
Go forward from the first step to the *atamagala!*

STEP 7

Concentrating on the *satya* (truth) *paramita* may there be success.
In the seventh week of his Enlightenment the Buddha meditated beneath the Kiri-Palu-Nuga-Ruka tree.
By this action may there be victory.

The *vina* was made by drawing the fatal (*mara*) letter.
Stop this sorcery with the power of the Sat (seven) Pattini.
The patient takes his step to the north, as did the Buddha when he made the seventh step.
With the power of Maitri may the *vina* be finished.

> The body burns like fire. Kali stop the burning!
> With the power of Kali may the *vina* be removed.

> (Exorcist cuts the lime down the patient's body; food packet placed
> in lotus altar.)

> The limbs are numb, the teeth are loose. The victim vomits blood. O
> *vina yaka* accept the *dola* and remove the *dosa*.

> Lord Buddha spent the seventh week after the Enlightenment in the
> Kiripalu jungle.
> By this power may the numbness of the limbs be removed and the ag-
> onizing pain (*vedana*) at the fingernails and toenails. Go into the
> *atamagala!*
> Long Life! Long Life! (these exclamations are made by the *adura* and
> the audience).

The consummation of the entire *hatadiya* has now been reached: the entrance and seating of the patient within the *atamagala*. It is now approaching 3 A.M. toward the end of the period of the midnight watch
and the start of the morning watch, which extends through daybreak—
a time of reawakening.

When the patient enters the *atamagala*, he comes within a pure and
untouched space, a new place of habitation. He is himself cleansed and
purified. The metaphors of the rite and especially of this moment are of
a woman purified of the defilement of her menstruation (or of rape?) and
also of a woman approaching her bridal bed. The patient may be said to
be like the bride, a pure and perfect gift and one of recreative potency.
In a powerful sense, the victim within the *atamagala* is a body of sacrifice
who in sacrifice will be regenerate and regenerating and bountiful. The
victim comes to sit upon a rush mat (which some *adura*s describe as a
marriage mat (*hangala padura*, twin or double mat). The place where the
patient is seated is the axial center of the universe, the pivotal point, as
the name of the yantra (*kaksaputa*; see Chapter 4 n 12) suggests, the site
of the union of Mahasammata, the world ruler, and Manikpala. It is also
the lotus seat, the place of knowledge, of Being (*sat*) in a state of full
conscious awareness of itself, a locus of Buddhist meditation, a point at
the farthest extension of existence, at the edge of ultimate release from
suffering.

Victims and exorcists are in some awe of the extraordinary potency
concentrating in the *atamagala* upon the victim's entry. *Adura*s say that
when some patients come within the *atamagala*, they become faint and
shudder as if entranced by the gods (*devarude*) or in an extreme heightened condition of excitement (*salita venava*, also used in reference to or-

gasm). Such experience manifests, I suggest, the ascent, bubbling up, or effervescence of potency and not its destruction or draining, like the collapse of Manikpala on Vasavarti's attack. This empowerment is also a repositioning at the crux of cosmic force, as well as a radical reorientation of the victim. Seated within the *atamagala,* the patient is made to face back along the path on which he has come. In this reorientation and repotentiated, the victim confronts his world in a manner both reconstituting and regenerating.

The victim's entrance into the *atamagala* is preceded by a song indicating some of the potent import of the first of the two yantras on which the patient will be seated.[39] The verses tell how when Manikpala fell unconscious, Oddisa burst through the earth and chose the spot where Visvakarma should draw the yantra with four different kinds of ash.[40] Drawn on the ground, it is filled with the power of Bumi Devi (Polova Mahi Kantava), the earth goddess. The verses tell that the signs of the gods must be drawn, with the one for Maha Brahma (Purusa, Cosmic Man) placed at the center, and that five colors (*panca varna*) must be present.

After preparing eight oil lamps to be placed on the pots (*punkalas*) at either side of the four doorways into the *atamagala,* the patient takes a lighted torch with which to burn the threads (*kanya nul,* virgin threads) that crisscross the front entrance. The master exorcist and the other *adura*s sing:

> May the patient live five thousand years!
> May the demoness who waits at the entrance not bar the way!
> With the knowledge of Buddha's victory over Mara, may the patient enter!

The *adura*s sing briefly of events from popular tales concerning the Buddha: of Buddha's birth as a bird, the Sandakinduru Jataka, who was killed by the Vadda King,[41] an incarnation of Buddha's chief adversary, Devadatta, but restored to life by Sakra, who was moved by the lamentations of the bird's wife. The story of the hare is repeated, as well as the story of Buddha's victory over the demon hordes of Mara. The theme of Manikpala's cure is quickly returned to:

> Threads were tied at the doors of the *atamagala.*
> Queen Manikpala burned the threads.
> Buddha placed his footprint at Mecca.
> With this power may the patient come to the *atamagala!*

The patient, crouching down, burns the threads and crawls (right strong side first) through the tiny entrance into the *atamagala.* As he does so, the exorcists chant the *Astaka*[42] *Sloka* (chanted at wedding ceremonies) and then intone the Three Refuges (Buddha, Dhamma, Sangha). Simultaneously, a kinsman of the patient, appropriately in the relation of mother's brother (*mama*), smashes a coconut on the ground. (The mother's brother performs similar ritual functions at rites of first menstruation and at marriages). This is an auspicious act, the breaking of the coconut (*polgediya*) indicating the success of the rite as well as the force of the moment. As the patient disappears from view, the master exorcist loudly exclaims, "Pura! Pura!" (Fill! Fill!). The cry is at once a reference to the auspicious or prosperous period of the ascendant moon (the period of the new moon) and also (as explained later by the *adura*) a call to distract the gaze, at this vulnerable moment, of demons who are lurking at the entrance.

Once inside the *atamagala,* the victim lights the wicks of eight oil lamps, one for each of the pots at the four doorways. As he does so, the exorcists sing of events in the life and former lives of the Buddha: of the King Kusa, shunned for his ugliness, who was nevertheless able to marry the beautiful Queen Pabavati, who saw the truth behind his ugliness; of Sumeda's protective prostration before Dipamkara; of Buddha's unmoving and unswerving concentration in the face of Mara's hordes; of Prince Siddharta's ordination at the birth of his son; of the impotency of the demon Alavaka, whose spear could not penetrate the Buddha's power, and so forth. These verses are understood to subdue the female demons, attendants of the demon Suniyam, who are attracted to the pots.

A chair to be used as an offering table is placed outside the entrance into the *atamagala,* and an offering basket (*Suniyam vattiya*) set upon it, into which the patient places offerings for Suniyam and his retinue of female demons.[43] Sixteen small offering plates (*aile*) are in the basket, the number indicative of independent conscious awareness and of Suniyam's power to destroy it. These offerings externalize Suniyam and firmly define him as a demon of the outside. The victim, in the *atamagala* and positioned within the defensive lines or barriers of the yantra, is distanced from the destructive essences (an important aspect of the food offerings) of sorcery. The offerings are indeed conceived by *adura*s as disgusting (*pilikul*), such a sense contributing to the victim's distancing (see Chapter 7).[44] When finished they are taken to the place where the Suniyam clay image (*baliya*) is laid, well outside the boundary of the arena and the light of the performance.

The song that accompanies these actions tells of the birth of Oddisa from Queen Yawudagiri, of his terrible mien, and of the offerings that should be given to him and to the demon Suniyam. The verses play on the Suniyam-Oddisa ambiguity and the transformational moment that this ambiguity signals. Ambiguity is the structure of transformational dynamics. In this context, Oddisa is emergent from the guise of Suniyam in the process of the latter's externalization. Here are some of the key verses:

> Appearing in his *yaka* form, Oddi left the Palace.
> He ran to Hirandana jungle, where he saw a golden anthill.
> He clothed himself with cobras.
> Offer Suniyam roasted grains and sea and land flesh.
> The rice is colored red and blue.
> Make a *torana* with banana bark, tie it with a black cloth. Offer a cock.
> Give this *bili* to Suniyam god (*devatava*).
>
> Oddi, look (*disti*) at your offerings and heal the illness.
> Oddi dwells at deserted houses.
> He lives at resting places.
> He lives at places of conflict.
> He eats fish and sweetmeats.
> He comes to the smell of sandalwood.
> O Oddi friend (*machang*),[45] heal the patient.
> Oddi gathers his demon troops.
> His body glistens with power (*bala*).
> Suniyam Yaka is coming!
> He traps tusked elephants and eats them.
> He enjoys the fiery heat of his body.
> O Suniyam take the offerings.
> Come and cut the cruel bonds.
> We do not sleep, the sorcery is so powerful.
> O Oddi Yaka who flies through the air
> Come to the lights of the torches.

With these songs and offerings, the *hatadiya* is ended. There is now a long break (the *maha te,* or great refreshment break) that lasts some forty-five minutes.

Overall, the *hatadiya* is an obliteration of the line of the sorcerer, a separation of the power of sorcery from the life course of the victim (expressed in the ambiguities and the actions and metaphors of inside/outside of the closing events), a new beginning, a radical recentering and reorientation of the victim within regenerative cosmic forces, and a reempowerment enabling him to face back reconstitutively toward his life world.

The progress of the seven lotus steps engages the hierarchical powers of the cosmos in overcoming the transgressive, flattening totalization of the sorcerer. The hierarchical and differentiating powers—expressed in the songs, offerings, and numerous other gestures—are themselves productive or recreative of hierarchical differentiation. The boundaries and limits of such regenerating and reordering process are vital in expelling the sorcerer's transgression (see Chapters 6 and 8).

Above all, the *hatadiya* is a radical reawakening, development, and efflorescence of full embodied consciousness. This is commanded and encompassed by a projection toward the Buddha's example and qualities. This projection ensures the reequilibration and reharmonization of the victim's mental and physical being, which in the Buddhist world of the Suniyama's ritual practice are always in union.

Mahasammata's palace may be understood as a temple, the *atamagala* being its womb, or *garbha*. The victim becomes revitalized in his progression toward it. Although he is located at a supremely potent center, he is himself repotentiating.

The palace, a center of cosmic forces, also becomes a potent place because of the victim's presence within it. The victim is constituted as a body of sacrifice and himself a pure gift. From the victim's perspective within the *atamagala,* he is surrounded by offerings to the ordering gods of the universe and in a sense is one with these offerings. The lighting of the lamps within the *atamagala* may be interpreted as a self-presenting sacrificial act that marks him as a conscious body filled with the life-giving potency of sacrifice. Moreover, reoriented toward the world of human beings, the victim is more than a being regenerate; he is also an agent or being for the regeneration of others, for world regeneration. He becomes the revitalizing force of the temple/palace/world in whose vital center he sits and a recreative energy source of what is around him. He is both world center and world creator. As the patient achieves the place of knowledge and of conscious being, so does the world around him, which explodes into regenerative action.

This is a theme of the wonderful events of the *vadiga patuna* comedy, which occupies much of the morning watch. It starts shortly after the end of the *maha te,* in this performance at around 4:30 A.M. The *vadiga patuna* and other concluding events of the Suniyama develop and give further expression to processes already apparent in the rite as a whole.

The Events of the Morning and Midday Watches

I concentrate the description on four major ritual events leading to the conclusion of the Suniyama in the period of the midday watch (*iramudun*) at around 1:30 P.M. The events are: (1) the *vadiga patuna* (the arrival of the Brahmins); (2) the *valvalalu* (the binding and freeing of the patient); (3) the *chedana vidiya* (the destruction of the palace); (4) the *puhul kapima* (the cutting of the ash pumpkin, the victim as sacrificer). These events demonstrate, as they effect it, the victim's release from the bonds of sorcery and are regarded by exorcists as critical destructions or finishings of sorcery and the sorcerer. *Aduras* always include them in the *solos tinduva*, the sixteen destructions (judgments) which comprise the Suniyama.

A key theme of the closing events of the Suniyama—immanent in the climactic moments of the *hatadiya*—is human being as the focal center of the universe, and most of all, human beings as the constitutive, ordering, and generative force of their human realities. The victim becomes in effect the embodied potency of what may be described as the constituting consciousness of humankind: a consciousness formed in the process of action and now a consciousness on the threshold of further constituting action. One expression and power of such constituting consciousness is speech (*vacana*); the creative and destructive power of human beings as the articulators of speech is a major theme of the *vadiga patuna*.

The audience has swelled in size with the expectation that the highly popular *vadiga patuna* is about to start. Just before it begins, offering stands (*kattirikka*) are placed before the *atamagala*, and offering trays (*tattu*) are set on them for the three main demons associated with the sorcery attack (Mahasona, Riri Yaka, Sanni Yaka). Mantras are uttered, and the stands and trays are quickly taken away, actions which remove the main demons that might block the victim's outlook. These demons are the epitome of voracious greed and jealousy, especially of each other. Exorcists say that they are likely to be envious of the attention heaped on Suniyam and therefore should have their envy assuaged with their own offerings, or else their energy will continue to inhibit the victim's progress. The fact that they may block the patient's gaze, which is the feature of this episode—for the offering stands interrupt the victim's line of sight—is highly significant.

Seeing is an act of consciousness which is constitutive of the process of coming into being. A demonic blocking of the victim's line of sight confines the victim's constitutive gaze and prevents its extension out on the world and therefore the engagement of the patient's regenerate powers of consciousness in the reconstitution of his reality.

Reoriented within the *atamagala,* the patient looks out on the world. My own experience from the same position within the *atamagala* can be likened to peering out toward the horizons of the world through a narrow opening in the fingers or indeed a crack in a doorway. The sensation is simultaneously one of concentrated focus (a dimension of confinement) and of an opening out, of a great vista spreading out before one. There is a feeling of being drawn out toward that which is seen, that if you move out a little further, push the door more open, and widen the gap, more of the world will be revealed. In effect, there is a sense of being drawn into the world and also of creating the world in one's own motional action toward it. This, I think, is an experiential import of the patient's reorientation within the *atamagala*. The narrowing, or concentration, of the focus on the palace and the *atamagala* in the previous events is a process of revisioning the patient, in fact, correcting the sight dimension of consciousness. The reorientation of the patient, his opening and reextension toward the actual world, is an act which instantly engages the victim in a process of reconstitution through the action of a corrected consciousness. The world is brought back into existence for him and by him.

A Farce of Brahmins: The Vadiga Patuna and the Celebration of Consciousness

The *vadiga patuna* opens with a brief prologue by the master exorcist. He declares that it is a book (*potak*) written by Oddisa on the command of god Sakra, and written in different scripts, it has passed down the generations into the hands of present-day *adura*s. With the knowledge of Sakra's command and by the authority vested in Oddisa, the exorcist announces, the *vadiga patuna* is to be performed. The exorcist-drummers beat out a loud rhythm, and they and the other exorcists sing of the origin of the *vadiga patuna* book. They tell how it was written in ten different languages and was brought in procession, shrouded in a pure white cloth on the back of Sakra's royal elephant, to Oddisa's cave (*ratgal,* red rock). The singing ends telling how Oddisa makes his sacrifice dressed in his turban (*mundasana*), his necklace of the nine qualities (*navaguna vala*), his sacred thread (*punanula*), and other body ornaments (*abarana*). "Dressed like this," sing the exorcists, "he is known as *sastradari,* a man of knowledge and learning, and he repels the *dosa.*"

Now the comedy starts. It begins as a mime. The gradual appearance of the Brahmins, their at-first hesitant motion toward the world and the opening up of the horizons of the world to them as they move toward it, gains some of its significance in terms of my discussion on the gaze and sight as a constituting force of consciousness. The opening comedy is a mimesis of the victim's process, of his constitution and opening out to the world through sight.

The drummers quicken their rhythm. A Brahmin quickly shows his face at one side of Mahasammata's palace. He disappears and another Brahmin, half-hidden, peers around the other side of the palace. No words are spoken. The mime continues until one gathers his courage and strides into the arena. He is dressed in a yellow turban and a yellow smock. His face is lightened with powder, and he sports a neat black beard and waxed mustache. The Brahmin is dressed very much like a Sikh from the Punjab. He carries a rolled black umbrella under his arm. The Brahmin suddenly stops short, as if he is astounded to find himself in the midst of the audience. He beats a hasty retreat behind the palace. The other Brahmin now makes his full appearance in the same fashion. These actions are repeated a number of times, and the audience is greatly amused. Some sing out abuse, calling them to come and talk.

At last the Brahmins come and stay in the arena. They gaze in apparent amazement at Mahasammata's palace. They look this way and that, examining the decorations, bending down to peer at the patient. They gesture in recognition that the palace is their own handiwork. The Brahmins stagger around talking a nonsense language. They walk into the audience and are pushed away. One Brahmin rushes back, falling into the crowd, evoking great cries of thrilled amusement.

These actions, given their context, are indicative of the pushing back and always-shifting horizons of the life world, which comedy, of all the dramatic forms invented by human beings, achieves the most excellently. The creation and testing of boundaries so apparent in the *vadiga patuna* can be grasped as the reemergent flux of the ordering processes of social life, their alternating dynamic of mutual transgression and simultaneous assertion of personal boundaries.

The comedy now adds speech to its mime and is a veritable apotheosis of the constitutive powers of the consciousness of human beings through speech.

An exorcist dancer and one of the drummers, playing the role of Sinhalese Everyman, try to interact with the Brahmins. The drummer in mock anger demands to know what the Brahmins are saying (*Moko megolla me kiyanne*). The dancer suggests that they ask and goes up to the Brahmins. There is a short exchange between drummer and dancer to discover the best way of entering into a conversation with the Brahmins. "Ask them where they are going and what they are doing," suggests the beater.

Dancer: (shouting) Where are you going?
What . . . why? *Hello* (he uses the English word).

> Where are you going! (Turning to the drummer)
> This fellow doesn't know Sinhala.

Drummer: Try English.

Dancer: How can I do this?

Drummer: Just say, "Hello Johnny, give me one cigarette?"

Dancer: (in English): Hello Johnny, one cigarette?
          (The Brahmins stare dumbfounded at the dancer.)
          They don't understand English! (The dancer dashes the palm of
          his hand against his forehead in a gesture of despair.)

Drummer: Try Tamil.

Dancer: (in Sinhala to the Brahmins): Where are you going in Tamil lan-
          guage (*Demala basaven koheda yanne?*).

Drummer: Don't be so foolish . . . Ask respectfully. Call him *aiya.*

The dancer follows the drummer's suggestion, but there is still no response. The Brahmins, abashed, take a couple of steps backward. The
drummer then suggests that the dancer attempt Elu, the Sinhala of the
medieval Sinhalese kings, which many village Sinhalese consider to be
uncorrupted by foreign influence. "*Golu basaven koheda yanne?*" says
the dancer. The audience laughs at the use of the word *golu* (dumb) instead of *Elu.* It is apt comment on the speechlessness of the Brahmins.
The dancer perseveres, and eventually the Brahmins start to respond. At
first they stammer (which causes the audience to howl with laughter), but
as they break into communication with dancer and drummer, they make
all manner of spoonerisms and confused utterances, usually with grossly
obscene implications, much to the added delight of the audience.

> Brahmin: (in response to a question "Where are you from?") I am from
>   a Brahmin village to the south of the cave of Ratgalgiri. We
>   are Kondapala, Bimbisara, Agrajoti, Vimalajoti, Suwandagiri,
>   Kirtijoti. The Brahmins who came to heal the queen. We have
>   come by ship.
>
> Drummer: What! You have come with a truck load of tomatoes!
>
> Brahmin: No, no. We have come to Sri Lanka to worship at the temple
>   (*caitiya*).

More horseplay occurs, but eventually the Brahmins come to speak in
ordinary colloquial Sinhala, declare what they see before them, and de-
part from the scene. They leave after giving homage to the Buddha and
to the patient.

Comedy, Consciousness, and Sociality

The comedy of the *vadiga patuna* is centered in the potency of speech
and the embodied gestures of speech. The numerous devices of comedy

which make the drama of the Brahmins recognizable as comedy (the language plays, misrecognitions, paradoxes, parodies, stereotypic absurdity, buffoonery, obscenities, etc.) are used to demonstrate and explore the constitutive powers of consciousness in speech and other gestures. The *vadiga patuna* is a demonstration of what comedy can be (and perhaps why human beings almost everywhere are drawn to it), which is no more nor less than the luxuriating of human beings in their powers of consciousness achieved in their mastery of language and speech. In the *vadiga patuna,* and perhaps in comedy generally, is realized the apotheosis of human beings as constitutive of their own realities, of the ebb and flow of their own life worlds.

The comedy is a bubbling up, a boiling over of regenerative life,[46] but perhaps more immediately, a demonstration of the socially creative force of a thoroughly grounded and embodied consciousness of human being (which the progress of the *hatadiya* achieves). The visceral energy of comedy, its obscenity and the gut response of the laughter evoked, attests the embodiment of constitutive consciousness and its nonethereal nature (no mind-body dualism here).

The progress of the Brahmins is iconic with the development of consciousness through acts of consciousness: they gradually come to see what is before them, are increasingly drawn into the world (as they simultaneously form it) through their seeing action, which leads to speech and the full efflorescence of consciousness, by which practice the social realities and communities of human beings are defined. The Brahmins move from being outsiders to being insiders, and this shift, effected through their formation of consciousness, also gives rise to the social community, the Sinhala speech community, and establishes its boundaries. The *vadiga patuna* comes to an end at the point of the realization of the social community, with the final salutations by the actors before the patient and their homage to the Buddha. In this context of the *vadiga patuna,* such final action is not only recentering but also indicative of the broader message of the comedy, that it is human consciousness that is at the seat of sociality and community.

The passage of the Brahmins is also mimetic of the import of the victim's return to full consciousness and separation from sorcery. The ritual progression of the patient is one that actually follows a path from a point external to society and community toward its generative inner center. As the victim becomes an insider, he brings his community and society back to life, as the resurgence of community and society revitalizes the patient.

The *vadiga patuna* (and indeed the Suniyama as a whole) does not reduce sociality, social process, or social orders of human life to consciousness. Nor does it separate consciousness from the social in the

Durkheimian sense of the social, for example, society as irreducible and sui generis. Social realities and consciousness are indivisible, as are individual and social consciousness. They are mutually systematic, the one being a process of the other. Thus, the coming to consciousness of the victim simultaneously initiates and makes possible the resurgence of social existence, which in its elaboration, works back on the patient, further extending the consciousness of the patient, which is also part of the growing elaboration of human social life by means of consciousness.

The comic process of the *vadiga patuna* is an expression of the immanence in consciousness of social life and its life-sustaining orders. Moreover, the *vadiga patuna* shows that human beings, by manifesting a particular growth in consciousness and then exerting it, can constitute aspects of their social existence. The *vadiga patuna* is a demonstration of such a process and a practice of it. The audience, the patient's community, engages the actors, responding to their action and *commanding* them to act or behave in particular ways. The fun of the comedy, the pleasure and wonder of it, is in the exercise of consciousness and its constructive dynamic per se.

There are few better vehicles than comedy for demonstrating consciousness as an object to itself, the constitutive powers of consciousness, and the immanence and development of social life through acts of consciousness. The comic process loosens consciousness from its embeddedness in means-end schemata, from structure and rule. This is a feature of its amorality, irrationality, and transgression. So disconnected, consciousness becomes itself revealed as an object. This is a significance of the wordplay in comedy and the source of much of its pleasure. In the *vadiga patuna,* language and speech, the mediums of consciousness, are themselves revealed as objects of consciousness. Furthermore, their inappropriate usage, the breaking of ordinary rules of speech practice, reveals the rules, conventions, and means-end schemata of language as themselves objects of consciousness. Shown as an object, consciousness is used in its objectness, as, for example, when the exorcist-straightmen attempt to talk with the Brahmins.

The creation of consciousness as an object to itself in comedy simultaneously opens consciousness up to an intense display of its objectifying or constituting powers. This is an aspect of the fantasy and invention attendant on comedy. These result from the passion those given up to the comic process have for reveling both in consciousness for itself and in the powers of comedy to create the objects by means of which consciousness is objectified. There is a voracity for objects in comedy—evident in its rhythm of creation and destruction (the line and punch of the joke) and its *quick* darting from subject to subject. This is vital to the sustaining of the objectness of consciousness and to the immersion in consciousness for itself which provides much of the fun of comedy, even when it is not funny. It is the hunger for objects demanded in comedy that is its generative force, as well as its quality for immanence or its capacity to present consciousness as the energy which creates and constitutes the realities of human social existence and experience. Comedy, it may be added, is fundamentally aimed at, and encourages, physical reaction—laughter and other gestures of the body. These are immanent social acts, signs of the production of shared understanding, and indication that such consciousness and understanding well up from the depth and ground of Being.

Both the comedy of the *vadiga patuna* and sorcery are founded in similar processes and problematics. They live off victims. Their force and dynamic are located in a failure of consciousness or awareness. The sorcerer is most potent when he catches his victim unawares. The comedy lives in a lack of awareness; the fun continues until mutual awareness and a shared consciousness dawns. Sorcery and comedy are both transgressive; they both revel in filth and the obscene. Power is the energy of sorcery and is infused through the dynamics of comedy. Comedy and sorcery occupy much of the same ground. However, they work these processes in counteractive directions. In other words, comedy is an antidote for sorcery.

For example, consciousness is provoked in the comedy. The Brahmins are excited into becoming aware and fully conscious and communicative. In a sense the Brahmin butts/victims are incited to cast off their victimhood and extend themselves toward the world. There is a mutuality in the transgression of the comedy, whereas that of the sorcerer is a one-way street. When the Brahmins fall into the audience they are pushed back. The sorcerer overwhelms and intrudes within his victim and in a sense becomes his victim. In the comedy there is a play with boundaries so that they are made apparent rather than dissolved. The transgression of the sorcerer flattens and eradicates difference and the hierarchies that sustain difference. In the comedy, difference and hierarchy become elements of the absurd, but they are brought into play rather than denied, and frequently celebrated. The failure to recognize difference and the thrill of playing with the forces of power provide some of the fun in the comedy. The order and power of the everyday social world is made vitally present in the comedy.

Thus, the jokes of the *vadiga patuna* concentrate on the hierarchies of language and speech, in effect connecting their hierarchical power in the rite with that of ordinary social and political experience. The power of language and speech in everyday life underscores the power of language and the hierarchies of language, in the rite and vice versa. The comedy makes apparent, within the context of the rite, the boundaries and hierarchies of social distinction, the power of lived-in social realities, and speech as constitutive of such social divisions, as it is also expressive of them.

The comedy identifies Tamil with the language of the outsider and the danger and power of the outsider, all of which are integral to the diminishing and reductive force of the humor. Tamil words are part of the mantras used to speak with and command dangerous and demonic forces within the rite. In the *vadiga patuna,* on this and other occasions, reference is made to the current Tamil-Sinhala ethnic war and the dangers of visiting the shrine of the Bo tree at the ancient city of Anuradhapura. The fun derived from addressing the Brahmins in English comes from the deep ambivalences that Sinhala-speaking communities have to this language. It is, of course, the language of the outside, of foreign wealth and power. The request for cigarettes in this performance plays on the commodity and consumer power of tourists relative to the impoverishment of Sinhalese villagers. But English was the language of colonial power and continues to be the language of political and social elites in Sri Lanka. In colloquial speech, English is referred to as *kaduva,* the sword of state, which judges, orders, and separates and divides those who are socially and politically powerful from the weak.[47] Ordering power, the force that structures internal political and social relations, has the quality of externality or outsideness—a feature of the ideologies and metaphors of kingship in South Asian and other contexts and a theme in the myths and discourse of the Suniyama and other rites (Frazer 1890; Hocart, 1936; de Heusch 1985; Sahlins 1981; Obeyesekere 1984a; Kapferer 1988a; Tambiah 1992).

The *vadiga patuna* is a discourse of power. Comedy (like the jester in the court traditions of Europe, or Lear's fool) lives in the situation of power, uncovering its posturings and testing its claims. This is a central dynamic of the *vadiga patuna.* The *adura*s in their comic antics manifest key dimensions of their role as manipulators of cosmic forces, as persons who must confront the primordial energy of sorcery, as controllers and alchemists of potencies, and as architects and articulators of the hierarchical ordering of power. The exorcists reveal themselves as the fools and the jesters in the court of ritually invoked powers who discover the absurdities and falsities of power as well as its legitimate claimants.

The entire comedy of the *vadiga patuna* is centered on a joke of power.

The Brahmins at the focus of the fun are *failed healers*. When Manikpala fell sick because of Vasavarti's sorcery, Brahmins were summoned, so the stories go, but they could not cure the queen. Only Oddisa succeeded, the last of the Brahmins summoned and the encompassing form, the master healer and sacrificer who subsumes all the others. The Brahmins in the *vadiga patuna* present an authority and a power that they do not have. They are absurd in this fact.

The absurdity of the Brahmins is explicitly conveyed in their strutting and striding around the performance arena. Their insignia of power—the rolled black umbrellas that they carry like a drill sergeant's stick, their waxed handlebar mustaches, their dark glasses[48]—are of a false or impotent power. They wear saffron tunics; saffron, in this context, is the color of impotence (or of the negation of impotence, the power that overrides power, the color of Suniyam). When the Brahmins leave the arena, they do so in a manner that acknowledges actual power—that of the Sinhala community they have entered and have brought to life, of the patient reempowered, and of the Buddha. Furthermore, the comedy, in its dynamic of exposure and of Brahmin rejection, gives rise once again to the emergence of the authority of the *adura*, the power of Oddisa. The *vadiga patuna* is a practice that emphasizes the claim of the master *adura* at the start of the comedy to possess the authority and knowledge of Oddisa.

An implication of the absurdity of the Brahmins, another dimension of what is immanent in the comedy, is that the patient will achieve the potency that eludes the Brahmins, that the real power is what is germinal within the *atamagala* and waiting to break out.

Exorcists say that one of the purposes of the *vadiga patuna* is to cool, please, and soothe the patient's mind (*sita pinavanava*). This superficially simple understanding condenses the great transformational potency that inheres in the *vadiga patuna* as a practice and its power as a demonstration of the processes in train within the rite as a whole. The exorcists insist that the *vadiga patuna* is one of the critical judgments (*tinduva*) of the Suniyama, and the comedy is the power of such a judgment, one aspect of which is to separate impotency (the force of sorcery) from life-generating power. The *vadiga patuna* in many respects manifests the punishing possibility of comedy and fun. The Brahmins as butts of the jokes are punished for their ignorance and posturing. What happens to them is a metaphor for the punishment of the sorcerer that the Suniyama will effect.

Overall, the farce of the Brahmins is the full unfolding of the power of consciousness: a consciousness that has human being as its vital center and that is the force through which human beings make and break their realities. This is the meaning of the comedy within the context of the rite: the *vadiga patuna* revealing the great potentiality of the dynamic of the comic process to objectify consciousness as a thing in itself. The delight and pleasure of the audience in the comedy—a pleasure of the body, its shaking in laughter, virtually an orgasmic excitement, a heightening rather than a release—is one born of a simultaneous immersion within and realization of the flow of consciousness.

There is one further aspect of the *vadiga patuna* that I stress. Although it can be understood as an opening up of the life world before the patient, this opening up is not independent of the victim's progress. That is, the victim is made the enlivening presence in the space-womb at the heart of the *atamagala* (as much as he is enlivened by his location in this space). In other words, in the course of the *hatadiya*, the victim is himself made into a pulsating life force that is generative of the explosion of a life world around him in the process of the *vadiga patuna* comedy. This world, the community brought to life in the comedy, is not reducible to the patient. Nor is it a world apart or separate from the patient, or a world that the patient must step back into or rejoin. Such an interpretation would, in my opinion, miss the sense that it is the reextension of the victim toward the horizons of a life world, effected, for example, in the *hatadiya*, that is a central force in the creation of the world which he rejoins.

The coming back to full consciousness of the patient is a force emergent in the victim that draws him to the world (a drawing toward that is virtually a recreation), but simultaneously such a world—as it opens out in the patient's motion of consciousness toward it—actively draws the patient into its domain. The process is similar to what I discussed earlier concerning the action of seeing that involves being drawn by the what-is-seen (or by the power of what appears to be all around but is not yet in view) as much as by a self-originating extension toward the world of the seen. The comedy of the *vadiga patuna* is a greater elaboration of the process. The life world of the comedy has a dynamic connection with the patient's reemergence to consciousness. It is a manifestation of the victim's growth in consciousness and also toward consciousness. But the world coming to life in consciousness also draws the patient into it. This is the force of the chaotic and fractal-like motion of the comedy, often, I suggest, a tantalizing force, for it extends at the periphery and at the limits of the patient's gaze. Through the dynamic of the comedy not only is there an expansion of the victim's consciousness, but this is also systematic with an increasing remotioning of the body, or the capacity of the body of consciousness to move out in the world.

All that is immanent within the *vadiga patuna*—the constituting force of consciousness within a mobile body, the generation of the social community through the power of consciousness, the impotence, retreat, and destruction of the sorcerer before the ordering of human being—are actualized in the last acts of the Suniyama.

From Victim to World Maker

The closing events of the Suniyama—principal among them the *valvalalu tinduva,* the *chedana vidiya tinduva,* and the *puhul tinduva*—express the release of the victim from the bonds of sorcery and the impotence of the sorcerer and engage the victim in reconstitutive sacrificial action. The power of consciousness is expressed as being vital within a reequilibrated and mobile body and integral to the action of the patient now as sacrificer and not the sacrificed. In effect, the patient is in the position of Mahasammata the world maker rather than of Manikpala the world-destroyed, and also manifests the potency of the Mahasammata-Manikpala harmonic and regenerative conjunction.

Valvalalu Tinduva: The Cutting of Sorcery's Bonds

It is around 5:45 A.M., well into the morning watch, when the *vadiga patuna* finishes and the events of the *valvalalu* begin. The scene is bathed in the fresh light of dawn. The audience has grown in number with early risers, getting ready for the tasks of the day, and curious passersby on their way to work. The *valvalalu,* which includes other ritual acts of judgment or sentence (*tinduva*), lasts the better part of an hour, most of this time spent on binding the patient seated within the *atamagala.*

The key acts of the *valvalalu* involve shackling the patient in the poisonous coils or vines of sorcery. The master exorcist places bonds or hoops (*valalu*) over the patient's body, pinning his arms to his sides. His wrists are cuffed with small hoops, as are the patient's legs and ankles. Ideally eighteen (here a number symbolic of the totalizing destruction of the order of human beings) such hoops should bind the patient's body. These hoops are the vines or poisonous ties of the sorcerer.[49]

Before the hoops are placed around the victim's body, the master exorcist takes a crown (*otunna,* woven with coconut leaves and garlanded, the gems of the crown), and executing a short dance, sings of its origin (*otunu upata*). He tells that it is the crown of the Naga king, the primordial serpent, and is made from 108 poisonous vines. The exorcist sings about how the Naga king, wearing this insignia of total destructive and ordering power, ended a fight among his Naga subjects at Kelaniya, a place at the northern outskirts of modern-day Colombo.[50] Other verses sung by the exorcist (and his companions in refrain) declare that it is also the crown of Manikpala as well as of Mahasammata. This crown is worn by the patient throughout the *valvalalu* and condenses much of the transformational import of the event.

The victim is hot with potency and regenerative energy and is simultaneously in the position of destruction and creation. The ambiguities condensed into the crown indicate this. The binding of the victim expresses the immobile body, the body rigid in the poisonous heat, and the terror of sorcery attack. He is made to relive the constriction and confinement of sorcery. But it is also the confinement before birth.

In the well-known legends of the origination and reoriginating process of Sinhala kings (Sinhabahu, Vijaya, and Dutthagamini, whose exploits figure in the songs of exorcist tradition and in the written chronicles of the *Mahavamsa*), the metaphors of confinement (caves, the fetus) indicate a potent rebirth. In the verses sung at this performance, the Naga king quells the fighting Nagas at Kelaniya. Kelaniya in other important legends is a place of transgression and turbulence from which new orders grow. Viharamahadevi, the mother of the famous Prince Dutthagamini (who in ancient times, breaks out from his own confinement to conquer the Tamil king Elara and reestablishes Sinhala hegemony), is herself born from the chaos of destruction. This is caused by her father, the king of Kelaniya, who in a fit of jealous rage kills an innocent Buddhist priest, bringing the fury of the elements. King and people are engulfed by the sea, and only Viharamahadevi is spared (see *Mahavamsa* 1934; also Kapferer 1988a:28).

While binding the patient's body, the master *adura* takes a spray of mango leaves (which have been hanging inside the *atamagala,* on the left, or moonside, of the structure) and brushes them repeatedly, head to foot, down the patient's body. As he does so he utters a mantra (*ambakola atta matirima*). These actions cool the patient and balance the body humors (*va, pit, sem*) disturbed by sorcery attack. They also sweep the body clean of the pollution of sorcery, of eye, mouth, and thought poison, of the fire of curses, and, so the exorcist intones, dispel the ten fears of sorcery.[51] These actions are not just the cleansing of sorcery but purifications attendant at the dangers of birthing, a birthing of a new conscious body from the primordial ground of Being which is a thorough counteraction and overcoming of the sorcerer. The actions of the *ambakola atta matirima* are sometimes performed by exorcists during childbirth.

Themes of primordial and potent birthing and regeneration are pursued in other songs of the *valvalalu*. They deal with the regenerate powers of rebirth and with the heat, destruction, and uncertainty of the forces engaged at birth.

The exorcists sing verses telling of the birth of the goddess Pattini and of Prince Oddisa's birth from Queen Yawudagiri. One song relates the story of Pattini's birth from the mango that Sakra, the king of the gods, gave to Buddha to eat. Sakra plants the stone in the land of the evil king of Pandi. Pattini is born from this stone and puts out the third eye of the cruel king. Another song tells how Pattini destroys the city of Madurai as punishment for the unjust killing of her husband, Palanga, whom she raises from the dead (see Obeyesekere 1984a for other accounts of the births of Pattini). Yawudagiri's story is recounted: her marriage to the king of Vadiga, the conception of Oddi as a result of her unwitting intercourse with a lustful god while she was bathing (during her menstrual period, *kili mala*), her pregnancy cravings, Oddi's birth, his rage and leaving of Vadiga city, his reaching into the bowels of the earth through the golden anthill, and his extraction of the cobras and vipers with which he adorns his body (see Chapter 3). The verses describe how Oddi drinks the snake venom, changing its poison into the antidote of sorcery.

Once the patient is bound, the *adura* immediately cuts the bonds. The *valalu* are quickly placed in a sack and thrown away at the margins of habitation. They are dangerous and polluting. In a sense, like other materials used in this rite, they are virtually the afterbirth. In effect, I suggest, the *adura,* when he cuts the patient's bonds, acts as a midwife to the patient's regenerative metamorphosis.

This binding and releasing of the patient engages the body in the direct experience of the reconstitutive and liberating project of the Suniyama. Perhaps it gathers greater intensity coming as it does after the *vadiga patuna*. There is a life-death explosiveness and shock in the dynamic of comedy (see Douglas 1975; and with reference to exorcism, Kapferer 1983), and such import of the process is imaged on the patient's body. Furthermore, given the ritual context of birthing and the explosiveness of comedy, the patient is not so much released from his bonds as he himself bursts them open. This is consistent with the rebalancing of body and mind, the repotentiating of consciousness, that has been occurring throughout the rite.

Moreover, the patient in breaking his bonds springs back into the life world. I remark on the building of tension in the *valvalalu*, the slowness of the binding relative to the quickness of the cutting. The cutting of the bonds enables the victim to leap back toward the world with the full motional force of his emobodied consciousness. The energy of the victim's reextension turns back the destructive transgressive leap of the sorcerer.

The *valvalalu tinduva* (or *kapuma*) is followed by four other acts of judgment (sentence). These indicate the repotentiation of the patient and his active role in turning back the sorcery. They are mimetic of specific rites of sorcery attack but are now aimed at the sorcerer. These rites include the *annakka,* or pineapple *tinduva;* the *hondala-ala tinduva,*[52] the *tambili,* or red coconut, and *tambili mal,* or coconut flower, *tinduva);* they are performed at the western door of the *atamagala,* the exorcist and the patient together holding the machete that cuts through the objects. The *adura* instructs the patient in the action but also takes on his own body the dangers inherent in such practice.

I will later (Chapters 6 and 7) discuss the formation of consciousness as integral to the intentional and mobile body. This is a powerful aspect of the practice and project of the Suniyama as a whole and is condensed in the events of the *valvalalu.* In the condition of sorcery the victim is confined to the physical body and cannot move. So chained, the patient is given up to the intensity of his fears, and like Manikpala, is in danger of losing consciousness. Some patients have described their experience while shackled in the *atamagala* as one of consuming fear, and occasionally, as I have witnessed, the victim seems almost overcome with fright. The *valvalalu* expresses the full repotentiation of consciousness in a motional body, the interdependence of consciousness and the motional extension of the body, and that it is in a fully motional body that consciousness expands.

Above all, in my interpretation, the *valvalalu* images the fruition of the victim's progress as rebirth in a most powerful and primordial sense. The victim is reborn from *out of himself* and out of the very primordial ground from which his substance and physical being are formed. The *valvalalu* is the reemergence of the microcosm from the macrocosm. The bonds of the *valvalalu* are not merely the ties of sorcery but in another sense also the coils of time (and of space), such symbolism being dense in the practice of this rite and in the wider Sinhala Buddhist cultural context of the Suniyama's performance. The progress of the *hatadiya* is a progression through time and space. The victim may be understood as embodying the potentiality of time and space. The cutting of the bonds, in my interpretation (it is not advanced by the exorcists but is nonetheless consistent with much of their practice), is an actualizing or opening out of the victim toward the reinstantiation of time-space fundamental in existence and integral to the dynamic of social and political relations of human beings.

The rebirth of the victim also manifests the sorcerer. This is because the rebirth involves a separation from the sorcerer. Before the rebirth, the sorcerer or sorcery exists within the body and circumstance of the victim. With the victim's rebirth, the sorcerer and sorcery are objectified as distinct and opposed to the victim. The acts of cutting and judgment that the victim performs at the end of the *valvalalu* address the objectifications of sorcery which, significantly, appear after the victim bursts his bonds. The most intense and greatest manifestation of sorcery and the sorcerer is to be expected when the reborn victim assumes the height of his constituting consciousness and is freed to reinstantiate his political and social actualities. Liberated, the patient is virtually in the position of the world-ordering King Mahasammata. Like Mahasammata, the erstwhile victim is capable of reinstituting a division in the totalization of his existence and of excluding and resisting the forces of destruction. These assume their most encompassing and violent form, that of Vasavarti Maraya himself. This is the central theme of the extraordinary ritual drama that is now performed, the *chedana vidiya,* or the destruction of the palace.

The Final Judgments: The Impotence and Destruction of the Sorcerer

The *chedana vidiya* demonstrates the fury of the destructive and transgressive energies that surround the political and social order within which the patient is situated. The internalization of the victim generates the externalization of violent destructive forces. The action shows the nature of the extreme totalizing power that sorcery manifests, that of furious fragmentation that breaks down hierarchy and the hierarchical ordering of difference. This power fails before the force of world-reordering embodied consciousness.

A loud drumming announces the start of the *chedana vidiya,* as three exorcist-dancers shoot clouds of burning resin (*dummala*) in the air and toward the palace. Simultaneously, the master *adura* boils eight limes and eight small lime branches (*pangiri kotu atta*) in an earthen pot at the side of the palace. The branches and limes are taken from the top of the *atamagala.* Their boiling is the making of *nanu,* the paste with which the patient was consecrated at the start of the Suniyama and, significantly in this context, with which the king was anointed at ceremonies of installation and reempowerment. The boiling of the limes and sticks (the poisons of the viper of sorcery) is a transformation of their destructive essence into that which is cleansing, healing, and protective. The action indicates that the victim is in the position of the consecrated King Maha-sammata, the *cakravartin* who institutes the hierarchy of the world order. The patient no longer wears Manikpala's shawl, the *mottakkili,* and is healed. This is conveyed in the name of the event, the *candragane tinduva,* which suggests the return to brilliant constellational unity (*gane*) of the moon (*candra,* Manikpala). Here is also the sense (in the term *tinduva*) of both judgment or justice having been passed and order reconstituted.

The three exorcist-dancers, each carrying a machete (sword), come before the audience. One rolls out a coconut leaf and mimes reading a horoscope. He declares that they must hunt the boar. The drumming quickens, and the dancers, running around the performance arena and through and behind the palace, chase after the exorcists' assistant (*madu puraya*), who is the pig. The pig scuttles away, first in this direction, then that.[53] The palace shakes, bits fall off, and the dancers sometimes halt to take a desultory chop at part of the building. There is a comic tension, and the audience thrills to the fun. At last the chasing ends, and the dancers come before the patient, virtually hidden inside the *atamagala,* and give their obeisances.

Suniyam has the face of a pig (and the forehead of a bull) and is represented as such on his clay image which is laid on the ground outside the performance area. The Buddha dies after a meal of pork, and the pig in some popular conceptions is the animal of indiscriminate greed. The chasing of the pig is a hunting for the sorcerer, a flushing out of the pig of sorcery from his hiding place. It is the manifesting of the sorcerer.

The sorcerer is now revealed and his furious potency displayed. His manner and form is mimed by one of the dancers, in this performance, the eldest son of the master *adura.* He and his father are dressed similarly. The other dancers are in the dress of Oddisa. But both the master *adura* and the sorcerer are attired in the traditional working garb of the exorcist, bare-chested and wearing white sarongs. The only distinction is that the sorcerer wears a red cummerbund (*paccavadam*) and a red head cloth, indicative of his hot and destructive condition. The sorcerer is the counterpart of the *adura* (the double aspect of all *adura*s), with whom, in effect, the master exorcist has been joined in struggle throughout the rite. The Suniyama is an organization of rites that mimic the practice of destructive sorcery but in actuality are its antidote or counteraction. Here the master sorcerer can be seen as confronting his own alternative possibility and also the ritual power of that antidotal and controlling possibility.

The sorcerer brandishes a large machete, the destructive sword (*ka-*

duva) of Suniyam. He rushes toward the palace, transgresses its space, reaches through the doorway into the *atamagala*, and takes the rice pounder (*molgaha*) resting by the feet of the patient. The sorcerer removes a major barrier between the patient and the force of destruction. In the conception of exorcists, the rice pounder is a weapon for clubbing and warding off demons. The sorcerer (Suniyam/Vasavarti) has breached the patient's line of ritual protection and the defenses of Mahasammata's palace/fortress. The patient is alone and vulnerable with nothing between him and the sorcerer's anger. The only defence or protection is the harmony and unity and potency of the patient's embodied consciousness.

The sorcerer screams. Suniyam/Vasavarti lurches and staggers drunkenly. He is crazed and wild, the image of decomposition in himself. His head scarf falls and his hair is disheveled. Freezing before the *atamagala*, the sorcerer glares fixedly at his victim. He screams once more, and reeling, encircles the palace. He sees the image of Suniyam at the apex of the palace's central tower, and reaching up, hacks it down with his machete. He stabs at other demonic representations of himself. These images, facing out, are protective, but the sorcerer destroys them. He attacks the representations of order and regeneration, the emblems of the Sun and the Moon at the side towers of the palace, and erases their form (as his own manifestation as the serpent of sorcery was erased in the course of the *hatadiya*).

Inside the *atamagala*, the victim looks nervously about him as the sorcerer crashes through the palace, ripping it down. At times, the blade of his machete brushes past the patient. The other dancers join the sorcerer in cutting away the palace. As the building tumbles around him, the patient, unscathed, appears to rise out of the debris, which is quickly swept up so that no pieces remain, and like the *valalu* earlier, either put in a sack or carried away to be thrown in a roadside ditch. The patient appears resolute in his consciousness, as in the well-known popular story of the Buddha at the time of Enlightenment; he was not moved from his way before the furious demonic hordes of Mara.

The patient is made to live the danger of sorcery. I can only speculate about what the potentialities of the experience are likely to be. I stress the enclosed nature of the space within the *atamagala* and the fact that the patient can see little from his position but can hear the clamor about him, occasionally flinching from falling pieces of the structure or dodging the sorcerer's blade. Patients acknowledge that they feel uncertain about their safety. The destruction of the palace seems a tense enough moment judging from my own experience in the audience. Quite possibly there is a sense of relief as the building is cut away and the victim emerges, as if from a chrysalis, into clear and open space and for the first time in over four hours is able to see all around him.

The *chedana vidiya* concentrates and develops themes already apparent in the rite as a whole. The single most important and significant feature is the destruction of the palace. It absorbs the destructive fury of sorcery and as a result becomes contaminated and dangerous. This is one reason for the immediate cleaning of the fragments from the ritual area. Exorcists understand the destruction of the palace as itself a major event in the cutting of sorcery. Because the heat of sorcery infuses the palace, it becomes a materialization of sorcery's power, and its destruction is the annihilation of that power.

This culminating force of the *chedana vidiya* extends into the final ritual acts surrounding the cutting of the ash pumpkin, the *puhul tinduva*. These are performed over the midday period (*iramudun*), when the sun is at its zenith, and draw their potency from this fact. They are the final judging acts when the sorcerer is killed or finally cut away from his relation to the victim. This action is performed by the erstwhile victim on the body of the exorcist, who is both a victim surrogate and an embodiment of both the agency or instrumentality of sorcery and its potency. This action is (see Chapter 6) a quintessential dimension of sacrifice, an act of reconstitutive division whereby human being remakes itself and the social realities upon which life depends. The *puhul tinduva*, as a rite leading from the *chedana vidiya*, is, like so much else in the Suniyama, the actualization through human action of microcosmic forces immanent within macrocosmic processes.

In the *puhul tinduva*, the master *adura* lies down on a rush mat before the patient. His attitude is that of a corpse; his head is oriented toward the west, in the direction of death, and rests on the rolled end of the mat (where the head of a corpse is placed). At the instruction of the exorcist, the patient makes three obeisances (for the Triple Gem: Buddha, Dhamma, Sangha) to a new white cloth which is spread over the exorcist's body.

The *adura* is in the position of the body of sorcery which is similar to the position of the victim at the very start of the rite. The exorcist is also the body on to which the attention of the sorcerer is deflected, as at previous times in the course of the rite. The cloth, like the *mottakkili*, symbolically condenses notions of death and regeneration and is an object of protective purity, intervening between the *adura* and the energy of sorcery. The mimesis is integral to the exorcist's role. He pretends to be the victim to trap the sorcerer and his energy; these are then subordinated to the *adura*'s own knowledge and skill as an antisorcerer. The *adura* here, as he does throughout the rite, works his powers in the ambiguous spaces of his own position as a master ritualist and in the ambiguities generated in the course of the ritual process.

A basket of offerings is set on the exorcist's stomach, on which an ash pumpkin is placed. This is conceived of by exorcists as a human being surrogate that becomes the object and embodiment of sorcery. The patient takes the handle of a machete and slowly starts to cut the ash pumpkin in half, the exorcist pressing down on top of the blade, all the while uttering a mantra that powers the force of the blade and cuts the sorcery. At the *adura*'s feet, an egg is cooked in the cranium of a human skull (the *nicakula tinduva,* the low- or outside-caste judgment or sentencing act), an act of destruction (and of radical externalization, as indicated in the name of the event) of the germinal center of the life of the sorcerer within the very receptacle of consciousness.

This action in particular is viewed with disgust and some awe by exorcists and audience alike. It is a compression of much of the import of the Suniyama as a whole, the birth-to-consciousness process in one event, but in a reverse direction. The consciousness of the sorcerer is destroyed at the source. A contrast might be drawn between the diminishing, shutting-down force of this action—in my view, one that contains in its tension the entire terrible potential of sorcery—and the rebirth, the bursting of consciousness, and its opening toward the world, of the events of the *valvalalu* and the *chedana vidiya.*

The acts of the *puhul tinduva* mark the transition of the victim from a relatively passive role in the process to one of being an active world maker. He engages in sacrificial action and is no longer the object of sacrifice. He partly takes over from the *adura.* The *adura* must also be committed to such action, for he thus cuts the intimacy of his own relation with the sorcerer established in the earlier event of the *doratu panima,* before the entry of the victim into the *atamagala.* Furthermore, the exorcist maintains a sacrificial role, for the power of the event is in the trap he sets and his being disclosed, in opposition to the energy of sorcery, as an antisorcerer. Also, in continuing his sacrificial role, the *adura* bears the risk that attaches to the killing action.

It is the exorcist and his companions who are responsible, I suggest, for the violence of the sacrifice, and not the patient. Thus, the patient's involvement in immoral action is reduced in this Buddhist universe; he is separated from acts of killing and instead is given to constitutive and regenerative action. The exorcist stands between this process and the destruction from which regenerative action cannot otherwise be separated.

It is the exorcist who remains open to the brunt of reciprocal revenge and runs the full danger of immoral action (see Chapter 6).

Apart from concluding salutations to the Buddha and the deities, the Suniyama is now over, after almost a day and a half of constant and intense ritual activity. Most of the audience had departed at the end of the *chedana vidiya*. Before this, the dramatic excitement of the event had kept their attention. The rite finishes quietly, dissolving and merging almost imperceptibly into the routine of everyday life.

Ritual Practice: Virtuality and Actuality

I have explored the logic of the Suniyama through a description of its key practices in one performance.[54] Although there are always some differences, even marked ones, in most other performances that I have witnessed, the actions are routinely repeated. It is in the structures of practice that the significance of the ritual events is revealed.

The practices embed the *doxa* of the rite, or the principles that underlie its direction. *Adura* can and do reflect, independently of the contexts of their performances, on the meaning and structure of their practice. But like human beings everywhere, they cannot verbalize the significance of all that they do. Indeed, it is impossible for me to transform into a text all that I saw and heard and experienced. Exorcists are selective in what they reveal in words, like anthropologists who textualize ethnographic material, although the unconscious (unreflected social and psychological) and conscious processes involved are different. All this is obvious.

However, I stress the logic of ritual practice as it exists qua practice, as a set of activities whose design, or the way specific activities are routinely interrelated, embeds organizational principles. These principles are tied to the activities and can be only partially abstracted from them. Exorcists know the schema of a Suniyama, the sequencing of particular named events, the content of acts, and so forth, that should be enacted in any specific performance of a Suniyama. However, they cannot give, abstractly or independently of concrete ritual practice, more than the most general outline. Only in exceptional cases can they give a statement on the reason for the design or logic. They operate a practical logic present in the activities of constituting the production of a Suniyama and emergent in its course. The rite does not develop from a logic so much as it generates it in its practical motion.

Patients at the focus of Suniyamas may be said to arrive at a position where they may have a reflexive grasp of the meaning of their acts, both past and future. The achievement of such meaning on the part of the patient and others is a concern of the *aduras*. However, this meaning and the meaning or import of the activities of the rite are not independent of the body but coextensive with it, inscribed on it through the involvement of the body as both the instrument and the site of practice. Throughout the rite patients are instructed in the practical activity of the Suniyama. They and the exorcists do the meaning of the rite in their manifold activities, which also constitute what may be called the practice structures of the exorcism (the dance, the comedy, the pattern of songs and mantras, the manner of gifting, the ritual orienting and reorienting of the patient's body, the manipulation of perception). The priority that I give here to knowledge and meaning as generated in and through practice—a lived knowledge and meaning—bears close affinity to Bourdieu's discussion (1977, 1990) and those who have influenced him (Heidegger 1962 and his "hammering"; Merleau-Ponty's 1962 "activities"). But the primacy of practice is basic to exorcists' own orientations to their work.

The power of the Suniyama is in *prayoga*, practice. It is in the activities productive of the Suniyama—in the making of the rite—that the recreative energies of the rite become present and potent. Much discussion of ritual understands its potencies to ultimately reside in belief. Although what people believe is certainly crucial, I stress the potencies of the activities or organizations of ritual practice in themselves. The practice constitutes the force of the belief by making belief coincident with the oriented activities of the body—the body as belief. The regenerative force of the Suniyama—its formation of being and consciousness—is through the performative dynamic of its practices.[55]

The *aduras* insist at intervals throughout the rite that they are representing the Suniyama as it was performed the first time. They are not repeating the initial rite but in effect recreating the rite with all the reoriginating potencies that were present in the first rite. In other words, every performance of the Suniyama is always a first performance. It is not a mimetic recreation or a copy, and thus not a duplication or mere repetition of the first rite. Every performance of a Suniyama is an original repetition—always new and in possession of all the vitalizing potencies of the first, because *it is the first rite*. The power of every performance of a Suniyama is not a result of its being continuous with tradition—with what was successful in the past—which brings the powers of the past into the present. This would yield to tradition a mystical potency that I think would obscure an understanding of the force of rites such as the Suniyama and might also distort the import of exorcists' assertions about what they are doing. Moreover, the view that something is powerful because it was powerful in the past places a huge onus on the potencies of belief: a ritual is effective because people believe it is effective. This orientation (around which debates are formed in anthropology concerning the efficacy of symbols, the rationality or irrationality of ritual, and the reasons why people believe) displaces a focus on practice, the importance of which is continually emphasized by exorcists.

The importance that the exorcists give to the correctness and detail of their activities—they say that they are precisely those of the first rite—underscores the originary force of their repetition. Every Suniyama is always the first rite. *Aduras* say that their ritual will not work unless it is correct in every detail. An improperly recreated rite may deepen the destruction of sorcery and backfire disastrously on exorcists and patients alike. Exorcists attribute the failure of their rites to faults and omissions in practice or to misapplications (inappropriate acts). They are asserting that originating force is contained not just in practices but in the exactitude, precision, and technique of these practices. In other words, the insistence that the first rite is being repeated is an assertion that practices appropriate to the matter at hand are being carried out correctly. Furthermore, these practices in the original repetition of the Suniyama are not merely a means to an end but have inherent in them and their organization their originating force, their poiesis, or capacity to bring forth.[56]

Anthropologists have frequently defined ritual in terms of its stereotypy, repetitiveness, obsession with detail, and liturgical form (see Rappaport 1979 for a survey of such positions). These are treated as among the conventions of rite, the obvious aspects of rite by which ritual is recognized as being ritual. As Handelman (1990) and Humphrey and Laidlaw (1994) have noted, such a perspective has not greatly increased the understanding of the force of ritual. Lévi-Strauss (1981), more than many, recognizes the technical importance of such aspects, specifically repetition, and recognizes that they have importance for much more than being definitional of rite or functional for the communication of its message or meaning. But his preference for abstract operations of the intellect (myth) rather than those of practice (rite) leads him to reduce the significance of his own insight regarding the technology of ritual. The conventions and repetitions of ritual (for Lévi-Strauss 1981: 674, the method by which ritual reduces, fragments, and "parcels out" meaning) produce meaninglessness (relative to the meaningfulness of myth). But what is seen as repetition, the apparent obsession with detail, precision, and so forth, is an expression of the constitutive and generative aspects of practice: that is, practice not as a representation of meanings but the very dynamic of their constitution.

The practices that the Suniyama composes refer preeminently to the cosmological and ontogenetic reality that it encloses. Other realities—those of the everyday working world of the patient and household—are backgrounded. They recede or intrude in relation to the focal activities of the Suniyama. The Suniyama's ritual process, the dynamic of its events, governs the nature of the inclusion of activities that may be seen as part of routine life in the structure of the rite and to varying degrees makes them conform to the modalities of the ritual activities (e.g., everyday episodes that form part of the comedy and excitement of the *vadiga patuna* and the destructive acts of the *chedana vidiya* are integral to reinvoking the dominant realities of everyday life). Broadly, the practices of the Suniyama constitute their own space and time and are oriented in terms of their own means-end schema. They are simultaneously their own objective and the method for achieving it. The activities in rite thus become revealed in their density and dynamic, as practice qua practice.

The implications of what I am saying may be better grasped if the Suniyama (and possibly ritual in general) is understood as a practice in virtuality. The Suniyama is a virtuality in the sense that it is an organization of activities that are integral to the routine activities of the lived-in life world but not subject to the indeterminacies of its processes. These flow from what may be called the forces of actuality or the energies born, for example, of historical events, political and economic occurrences (global and local) that play on particular lived sites of everyday existence and that form the diversities and manifold directions of daily life. Actuality is indeterminate, but virtuality is determinate and repeatable. The practices of the Suniyama are oriented to the generation of the projects defined internal to the Suniyama. Each act is organized in a sequence that has a predictive, almost musical, pattern to it, so that the next event is indicated by what preceded it. The apparent repetitiveness of rite is something that intensifies this quality of ritual practices and also their determinacy. The indeterminacy that ritual avoids is of course present in actuality, where the forces affecting the victim's context cannot be so controlled.

In the Suniyama, the reactualization of the ordinary world amid the virtuality of the rite is a moment of intense anxiety because of the resurgence of the circumstances of indeterminacy. This is fully exemplified in the events of the *chedana vidiya,* whose tension is connected not merely with the presence of the destructive force of the demonic but also with the reemergence of the victim into a reactualized everyday world. The manifestation of the sorcerer in this culminating event of the rite carries with it the sense of the indeterminacies, transgressions, and threats potent in actuality.

I should make it clear that I conceive of actuality as far more than the constructions created by human beings to grasp actuality or to control it. The life world is not reducible to the constructions that human beings place upon it and always moves beyond their grasp. This view is implicit in the Mahasammata story and the Suniyama. Mahasammata cannot totalize existence and the dynamics of chaotic actuality which form a part of it and can disruptively intrude within the order that he constructs.[57]

The virtuality of the Suniyama is a compression of the forces that are vital to the way human beings make themselves, form their realities, and apprehend the actualities of their existence. The Suniyama operates in its own space-time, but it is not a space-time that is radically distinct or apart from ordinary lived space-time as a construction immanent in human activity. The virtuality of the Suniyama enters within the dynamics of the space-time construction (e.g., the *hatadiya*) of the ordinary world. The density of the virtuality of the Suniyama may be said to be a radical slowing down and entry within the constructional moments in which human beings realize themselves and their worlds. The Suniyama may be seen as akin to what Deleuze and Guattari (1994:118) describe as a dimension of scientific practice. The virtuality of the Suniyama is a "primordial slowing down" which impedes the chaos of the circumstances of life, a world that is always in flux; it attempts to set or reset the conditions from which the world develops or extends in all its changeability and expanding difference. This has some degree of fit with what the *adura*s say when they describe their practice as correctional. In the virtual time-space of the rite, they reset their patients within the space-time of reality construction.

It should be clear that the Suniyama is not a model of or for reality (see Geertz 1965). To offer description along such anthropological lines would indicate that the Suniyama both represents the way ordinary existence works and ultimately refers to the world external to its reality.[58] The Suniyama is a simulacrum, not in the Platonic sense of a copy of external reality, but a reality complete unto itself and with no reference other than itself. It is its own reality and is lived as such. It does not model the external dynamics of the processes of everyday life but is a magnification of them. These dynamics are extensive with those in the routine life world and are productive of its realities. In this sense the rite does not play with reality but rather is the dynamic play from which the constructions of reality take form. The Suniyama not only recenters victims in the routine world but by immersing them in the dynamics of its practices enables them to regenerate their life world. As virtuality, the rite does not simply dissolve into reality but brings it forth.

The virtuality of the Suniyama should not be confused with computer-based contemporary notions of virtual reality: that is, something that attempts to create the semblance of real experience or that models reality. Such virtual reality works representationally and referentially. There is an attempt to match experience with a series of representations, to copy the shapes of external realities, and to make participants live these copies as if they are real or actual. Such processes bear no connection to the kind of virtuality that the Suniyama constitutes, which is its own reality.[59]

There might appear to be a similarity between virtual reality machines and the Suniyama in the sense, for example, that in both the orientation and motility of the body is engaged in generating shifts and changes in the parameters of the reality in which they are engaged. However, in the case of the virtual reality machine, what can be generated is constrained to the capacity of the machine. The ability of the human being to create realities and to alter them is always machine linked. In effect, the realities that may be invented are a function of machine adjustments and responses. The Suniyama, however, is nothing like a machine. It is not a form that responds and adjusts to the activities of the human beings locked within its frame. Most important, the generative practices of exorcists, and especially their patients, are capable of creating realities that extend well beyond the Suniyama, realities that burst through the bonds, boundaries, and other limitations and constraints of the rite.[60]

The Suniyama's process is not confined to the production of realities within its space-time parameters. It is ultimately oriented to generating the capacity of victims to generate in actuality and not in virtuality. Thus, the rite immerses victims in a welter of activities that instruct patients and engage them in action by means of which they can regenerate themselves and participate in the routine generation of relations in the world. The activities of the rite open up the perceptual faculties of victims, which are keys to the intentional direction of victims into the world and the full elaboration of consciousness. The consciousness of the patient developed through the activities in virtual space-time burst the confines of the rite and fling the patient back into actuality. The virtuality of rite, at least with reference to the Suniyama, does not exist to represent or generate representations that are to be experienced as actual (as in virtual reality) but to engender activities essential to the participation of the patient in actuality.

My stress on the virtuality of the Suniyama is to highlight it as a site for the production of generative practice which does not subordinate the process of the rite to the function of representation and the reflection on representation.

Conclusion: The Suniyama and the Enormity of Sorcery

Overall, the Suniyama addresses sorcery as nothing less than a total outrage against human existence that is founded in the circumstances of existence itself. The depth and ground of the horror of sorcery, what sorcery is the expression of, is demonstrated through the reconstructive dynamics of the ritual practice: the reharmonization of the body, the reinstitution of consciousness, the return to speech silenced in the attack and terror of sorcery, the breaking free of mind/body from the constraining bonds of sorcery, the return of world-making potency, and so forth. The Suniyama in its sheer primordial expanse and its placing of the victim at the world center, at the vortex of the regeneration of social and political order, makes the enormity of sorcery clear.

It is an enormity the potential dimensions of which dwarf and surpass terms such as alienation, misfortune, and suffering, which in the context of this magnificent rite appear trivial. Alternatively, the structures of practice of the Suniyama expose the depth of experience that is the excess, indeed the meaning, that such terms may reach toward but can never capture.

The Suniyama, in my view, is a rite that can embrace all manner of existential crises that human beings may encounter as a result of their actions in the world and of the actions of others toward them: what, after all, is the overburdening sense of the words translated as sorcery in Sri Lanka and in most other parts of the world. The Suniyama can gather within its compass the depth and uniqueness of individual experience grasped as sorcery. The forces it enlivens are simultaneously focused on the victim whose manifold specificities of experience, many dimly present in awareness, discover and may expand their form and depth in the cosmic immensity of the Suniyama. The Suniyama is a rite that individualizes as it universalizes, and experientializes as it structures.

Suniyama performances represent aspects of the social and political situation of the sorcery victim within local communities. The rites express the potential power of re-presentation. That is, their performance intervenes in the definition of social and political relations centering on specific households—for example, when household members have newfound wealth. Such functions of the rite are important, especially because of the nature of the problematics to which the Suniyama directly attends. It addresses as central issues the fundamental dilemmas of existence and suffering whether this is born of lack or of success. The Suniyama is concerned with the problematics of the materiality of power and of wealth. Few other rites engage so directly the predicaments of daily life and make socioeconomic and political forces, and the anxieties of human beings at their vortex, so focal. The potentiality of the Suniyama as a representation of social and political processes, even redefining them, at least as these relate to patient and household, cannot be overemphasized. The Suniyama is directed to the lived-in world. This is its impetus, even in aspects of its performance that appear to be apart from the life world or even to transcend it. I stress the repeated occurrence of actions integral to the rite that tie it to the habitual world of the house and the activities that are vital in the house and emanate from it. The fact that the Suniyama is a rite founded in the midst of social actualities and gives them expression makes the Suniyama as a practice quintessentially concerned with the dynamics of psychological and social construction whereby human beings make their realities and pursue their lives.

I cannot overstress the human-centeredness of the Suniyama. Not only is it an antisorcery rite but it is ultimately an antiritual. This is because it aims to refound human being as a being that in its motioning toward the horizons of its own existence brings the worlds of its life and sustenance into existence. The Suniyama demonstrates that human beings make their worlds. Although human beings are formed in the motion of the cosmos, they are not simply determined but are themselves constitutive and determining, embodying the powers of the gods rather than being in subjection to them. The Buddha is above all a human being, and his knowledge encompasses the universe and defines its process. Something of this understanding is apparent in the Suniyama when patients burst their bonds in the *valvalalu* and in the destruction of the Mahasammata palace. Here there are strong implications of the reemergence of human being, of a being who can exist in the world and pursue a path regardless of the furies that rage and tear about. Furthermore, the human being does this even without the edifices of rite that have hitherto enclosed and protected, edifices out of whose rubble a human being emerges renewed in potency.

The Suniyama set in the world and directed to the conditionality of human being is far more than a representation, an expression, or even an idiom of personal anxieties and social and political processes. It is centrally concerned with the practices through which human beings form and reform themselves within the life world. In the Suniyama, *adura*s systematically engage victims in the foundational practices that are embedded, and therefore hidden, within the surface relations of ongoing social and political life and which are vital in their generation. The Suniyama immerses victims within the activity of constructional practice that flows in consciousness and is manifest as the constitutive sociality of human beings integral to the realization of their diverse and continually changing life projects.

The major images and metaphors of sorcery that flood the Suniyama and other rites are those of barriers and blocks to the extension of human beings toward the horizons of their existence. These barriers, part of the existential realities of human beings, impede the life chances of victims, confining them and destroying their consciousness, indeed, ultimately attacking it at root. The antidote that the practitioners of the Suniyama provide is to plunge the victim into the wellsprings of consciousness and the vitalizing practices of consciousness by means of which the victim can return to the world. The relations of human beings with others are integral to their extension into the world. The Suniyama engages in practices that not only remove obstacles to the development of relations but are foundational in the very formation of relations.

This is the central feature of the Suniyama with which I am now concerned. The Suniyama is preeminently a structuring of practices foundational not just to the life world of human beings but to their sociality within it: to the life-seeking and sustaining capacity of human beings to constitute or form their social and political relations and thus to achieve the potential of the full growth of their consciousness as human beings. Such sociality has the power to create relations where there were none and to generate them even against the forces of human action that throw up barriers to their formation. This is the creative and productive dimension of human action that is an incorporating, including, internalizing process—all key metaphors of the Suniyama counteracting sorcery. The Suniyama, as an organization of the practices of sociality, manifests an indigenous sociology, which, however, does not engage in a rupturing of human being and its formations of existence along the lines of so much academic sociology in the West. I refer, for example, to the Durkheim heritage, which posits a separation of the individual from society and posits either the priority of society or else the priority of the individual. The sociology of the Suniyama is a major focus of the following chapter, which concentrates on the Suniyama as a sacrifice.

6

Sorcery and Sacrifice
Victims, Gifts, and Violence

The noble king Vessantara, after so much giving, at the disso-
lution of his body, full of wisdom, was reborn in heaven.
From *The Perfect Generosity of Prince Vessantara,* Gombrich and Cone 1977

THE SUNIYAMA IS A SACRIFICE that restores social agency to the
victim. The victim becomes a world maker who simultaneously engages
in acts of self-recreation and is endowed with the capacity to constitute
and reshape relationships in the world as these affect the victim's life
chances. In this process, the victim shifts from being the subject of sacrifice to being the sacrificer. It is as a sacrificer that the victim is empowered
with social agency and the potency of sociality.

Sociality, in my usage, is immanent in human existence or in the fact
that one human being always presupposes the existence of others and in
one way or another is already oriented to them and vice versa. Human
beings realize their sociality or what is already immanent in their existence in their capacity to act and to effect their life course through activities involving their interrelation with other human beings. This is the
sense in which I also use the terms *agent* and *agency,* which focus not
on human beings alone (or the individual as independently constructive
or constitutive) but as always rooted in-the-world which is inhabited by
others toward whom they are thrown and mutually oriented or acting.
Human beings as agents simultaneously bring forth their realities and are
brought forth by them. The regeneration of human beings in this sense
is at the heart of my concentration on sacrifice—the reconstitution of
human beings as beings capable of manifesting a sociality that is immanent in existence.

The main myths of the Suniyama (e.g., the myths of Mahasammata-Manikpala, Vijaya-Kuveni) underline the Suniyama as a rite of cosmogonic and ontogenetic proportions in which human beings become the agents of the political and social realities in which they are potentially constitutive as well as simultaneously constituted. This relates to the strong sense in which I use the word *sociality*—that is, the capacity to form and participate in the processes of world construction and even against the forces that are integral to such processes but may blast apart both the constructions of the world and the human beings within it. The ritual dynamics that produce this sociality are the chief concern of this chapter.

The Suniyama is obviously a powerful rite of physical, psychological, and social renewal. It is more than equal to the radical unmaking of human being of the sorcerer, whose extreme violence destroys social relations, sets up barriers to their creation, and reaches into the body and mind of his victims, dissolving and fragmenting them in dis-ease. The sorcerer attacks the ground of Being and of the social formations of human beings. Thus, the Suniyama must repeat the primordial acts of re-origination in which the orders of body and world, a world in which human beings are at the vital center, can be restored. In doing this the Suniyama engages processes that develop and make whole once more fragmented human beings and transform them into world makers, or beings of sociality.

I expand the analysis of the preceding chapter and explore a number of other themes. Both sacrifice and sorcery are violent acts. I discuss this violence in the context of the Suniyama as above all a Buddhist rite that aims to overcome violence and its repetition. I discuss the relation between sacrifice, sorcery, and violence and their relevance for understanding wider processes of political violence in Sri Lanka and elsewhere.

More specifically, I examine the constitutive dynamics of sacrifice involving acts of classification, differentiation, and giving (acts that often have a violent symbolic form or have violent effects). These, especially the gift and reciprocity, have consumed some anthropological interest as being at the center of social formation. The Suniyama can be seen as a practical discourse on the constitutive and transformational powers of the gift. Obviously, this expresses the Suniyama's historical/cultural context and its Buddhist ideological direction. Nonetheless, this has import beyond a relativized world of its production. I place the Suniyama into a dialogue with a philosophy and a social science that might otherwise impose their models and understandings on the dynamics of the Suniyama.

In other words, the Suniyama and its practitioners have authority not just for the actualities in which they work but also for a more general understanding of the practices of human beings. The Suniyama, in its overcoming of the sorcerer, addresses the problem of human intentionality and lays out the dynamics of its structure and the process of its socially generative transformation. The broad implication of my discussion of this practice is that it has general significance for the understanding of human action.

Sacrifice as the Total Act

There are numerous approaches to sacrifice, and these have been well surveyed (e.g., de Heusch 1985; Valeri 1985). My own position is, like that of most ethnographers, highly influenced by the materials of which I have firsthand experience. Therefore, at some risk, I regard sacrifice as a total act of (re)origination by means of which human beings radically reconstitute, remake, or maintain their life and its circumstances. It is in my view *the* total act which condenses or has immanent within it qua act the generative processes constitutive of human beings and their life worlds. The diverse pragmatic functions of particular sacrificial action (to heal, to win favor, to achieve protection, etc.) are possible only because of the foundational dynamic of sacrifice as a total act of (re)constitution or (re)origination.

Theories of sacrifice have concentrated on one or more central features. Thus, sacrifice has been discussed as focused around destruction or violence, as articulating the dynamics of the gift, as communion, communication, cooking, and so forth. One or another basic dimension of sacrifice is stressed, depending on the cultural or religious standpoint of the theorist. Anthropologists widely agree that a general theory of sacrifice is impossible (see Lévi-Strauss 1962; de Heusch 1985, Bloch 1992). This is also my own opinion. However, such theoretical concerns have left their legacy in a compartmentalization of the phenomenon by anthropologists and other scholars and its reduction to one or another key elements. Such a reduction obscures its force as a total act and the import of the dynamic complexity of its process, often condensed into overt acts of great and sometimes dramatic simplicity.

Hubert and Mauss ([1899] 1964), in their classic study, at least implicitly recognized sacrifice as a total phenomenon. This notion, of course, was developed more strongly later by Mauss ([1950] 1990) in his highly influential study *The Gift*. I follow their lead but not their execution. Hubert and Mauss, in the context of a Durkheimian sociology, are eager to demonstrate sacrifice as a social fact. The person for whom the sacrifice is performed enters the domain of the Sacred and then rejoins the Profane world which is separate from the Sacred, though conditioned by it. Effectively, the Sacred is the potency of Society.

Their sacred-profane dichotomy is crucial in the general model they develop of the sacrificial process. This is similar to that worked out by Van Gennep ([1909] 1960) for life crisis rituals in general, and elaborated by Victor Turner (1967, 1969). These later approaches may be seen to be commanded by a similar dualism, although they develop an indeterminate middle term, the *marginal,* or *liminal.* Broadly, the marginality Van Gennep and Turner describe shares characteristics with both the sacred and the profane that Hubert and Mauss keep separate. The importance of Turner's development of Van Gennep is that he introduces a greater dynamics into the analysis of rite, a sense of human agency, and a far less determined view of the sociality of human beings.[1] He reveals the fundamental stasis of the Hubert and Mauss approach. The dualism of their perspective persists in recent theories of rite. Bloch (1992), for example, engages it but refuses the separation of Hubert and Mauss, arguing for a continuity and expansion of the dynamic of the sacred (which Bloch sees as transcendent or above the mundane) as the violence of the political world.

In this discussion of the Suniyama I am not concerned with applying anthropological dualist or triadic models of the ritual process. The sacrificial process of the rite is a continuous one, oriented in a singular direction and toward the restitution of the social, or social agency. The ultimate sacred space of the Suniyama, the *atamagala,* is reached through a cosmogenic and socially regenerative process. It is the culmination of the process, its totalization, end, and beginning, which conditions and in fact sets the whole regenerative process in motion. The victims are not separated from society, put in the realm of the sacred, and then put back in the profane world. They are from the start of the rite put in motion with the process of the totality and are recentered in the world, the significance of the events of the *atamagala.*

The process of the Suniyama is never a totalization of society as the sacred apart from and determining of the individual, as it might appear in a Durkheimian representation. The Mahasammata palace is not a representation of society. Instead, it is an image, a materialization of the forces or ordering principles behind social and political life that engender and are simultaneously engendered by victims in their progress: forces integral to the ordering of their bodymind, their regaining of agency, and their restructuring of their world.

Hubert and Mauss are criticized both for their Judeo-Christian bias (which is integral to the sacred-profane dichotomy) and for the distortions in their understanding because of their reliance on Brahmanic materials (de Heusch 1985; Detienne and Vernant 1979). De Heusch (1985) is among the more severe in his attacks along these lines. He asserts that the African sacrifices he examines are more concerned with *having* than with Brahmanic Being. Indeed, he suggests, using the work of scholars of Indian sacrifice, a notion of sacrifice as cooking rather than as being might be more appropriate—sacrifice as a cuisine. Here I have some sympathy with Hubert and Mauss, and this is not because the Buddhist materials with which I deal are related to Vedic sacrifice.

In my view, sacrifice must always be about Being. This is so because sacrifice is first and foremost action. It is a primordial act, an act of instantiation par excellence, and in this sense a total act. The ethnography of sacrifice everywhere seems to point to this fact through the cosmogonic significance which generally attaches to sacrifice. To act is to be, and it is this being of the act which the whole process of ritual understood as sacrifice unfolds. This is preeminently the force of sacrifice as constitutive both of the being of the person at the center of the sacrifice and of the person as himself or herself a being who constitutes. This is what I mean by sacrifice as the total act.

More broadly—and I think this is a reason why Hubert and Mauss were drawn to the study of sacrifice—I think it is possible to regard sacrifice as the core process in most forms that anthropologists study as ritual. This might explain the ubiquity of sacrifice, the reason why such action crops up in numerous areas where human beings encounter challenges to their existence. It may also explain the great variety of forms that sacrificial action takes even within the one culture-historical context. Sinhalese exorcists consider the Suniyama one of the most important of the rites they perform. Those who are specialists in it are regarded as of high status. This, I suggest, is not only because of the Suniyama's major Buddhist themes but also because of its thorough sacrificial structure.

Sacrifice and the Violence of the Total Act

Hubert and Mauss, along with most students of sacrifice after them, take the destruction and violence of sacrifice, often but not necessarily acts of killing, to be definitive of sacrifice. In my view, the violence of sacrifice underlines sacrifice as the total act: an act that can have immanent within its process the entire potential and process of human being. The violence of sacrifice is consistent with its primordialism, with a (re)originating act that condenses the total potential of all action. Such an act is potent with ambiguity which is manifested in the turbulence of violence. Violence is quintessentially the form of totalizing action, the explosion of possibility and of possibility exploded.

The act of killing *in sacrifice* is a compression of the totalizing potentiality of action as action. It is filled with the ambiguity of potency. I stress the process and not the finality of killing. The action itself is a conjunction of the force of life with death, and of the separation of life from death. This conjunctive/disjunctive energy is the vital force of sacrifice. The motion toward killing is the conjunction, a violent conjunction, of death with life. The moment of killing, the peak of the death-life conjunction, is also the radical separation, the disjunction of life from death. These forces or energies are expressed in violent forms. The physical act of killing is just one form, perhaps the most common, and the act that most frequently comes to mind when the topic of sacrifice is discussed.

Physical killing is not necessary for a sacrifice to be a sacrifice or for such themes to be made apparent in practice. This is the case even in societies where the act of killing is valued. Consider the classic examples of vegetable sacrifice among Nuer and Dinka (Evans-Pritchard 1956; Lienhardt 1962). Buddhist societies for whom killing is radically disvalued make the point explicit but nonetheless engage in complex substitutions. The ash pumpkin is a substitute for a human in the Suniyama. The cock (rarely killed) is a blood sacrifice and a human surrogate in the Suniyama and other exorcism rites. Such substitution or the suppression of actual killing within the rite places the accent on the dynamic present in the sacrificial act of killing obscured by the fact of killing.

The violence of sacrifice is emergent in the (re)originating conjunctive/disjunctive dynamic of the action. Violence is the totality of such an act. In the cultural context of the Suniyama (but extendable to others, though doubtless with different cultural configuration), it is the force of the fusion of death and life and of their rupture, the severance of life from death: the release of life from death's grip (or containment) and the creation, through radical disjunction, of a life space. In other words, the action of reorigination is productive of totalizing forces whose violent shape is the product of their tension.

Violence is integral to both structuring and destructuring dynamics. This, I think, is the strong implication of Sinhalese sorcery myths. The Mahasammata-Manikpala myth identifies the most dreadful destructuring violence of sorcery as arising at the instant of the constitution of the sociopolitical order (Chapter 4). This is a theme repeated in the Vijaya-Kuveni story and other myths of sorcery and social origination. The constitution of the sociopolitical order involves a rupture in the totality of existence, and violence is refigured as the oppositional force of interiority (the sociopolitical order) and of what is exterior to it. The violence of exteriority is a refusal of the externalizing act of social creation. This generative act is also in a broad sense an act of rupture. Suniyam (rather than Vasavarti) is the divided form of exteriorizing and interiorizing forces, an aspect to which the sorcery shrines give vivid expression (see Chapter 7). The Suniyama rite demonstrates the violent force in both structuring and deconstructing processes.

Sacrifice and violence is an issue of debate among scholars: a debate that often takes an essentialist or functionalist turn. More specifically, the problem of violence, and of killing in particular, in sacrifice is frequently an agonistic dimension for those peoples who engage in sacrificial practice. It is an aspect that is relevant, as might be expected, in the anti-sorcery sacrifices of Sinhalese Buddhists. This problematic—a profound ethical and moral issue in Sinhala Buddhist practice—is at the center of the Suniyama's dynamic. The Suniyama is a nonviolent, antiblood sacrifice. It affirms life and is centered on the paradox present in any practice, even its own, that must take life in order to secure life. The difference of the Suniyama from violent blood sacrifice, the Suniyama's active opposition to violence that is the practical discourse of the Suniyama, gives the rite a key significance in a discussion of violence and sacrifice. This significance, moreover, relates to the Suniyama's disclosure of the life-constitutive forces of sacrifice that may be otherwise embedded and hidden in sacrifices that appear to derive their force from the violence of killing in itself.

Victim, Violence, and Intentionality

Victims of sorcery are already the centers of violent action. The extreme of this action effectively positions them as the victims of a blood sacrifice. Thus, in the Suniyama (and in other exorcisms that involve the dynamic of sacrifice), a bound cock, a two-legged creature of domestic space, is kept near victims as their blood surrogate. The Suniyama is practically oriented to overcome such death-dealing violence. The discourse of the Suniyama emphasizes that victims of sorcery are in the determined position of those victims of sacrifice who against their will are exposed to the destructive and ultimately annihilating forces of the action of other human beings. Therefore, the Suniyama is directed to reveal the hidden sacrificial violence as the condition of sorcery victims and to convert such violence into a willing sacrifice that is life-giving and -releasing.

The Suniyama expresses other key dimensions of sorcery that may be at the center of victim outrage: its violation of body and world, and that the forces of sorcery are integral to the activities, relations, and intimacies of the life space. Manikpala raped is one expression and Vasavarti Maraya, another. Vasavarti (world poisoner, world destroyer, harbinger of death) is commonly associated with Devadatta, a kinsman of the Buddha who deserts the Buddha's Path. Not only is he a supreme figuration of all that undermines the Buddha's truth, but he is also an image of the life world in its actions and intimacies turned against itself.

The symbolism of the Suniyama is filled with notions that sorcery victims are subject to alienating and externalizing forces emanating from within the field of their lived-in realities. The externalizing energies of sorcery become radically interior. They drive into the physical being of victims, striking at all the major points of articulation within the body, and flow through all the veins, the routes of the body. This is what the mantras and songs of the Suniyama express (see Chapter 5). The boundaries, lines, or striations between outer and inner, upper and lower, become dangerously blurred and destructively breached. Victims present as their own sorcery experiences a violence that courses along the lines of their social affiliations and associations. The vital nodal points of their networks of kinship and friendship are attacked (see Chapters 7 and 8).

The Suniyama and other rites and experiences of sorcery indicate the transmutation of a life world into a space of dangerous and threatening realities and ultimately into a space of death. The attachments and diverse features of ordinary life, in the experience of sorcery, become the instrumentalities of destruction and intense suffering. The ways and means by which human beings live and make their lives endanger them and threaten to extinguish them. Even the victim and the victim's victimness become an agent and agency of the destruction of the victim's life condition. A certain affinity between sorcery and torture expands these points.

The horror of torture, like that of sorcery, is the turning against the victim, as the instruments of pain, of all that is familiar, pleasurable, safe, and secure (Scarry 1985). A bed, a table, a chair, and so forth, become the tools of the torturer. Likewise, in sorcery a victim's house is the object of attack. Considerable ritual precautions in Sri Lanka, and elsewhere where sorcery is rife, are taken to guard houses against sorcery. In the accounts of victims, objects of pleasure and success—a television, a radio—become the focus of envious sorcery, and thus become the weapons of pain.

Moreover, in both torture and sorcery, rationality and reason are engaged to the service of painful destruction. Scarry (1985) elaborates this point brilliantly for torture in the context of a criticism of those who effectively sanitize torture by regarding it as an information-gathering technique. This view, she says, extends a rationality or reason to torture that has, in fact, no other reason than the horrific demonstration of the unreason of power via the mutilation of human bodies (see Chapter 8). The torturer's insistence on information, indeed an unquenchable thirst for it, is little else than the engagement of information as a rationale for the infliction of more and more pain, the torturer's prime interest.[2] A similar observation may be made regarding the absurd use of torture by the witch hunters of European history.

In Sri Lanka victims of sorcery are often obsessed with the search for the rationale behind their ensorcellment, and similar reactions are recorded by ethnographers for other societies. There can be sound foundation for their concern, but as with the torturer, their search for reason becomes an instrument in the expansion of their anguish as victims of sorcery.

Scarry (1983; also Saez 1992) describes how the torturer's lust for information transforms the relation of victims to their worlds. The tortured and their erstwhile life worlds are brought into a mutual relation of hostility. Forced to inform on friends and acquaintances, the tortured can come to see these persons as agents of their pain. Simultaneously, the friends and acquaintances of the victim can see the victim as existing in a threatening and destructive relation toward them.

Victims of sorcery are similarly oriented to their daily realities as the source of their pain. In Sri Lanka some people stay away from antisorcery rites, especially if the victim is expected to enter a trance, because they fear being named as attackers. There is a tendency, widely recorded in ethnography, for those who are victims of sorcery to blame those who stand in a relation of real or potential conflict and competition with them. Victims of sorcery (and possibly victims more generally) are a double sign of destruction (passive and active). They express the ruinous and ultimately annihilating relation of their worlds to them. However, they also refract such destruction back upon their realities. Sorcery victims themselves become agents for the perpetration of destruction. This is not simply a fact of their reaction against attack but integral to their condition as sorcery victims.

Other parallels may be drawn between torture as discussed by Scarry and sorcery. The bodies of victims are breached and determined by forces coming from outside themselves. Their pain drives against consciousness and the capacity of victims to extend themselves into the world of ordinary activity (see Chapter 7). In torture, speech is used to drive speech from the body of the tortured and ultimately to exhaust or prevent the ability to speak. So too, the words and speech of sorcery aim to silence its victims (see Favret-Saada 1977).

My comparison of sorcery and torture stresses the dehumanizing potential of sorcery attack. The Suniyama represents sorcery victims as returned to a primordial condition. At the start of the rite they are located at the margins of Mahasammata's cosmic city. With the sorcerer's viper at their genitals, victims represent a peak of human suffering. They may be described as a dense and ambiguous fusion of the forces of life and death, each one fueling the other. Oriented toward the life source, the *atamagala* and the Mahasammata palace, victims are yet at the perimeter of their life-giving compass, externalized and withdrawn. They are figuratively at that moment in space/time in the cosmic formation of human being that is before the efflorescence of consciousness and knowledge, which are the potencies of social creation and forces for the overpowering of ignorance and suffering. Still overridingly determined and in the space of death, victims are poised, nonetheless, to replay processes of cosmic creation in which they regain their humanity. Thus, the Suniyama sacrifice is a powerful discourse on the construction of human agency and sociality, on how, in the context of the sorcerer's dehumanizing action, human beings can regain their capacity to act, to form the order of their life world, and to follow a life course untroubled and unimpeded by the actions of others.

Critical in the Suniyama's sacrificial process is the restoration of victims to full consciousness, which is fundamental to their sociality, and the separation from forces that destroy consciousness. The Suniyama is conceived of as comprising sixteen (*solos tindua*) main sacrificial events that aim to restore victims to an independent capacity to participate actively in their life course, and without encountering barriers to it (see Chapter 5). I focus on one aspect of the formation of a complete or full consciousness with reference to what I call a dynamic of intentionality. This is most explicit in the Suniyama's main sacrificial events, starting with the *hatadiya*.

By intentionality I refer merely to the fact that human beings are directed out into the world and to the horizons of their existence. Human beings exist immediately in the context of other human beings and are intentionally embroiled with them. My use of the term *intentionality* does not include notions of motivation, reason, or value. These extend from the ground of human intentionality. For example, motivations emerge within the intentional trajectory and become vital in focusing its aim. This is an understanding that could be used to interpret some of the events in the sorcery myths. In one, Suniyam flying overhead espies a beautiful princess (Manikpala), and intentionally aware of her presence, then desires her and lusts to possess her: the motivation of the sorcerer to possess forms on the basis of a directedness, an intentionality that is already there.

Following Husserl and others, I see intentionality as fundamental to consciousness. Consciousness is not something in itself but emerges *in relation to something.* Almost all activity is awareness or consciousness in this sense, but the sorcerer's attack can virtually freeze such intentional consciousness, as the event of the *valvalalu* indicates (see Chapter 5; also Chapter 7). The Suniyama, however, aims to bring victims into full world-making potency, to manifest that creative social constructive capacity symbolized by Mahasammata's life-ordering gesture.

The *hatadiya* centers on the fundamental paradox of intentionality, that it is ambivalent: on the one hand, potentially destructive of consciousness, and on the other hand, germinal of consciousness and vital in the forming of the protective orders of lived reality. From the standpoint of the Buddhism of the Suniyama, intentionality can give rise to desire and greed that, like Vasavarti, overcome consciousness and are destructive of relations and disruptive of harmony. Varsavarti can reproduce only himself, and the relational burst of his leap to Manikpala cannot develop and flower as does the relational harmony of Mahasammata and Manikpala.

The process of the *hatadiya* is to eliminate the paradox of intentionality, to erase the line of the sorcerer's serpent, and to subdue and exclude its destructive possibility. This is achieved through the constant recitation of the Buddha's virtues, which both ethicizes the intentional path of the patient into the Mahasammata palace and is a force of the victim's motion, enabling the victim to cross the sorcerer's barriers.

Overall, the dynamic of the *hatadiya* is a progressive and regenerative dividing out and externalization of the intentional potencies of the sorcerer from their overriding and consciousness-destroying fusion with the patient. This dynamic is an equivalent of the restorative sacrificial rupture that blood sacrifice otherwise effects. Moreover, it converts or transmutes human destructive, fragmenting, and ahierarchical energy (sorcery or Suniyam malevolent) into generative and hierarchializing force (the representation of Suniyam at the apex of the palace, Suniyam protective).

Although the *hatadiya* may seem to fit Husserl's notion of intentional consciousness, the *hatadiya* and later events diverge significantly from key aspects of this perspective. Among the strongest criticisms by other philosophers of Husserl's concept of intentionality (not least Heidegger,

who barely mentions the concept, without necessarily completely abandoning it; see Hall 1993) is that he sustains a subject/object dualism of
a Kantian kind. Husserl did aim at a nondualism treating subject and
object as coextensive and arising from each other. But this approach
maintains a subject/object dialectic common in various forms in Western
philosophy and social science. Ultimately, Husserl does not escape a reductive subjectivism, and he even entrenches it in a transcendentalism
(e.g., his concept of the transcendental ego, a kind of Freudian egoic force
within, which is made into an externalized reflected objectivated force—
a cogito—through which the subjectivity of the subject is generated; see
Husserl 1952; Ricoeur 1967:220–233). Husserl's subjectivism and transcendentalism are seen by his critics to defeat his aim to understand the
phenomena of human creation through their grounding in the lived-in
world. This informs a major critique by Sartre (1962, 1976) and relates
to Heidegger's (e.g., 1962, 1977) phenomenological redirection, away
from a focus on reflection and representation, to practice.

The *hatadiya* and the events that follow can in no way be reduced to
the terms of the kinds of Western philosophical debate to which I have
referred. The Suniyama and its world of practices are their own authority and have their own authenticity and truth regardless of how I might
explore them through concepts and concerns far away from the matters at hand of exorcists, victims, and their kin. Such philosophical debates as I have intimated, however, point up some of the significance
of what I see to be the practical argument of the events of Suniyama
sacrifice.

The power behind the motioning of the victim toward the palace is
in the orientation of the patient toward the palace, a representation of
Mahasammata's world order and of the force of the Buddha idea that
conditions Mahasammata's cosmic structure. The orientation is motioning as a combination of the patient's own forward move and the powerful attraction of the ordering energies that the palace presents. The palace is an object that may be seen to pull the patient toward it and through
which the subjectivity of the patient is restored. The palace, of course, is
a representation of the sociopolitical cosmic order established by human
beings when they achieved a constituting consciousness by which they
recognized the orders of life around them. In this recognition they imagined and created their own political and cosmic ordering into existence
(see Chapter 3 and Chapter 5). The suffering of human beings impels
them toward the collective choice for society, but the object of the order
to which they are directed is not an externalization of that which is within
but is in the worlds outside and surrounding human beings. The invention

of society by human beings is a copy (see Chapter 3) of an idea already present to human beings in the hierarchical natural orderings of other forms of life—creatures of the sea, land, and air. The idea is foundationally grounded in being-in-the-world and informs Mahasammata's creation of the original human society. The orientation of the patient toward Mahasammata's construction indicates the power of the idea and the imaginary in drawing the patient into action from out of the paralyzing condition of sorcery. Through the power of the idea, it may be said, patients become committed to their own recreation and the reinvention of the order of life.

However, the idea of the palace is not necessarily a fully formed or cognized meaningful reflection before patients at the start of their journey. In the discourse of the Suniyama, it is more an awareness in a field of developing consciousness of which patients are the center. The full meaning of the idea of the palace is developed in the course of the patient's motioning along the lotus path. The potency of the idea develops through the action of patients as they progress.

The *hatadiya* is in effect directed to the dynamic within the space/time of the intentional relation. It is not expressing a subject/object dialectic of a Husserlian kind but rather focuses on the intentional dynamic itself, a dynamic of practice. What is subject and object and their complexities are emergent from practice and achieve their completeness simultaneously and in conjunction. The potency of the subject and of the object are produced in their union, with the patient's entry into the palace. The idea arises from the ground and achieves its full meaningful objectification as an idea of consciousness when the patient by means of practice enters the *atamagala* (see Chapter 5).

Rawson describes the slowness of the process of the creation of being into consciousness in some tantric rites as "the boredom of the immensity" (1973:141)—a boredom that some Sinhalese certainly feel. It is during the performance of the *hatadiya* that many people, including some of the exorcists, leave to sleep. The slowness is equal to the cosmic scale of the *hatadiya* in its rebuilding of victim consciousness so that they are imbued once again with the potencies of sociality, of social restoration both of themselves and of the orders of their lived-in realities.

I think the Suniyama, as the *hatadiya* demonstrates, escapes an idealism of the kind that Western philosophers and social scientists complain about in their own worlds. The Buddha ideal and the ideal order that the palace images and comes to express through the action of the patient are not abstract, above or external to practice. The potency of the ideas is thoroughly embedded in the activities, in the doing, and is remanufactured through the patient practice under exorcist instruction. The idea grows in the body of patients in their progress, which is effected by their reacquiring the skills vital to life and the reinvention of its orders. The idea is embodied and produced through practice, which is right ethical and moral practice in the Buddhism of the Suniyama.

The idea not only emerges or is made absolutely manifest through practice (culminating in the in-dwelling of the patient in the space of the *atamagala*) but effectively dissolves back into the life world upon the completion of the patient's restoration to consciousness. Thus, a major significance of the event of the *chedana vidiya* is when the palace enclosing the patient is hacked down by the now impotent sorcerer. This event occurs after the event of the *valvalalu* when the patient, once more a creative body of consciousness, bursts the confining and restrictive bonds of the sorcerer and is reborn as a constitutive agent in the world.

The bits and pieces of the palace are rapidly cleared away and the place where it stood is swept clean. I described this as a removal of the sorcerer's pollution, which clings to the fragments. This event may also be seen as a clearing, in a Heideggerian sense, a reopening and reextension of patients into the world in which they are now reconstituted and reconstituting beings with all the potency of the world-making, world-renewing sacrificer.

My analysis of the Suniyama sacrifice suggests an understanding different from Hubert and Mauss's view of sacrifice. Their notions of the sacred and the profane express the dualism of a Western idealism. The events of the *hatadiya* and the progress into the palace are not a removal from the everyday world and the entry into space apart from it. Rather, they are a motioning into the vortex of the forces that are at the center of lived-in realities and at the heart of regenerative dynamics. To enter the palace is to regain the world and in effect to reinstitute its everydayness (an aspect of the events of the *vadiga patuna*). Life and the potency of human consciousness repel the forces of suffering and death.

The philosopher Searle has asserted: "Language is derived from Intentionality and not conversely. The direction of pedagogy is to explain Intentionality in terms of language; the direction of logical analysis is to explain language in terms of Intentionality" (Searle 1983, 5). Exorcists are not interested in explanations of the academic kind, but their practice indicates a similar claim. The intentional trajectory of the *hatadiya* is explicitly directed to the restoration to speech of the victim silenced by the sorcerer's attack. Furthermore, exorcists introduce their patients into the very dynamics of the intentional process from which a consciousness-developing speech is produced.

Sacrifice, the Gift, and the Dynamics of Totality

The sacrifice of the Suniyama is a gift or achieves its force under the total sign of the gift. It is a *total prestation,* as I have already suggested, in the sense discussed by Mauss. Through the acts of giving the differentiated totality of existence and its hierarchical unity are symbolized and formed. The full potentiality of the gift is unfolded in the Suniyama: the gift as poisonous, as negating and separating, and as constitutive of relations and of life within the space of these relations. The Suniyama develops its force through the material/immaterial qualities of the gift, the gift as something consumable and also beyond consumption. The Suniyama centers much of its process around the food of the gift. But the quality of the gift, of the *spirit,* or what I will discuss as the *givenness* of the gift, infuses much else of the Suniyama. The music, song, dance, and drama are gifts and engage the potency of the gift.

The sacrificial destruction of gifts and offerings in the rite is fundamental to the generative power of its ritual events. Here is one further significance of the destruction of Mahasammata's palace. The palace is an organization of the hierarchical force of state/society which the victim reaches through the generative force of the gift. It is the form of the total prestation. Its destruction releases the power of the gift. This power is embodied in the patient, who has been made into a willing sacrificial gift. The patient as the power of the gift is filled with the potency to reestablish the action and relations of the social world.

I note a similarity between the destruction of the palace and the institution of the potlatch. The Suniyama is an overt display of wealth, power, and status. The beautiful, glittering, and bounteous splendor of Mahasammata's palace and the space of his city is quite explicitly an expression of this fact. It asserts both the world of Mahasammata and that of the victim and his household as foci of desire. The destruction of the palace signifies the end of desire: victim and household as no longer the object of the sorcerer's envy or jealousy. Moreover, I suggest that the violence of the event—an event simultaneously of death and rebirth—draws some of its intensity from its being a radical dematerialization of the very objectness that is the cause of ruinous desire and interest.

The agon of the destruction might be understood as the killing of what Mauss (the Sanskritist influenced by Brahmanic sacrifice, a practice obviously relevant to the Suniyama) recognized as the interest in the gift. This sacrifice of interest, the source of suffering epitomized by the sorcerer's attack, is conquered by noninterest, nonattachment, and in effect, nonaction (the victim reconstituted in the *atamagala* and in the situation of meditative contemplation)—the qualities of the Buddha to which his path leads. The sorcerer's attack on the palace as a killing of the interest in the gift is a killing of himself.

The Suniyama is a preeminent practice of the gift. It takes the gift and the acts of giving as fundamental in the construction of cosmic and social relations. The victim in the rite is made to live the practice of the gift. The Suniyama might be understood as the *habitus* of the gift (Bourdieu 1977), and the victim is taken through what might be called the exercises (or the discipline) of the gift. Thus, the *doxa,* the routine logics of practice, the taken-for-granted and not consciously reflected-on processes engaged in the daily construction and reconstruction of daily life worlds—life worlds threatened and made acutely problematic by the sorcerer's attack—are revealed and practiced in a context, that of rite, in which their full structuring force is made apparent in and before experience.

The exercises of the gift in the Suniyama are directed to the embodiment of the processes that they reveal. The victim is made into a body of the gift and therefore a source of its regenerate qualities and its structuring potency. One dimension of this is a negation of the alienation of the condition of the ensorcelled. That is, the exteriorization of the sorcery attack is a separation of victims from society in a most radical sense: they are placed outside the machinery of its force. Society becomes an abstraction. Through the Suniyama, the abstract is made concrete and victims are made agents in social life. So reconstituted, victims as bodies of cosmic and social force are able to turn back on the line of their own determination, now as themselves determining.

The practice of the gift is in itself differentiating, classifying, and hierarchializing as well as a process of the formation of relations. Luc de Heusch (1985), who gives primacy to the classifying and structuring process of sacrifice and the gift in sacrifice, has pointed to the banality of so much anthropological analysis of sacrifice which concentrates on sacrifice as mere offering to, or communication with, the gods through acts of killing and the like.

The content and structure of the offerings operate in accordance with the differentiation and hierarchialization of the cosmic and social whole prefigured as the totality of Mahasammata's palace. Different categories of beings are marked out by the kinds of offerings they are given. Thus, the lowest (ghosts, demons) receive fragmented flower petals, roasted grains, curries with meat, and pollutants such as fecal matter and stimulants; the higher gods are given whole flower petals, boiled (often with

milk) rice, uncooked grains, and so forth. Other dimensions of the offerings—dance, music (drumming), smell, verbal invocation, poem, and
song—operate in similar ways (see Kapferer 1983, especially Chapter 5).

I should add that similar processes (that is, of differentiation and hierarchy) that underlie the formation of the cosmic order are also engaged
to social re-formation. The process of cosmic ordering and the formation
of social relations are placed in symbolic alignment, in the context of the
Suniyama and in most other Sinhala ritual events. They exchange meaning. Each carries the import of the other, and both consequently achieve
a heightening of symbolic significance.

The Suniyama is a hive of social activity, and a key aspect of this activity is a reassertion and redefinition of social relations as these center on
the victim and household. This is expressed largely in acts of commensality (as it is at other large exorcisms; see Kapferer 1983). In the course
of the process of the rite, members of the audience are invited inside the
house to eat meals. Those high in status typically receive precedence both
in invitation to eat and in the order of being served. The acts of commensality (in themselves consistent with a dominant theme of generosity) and
the acceptance of the gift of food define social relations. They indicate a
restructuring of victim and household in a set of social relations. The
acceptance of food also is a social recognition that the danger of sorcery
is removed, or is being removed, from the victim and the victim's household.

Through the practice of the gift, victims recenter themselves and their
household in a complex of cosmic and social relations. The *hatadiya* is
the key process of this centering and effects an upsurge of Being through
the transformation of a nondifferentiated totality (*prakriti,* the formless
void or ground of existence) into one of hierarchialized differentiation.
Most vitally, by means of the instrumentality of the gift, victims generate
relations between themselves and other beings of varying quality, distance
(spatiality), and duration (temporality). In the process of giving, the person of the victim is progressively recreated. The person is not prior to
the gift or to the relation but is (re)constituted through giving and the
relation formed.

The connection between sorcerer and victim is a demonic connection.
That is, it is in fact nonrelational. It is a fusion of victim and assailant,
in which the victim has no agency, no capacity for action. Demons (and
Suniyam; see Chapter 3) are forbidden by the Buddha to eat human beings, but this prohibition is a recognition of what the demonic is, a destroyer of relations and a cannibal of persons. Demons and the sorcerer

are absolute beings of consumption. They bloat themselves in the incorporation of all around them. The binding (*valvalalu*) of the victim in the *atamagala* is the totalization of the sorcerer, a covering of the victim in the sorcerer's poison.

Through the gift a fused bond is opened into a relation. The relation becomes a space for action of the victim. It becomes a space in which the terms for the continuity or ending of the relation can be negotiated. Thus the acceptance by the demonic of gifts from their victims in the Suniyama and other exorcisms is an act separating the demonic from the victims. They receive back the pollution of their destructive consumption. They are tricked into this (trapped by their own greed) by the smells, tastes, and beautiful baskets in which their gifts are presented (see Kapferer 1983). Moreover, they are constrained to the magical power of the gift (the baskets are in the form of yantras) which is the constraint of the relation formed. Within this relation, a bargain is struck. The demon will leave the victim, and thus the bond made into a relation is ended or cut.

There is a sociability in the demon-victim connection. This is manifested in the comic dramas of exorcisms, where demons make their masked appearance (see Kapferer 1983). The fragility and speed of the humor in some ways match the changes occurring within the connection and its short-lived nature.

The *vadiga patuna* has much in common with the demon dramas of the other exorcisms. Similarly, it might be seen as a sociability of the victim, or at least of those in the victim's field of social relations (the audience), with the sorcerer (the Brahmins as manifestations of Odissa). In the course of the drama, the making of the sorcerer into a being interior to state/society submits him to its constraint. The closing gifts to the Brahmins (as to demons, at which time they leave the performance arena) end the relation. In fact, they signify the closing of the contract between the victim and the Brahmins to rid the victim of sorcery. By extension, they also indicate the end of the connection between sorcerer and victim by making it into a social relation, one in which the victim now has agency, the power to break the relation as well as to make it, and precisely because it is a social relation in which the victim is in conscious command, one in which the sorcerer is divested of determining power.

This discussion should give a sense of the dynamics of the *hatadiya* and the succeeding events as not only breaking the bond between sorcerer and victim but also as transmuting intentionality into a social relation. The line of the viper is retraced and through the gift becomes the time and space of the total social relation.

The Agony of the Gift: Beyond Reciprocity

The events of the *hatadiya* and the following events support aspects of Mauss's argument concerning the power of the gift but also go beyond it. Mauss has been accused of mysticism in his discussion of the spirit or force of the gift. For some (e.g., Bourdieu 1977), he mystifies society (deifies it in the notion of the total prestation) or capitulates to indigenous magical explanation—in his celebrated example, the logic of the Maori *hau*. Sahlins (1974: 155) comments that if this is so, then the explanation is in fact more French than Maori. That is, Mauss's mysticism has more to do with the mysticism of rationalist economism than with the magicality of the *hau*. In other words, Mauss fails to realize the full import of his own insights in his study of the gift (see also Lévi-Strauss 1966; Dumont 1986). He does not sufficiently underscore either the radical distinction of archaic systems of gift exchange from those of contemporary economic systems or the import of such archaic systems in the general understanding of the role of the gift in the formation and practice of the social relations of human beings.

A difficulty of Mauss's rationalism may be in tying the gift too closely to the problem of reciprocity (see Derrida 1992). Focusing on the issue of reciprocity as the basis of sociality, he is led to assertions of an often quasi-mystical nature. Thus, the gift is returned because of the force of the person in the gift. This has a very Christian flavor to it and further supports similar criticism of Hubert and Mauss's earlier study of sacrifice.

For Mauss, the gift is always an interested gift and oriented toward reciprocity, return, or reward. Reciprocity is the key to the sociality of the gift, its capacity to create relations between individuals—a position that Sahlins notes brings him close to the rationalism of Hobbes. One force that engenders the return is the person in the gift. The confusion, in Mauss's view (also Marx's), that archaic systems make between persons and things is an aspect of the energy or spirit (*hau*) of the gift. In the context of the Suniyama and of sorcery, it is precisely this aspect that might be seen as the negative force of the gift—a fact that Mauss allows. But it is this negative force that the Suniyama is directed to overcome, and the Suniyama engages a rather different logic of the gift as the force of sociality.

The progress of the *hatadiya*, during which the victim is fully (re)centered and repotentiated as an agentive being, radically separates the gift from interest and reciprocity. The victim is oriented toward the pure gift and situated in process toward the Buddha ideal. The pure gift in this

Buddhism of the Suniyama is outside of a notion of material return and is exemplary of nonattachment and non-self-interest. These are the dominant messages of the *jataka* tales of Prince Vessantara and of the hare (*Sasa Jataka*) recounted in the *hatadiya*.

The power of the pure gift, of the Nothingness (infinitude) of the Buddha, encompasses state/society. The orientation of state/society to the pure gift (the Buddha ideal), like that of the victim, is the force which (re)generates them. Insofar as material reward is achieved, this is more along the lines of Sahlins's reinterpretation of the Maori *hau* as yield. The yield of the pure gift (the return to Vessantara of his family and riches, the emblazoning of the hare on the Moon) is a consequence of noninterest and of no concern for reciprocity. Yield, then, is also free from the danger of sorcery or of destruction born of the interested glance.

This extends an import of the young fruits that bedeck the struts of the hut (*maduva*) that covers Mahasammata's palace and the space of his city. More than symbolic of rebirth and renewal, the fruits are the yield of what can be called the pure or perfect gift. This Buddhism of the Suniyama adds to an understanding of why these rituals are often performed by entrepreneurs and traders, apart from their being occasions for the display of wealth and status. In a sense they purify wealth and so protect it from the sorcerer.

The *hatadiya* immerses the victim in the quality of the gift, or what Derrida (1992) identifies as the givenness of the gift. The victim is not a body to be sacrificed but progressively, as he or she advances or transmutes the line of the serpent, the quality of the force that in another system might be released in an act of blood sacrifice. Victims materialize in the upsurge of their being and in the course of their transformational passage the full power of the givenness of the gift. The power of the gift is not an immaterial spirit (Derrida's key point) but a thorough materiality which the *hatadiya* expresses and develops. Indeed, it is the materialization of the power of the gift that is the feature of much ceremonial exchange or ritual-symbolic gift giving as described in ethnography. The givenness or quality of the gift, its power, although it appears intangible, is experienced as a force in the constitution of relations.

This, I suggest, is a general human experience, the factuality of the existence of human being. Although social science analysis focuses on the evidently concrete, the formal and objective properties of exchange systems (the units of exchange, the quantities exchanged, the mechanics of the wider system as a flow of goods and services, and the creation of balances and imbalances in such flow), when applied to the dynamic of social relations such an approach is not the whole story. This is Mauss's argument. The *hatadiya* makes evident the concrete power of the gift in itself, and the victim is made the agent and agency of its dynamics qua dynamics.

Adopting a Heideggerian stance (which might further demonstrate how developments in Western philosophy are prefigured in Asian systems; see Zimmerman 1993; Loy 1988; Parkes 1987), Derrida asserts that any kind of objectification or identification of the gift *as a gift* annuls or negates the gift. Derrida pushes the paradox that Mauss himself recognized about reciprocity (that the return of the gift breaks the bond of the gift) in order to demonstrate that the creative and socially generative force of the gift is not aimed at reciprocity. If anything, it is antagonistic to the return.[3] The most powerful gift is that which projects toward the horizons of existence and beyond, and which transcends an orientation to interest and return. Within the orbit or span of such a gift, all time and space is included, as well as cosmic and social relations of varying temporality and spatiality.

The line of orientation of the *hatadiya* toward the *atamagala,* the place of the totality of Being and of infinitude (of Maha Brahma, Maha Purusa, Buddha) is encompassing and generative of the totality of ordered existence and of the givenness of the gift. Essentially, it has no object (the Buddha as nonexistent cannot recognize the gift as a gift). The subject or the egoity of the victim might also be seen as subsumed in the process. The victim starts the journey of the *hatadiya* in the heat of existence. With the head of the serpent at his genitals, the victim is understood by exorcists to be in the situation of creative-destructive sexual heat (the heat of origination).

This expresses an *I-ness,* perhaps an acuteness of the physical, visceral awareness of being, instantiated at the moment of greatest threat to physical existence, and is ultimately developed (in the words of the exorcists, "cooled") into the power of the constituting gift, the total force of the betweenness and sustenance of relations, the time and space of this betweenness. The victim transcends body, person, and self. The *atamagala* is the space of *sattva* (of the radiance of being). I note that the victim is not merely inside the edifice of the cosmic state but is virtually *hidden* within it. The subjective egoity of the victim and the emergent self are transcended as the force, the givenness of the gift, that encompasses and governs the entire process. Hidden within Mahasammata's palace, the victim is essentially a manifestation of the power interior to it but also of the power that generates it. Thus the victim shifts from being a body of sacrifice (subject to the violence of the sorcerer) into a being of the force of the gift, who can release through sacrifice the energies of cosmic and world recreation—the theme of many of the events following the *hatadiya.*

The entrance into the *atamagala* is an act that is a symbolic excess of meaning. In one sense, it can be seen as an act of transcendence. If it is an act of transcendence, however, it is not a removal from the world of social existence or even a rising above it in some common uses of the term. Rather, it is a *transcendence in-the-world* and from a position that is in alignment with its vital core and directionality. The victim is seated in the *atamagala* on the world axis. In the conditionality of the pure gift, as the force of the cosmic and social totality, the victim is the ordering and structuring potency of the world itself. Moreover, as the totality, the victim might be seen as now completely open to the world and able to confront it and form it in relation to his or her own being. Thus victims manifest a major meaning of the notion of the bodhisattva which the rebirth of the victim appears to manifest.

Sacrifice and the Paradox of Violence

The Suniyama addresses the paradox of violence, that it is both a generative and destructive force in the world of human beings. Its sacrificial dynamic is centered around this paradox and is oriented toward its resolution—the conquest of violence or separation from it. The gift, which is so central in the Suniyama (and comparative ethnography would suggest in all sacrifice), appears to negate itself; the same often appears to be true of sacrifice. Derrida draws attention to the "madness" of the gift at least to the ratiocinating mind. Lévi-Strauss (1962) declares sacrifice is absurd; one aspect of this might be its engagement of destruction to creation. The very craziness of the gift and of sacrifice have do with the extreme paradox of their foundational dynamics, in which the very process whereby human being makes itself is thwarted by the selfsame dynamic of its own construction.

The Suniyama engages violent techniques in the reconstitution of the victim. Not only is the violence of the sorcerer made to rebound upon himself but also the reempowering of the victim is expressed in an apparently explicit act of violence enacted by the victim.

Acts of cutting, severing, destruction, and the like are executed throughout the Suniyama. They both indicate and are actions which in themselves effect the ending of malign connections with demons and with the sorcerer. Moreover, the actions of cutting accompany gifts. They sever the relation created through the gift and thus cut the demonic bond. The action of cutting might also be understood to indicate the power of the gift simultaneously to create and to separate. Cutting, severing, and violent acts of destruction mark moments in the development of the Suniyama as a whole and, as Hubert and Mauss asserted long ago, demonstrate that sacrifice is that ritual action which above all engages destruction to regeneration and transformation. They concentrated on the role of such acts in changing the status of the *sacrifier,* and the Suniyama is largely a confirmation of their point.

The term *violence* in application to these actions subsumes too much. This is a general problem with the word, which tends to be abused through overuse and can activate a potentially blind and inappropriate moralism, especially in contemporary political climates of vast human destruction. More specifically, in the context of rite, it obscures what is *hidden* within an overtly violent act.

Thus the acts of cutting and severing are performatives, in Austin's (1962) sense, doing what is also being done by other acts (e.g., mantras bind and cut and are the saying of the doing). They, like much else in the Suniyama, are mimetic acts which in their performative contact with the body make the meaning of the act, the act *as its experience* and thus potentially its efficacy. Thus, in the *hatadiya* the limes are cut against the vital points of the victim's body. The cutting of the bonds binding the victim in the *atamagala* has similar import.

The cutting, severing, and destruction are indicative, in my view, of the classifying and differentiating process of cosmic and social constitution. They are equal to their symbolic significance as negative acts of deconstruction and decomposition. They cut away the forces that bring disease, suffering, and death. There is a powerful violence in this which implicitly recognizes the gargantuan (and finally impossible) effort involved in such a task. The forces of demonic destruction are in fusion with the body, and they do not leave voluntarily. In the Suniyama and other exorcisms, not only must demons be beguiled into taking the gift, but they must be cajoled and aggressively forced to comply with the contract. The story of Prince Oddisa (see Chapter 3) suggests that even Buddha, in his encounter with the sorcerer, an encounter with the counter-rational supreme, is himself driven to resort to violent acts.[4]

But I stress the violence of the cutting as a dividing action thematic of that originary action of human consciousness whereby the social and political ordering is instantiated and cut away from the totalization of existence. It is this *dividing* of the violent act—a feature also of killing—that is a vital aspect of violence in sacrifice. The distribution and division of food at sacrifices, integral to the commensality of sacrifices, shares symbolically with killing and other violent acts in their divisive significance. Both acts (killing and food distribution) can be seen to be *classifying and differentiating acts of cosmic and social (re)origination and (re)constitution.* In other words, the distribution of the food of sacrifice according to particular categories and classes of relation unfolds what is already immanent in acts of killing, cutting, and so on.

It should be clear that the violence of the Suniyama sacrifice is of considerable complexity and valency. This is not to diminish the violence of the rite but to expand a sense of the forces which violent acts subsume. Moreover, what I have to say does not diminish the paradox of violence on which the rite is premised.

The Suniyama is heavy with the metaphors of violent killing and allows for a connection between its action and the death or killing of another human being. When the drunken Vasavarti (drunk on soma) is about to destroy the palace, he is hunted (see Chapter 4). This occurs after the reempowering of the victim and would appear to agree with Bloch's (1992) thesis that understands the *transcendental* events of rite as converting prey (i.e., ritual subjects) into hunters (who can now themselves search for victims and prey). The cutting of the ash pumpkin near the end of the rite is sometimes seen by nonexorcist participants as a nonviolent equivalent of the sacrifice of a human being. In the dark and away from the light of the ritual performance, a straw dummy, a surrogate for the sorcerer, is driven with needles and killed. Victims frequently expect (see Obeyesekere 1975, for the action at the sorcery shrines) those who have caused their suffering to experience similar suffering or be brought to their death as a function of a Suniyama performance.

These features of the Suniyama performance could be seen as a metadiscourse on suffering and violence. Human beings can overcome violent acts toward them through an orientation to the Buddha ideal. Because they remain bound to existence, however, they must continue as both the subject of suffering and the cause of harm to others, although indirectly. This is a theme that is consistent with Buddhist ideology.

The structure of the rite and the organization of the participation of the victim in its process directs the victim away from responsibility for any ensuing violence. When Vasavarti is hunted in the action surrounding the *atamagala,* it is not by the victim but by Vasavarti's cosorcerers, the exorcists. Vasavarti is destroyed by his own action. The victim is virtually inactive and irresolute in the midst of Vasavarti's rage. The victim has conquered fear. The killing work is done by the exorcists, who must themselves bear the risks of their action; this is a reason for their lowly position in the social hierarchy and for why they must be paid.

The event of the ash pumpkin is a cutting of the final dangerous relation of the victim with the exorcist. In fact it dissociates the victim from killing. But it remains significant as a highly potent act signifying the victim's socially constitutive force. A view of nonexorcists that the action is a killing act is in my analysis a commonsense Sinhalese view (and the view of human beings generally) which associates the strongest power with killing. It also is an implicit acknowledgment of the extreme sense of vengeance contained in such acts; this sense of vengeance is suppressed in a ritual discourse of nonviolence. The act *is*, in fact, a sentencing verdict canceling out the force and agent of sorcery.

That the act is ordinarily viewed as one of great potency, indeed of extraordinary potency, is indicated by the way it is sometimes described by persons away from the context of a Suniyama performance. Thus, on four separate occasions I have been told that the victim brings the machete down with great force on the pumpkin, severing it at a stroke but, amazingly, causing not even a scratch on the exorcist's stomach. I have seen a great many Suniyamas and have never seen the act performed in this way. It would be highly unlikely, because during the event the exorcist intones mantras while slowly pressing the victim's hand down on the machete. The victims, probably significantly, use hardly any active force of their own.

The final sacrificial acts of the Suniyama are directed to separating power from violence and also to removing the grounds for any return of the sorcerer's violent attraction. The possibility of revenge is reduced by the fact that the sorcerer is rarely named (the sorcerer is a generalized other). Furthermore, the victim at the center of the Suniyama is disconnected from being a direct agent of an attacker's suffering.

The paradox of violence in the Suniyama is above all a matter of pragmatic concern. It addresses the circumstances generating violence and the consequence of violence, the incapacity to act in the world. Moreover, it is directed to punish the sorcerer but in a way that interrupts a cycle of violence and reduces the danger of the sorcerer's violent vengeful return. The paradox of violence is of particular pragmatic concern in the context of sorcery, emergent as it is within a social world, not merely because the context of the Suniyama is a Buddhist one in which nonviolence (*ahimsa*) is a major moral value.

Buddhism, of course, takes violence as critically problematic in a way that many other cultures and worldviews do not. Indeed, some peoples see violence as simply a fact of existence (as many Buddhists do too) and regard it positively rather than negatively (see Mimica 1991; Harrison 1993). Buddhist philosophy explores the sources of human suffering and suffering's extreme expression in violence. The Suniyama can be seen as an excellent practical demonstration, for the victim of sorcery at least, of the triumph of Buddhist nonviolence over the violence of the sorcerer. Some people who hold a Suniyama for themselves are clearly using it to demonstrate this ideological aspect. More overtly, Buddhist monks and lay officials of local temples may organize the performance of Suniyamas in temple grounds explicitly as a demonstration of Buddhist ethics as well as a form of popular entertainment. Although they are undoubtedly influenced by a renewed ethical emphasis on nonviolence as part of Buddhist revitalization, this is their manipulation of a discourse that is fundamental in the logic of transformation of the rite.

The aim of the rite in its routine practice, however, is directed to overcome the pain and suffering of a victim and household. It is concerned with pragmatics or with ideals as ultimately of use in overcoming immediate personal problems and circumventing their return. Morality is the *means* and not the *object*. Furthermore, the Suniyama and the moral outrage its process details does not involve outrage against violence or its social disorder in some abstract or intellectualist understanding detached from the practicalities of daily action. Its pragmatic concern is with the impediments to social existence and the prevention of a capacity to act in the full psychological and social sense of human being; it is concerned with what is signified symbolically in violence rather than with violence itself as an object of moral condemnation independent of its figurations and experience in everyday life.

Other Approaches to the Violence of Sacrifice: A Note

Girard (1977) especially, and more recently Bloch (1992), explore the relation of sacrifice to violence in general terms. Their work is of interest because they raise the question of the nature of violence in rite and its functional role. Most important, they are concerned with the connection between the violence within the rite and wider social and political processes. This is also my concern and is a major theme of the rest of the book.

Girard and Bloch are interested in asserting general theories. Broadly, Girard sees in sacrifice the basis of a general functional theory of society and an argument for a resolution of the inherent violence of society (the "sacrificial crisis"). He values ritual as essentially bringing social harmony. This is a common argument in functionalist sociology. Bloch's argument reverses most of the central terms of Girard. He asserts that rite and sacrifice are not only centered on violence but expand its force.

Girard has been effectively criticized by others, specifically with reference to his use of ethnographic materials (see Valeri 1985; de Heusch 1985; Detienne and Vernant 1979). The critics find fault with the clear Christian bias of his approach and an essentialism that asserts that violence is rooted in human being per se. Bloch steers clear of these pitfalls, though he is unashamedly universalist (which can be close to essentialism, for universal truth is the essentialist's dream). He essays a general structure to all rite. His structure develops upon, as it challenges, other well-known general theories (e.g., Hubert and Mauss [1899] 1964; Van Gennep [1909] 1960; Turner 1967, 1969). In many ways Girard and Bloch are open to similar criticisms, not least for their symbolically impoverished vision of violence in the context of rite (see Valeri 1985; Hoskins 1993).

Girard builds his argument around the concept of mimetic desire (i.e., human beings want the things that other human beings want, leading to a basic war of all against all) and says that violence is natural to human being. Sacrifice is the socially generative violence organized by human beings to overcome their natural violence. It is the violence that ends violence.[5] Sacrifice does this through a process whereby the destructive processes interior to a community are externalized by being focused on a single victim, the scapegoat for the community. By means of the scapegoat, the disorder that is in fact internal to the community is expressed as an outside threat. The idea of the outsider as the threat is a fiction, the falsity of which the community hides from itself. The complicity of the scapegoat, Girard suggests, sustains the view that violence is external and encourages the collective action of the community to expunge it.

The victim/scapegoat takes back the violence that has entered the community, and the killing of the scapegoat is the final extinguishing of the violence. Moreover, because the victim is an outsider (in Girard's analysis, echoing Frazer, kings are virtually outsiders in their own communities and can therefore function as scapegoats in sacrifice) and isolated from other relations, the violence done to the scapegoat avoids the dangers of revenge. The reciprocity of violence (Girard 1977), the cycle of revenge within the community and possibly between communities, is broken and exhausted on the victim as scapegoat. In this positive view of sacrifice, the ritual and social communities are identical. Thus contained, the violence does not spill over and can be resolved ritually.

Girard distinguishes the violence that is socially destructive from that which is socially generative. Destructive violence erases distinction and difference. Reconstitutive violence restores the difference and distinction on which he sees societies as being based. Bloch rejects such a rosy picture. The violence of sacrifice has nothing to do with social harmonics.

Violence is power, and the violence of sacrifice has to do fundamentally with reempowering. Power and violence are not separable but grow in their dialectical unity.

In Bloch's general theory of rite, there are two vital moments of violence. The first is directed toward those who are the central ritual subjects. They are the prey of violent power. Second, there is a process in which the subjects of the rite are taken outside of society into a space of transcendent power which is external to, or outside of, social and political relations. This transcendent power somehow attaches to the subjects, for example, by acts of consumption, and ritual participants are changed from being "prey into hunters" (Bloch 1992). The second violent power is stronger than the first, on which its emergence nonetheless depends. There is no scapegoat theory here and no violence that ends violence. Rather, it is a view of ritual as generating violence and as being instrumental in the expansion of its destructive potential beyond any boundaries of containment. The violence does not function to reharmonize communities but if anything turns people against each other. For Girard, Thomas Hobbes's ([1651] 1962) "the war of all against all" is subdued in the collectivizing and differentiating reordering of sacrifice. For Bloch, Hobbes I leads to Hobbes II: the weakening of society and the individual leads to a process of ritual (re)constitution which generates violence of group against group.

These broad perspectives have some limited resonance with the dynamic of the Suniyama. One aspect of the Suniyama is a reharmonization of social relations. A *community* is defined and structured in relation to the household through the progress of the victim. But the community defined by the rite is largely limited to the duration of the rite. Such rites can be socially divisive by virtue of those who are absent. The rite is concerned not so much with reconstituting a social order as with the restitution of the socially generating capacity of the victim and household.

The community restored is a symbolic community and has a value similar in the context of the rite to the symbolism of Mahasammata's city, whose space the audience, the community of the rite, occupies. The audience is functional to the subject of the rite. It is the society toward which the victim moves from the very start of the rite and is the society whose audience participation in the rite is instrumental to this transformation (e.g., in the *vadiga patuna;* see Kapferer 1983 for other exorcisms).

Girard's scapegoat function has reduced relevance. Anger and suffering may be displaced onto the sorcerer as a generalized scapegoat. And the violence of the sorcery that has entered the body of the victim is *taken back* by the sorcerer and the demonic through the mediation of the gift (a dimension that Girard does not explore). But the force of the rite as a whole is directed to the transmutation of the violent angry relation. The transformation is not effected through catharsis (although this is far more apparent in other demon exorcisms); rather, the anger and violence are dispelled as a function of a reordering, restructuring dynamic. Violent destruction in the rite is not the means of the transformation (as it is for Girard) but is a dynamic in the transformation and even a result of the transformation. The sorcerer becomes the figure of manifest violence at his exclusion on the reconstitution. Externalized, the violent power of the sorcerer is rendered impotent, but still always threatening.

Bloch's approach also has a degree of fit with the Suniyama. The movement to the ultimate place of nonviolence (the *atamagala*) involves events that are the exact inversion of an act that might outwardly appear as a building of violence. The final acts of sacrifice (e.g., the cutting of the ash pumpkin) can be understood as a negation of an event which otherwise would be a greater violence overcoming an initial lesser violence. The rite in its Buddhism has anticipated Bloch and has produced a diagnosis of a major cause of violence, the link of power with violence, of which the sorcerer and the demonic are the extreme actualizations. In the Suniyama, nonviolent power is the greater power and conquers violent power.

There is much in Bloch's argument that is already familiar in discussion of the rites of kingship and the myths of premodern state formation. This is especially true with regard to their notion that power and its violence come from a source external to the state, or that the state is the result of conquest from the outside (see Hocart 1927; Gluckman 1954; Sahlins 1981; Valeri 1985). The regeneration of state and society is achieved through the repetition of this externality: the forces of internal social order are exteriorized and engage in a process of reconquest (see also Kapferer 1988a). The externalization is not primarily a catharsis (though such a psychological possibility is not ruled out) but a reorigination—a return to the source of the violent imposition of order—from which the differentiated order of society grows and then rebounds regeneratively. That such violence continues within regenerate orders and places them in a potentially aggressive relation to other groups is certainly implicit and often fairly explicit in the ethnographies that use such an approach.

Sacrificial Violence and Contemporary Politics

Bloch identifies the transcendental properties of such rebounding power as a major force of expanding violence. He suggests that it is an ingredient in contemporary political violence, in which religious ideologies often appear as frames and idioms for violence and may even have a role in promoting it. Distancing himself from Girard (and Burkert), Bloch states: "I do not base myself on some innate propensity to violence but argue that violence is itself a result of the attempt to create the transcendental in religion and politics" (Bloch 1992: 7). There is much to agree with in Bloch with respect to the force of religious discourse or ideologies in contemporary politics. I have argued along similar lines with regard to the role of ritual and religious mythology as an idiom for some of the recent Tamil-Sinhala ethnic violence and as contributing to its impetus (Kapferer 1988a, 1989, 1993; see also Chapter 8). A logic of the myths drawn from the ancient religious chronicles and used by ideologists of Sinhala nationalism (myths which are also part of everyday ritual, such as the story of Prince Vijaya, having additional popular import because of this) is the notion that the regeneration of state/society is achieved by the state/society becoming external to itself.

In this argument of the myths, a violent externality is encompassed and drawn within state/society in a process of rehierarchialization. This subdues and either relocates violent forces at the base of the social order or makes them external to it. This process of the myths is evident in the Suniyama as part of its internal dynamic. Insofar as it applies to the Sinhala-Tamil situation, however, the argument is valid only because of the social and political circumstances of contemporary Sri Lanka, which both transmute the significance of the myths and give them particular aim and potency. Bloch makes much the same point.

Put another way, it is impossible to argue directly from the logic of myth and rite to the process of contemporary political violence. First and most important, the relation is dependent on mediating factors: the political and socioeconomic context in which the myths and rites are made relevant and which gives them their direction and meaning. Second, myths and rites are totalizations. That is, they compose and constitute all the elements that they interrelate and transform. I consider this to be the major factor that contributes to the efficacy of rites. The transformational power of rites as fully embodied experiencing is founded in this fact. The Suniyama does not change the structure of social relationships in the environment of the victim outside the context of the ritual performance. What it might achieve is a shift in the orientation of victims to their world as this is experienced as centering on them. Rites do not totalize or represent the world of actual ongoing daily relations outside their performance. The attempt to totalize rite (myth)—a feature of recent state-sponsored ideological practice in Sri Lanka—has contributed to some of the recent interethnic strife.

If the process of the Suniyama were transferred into the contemporary context, however, violence would likely be inhibited and not exacerbated. Violent action is systematically suppressed and negated. The rebounding of the victim back into the world is an act of community restoration and the reestablishment of its boundaries.

I do not overlook more cynical interpretations. The Suniyama dissociates from violent action the person at the center of the rite, who comes to embody the power of state/society. Those low in status, the exorcists, do all the violent work. This is a dynamic of the rite which might be seen as a metaphor of much of the contemporary suffering in Sri Lanka. It is the urban poor and peasants among the Tamils and Sinhalese who have borne much of the brunt of the ethnic hostilities, and the urban elites at the center of state power have been largely distanced from them—until the recent JVP (Peoples Liberation Front) uprising (see Kapferer 1994a, 1994b; Chapter 7). Members of these elites have also been vocal in their assertion of the values of Buddhist nonviolence.

The rites and the myths are not causes of political violence. They can provide metaphors for those engaged in political violence to understand it. Insofar as these metaphors are made to express social and political actualities through the artifice of contemporary state and social processes, they can have dangerous consequence. Furthermore, the dynamics of rite and myth can provide insight into the forces engaged in human political and social practices in their own right and not merely as a demonstration of the abstract theories of philosophers and social scientists. This is not to argue that the dynamics of rite and myth is replicated in other social and political practice. We should use the dynamics that are apparent in rite and myth as means for exploring the possibilities of comparable dynamics in other arenas of practice, but in a way which does not reduce rite to politics or politics to rite.

Bloch's insight, that the transcendental aspects of rite and myth may be implicated in the production of violence, draws on Hubert and Mauss's sacred-profane dualism in their study of sacrifice. Their notion of the sacred is highly mystical (related to a Western rationalism that produced such dichotomies) and one to which I think Bloch remains committed. Durkheim and Mauss tried to demystify their notion of the sacred by identifying it as actually society. Durkheim and Mauss were knowledgable about Buddhism, probably a Westernized Buddhism, and drew on it in developing their social theories. But they maintained their dichotomies. Within the context of some rites, certainly the Suniyama, such dichotomy and opposition would miss the point that the motion toward the central sacred space of the *atamagala* is both a movement toward the power of social existence and a move beyond it. The sacred and the profane are coterminous, the profane being generated through the sacred, which is the premise of the profane. It is the motion toward the sacred, which is *not* society in Durkheim's sense but its conditionality, that recreates the orders of daily life. When the victim reaches the *atamagala*, this is the apogee of the process. The victim does not enter the *atamagala* to start the process of social (re)constitution in some kind of magical, mystical empowered state. The victim is not located in a place of mysteries but in the space of knowledge. The victim is at the height of ordering potency, totally reordered in himself or herself, and ideally fully in command of his or her reason (which is nonetheless able to generate extraordinary powers beyond ordinary human capacity). The victim is at the center of cosmos, state, and society and not in the dangerous space outside it. Furthermore, the victim is cleansed of violence.

Bloch (1992:46–64) centers some of his discussion on Buddhist (and Shinto) practices in Japan. He raises the issue of pilgrimage, the alignment of temples along the Buddha's path, memorials, and so forth, as places and lines of passage for the renewal of vitality in accordance with his thesis of rebounding violence. These, Bloch indicates, can give emotional force and legitimation to modern, often violent, political movements and can find continuing and new import in changing political contexts. In contemporary nationalism, for example, the kinds of phenomena that Bloch mentions are adaptable to a politics of sovereignty and space. I examine this aspect of the transcendental, a process that is in itself powerful because of the dynamics of its motion (and not as a rebounding of violent power renewed with the strength of the outside or beyond). I concentrate on the journey *toward* the transcendental point as the vital conquest, rather than the journey back, or the rebounding return.

One feature of a transcendental process is its crossing and negation of boundaries. Moreover, the process surpasses the limitations of space and in effect deterritorializes. This is not the same as transgression, which is destructive and violent, although the difference indicates a similarity. In the *hatadiya*, the progress toward the palace is simultaneously transgressive, clearing, and preparatory for the establishment of new boundaries (the dualism of Suniyam's symbolism is of a demon who transgresses and guards the boundaries). Like the *hatadiya*, a transcendent process is normally highly ethical and moral in its assertions. It transgresses with the force of morality and breaks through and clears the space of the routine social and political world by virtue of its morality. This moral deterritorialization (indicated in the *hatadiya* by the erasure of the line of the snake and the fiery, *ira*, barriers, and by the placing and removal of the lotuses) is a preparation for a recontouring and a remoralization of space.

All religions have aspects of such processes, but as Deleuze and Guattari (1988) note, religious forces in a missionizing and proselytizing mood are deterritorializing in the extreme. This explains the integral role of missionary Christianity in imperial expansion and the formation of colonial states. I suggest that this impetus toward deterritorialization is a factor that makes radical Islam currently both internally threatening to state orders and a vital force in particular state expansionist interests. In Sri Lanka, the revitalization of Buddhism as part of an anticolonialist nationalist politics also switched Buddhism into a missionizing and proselytizing mode.

The conscious striving to be Buddhist (especially among the highly Westernized and urbanized bourgeoisie) is expressed in a growth in pilgrimage and the creation of new pilgrimage centers, often sites of ancient importance to Sinhalese. Pilgrimage is a dynamic of deterritorialization which, associated as it is in Sri Lanka with state-directed religiously defined nationalist interest, becomes a critical element in a reterritorialization and a redrawing of spatial boundaries. Other kinds of demarcation or the bounding of space can be seen as dangerous obstacles (like the barriers of the sorcerer) that should be either broken down (the Ayodhya mosque; see Van der Veer 1988) or otherwise transformed (the shrine at Kataragama in southeast Sri Lanka was changed into a dominantly Buddhist shrine in which its important Hindu Tamil significance is reduced). It is not the transcendental aspects of religion or politics in its mystifying or antirationalist sense (as a locus of powers) that is productive of the violence; rather its deterritorializing dynamic becomes tied to (and may be generative of) a pragmatic interest in redrawing boundaries (see Chapter 7).

As with Bloch's perspective, there are implications in Girard's perspective (despite his religious commitments) that can be extended to contemporary social and political circumstances. As is true for much functionalism (but not that of Bloch, who identifies the disharmonies with the harmonies), however, it is the negativizing of previous positivities that produces the dire results. In Girard's terms the present violence in Sri Lanka would be described as a *sacrificial crisis* (Girard 1977). The forces of dissension and division within Sri Lanka—poverty, unemployment, class conflict, regionalism (southerners against the hegemony of Kandy-centered elites)—are displaced by the Sinhalese onto Tamils as scapegoats (and by Tamils onto Sinhalese). As in ritual sacrifice, as interpreted by Girard, they are made into a singular exteriorized manifestation of internal disruption. For example, Tamils were presented as a category inequitably favored for jobs, as against the Sinhalese, in the colonial and postcolonial state (Committee for Rational Development 1983; Tambiah 1986, 1992). Such a fiction in the rhetoric of nationalism (the rite of nationalism) is not ritually contained but rather becomes the factuality of everyday political and social realities defined in the ritualized space of nationalist assertions.

Moreover, the scapegoating of the ethnic process (its categorizing dynamic) makes Tamils and Sinhalese internally undifferentiated unities. They assume a violent form and mimetically and mutually refract the violence of themselves onto the other. Consequently, no regeneration of the social as an internally differentiated totality occurs by means of the scapegoat, and a continuous and expanding cycle of violence is created. Each becomes the scapegoat of the other and they descend into an ever-deepening maelstrom of violence. Furthermore, the scapegoat of Girard's sacrifice is self-contained, specific to itself, and isolated from the world. This is a property of the constitution of the scapegoat in ritual. The same dynamic outside the ritually circumscribed context does not impede or negate a reciprocity of violence; instead it exacerbates the violence.

It is at least implicit in Girard that the extension of ritual metaphors and processes into the contemporary contexts of mass society is likely to generate violence. This position is not too distant from Bloch's. The prime distinction is that Girard thinks that the sacrificial solution is valuable but only if its principles are transformed into judicial and other state institutions. He might argue, again in the common mood of much sociological functionalism, that in the Sri Lanka case and in numerous others, there has not been a successful transformation of archaic forms of social control and ordering into the modern form. This is a major problem with Girard's perspective, in addition to its essentialism. His stress is on the malfunctioning of what he deems a universal sacrificial dynamic of social (re)origination and purification in human being. His is largely a Christian perspective (and therefore not universal even across a diversity of ritual practices that might be defined as sacrifices). More important, the processes he discovers, particularly if applied to contemporary societies, are not the malfunctioning of a basic underlying mechanism but involve the assemblage of forces and their dynamics (as much part of their function as dysfunction) within modern states and the nature of the global articulation of these states.

Both Bloch and Girard provide insights into contemporary social and political actualities by investigating sacrifice and other ritual practices. They continue a well-established tradition in western philosophy and social science of validating their theories by examining exotic (i.e., non-Western or historical, usually ancient) materials. My own analysis is far from free of this feature. Their problem is not that they use such material but that they impose models on their data that refuse the subtleties of that material, subtleties that might enable other interpretations and understandings of the dynamics of human action. They shut out the possibilities in ritual action for understanding the dynamics of human practices and the manifold directions in which their ambiguities might lead. Despite their opposed positions (and leaving aside charges like Christian bias, essentialism, etc., which can obscure some of the points that Girard and Bloch are making), both perspectives can be applied to the Suniyama material. But even together their perspectives remain limited, a limitation not of the material (of their own as well as mine) but of the kinds of sociological functionalism that both these scholars espouse.

From Rite to Shrine

The sacrifice of the Suniyama reconstitutes the social being of the victim. It demonstrates sacrifice, at least in this context, as a total act of recreation. In this act, the victim repeats that primordial action of human consciousness whereby human beings make a radical choice for society and bring its ordering into existence. The victim is imbued with social constituting power. In the process, which from the very start is a movement toward social existence and a transcendence within it, victims recreate themselves. They are removed from the condition of the sorcerer, a condition of violence and violated externality, and are radically recentered within a cosmic process so as to recover their socially constituting vitality.

The sociological dynamic of the rite transmutes the negative forces within human sociality: the intentionality of human action that is the force that simultaneously generates relations between human beings and destroys them. The process is one that opens up the space and time of social existence, progressively cuts away destructive relations, and converts the potential for destruction in intentional action into a regenerative and socially positive force.

In very condensed form, the dynamic of the Suniyama is also that of the shrines to the sorcery demon-gods, and in particular, Suniyam. These gods in their divided character are beings of the sacrificial rupture, which I consider the socially (re)originating act. The Suniyama expands an understanding of some aspects of the dynamics in these shrines. At least they are part of the same culture-historical and changing world. The action at the shrines is concerned with intentionality and the regenerative transmutation of its relations, or else their cutting away and destruction.

Of course, there are major differences between the action at the shrines and that in the Suniyama. For one thing, Buddhist morality is cut to a bare minimum at the shrines. At the Hindu temples, where Sinhalese Buddhists also go to overcome the anguish born of social existence, a Buddhist ethos is not present at all. But the key difference is in the action of the clients and victims. In the Suniyama, the victim is silent throughout. The victim is carried through the action of the rite and is not, relatively speaking, an aggressive center. The victim's emotional and passionate concerns, as a focus of sorcery attack, are taken over and stylized into the poetics of the rite and become the generalized possibility of all victims of sorcery, not of a particular one. At the shrines, the victims give full vent to what the meaning of sorcery is for them. It is at the shrines that the emotionality of sorcery screams out, of sorcery as the motion of anguish and anxiety in a historical world.

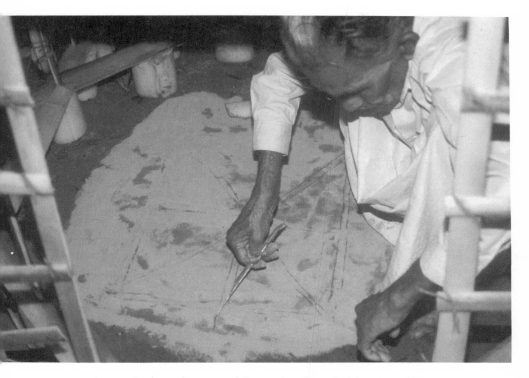

7. An exorcist draws the *yantra* of the cosmic order and of the origin of being

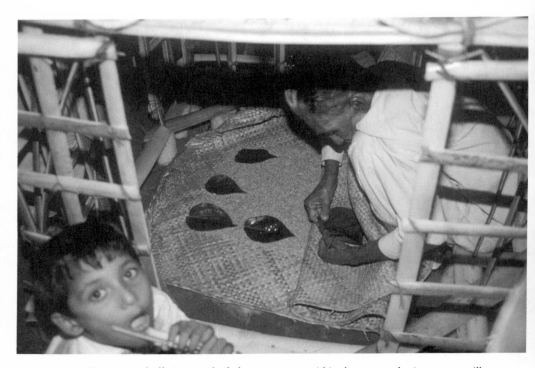

8. The setting of offerings on the *kaksaputa yantra* within the *atamagala*. A new mat will be placed over the offerings for the patient to sit on.

9. The *Suniyam baliya* is made

10. A patient with the *mottakkili* shawl oriented toward the Mahasammata Palace. Her young niece is beside her.

11. Dancers wearing Odissa's *kangul toppiya* exchange jokes

12. The god Vishnu makes his appearance

13. The *valvalalu:* in the coils of sorcery

14. The *vadiga patuna* Brahmins

15. *Vasavarti*

16. The destruction of the palace

17. The *puhul tinduva*

7

Sorcery's Passions
Fear, Loathing, and Anger in the World

> *How can I let these enemies of mine*
> *Escape all punishment, live free to mock me?*
> *No, I must face this act.*
> . . . .
> *Your sons are dead. Let it pierce your heart:*
> *Your sons are dead!*
>
> Euripides, Medea

MY MAIN CONCERN in this chapter is to present some sense of the experience and existential force of the world that is grasped and recognized through sorcery. I aim to demonstrate the power of sorcery beliefs and practice to disclose the nature of the forces in the world that can condition, prey on, and unsettle human beings in their life courses. I attempt to give some sense of the agony of sorcery, the way in which practices of sorcery enable the expression and management of the profoundest abjection and despair of human beings. These vital aspects of sorcery often seem to be lost in the various intellectualist and rationalist approaches to sorcery, especially those that are concerned with sorcery as a mode of explanation or that concentrate on its pragmatism.

I show how the articulation of the passions in the domain of sorcery practice opens up an understanding of the dynamics of human consciousness: an understanding that is not mentalist and that insists on its grounding in both the body and the world. In this examination of consciousness I intend to examine the kind of human anguish to which sorcery practices and beliefs can give the most poignant expression.

I see consciousness as both constituted and constituting. In my usage the term *consciousness* is a dimension of all human action and is not limited to that which is established reflectively or contemplatively. Human beings are conscious beings by virtue of their embodied existence in a life world. In the most basic sense, human beings are constituted as beings of consciousness, or have the potentiality of consciousness, as a function of their bodily presence for other human beings and their involvement with each other in activities functional to their organismic existence. In this view, consciousness is an emergent property of the interdependence of the individual organism and its life world and is not reducible to either one or the other. The reduction of consciousness to either the individual organism or the world somehow apart from the beings that inhabit it is not the direction of this analysis.

Thus, I attempt to avoid the dangers of philosophical dualism, which is the bugaboo of much discussion of consciousness, particularly in an anthropology inspired from recent Western history. I refer to mind-body dualisms and also to those approaches that seem to oppose a concern with subjective experience to those that concentrate on objective structures as not only constitutive of subjectivity but determinant and in some way independent or transcendent of the human beings that live them.

Central to my discussion is the idea that human beings do not have moods, emotions, or passions independent of their action among other human beings. That is, the emotionality of human beings is not integral to individual organisms apart from their field of existence with other human beings. A common assumption in a discourse largely centered in the West is that certain emotions or passionate dispositions—anxiety, fear, anger, violence, for instance—are foundational in the biopsychology of the individual organism, and these dispositions confuse rational and reflective thought: The mind must control the body. The notion is extended into ideas concerning social and political orders. Social and political orders are conceived of as having the properties of collective minds regnant over bodies. The perspective is evident in social philosophy from Hobbes to Durkheim and to contemporary political and social discourse. The orientation is active in debates that oppose the individual and society and in various resolutions of the debate that reduce the mind to the body (as physiological or chemical function and intrapsychic process) or that dissolve individual human beings into the structures of society.

Recent work in the neurological and biological sciences is questioning such a perspective. Thus Damasio (1994) criticizes the Cartesian dualism that asserts the value of reason over the passions. He argues for the centrality of the emotions in reasoning and states that reasoning fails in the condition of the destruction or excision of those brain centers that have a function in emotional behavior. Damasio's is but one attempt to overcome the Cartesian separation of body from mind and to insist on their unity, although he tends, like others, to overcome the Cartesian dichotomy by a reduction to the biological processes of the individual organism. That is, the body or the complexity of its internal organic structure, rather than expressing and developing its potentialities (and altering its organismic structure) through its presence in the world, is the originating source.[1] I resist such a reduction here.

In my analysis, the emotions or the passions are not things or objects located in parts of the brain or essential in the human organism. Rather they are forms of the expression of the fluid motion and unity of human beings in their world, emergent in the flow of action and vital in the perception and consciousness of the world. The emotions or moods are continuously engaged and shifting, and manifest the countless alterations in the ways that human beings meet their worlds and establish their unity with them. The emotions are the irreducible expressions of this unity. The more extreme emotions, what may be recognized culturally and felt as the experience of one's own being, such as fear, joy, anger, love, sympathy, hate, longing, pleasure, fury, and greed, manifest shifting dispositions and orientations of human beings in the world through which they move. They are integral to the motion of human beings and manifest themselves as attitudes of the body (e.g., in gestures, which include the physical experiences of illness and nausea). The emotions and moods of human beings are not merely reflections of their changing orientations within their life worlds but are vital to their perception and the formation of their conceptions and agency in the life world.

*Adura*s and other specialists in sorcery and related forms of demonic illness conceive of emotional or mood processes in ways similar to those I have outlined. Broadly, emotions are part of the ongoing activity of human beings in their everyday lives of which human beings are not usually aware. The emotions or moods are barely distinguishable in people's course of routine tasks and social interaction. Body and world form a relatively balanced sensory unity or flow together. The emotions or moods become apparent, or take on the appearance of objects, in processes that express some kind of disturbance in the human organism, its world, or their interrelations. In theory these cannot be separated. The source of emotional disturbance or imbalance is both in the body and in the world. Thus, demons are manifestations of extreme emotional dynamics. Mahasona, the great cemetery demon, is a creature of extraordinary violence. Kalu Yaka consumes the body in intense sexual longing. These demons are conceived of as attacking the body from the outside world. The demons manifest aspects of disturbance and destruction in the world and most of all in the particular relation that the specific victims, who become sites of demonic power, form with their world. The aim of exorcists is to cool the heat of emotional disturbance or excess. They do this by balancing the body humors (*tun dosa* or *tri dosa*) thrown out of kilter by demonic attack, and by reestablishing the fluid and harmonic unity that victims normally have with their worlds. The Suniyama is an example of such a process, and like other healing rites, is directed to end the emotional excess formed by the body as a function of disruptive energies encountered and attaching to human beings through their participation in the activities of their life worlds. Thus the demonic bond is broken that ties the disturbance in the organism to a disturbance in the world.

The passions of sorcery demonstrate the emergence of a reflective consciousness integral to an already *knowing* body active, productive, and responsive to the forces of human being-in-the-world. The ratiocinating human being is also and inseparably a passionate being whose passions or emotions emerge from within an involvement and commitment to the life world. Manifest through the body, the passions, emotionality, or constantly changing mood of human beings cannot be understood by a reduction to an individual human being but only by the way the individual is embroiled in the processes of the life world and involved in the activities of others. The individually manifest emotion or mood through the course of action in the world is vitally part of that human being's reflected and unreflected consciousness of that world.

My approach to consciousness is concerned with the structures of the life world which are the ground of its formation, as is the body. Emotion and mood are important in consciousness because consciousness is rooted in experience, and that experience is founded in the body which is active in social and political realities. Marxists have insisted on this, and most important, on the historical formation of experience and the consciousness of experience. Sorcery experiences and the anguish expressed in sorcery manifest a historical world and innumerable ways in which individuals are aligned or positioned within social and political processes.

I do not regard the passions of consciousness expressed as sorcery as unique to sorcery. Consciousness has no essential content, logic, or quality, and there is no essential consciousness in sorcery. The dynamics of consciousness in sorcery are like those in any other practice of human beings shaped in historical and cultural processes, even the consciousness of those committed to scientific practices or to the assertion of a rational understanding radically opposed to the practices of sorcery.

Anthropological and other scholarly discussions often imply that sorcery is a particular kind of consciousness. I refer to intellectualist and rationalist approaches (see Chapter 1) of various kinds that commonly depict sorcery belief and practice as instances and organizations of a flawed consciousness. Thus, sorcery beliefs obscure the nature of reality, demonstrate errors in reflective reasoning, are manifestations of psychosexual disturbances, and so forth. No doubt sorcery beliefs and practices can be symptoms of such processes. This is their potential. After all, they are explicitly directed to the problematics of experience in the world. The Suniyama and other practices of sorcery are directed to the discovery of fault. The consciousnesses of sorcery are about the faults in the human experience of existence, but the dynamics of this consciousness, the processes whereby it is formed in the world and potentially constructive of it, are not necessarily faulty as such.

Moreover, sorcery is not a unified coherent consciousness exhibiting a definite logic (e.g., Gluckman 1956; Horton 1967). Its representations, the demon Suniyam, for example, are organizations of contradiction, diversity, and rupture: totalizations of that manifold existential potential that cannot be brought within one coherent and ordered totalizing scheme. The demonic Vasavarti is excluded in the course of the ordering process of the Suniyama. The primordial themes of rite and shrine and their overarching cosmic span (the huge cosmic scheme of the Suniyama, the profusion of images of gods and demons that crowd the space of many of the major sorcery shrines), as a kind of symbolic excess, stretch to embrace the entire intensity and range of existential possibility. Sorcery does not manifest a particular type of consciousness; rather, in image and in practice it has the capacity to concentrate and focus a galaxy of consciousnesses of the problematics of everyday life.

Although sorcery is not a special kind of consciousness, neither is it necessarily a false or even mistaken consciousness of reality, as I will show. And although sorcery may not be an efficient means for achieving ends, this is relative to the available means and the kind of problem that must be addressed.

Sorcery is a power of the weak and the vulnerable, weakness and vulnerability being defined relative to the context and the immediate problem concerned. Persons who are in dominant positions of social and political power are vulnerable because of their situation. And the idea that sorcery courses along the path of envy works equally well for the strong and the weak. Undoubtedly, human beings through their sorcery practice suspect the wrong people of causing their distress and deflect attention from their own responsibility for their anxiety or suffering. But it is not the consciousness engaged in sorcery that is false but rather the empirical validity of its objectifications and the precise empirical detailing of the relations between cause and effect. However, the imagination of consciousness organized through sorcery can open persons to reflect on what are potential sources of anxiety and distress. The terms of sorcery can help people to grasp the empirical world.

Key notions that run through Sinhalese sorcery belief and practice, what Husserl would describe as "secondary reflections," are profound ideas about the nature of human consciousness. I refer to the insistence of sorcery practice that consciousness is embodied but also transcends its embodiment; to the implication in the Suniyama rite that a consciousness restricted to the body or bound within an immobilized body and unable to extend toward the horizons of its life world can be autodestructive; and to the notion that the consciousness of individual human beings is always embroiled with the consciousness of other human beings.

I will discuss these themes of sorcery and their importance for exploring the dynamics of the consciousness of human beings. I focus on the processes of fear and anger, the extremes of the retreat from the world and the extension toward it, which are heightened in sorcery belief and practice. The fear and anger of sorcery practice, given the cultural and historical context of Sri Lanka, yield some insight into aspects of the imaginary of consciousness, its process of autodestruction in the developing paralysis of fear, as well as the emergence of reflective consciousness and of the constitutive force of consciousness through radical extensions of the body into the world, as in the thrust of anger. At the end of this chapter I will consider the passions of consciousness in sorcery practice as expressions of political forces and as part of wider processes in the structuring of resistance.

Overall, I explore the passions of sorcery as relating to the fundamental urgency of human beings for sociality and social agency.

A Case of Sorcery's Fear

The experience of sorcery is often no less than total abjection, complete despair, and crushing helplessness and powerlessness. It is beyond comprehension and speech. The senses of the body which are central to reflective awareness but which are often experienced as peripheral in the action of reflection become dominant in experiential awareness. In sorcery or in that condition of total abjection in the world, the senses of the conscious body can overcome reflexivity and destroy thought: this is because the world as present to the sensate body is always more than can be grasped through acts of reflection. Alternatively, in the fear of sorcery, the sensing and knowing body and the process of reflection are engaged in mutual destruction. The world might be said to invade and subsume the body of the sufferer, a notion that I think is fairly explicit in Sinhala notions of the demonic. Moreover, the victim as the body of sorcery is given up to the senses which record the destruction, in the reflective acts of the imaginary, of their own condition of existence, the body itself. The extreme of sorcery and of the abject is the loss of consciousness and the body insensate. The body appears to dissolve inwardly upon itself. This is Manikpala's body, sorcery's body, the desolation of human beings in the world.

Siyadoris, a man of sixty, is a house builder who lives in a small town on the south coast, near the bustling center of Matara. Terrifying dreams broke his sleep. Three in particular crazed him with fear. In one he saw many of his relatives dead or dying. The image of his father's brother lying dead in a coffin (the man concerned is still very much alive) was especially vivid. He saw the mourners carrying the body and could feel himself overcome with grief as the coffin was lowered into the grave. Siyadoris awoke frightened from the experience of another dream, one in which he felt his teeth fall out. He dwelled on its significance, and his fear and shock intensified. Siyadoris thought it indicated the impending death of his son, Somasiri. Somasiri was suffering from crippling pains in his leg and was unable to walk. In another dream he was attacked by monkeys; they screamed and bit him and tore at his body. These, he felt, were the forms of *maruva,* the demon of death. Riri Yaka, the blood demon, has such a death form, and the face of Riri is that of a monkey. These dreams kept recurring. Siyadoris admits that he was inhabited by the terror of death, death to himself and to his kin.

The dreams were at the source of his growing fear. Siyadoris says that he could not stop himself from trying to grasp their meaning. Dreams are of vital import among Sinhalese, as in so many cultures. This is true specifically for exorcists. Perhaps the importance of dreams is increased in a Sinhalese Buddhist cultural world in which seeing is conceived as a fundamental dynamic of consciousness, as the force of the extension and projection of consciousness, and as a potency (*asvaha,* "poisonous glance") that can intrude within. This should be evident from the analysis of the Suniyama rite.

Siyadoris became ill. A terrible suffocating force bore down on his chest, and he had difficulty in breathing (*papuva tadavenava*). His body grew cold, and his limbs trembled (*anga sitalakala*). Overcome with fear, he fell unconscious (*sihiya vikaluma*).

Siyadoris's collapse brought him to the hospital. He was kept under observation for a few days, but nothing appeared to be physically wrong. He returned home, smarting a little from the 700-rupee doctor's bill.[2] He seemed recovered, but his wife and children became alarmed. Siyadoris's wife, Podinona, said that her husband would not stop talking about his dreams. He spoke constantly of death and dying.

Bound by his fear, Siyadoris refused to eat. He complained that Podinona's food stank and tasted rotten. Siyadoris did not wash and never changed his clothes. Later, Siyadoris and Podinona described their whole house as stinking of the viper (*polon ganda*), as reeking of the stench of Vasavarti Maraya. In despair, Podinona went with her sister to a *sastra kari*, a woman who specialized in reading horoscopes. The *sastra kari* confirmed their suspicions and declared that a *kodivina* had been made against Siyadoris. The *sastra kari* advised them to call an exorcist to cut the sorcery.

The exorcist took eight limes, cut them in half, and placed them in an earthen pot of water. The sixteen pieces are indicative of the action of consciousness (see Chapter 5). Sorcery is divined if some of the limes sink. A few of the limes sank to the bottom, so the presence of sorcery was definite. The exorcist recommended giving a special offering basket to Riri Yaka at the midday period (*iramudun*) and the performance of a nightlong *kapuma* the same evening. Siyadoris registered some improvement. His nightmares stopped, but he still shivered and trembled and the curries his wife served still stank.

The exorcist held another divination. Four limes were buried at the four corners of the house. When they were dug up the next day, three had gone rotten. This was an indication of the severity of the sorcery attack and, according to the exorcist, showed that a person outside of Siyadoris's kin and low in social standing had brought envious *vina* against Siyadoris's household. This agreed with Siyadoris and Podinona's suspicions about a next-door neighbor. This man and his family had moved in some months before. They were strangers from Matara and not members of Siyadoris's own caste community, which dominated the area. The exorcist said that two *kapuma*s must be combined: a *pita pantiya kapuma* for the forces of destruction coming from the outside and an *atul pantiya kapuma* for the destructive forces of the inside. The former *kapuma* was similar to ritual actions for ghosts (*preta*) and demons, the latter a fairly typical antisorcery *kapuma* incorporating the completing ritual acts (*tinduva*) of the Suniyama.[3] These rites ended Siyadoris's fear, at least while I was in the field.

The need to comprehend, to interpret the meaning of experience, or to explain the feeling and sense of embodied experience is particularly vital in the Sinhalese Buddhist context. The cultural emphases are quite explicit concerning the engagement of human beings in a complex web of actions born of existence. Siyadoris was driven, I suggest, to grasp the meaning of his experience. Possibly, as with human beings everywhere, his experience exceeded the meaning into which he could contain and structure it.

Dreams, or more appropriately nightmares, are a common indication that one is under attack by ghosts, demons, and human beings. They are obvious signs of malevolence. These terrors of the sign build more fear. Such fear, with rising intensity, as Siyadoris reported, is itself implicit recognition of the penetration of malignancy into the interior of the experiencing body. Manikpala invaded by Vasavarti, and Queen Yawudagiri inhabited by the sorcerer's fetus, are symbolic expressions of the body destroyed in fear, of the body open to the destructive energies of the world.

The meaning of nightmares could be said to be the terror of experiencing them and what they seem to indicate. Their indexes are integral to their terror (seeing death, experiencing the monkeys tearing at the body). However, the depth and intensity of the experience of nightmares, from all accounts, is packed with the portent which extends toward a meaning which is not yet there. Nightmares, like most dreams, are at the edge of meaning; they indicate a world immediately present in the dreamer that eludes comprehension. Nightmares or horrible daydreams as a function of the fear they cause impel those who experience them to search for their meaning, to seek beneath the surface of ordinary life for that which is hidden. In this sense, terrible nightmares and daydreams, especially when they insistently recur, constitute experience as an extension beyond meaning and sense, the overturning and upheaval of their structures. In this dynamic there is a spiraling of fear (fear itself being the agent of its own expansion).

Fear and the Play of the Imagination

Through the terrible play of the vital imaginary, the routine world of ordinary experience is broken down and its meanings and structures progressively dissolved. Alternatively, the gathering experience leads to the uncovering and construction of more and more hidden meanings and possibilities of life. Meaning and structure become exhausted in the dreadful press of the experience of fear. As Siyadoris implied, the experience of fear becomes all-consuming. The expressions of the body, the disruptions of the senses, the chills, and the trembling collapse and subsume meaning into the body of experience.

I note here the primordialism of the body in fear. Within it speech becomes silenced, or as Siyadoris's wife commented, speech—or rather the action of reflection—drives out meaning and becomes no longer the means for acting in the world. The victim in fear refuses to eat and to dress.

Consuming fear, as Siyadoris and other sorcery victims suggest, is a paralysis of the body. The senses of the body are reduced as the instruments of perception, the means for moving out on the world. Rather the senses are principally engaged in reception and become the means whereby that which is still outside and around floods into and overwhelms the lived-in body. When this occurs, the potential is there for the body's resistance finally to be broken. The conscious body is submerged and, like Siyadoris, loses consciousness.

The immobilizing of the body in fear progressively establishes the condition for a *world-within-being* rather than a *being-in-the-world*. The imagination plays within the space of the experiencing body withdrawn into itself. Encountering no resistance or modification from others in the world, toward whom the victim has ceased to move, the imagination of fear has no limitation apart from itself. The imagination moves freely, and like the other senses, it draws the possibilities of external realities within the body of experience and makes them real within the lived experience of the body. Different possibilities intermingle and merge in this creative play, combining perhaps into a single totalizing fantastic and monstrous shape. At this point the imagination of fear may explode itself. Either the terror created in the dynamic of the imaginary exceeds the experiential capacity of the body or the spin of the imaginary so consumes the realms of possibility that the imagination virtually dies from lack of fuel. In other words, the imagining consciousness runs out of a world or generates a world within which the body of the imagination can no longer live.

With the death of the imagination, the victim of sorcery might be conceived of as being taken to that dreadful region at the brink of the self-awareness of human being: that moment before the creation of political society imagined in the great myth of world origin and recounted in the context of Manikpala's terrible suffering. In this way, fear removes its victim from a world of meaning. Consciousness expanding and multiplying its fears must push or drive against itself. Siyadoris's falling unconscious and such imagery in the Sinhalese myths of terror are the escape of consciousness from itself. The body in fear, turned inward and trembling, is the final refuge, the last resistance against a destroying and voracious world. It is potentially a body given up to its own experience and perhaps only dimly aware of its own shuddering expression and of the world all around it within which the passage to fear took root.

I do not oppose the imaginary to the real, a common opposition. Sartre's (1966) approach to the imagination, aspects of which I use below, is an example of such a contrast. For him the imagination derealizes the real and comes into play in the absence of the real. As Dufrenne comments, Sartre mistakes "the part for the whole" (1973:357), for although the imaginary of consciousness may derealize the real, it is through the imagination that human beings adhere to or grasp the real or establish their existence in the world.[4] This notion is fundamental, I think, in Hindu and Buddhist concepts of illusion (*maya*), which understand the imagination as intrinsic to perception, whereby existence and attachment to existence are produced. The point can be put more strongly. The imagination as a dynamic of embodied consciousness is part of the real. It is constituted on the basis of the lived-in world and is the means by which the reality of this world is realized as real in experience. The imagination is integral to the process of the objectification of the world inhabited by and immediately present to the body.

It follows that dreams and dreaming are not the primary modes of the imagination, nor are they something apart from the actualities of the lived-in world. That is, dreams and dreaming are processes of the imagining consciousness, which is always active in wakefulness but is perhaps most apparent as one kind of imagination in repose, or in those moments that Bachelard (1969) examines as reverie and in the arousal from sleep. Furthermore, dreams, like all acts of the imagination of consciousness, result from the dwelling of human beings-in-the-world, no matter how fantastic or otherworldly the dreams may appear.[5]

Despite my reservations about Sartre's approach to the imagination of consciousness (he reduces the centrality of the imagination of consciousness in endowing the world with its reality, arguing that the imaginary is less real than the real),[6] his notion of the "chained consciousness" (Sartre 1966:52–71) is important for extending an understanding of the dynamics of the consciousness of fear which sorcery overshadows and of aspects of the fearing imagination and of the body in terror. A chained consciousness is one which develops in an immobile body.

Sartre makes his point by taking those moments between deep sleep and wakefulness as the periods when the excess and flights of the imagination seem most fully at play. This imagination of consciousness assumes its particular inventive and phantasmagoric character because the body of consciousness is immobile. That is, the motionlessness of the body disengages consciousness from its constant formation and reformation within the ongoing and changing structures of the life world: a process whereby the consciousness of individual human beings modifies and is continually being modified in contexts of action engaging others. Confined to the body, such a consciousness chained by fear not only can intensify its terrors but can attack its very ground of being, the body itself. Thus, the dreams of the ensorcelled, like those of Siyadoris, are of death and dying. These dreams, I suggest, are not simply born of a culture of sorcery and fear or of general human anxieties concerning death but are an expression of the very threat to consciousness that the immobility of the body in fear presents. The wish for death is produced by the paralysis of the body in fear.

Foucault, paradoxically echoing Sartre, argues that "the meaningfulness of all those dreams of violent death, of savage death, of horrified death," is a recognition of "a freedom up against the world" (1993: 54). In the last analysis, such dreams in the context of declarations and suspicions of sorcery may indeed be assertions of personal freedom and the right of an individual human existence against the press of the world. This is evident in sorcery action in which fear is converted into anger. But the dreams of death in sorcery should not necessarily be conceived in terms of a Foucauldian (or Sartrean) romanticism. Dreams of death express a consciousness (always an imagining consciousness) aware of its own extinction.

The dreams of death manifest the inseparability of consciousness from the body. They show that consciousness is integral to the motioning body, is always an activity of the body, and draws the body along with it through its direction into the world. It is in such direction, a transcendence of the physical boundaries of the body (through perceptual acts at least) into the world, that consciousness is sustained and grows. In dreams and in fear, consciousness afraid for itself can ultimately be sustained only by jolting the body into action, by means of which the body awakens and bursts the bonds of its confinement, to be extended once more toward the constantly changing horizons of its existence, the source of its imaginative sustenance.

Sartre understands the chaining of consciousness to be provoking the imagination, which ends once reality is reestablished. A different argument can be made. Consciousness is sparked in the motioning toward the horizons of existence, in the body increasingly drawn into the world by the projections of an imagining consciousness which are emergent in the movement of the body. This is how I interpreted a significance of the *hatadiya* in the Suniyama. The spin of the imagination of consciousness in the comedy of the *vadiga patuna* has its import in opening the victims of sorcery to the world and drawing them within it. But the chaining of the body in fear, or its immobilization or the blocking of action (a metaphor of sorcery), can destroy the consciousness engaging the imagination to such destruction. This is implicit in much of the episode of the *valvalalu* of the Suniyama, before the cutting of the victim's bonds. This suggests that embodied consciousness confined and enclosed within the body is potentially autodestructive both of consciousness and of the body with which it is in inseparable union. However, the cutting of the bonds symbolizes as it effects the capacity of consciousness to break the bonds of its self-closure, which limits consciousness to the body (the death of consciousness) and enables it to expand as agent-being into the world. The body of consciousness is opened and made to move toward the world, a world of the victim's existence which reenlivens the victim and to which the victim, reempowered in consciousness and once again active, also gives life.

The cultural constructions of sorcery, the beliefs and practices of sorcery, can participate in the intensification of fear. In Sri Lanka, where sorcery is a routine expectation, and the destruction of sorcery is apparent in practice and in representation (in temple and in shrine), the merest suggestion of its presence in experience is sufficient to spark an expanding fear. As Siyadoris and his kin increasingly recognized his experience as sorcery, his comprehension of his world through the lens of sorcery indications and projections intensified his fear.

But I do not wish to imply that fear of sorcery is a product of cultural constructions of sorcery. Rather these are the means through which individuals already in the condition of fearing come both to represent their fear and to recognize it as a function of the life world in which their being is constituted. That is, sorcery victims, through the agency of sorcery beliefs and practices, come to see their fear, expressed immediately as the unsettling of their bodies, as a fear of something in the world of their existence. In this sense, sorcery beliefs in articulating fearful experience express what is vital in human emotionality of whatever culturally recognizable kind as always emergent in the relations human beings have with their life worlds.

Through the constructions of sorcery, fear is contextualized. It is objectified and given diverse forms as a quality of social relations and events in the life world. The cultural constructions of sorcery operate to stimulate the imagination so that the world of existence is represented in negative mode. But when it is so represented, a distance and an intervention are established between fear as the immediate experience present in the body and the agencies blocking or destroying the capacity for action. The reimagination of the sources of the body's fear through sorcery beliefs and practices both reextends the individual in fear toward the world and starts a process whereby the agencies of fear can be objectified and externalized. In other words, a way is opened for the intimacy of the sources of fear with the body to be broken and their binding chains cut.

Sorcery has been described as a closed system of belief. That is, its assumptions are self-validating, so that it encloses all possibility. I regard this apparent closure as the dynamic of sorcery's totalization: its capacity to draw disconnected experiences into the one net. Sorcery is not necessarily to be contrasted with supposed open systems or systems whose assumptions can be invalidated and which must have their structure of understanding reformulated. This is a feature that some anthropologists and historians claim is the rationality of science. Rather, the imaginary of consciousness in the recognition of sorcery can be seen as potentially both closing and opening. As the experience of the life world comes to be understood and organized through the terms of sorcery, sorcery gives a meaning to reality which is at a distance from the experiencing body and which facilitates the opening up of victims to their life world and their reextension in it.

I have discussed the symbolic doubleness of sorcery: for example, it combines images of destruction and of restitution. It may be added that the doubleness of sorcery also shows that consciousness, in particular its imaginary, is both a force in the derealization and destruction of the meaning structures of the life world (as in the dynamic leading to Siyadoris's collapse) and a force in the re-realization of the life world. Other aspects of the definition of Siyadoris's situation through the constructions of sorcery illustrate this.

With the recognition of his ensorcellment, Siyadoris, his wife, and his other kin drew the various unsettling dimensions of their world into sharper focus. This occurred in the context of the divination and treatment of his troubles. The authority of the *sastra kari* whom Podinona visited depended on her ability to read the source of the problem before any suggestion from the client. When the soothsayer indicated the presence of *kodivina* the soothsayer (as was this *sastra kari*'s practice) proceeded to get further confirmation by asking Podinona a series of short questions (see Chapter 2). The exorcist's divinations followed a similar process. I stress, however, that the soothsayer and exorcist did not construct the context of fear out of thin air. Rather, they participated in giving a world already filled with terrible potential a particular form.

The ground for Siyadoris's fears had been long prepared. The house next door had been the setting of tragedy upon tragedy. Podinona's elder brother had lived there with his family. He had died some seven years before after a short illness. But barely a year after his death, his wife died. A few months later, the daughter was killed in a car accident. The son, the last surviving member of the household, then left the area to board with relatives in Colombo. The house has remained vacant and locked ever since. It is polluted with death, and as Podinona said, inhabited only by *preta* and *yakku*. Siyadoris said that the destruction of this household filled his thoughts. The exorcist's divination and the soothsayer's questions brought the tragedies into the foreground of his awareness. Siyadoris said that he could hear frightening screams coming from the house almost constantly. He took sleeping pills to get him through the night, especially around midnight, when the screaming was particularly bad. Siyadoris's frightening dream about the death of living relatives was grounded in the activities of the everyday life world.

Siyadoris's eldest son, a junior manager in a tourist hotel on the outskirts of Colombo, had bought a small plot of land two months before his father's crisis. He had obtained the land from a person who had a reputation for casting powerful mantras. The exorcist who treated Siyadoris was called in to clear the plot of any possible enchantment: the presence of protective charms which might attack strange new occupants.[7] The son had discussed this matter with his father and believed later that something buried on the land might have attacked Siyadoris. This possibility was brought to the forefront in the discussion surrounding the recognition of sorcery as instrumental in Siyadoris's collapse.

Anxiety, Fear, and Sociality

I have concentrated on the dynamics of fear because the specialists in sorcery—*aduras*, *sastra karayas* or soothsayers, *kapuralas* or shrine priests, *maniyos* or female attendants to demonic or sorcery gods—most frequently describe sorcery as having to do with fear (*baya*). Exorcists and priests outline and name a great variety of fears that are part of the expression and experience of sorcery. In my interpretation, the description of sorcery as fear indicates that it is the totalization and manifestation of extreme anxiety (*kansava*). That is, sorcery encompasses human beings' awareness of a whole gamut of forces in their life world that are potentially threatening to their ongoing existence. Fear and anxiety are psychological conditions in the sense that they must be centered in individual human beings. But they originate because human beings exist with others and are immersed in the activities of the world, because they are social beings. By this I do not mean that they are subordinate to society as some kind of transcendent structure but that they are engaged in the diverse social practices of the life world.

Sorcery, with its fear and anxiety, is the acute realization of being-in-the-world, of a self-consciousness which is aware of this fact. It is the dynamics of that world, integral to being, that have created a sense of being apart from the world of existence, within which the destruction of being is immanent. Sorcery, as I think the Suniyama rite shows so clearly, is a radical decentering of human beings from the practices of their own existence and world creation, a terrible cutting adrift by forces within the practices of the world on which existence depends. The fear and anxiety that sorcery beliefs and practices express are not founded in some original existential solitude or aloneness (which some might hold is fundamental to the human condition) but in the forces of existence that block or bar human participation in the activities of the life world or separate or isolate human beings in the life world. The fear expressed in sorcery experience and projected in belief relates to the dynamics of a world against being. The forces of existence deny and rage against the very body of existence.

Thus Siyadoris has the experience of his very life's breath being squeezed out by the dreadful press of the world against his body. A paralysis or semiparalysis of the body, otherwise inexplicable (victims and their kin usually have such symptoms medically checked), frequently accompanies sorcery attack. This is explicitly conceived of as a violent rejecting world forcing against the body. Thus, Jeanette, the wife of a poor farm shareholder, associated her paralysis (she could not move) with land inheritance struggles over seven years. Apart from her paralysis, the start of the attack was marked by poltergeist-like experiences: pots and plates would break and fly at her head, and, Jeanette commented, the stink of shit filled the air. At one time her small hut (built from cadjan palm) caught fire during one of these attacks. Her whole lived-in world was being destroyed, and her own life threatened to be extinguished. Jeanette frequently fell unconscious.

The onset of sorcery is commonly indicated by the throwing of stones against one's house. For example, Nandawathie, the forty-five-year-old wife of a brickmaker, experienced her attack of sorcery as the sweating and aching of her limbs and an immobilizing headache. No organic cause could be discovered by the local medical doctor. She felt that her body was collapsing against a world that was beating against her. Nandawathie's symptoms were not relieved, and a few days later, stones were thrown at her house from the thick undergrowth at the rear. The stones continued to be thrown at intervals for the next two weeks, and Nanda-wathie, as reported by her relatives, would cry in pain at each occurrence and express a feeling of impending death and a removal of her body from the world. As related by her kin, she would moan, "O mother, O father, someone is taking me away . . . lifting and dragging me" (*Budu ammo, budu tatte kavudo mava ussan yanavo*).

These examples are the extremes of anxiety in sorcery, of life at the brink of extinction as a function of forces striking at the body and at its dwelling: at the habitus of life's body, at the places of routine safety, of sustenance, and of the lived-in space of a taken-for-granted world (the inside world of the house) whose ordinary practices (the attack on Jeanette by her own cooking utensils, Siyadoris's feeling that his food was the substance of sorcery) are integral to the daily constitution and structuring of the life world. These vital features in the anxiety and fear of sorcery are of course the major concern of the Suniyama and of the less dramatic but often no less complex *kapuma*s to which all these victims resorted. Although these cases are extreme (but common), I submit that they are acute manifestations of the nature of anxiety that sorcery reveals and that its constant discoveries of envy and jealousy, and its expressions of lack, personal suffering, and conflicts and hatreds elaborate.

It should be clear that I am not engaging in psychologism of the kind distrusted by many social anthropologists in discussing the fear of sorcery as an organization of anxiety. Evans-Pritchard, echoed in Mary Douglas (1966), attacked perspectives that attempt to understand sorcery beliefs (and religion) as generated in fear: that is, the idea that sorcery grows in the conditions of fear and sustains it. Thus, the Azande, when they divine sorcery, are not afraid but indignant and outraged. This observation supports an insistence in social anthropology that sorcery is a phenomenon having to do with social relations and the structure of the social order and the process of its definition. Such a position is opposed, in the still-Durkheim-influenced ambience of much social anthropology (but not all), to approaches that proceed from psychological assumptions relating to individuals.[8] The perspective I have pursued is not Durkheimian (i.e., society is not treated as some kind of transcendent superstructure) nor is it reducible to the psychology of individuals somehow treated as isolable from their ongoing conditions of existence. Anxiety and fear in this discussion are not primary processes of the kind that formed the approaches to religion to which scholars such as Evans-Pritchard were sharply opposed. Anxiety and fear result from the fact that human beings are embroiled in the activities of their life worlds. The anxiety and fear of sorcery are not opposed to sociality or to the unity that human beings form with their worlds through their intentionality. They develop in the forces that attack or threaten the forms or orderings of the life world in which human existence is conditioned and defined. This is one implication of the Manikpala story and the practice of the Suniyama. Anxiety and fear are generated in the destruction and demolition of the world order in which the sorcerer's victims are contained and sustained. The fear and anxiety evident in sorcery beliefs and practices are an expression of the depth of anguish in human beings at losing connection with the ground of existence and the forms of life in the world on which being or individual life depends.

In fear, human beings are in flight from the world and are thereby threatened with a loss of consciousness. Anger, however, is a thrust toward the world. It is destructive, like the fury of Vasavarti, but also potentially regenerative. This is the case in the rite that Oddisa organizes for the stricken Manikpala when she is made to face back into the world order. Anger involves a dynamic that is both destructive of the sorcerer and regenerative of the victim's agent-consciousness or capacity to reconstitute a life world. The action at the sorcery shrines may be seen as repeating, though with clear differences, the themes of the Suniyama (see Chapter 2). The supplicants combine the roles of Oddisa and victim, for they are themselves the agents of destruction and of regeneration. Furthermore, the anger provoked in their anguish can be seen as the energy of human intentionality, a reconstitutive move back toward a world in which their lives have already been constituted but are now threatened by destructive forces immanent within their realities, by obstacles and by rejection. Through the intentional burst of their anger, the supplicants at the shrines can restore their sense of agency and recenter themselves in their social and political realities.

The Contexts of the Shrines: Spaces of Death and Rebirth

I discuss the action at some of the main sorcery shrines, describing them as turbulent centers, vertices of destructive and regenerative energies. They may be regarded as all the *cakra* points of the Suniyama rolled into one. At the main sorcery shrines, supplicants approach primordial ground: they are in spaces at the edge of existence, perhaps flung by the forces of social and political life to the fringe of their orders. Supplicants in the shrines become united with their energies, draw the power of the shrines to themselves, and through this power reextend themselves regeneratively toward the world of their anxiety and anguish. Within the space of the shrines, supplicants may be said to combine within themselves the transgressive boundary- and obstacle-removing force of a Vasavarti with the world-making powers of Mahasammata. Through the dynamic of the shrines, supplicants are able to reimagine, give shape to, and sharpen the outlines of their anxieties. Moreover, they can transmute their sense of lack or loss or incapacity for agency which fear expresses into an angry and often punishing regrasping of their hold on the world and on the source of their existence, and can reintervene in the life-giving processes of their realities.

The way the main sorcery shrines are articulated into cultural, social, and historical space is vital to their power and tends to distinguish them from shrines to other gods that are not usually the domains for cursing, personal reconstitution, or protection *through destruction*.[9] The most powerful shrines are those that are oriented to the everyday social and political world and that embrace or totalize the contradictions and diversities of the forces within it. In an almost Nietzschean sense they are beyond good and evil. They are chthonic in ambience, manifesting the turbulence of origination and reorigination, hence their sense and metaphors of sexuality and violence. The shrines are places of excess outside the orders of the life world, in spaces at the edge of existence or located in zones where existence is threatened or most volatile. Yet they are oriented to an ordering or reordering of life in existence.

The more potent shrines are in marginal geographical, ethnic, social, and political locations, at boundaries of transgression and of conversion. Some of the powerful demon-deities of sorcery are associated with trade. This is not merely because traders or entrepreneurs tend to have great recourse to such gods as a function of the real uncertainties of the world of their work. Many shrines have been established by the financial support of businessmen. However, I stress trade as a metaphor, a practice that transgresses and converts.

The sorcery shrines are centers of purity and pollution. They gain in their potency from the casting away of disease and the defiling forces in life within their space. The discarded pollution adheres to the shrines and becomes integral to their dangerous and destructive power and part of the dynamic force that throws supplicants back into their life worlds.

The sorcery shrines are grounded in the ordinary life world. They may be said to be transcendent *in* it rather than transcendent *of* it. This feature marks the shrines as distinct from those to other major gods in the Sinhala pantheon. The other gods generally describe a process whereby internal divisions and contradictions are resolved into an overarching coherent and unifying form. The unification to which they point is ultimately beyond existence. The sorcery gods do not offer any such ultimate transcendence; they exist as the contradictions of worldly existence and offer resolution only in the sense that they place their supplicants on the benign or just side of things. They invert fortunes but do not resolve the problematics of the life world. The demon-deities do not draw on higher powers so much as draw on the contrary forces that are integral to the life world of human beings. The sorcery shrines build their power directly on the particularities of their social and political location. Their power and popularity is highly sensitive to shifts in the social and political orders of the locales in which they are sited and to changes of other historical kinds (e.g., nationalist discourses in contemporary times have yielded new significance to the mythological history of certain shrines, leading to their increased popularity and potency). I will now describe some of the qualities that contribute to the experiential intensity of the shrines and their refractive force on the life world of supplicants.

The Qualities of the Shrines

Many priests (*kapuralas*) at Suniyam shrines say that they got their authority (*varam*) from the Suniyam shrine at Kabalava, the site of the originary, or *mul*, or root Suniyam. Currently there are two such shrines in the area, as the result of a succession dispute between rival *kapuralas* for control over the first shrine, which was established in the 1920s. Suniyam has his fundamental divided quality reinvented in this conflict. Kabalava is approximately thirty-five kilometers from Chilaw, near the town of Kuliyapitiya, where Sinhala-speaking communities give way to Tamil speakers, and it is the line of an ancient trade route. It is not far from the ancient city site of Panduvasnuvara (Parakramapura). This is named after Panduvas, who succeeded Vijaya, the legendary founder of Sinhala hegemony; this is the same Panduvas who suffered the curse of the spurned Kuveni. Atop the mountain behind the ruins of this largely thirteenth-century city is a recently reconstructed *tomb of Vijaya*. Halfway up the mountain is a small sorcery shrine (not Kabalava). The Kabalava shrine, although recently established, draws much of its potency from the mythological resonances which many people today believe attach to the area.

The main shrines to Suniyam in Colombo can also be conceived of as located in marginal social and political space. The Maligawatta (Dematagoda) shrine, currently perhaps the most popular, is located at the edge of the city, in an area of much ethnic and social mix (see Gombrich and Obeyesekere 1988: 107–12 for a description of this shrine). It is a place of considerable poverty and is famous for its violent crime. Maligawatta (established in 1958) began as an offshoot of Lunava, another famous Suniyama temple, located at the southern edge of Colombo's urban sprawl, in the urban district of Moratuwa. Lunava is on the coast, like other important sorcery places. Moratuwa is now populated largely by respectable members of the urban bourgeoisie, and the clientele of the shrine might be described as dominantly middle class. Perhaps it is less socially and politically marginal, and this may account for some of its decline in popularity. Its zone has cooled; it is not located in a site of hot turbulence, of transition and transgression, from which some of the other sorcery shrines draw their energy.

Entering into a major Suniyam shrine, at least for me, imparts a sense of entering primordial ground, of entering into the earth and the potentiality of being. At one Suniyam shrine near the boundary of Colombo municipality, supplicants enter the premises through the jaws of a lion, a representation of the lion of Sinhala, the lion of state at the ancient (fifth century C.E.) fortress site of Sigiri rock (see Kapferer 1988a, cover illustration). A model of a Buddha *dagaba* and the Wheel of the *dhamma* are also alongside it. Worshipers descend into a series of dark caverns, primal and womblike spaces. These may be said to give rise to the political and social and moral order on top of them (the lion of state, the Buddha *dagaba*). At the center of the shrine's inner chambers, besides Suniyam, are images of demons and gods who embody themes of destruction and regeneration. Bhadrakali is one, and the priest turns on a light that bathes her in a red light. An image of Pattini, the destroyer of Madurai, who also restores her husband to life, is nearby. A large statue of the devouring bearlike form of the great cemetery demon, Mahasona, has a prominent position. Mahasona, according to the myths of his rebirth, was destroyed in a violent quarrel and was restored to life, but in distorted and ruptured form, by Saturn, the planetary god (see Kapferer 1983). The priest explains that Mahasona is the commander-in-chief (*senadipati*) of Suniyam's army.[10]

This shrine gives extreme symbolic stress to destructive and regenerative power. It is significant that the shrine is supported largely by politically and economically powerful members of the urban bourgeoisie. The shrine in fact was built by the *kapurala*s with money from their clients; some clients sent money from as far away as America, England, and Australia in return for Suniyam's assistance. This shrine, like Lunava, mani-

fests sorcery as the anxiety and force of the dominant. The more fre-
quented and powerful shrines in Colombo attract their clientele from a
wider social spectrum, from the socially weak as well as the powerful.

But the chthonic aspects of this shrine are repeated in other shrines.
This is the case with the Maligawatta shrine, which was enlarged as a
consequence of its growing popularity and the donations of powerful
Colombo-based politicians and entrepreneurs. An upper story has been
added to a once-single-floored shrine where the main image of Suniyam
is kept, flanked on his left by a large glass cabinet encasing all the main
beings of the Sinhala pantheon. On the upper story have been placed a
large statue of the Buddha and images of the twelve guardian gods of Sri
Lanka. Suniyam is re-realized as the totalizing energy of the ground of
existence, which is contained or held down by more ordering and equable
representations.

Defilement, dirt, and disgust (*pilikul*) are integral to the cursing, destructive, and regenerative work of the shrines. There is a smell of decay
and the detritus of death in their space. Supplicants cast off the death
and poison of their distress which have clung to their bodies and in reoriginating themselves throw it back on the agents of their anxiety. At the
main shrine for Bhadrakali near the beach at Modera in Colombo, situated on the grounds of a Hindu temple dedicated to Ganesa (the remover
of obstacles), Buddhists, Christians, Muslims, and Hindus come to curse.
Bhadrakali is attended by male and female (*maniyo*) priests who are Sinhalese. A major kind of curse (*paligahima*) involves smashing eggs on
which the priest writes the name of the agent of suffering, sometimes in
the blood of the supplicant. Similar practices are now becoming increasingly popular at the main Suniyam shrines. Here some priests demand
the use of rancid coconut oil (*kunu pol*) in the cursing. The power of dirt
is harnessed to the violent work.[11]

A famous cursing shrine for the demon-deity Gale Bandara is filled
with an air of disgust. The shrine is situated outside the town of Kurunegala, in an area where for some centuries there have been settlements
of Muslim peasant farmers. Gale Bandara originated in the death of a
prince born of the union between a Sinhala king and his Muslim queen.[12]
The site is visited by Sinhalese Buddhists from all over the island, as well
as by Muslims. Its officiating priest is a Muslim. The relatively confined
space of the shrine is crowded with dogs, mangy and flea-bitten. These
were given by supplicants in return for the boons they were granted.
Those visiting the shrine have to pick their way through the dogs, which
for me, at any rate, was a slightly unsettling experience. Dogs, of course,

are loathsome to Muslims, which contributes to a sense of the place's filth.

There is a similar aspect, though less disgusting, at the popular shrine at Gatabaruya (for the demon-deity Rajjaruvo Bandara) in the southern foothills of the Morawaka District. This shrine is located near caves where the Sinhala king Valagamba is said to have taken refuge during a period of invasion from southern India. The shrine was declared a site of national heritage during the presidency of the late President Premadasa, presumed assassinated by Tamil Tigers. Rajjaruvo is famous for meting out judgments in quarrels and revealing thieves and liars. The area of the shrine is overrun with cocks given in return for favors done. They are Rajjaruvo's symbol but are also key sacrificial objects in exorcism; they are to be eaten by demons as surrogates for human beings.

Other major sorcery shrines variously repeat the ambience I have been describing. At Sinigama, on the south coast near the large town of Galle, people come to curse at the main shrine to Devol Deviyo, often grinding chilies and mustard seed mixed with broken glass as they make their curses. The main object used in cursing (*des*) is a seven-spouted pot, or *punava*, representing cobra hoods, conceived as holding disease and pollution.[13]

A flat totalized human world of often mutually antagonistic and swirling suffering is present before the demon-gods. They draw to themselves people from all walks of life whose anguish and anxiety—although it may arise from their particular social or political distinction or status in everyday life—engulfs and obliterates such differentiation.

The Pragmatics of the Shrines

In Sri Lanka and elsewhere, religious places have as their ethos notions of equality and humility before the godhead. Pilgrimage gives this especial emphasis. The distinctions and hierarchies of the everyday life world, however, particularly in relation to religious life at the urban and neighborhood temples, tends to shine through. The location of the temples, their clientele, controlling monks, and governing lay organizations (*dayaka saba*) refract social distinctions of class, caste, and political power.[14] The temples and the religious practices that center on them function in the expressions and interests of class power. Although persons who are subordinate in social life are by no means excluded from such practices, their participation at the temples of routine worship of the Buddha and the Guardian Gods is often a way to reexpress their subordination and integrate them within practices commanded by the powerful.

The sorcery temples cannot be separated from such social and political dynamics and can succumb to them. Sorcery shrines that come under the overriding control of particular communities, which may also influence an overroutinization of practice (i.e., reducing the diversity and invention of sorcery practices), might ultimately lead to the decline of the potency and popularity of the temple and its resident god. The popularity of the Bhadrakali shrine is likely to persist, because it is in a socially and religiously marginal situation and relative to other shrines (e.g., the Maligawatta Suniyam) is less likely to be captured, subsumed, and tamed to bourgeois interest alone.[15]

A visit to sorcery temples, however, has little to do with religious worship or devotion as expressed at other religious and ritual places. People do not express their social and political identity through their visits, in the sense that some patients express them in their performance of Suniyamas. Going to a powerful Suniyam *devale* or to the shrine of another demon-deity is not a display of virtuous Buddhist action. The devotees of Suniyam are generally persons who conceive of themselves in a constant situation of acute vulnerability or who have experienced repeated difficulties and distress.

Thus, Yasawati and her mother are enthusiastic followers of Suniyam. Yasawati, in particular, became involved after the murder of her father, a furniture salesman. His death left the family destitute, and the murderer was not caught. The father kept visiting Yasawati in her dreams, often appearing in the form of Suniyam. She was troubled by the dreams and sometimes became entranced. A number of small demon ceremonies were performed for her, including one for the violent Mahasona. Her two brothers then disappeared during the youth insurrection of 1989 against the Sri Lankan government. Mother and daughter thought the brothers may have been in one of the government detention camps. Both mother and daughter were distraught and took the daughter's dreams as signs that they should worship Suniyam (the authoritative and protective father?). They had done this for some six months before the interview, mother and daughter pleading continually for the safety of the brothers.

People go to the sorcery shrines and become devotees out of necessity: because their very circumstances of existence are threatened, because the social relations at the center of their lives are in some way destroyed, and so forth. The shrines are places to which persons are flung by forces in their political and social realities. Suppliants are impelled to visit the shrines rather than drawn to them because of their powers which transcend social and political orders. The most powerful Buddhist temples or sites are those to which pilgrimages are made. Ideally, on a pilgrimage, the devotees suspend their everyday social identities and become an undifferentiated body of worshipers, often in a celebratory mood. At the potent sorcery shrines, social distinctions and identity are not voluntarily yielded but are in danger of being lost or taken away. Such unity as may exist is one of abjection and the pushing of supplicants to the edge of social and political existence by the very orders and potencies of existence. The populations that gather at the more potent sorcery shrines are decentered from the world and in certain places appear as homogeneous communities of suffering.

The suffering is most visible at the Modera Bhadrakali temple. Unlike some of the other popular urban sorcery shrines, which can be approached at any time, the Bhadrakali shrine is opened at the limited times for *puja* (offering) only twice (Tuesday and Friday) a week.[16] Large crowds of mainly Buddhist and some Christian Sinhalese congregate. The urban poor and the struggling lower reaches of the extensive Sri Lankan middle class and urban bourgeoisie are present. So too are the powerful and the wealthy; their new Kombi vans, Mazdas, and an occasional Mercedes-Benz occupy the parking space at the shrine entrance. They come seeking assistance for all kinds of exigency: to ask for help in achieving a favorable judgment at court, to seek protection against employees or to attack an abusive and threatening boss or landlord, to wreak vengeance against an adulterous spouse, to punish a thief, to facilitate risky business deals, and so forth. The pleas and the curses, make the shrine seem to be a world against itself. At the Bhadrakali shrine and all the other potent shrines, the contradictions and conflicts of social and political realities become apparent: the mutual hostilities in the relations of class, the tensions of ethnic enmity, the fury and suspicion grounded in the complexities of kin relations and the problems of inheritance, and much else.

The images in the shrines are further potentiated as representations of turbulent fracture, of conflict and division in the context of anxiety and suffering that forms around them. There is, I suggest, a synergic building of power and violence in the mutuality of the gaze of the demon-deities and their supplicants. The gods are virtually alive, active in building the tension of those who come to them; as the anguish of the supplicants and their often murderous incantations grows, the powers of the gods also grow. There is a dynamic in the representations and the very ambience of the space of the shrines which augments the diverse experiences of anxiety and expands both the fear and the anger. In the presence of the sorcery gods and in generative interaction with them, supplicants are perhaps enabled to give greater reflective focus to their anxiety, to realize an intensity of interpretation of the nature of their suffering and its circumstance.

Priests (*kapurala*s; or *maniyo*s, female attendants), mediate the interaction between supplicants and the sorcery gods and, through their invocations and their performance, assist in the interpretation of distress and its intensification, or the reimagining and reexpression of the enormity of the anguish. Within the space of the shrines, supplicants can come to a deepened and highly dramatic sense of the forces that play against them and drive them to the edge of their life worlds.

The priests or other attendants at the potent sorcery shrines often embody (and this is sometimes expressed in the very attitude of their bodies) the fury of the gods. They can be a personification of their dynamic. There is a similarity and a difference here to the capacity of *adura*s in the Suniyama to manifest Oddisa's power: on the one hand, to assume or enter into direct struggle with the destructive energies of Suniyam, and on the other hand, to control them and to separate themselves from the forces of abjection. The *adura*s stress their powers of mimesis, as do many of the potent sorcery priests. But the *adura*s get their mimetic capacities primarily through learned knowledge and skill. The sorcery priests, however, often acquire their knowledge and powers through experiences involving Suniyam in daily life and through direct encounters with Suniyam. It can be said that in their performances at the shrines they are continually reliving their experience and their own intense relation with the forces of destruction and regeneration. Supplicants therefore enter into close and intimate connection with the forces relevant to their own anguish by means of the body and performance of some of the sorcery priests. The priests and the supplicants form an implicit union. The furious invocations of the priests may be said to be projections of the patient's condition and also lived by both supplicant and priest. They share in suffering and exchange powers. For a moment supplicants can become their own priests, able to control overcoming and rejecting forces.

The priests at the sorcery shrines are integral to the vitality of the shrine contexts. The popularity of the shrines often relates to their reputation. The *kapurala* at Gatabaruya is renowned for his powers, and during some of his invocations is virtually possessed by the violent punishing mien of the demon-deity he mediates. At some shrines, such as Maligawatta, there is a relatively high turnover of shrine priests; they are sometimes persons of low-caste backgrounds and people who had recent encounters with Suniyam's powers. Through such turnover, the potency of the shrine is continually revitalized. The *maniyo*s at the Modera Bhadrakali shrine express histories of personal suffering and the intervention of the goddess. The most powerful ones are from impoverished backgrounds and tend to live in shantytowns.

Several features of the contexts of the sorcery shrines—their marginality, their totalizing, chthonic, and turbulent dynamic, the divisive nature and world orientation of the central gods, the character of the priests and other attendants, and the collective distress of their clientele—combine to create the distinctive ambience of the sorcery temples. The temples collect those who are or feel themselves to be rejected and flung to the perimeters of existence by energies alive in the social and political realities of existence. The temples concentrate such force, and this is integral to their power. Thus, the shrines may be said to manifest a density of destructive and malignant force, an intensification of what is driving against supplicants, threatening them, and blocking or rejecting them from an ongoing involvement in diverse aspects of their life world. So intense is the destructive and ultimately life-taking quality of the shrines (the shrines are spaces of death, veritable killing fields), that their dynamic is to force the supplicants back into the world. Thus, the anger expressed in the shrines is partly generated by their context (as well as the supplicant's individual experience) and is integral to the motional force of the anger pushing supplicants back into the world.

I have referred to the disgust of the shrines and to their being places of defilement or pollution. Kristeva (1982) argues for the potency of disgust, as something that often resonates immediately and shockingly within the depths of physical being, operating beneath reflective awareness and acting as a fundamental perception and sensing of the body. The experience of disgust has force, thrusting the body back from a contact or union with the agent or agency of disgust.[17] This is, I suggest, one potentiality of the shrines for supplicants. The dualism of Suniyam, expressed in his imagery, is of the force of destruction joined to the energy of order: his death-dealing aspect clings to his life-ordering power. Supplicants seek in the shrines to separate themselves from the energies of destruction that cling to their bodies and to assert and sever the life-regenerating and ordering forces from the destructive and polluting forces. The action of flinging away the destructive forces becomes the power of the curses of priests and supplicants.

Boiling Anger and the Cursing of Despair

Most of the supplicants come alone, but some arrive in small family groups. The majority are women, but roughly one-third are men. Many of the men are small traders, but some of them are wealthy businessmen and politicians. In one instance, a prominent Buddhist priest and members of the lay association came to curse the robbers who had stolen from the temple treasure house, where gifts to the temple were on display. The high number of women is related to the high value of the household; women are not only the generative centers and source of existence but are particularly vulnerable to attack and sensitive to the forces that strike their families (see Kapferer 1983).

Sinhalese cultural values give women a heightened sense of responsibility for suffering and expand their own embodied feelings as centers of destruction and regeneration: an aspect to which the story of Manikpala's sorcery gives vivid expression. Their actions at the shrines and in other ritual contexts often seem to manifest the openness of their bodies, compared to those of men, to the expression of their own anguish and that of others. This is part of cultural expectation as well as of their culturally influenced and lived dispositions in everyday life. It is evident not only in the greater numbers of women that attend the shrines but in the form their cursing and supplication often takes before the demon-deities. A woman's whole body becomes transformed into the dynamics of the action. Thus, I have witnessed instances where women have become entranced before the sorcery god. Etched in my memory is the sight of a woman, distraught at being abandoned by her husband, who came before Suniyam and wildly let loose the braids of her hair. Her whole demeanor was wild and furious, she uttered curse after curse at the source of her distress.

Within contemporary Sri Lanka, women, in my view more than men, are at the center of destructive social and political forces in a context of growing poverty, especially along the densely settled urbanized coast. The withering away of state-supported social services, which has gathered pace since 1977, when the United National Party took power (replaced in August 1994 by Chandrika Kumaratunga's People's Alliance), has intensified problems for women, who are largely responsible for the routine organization of the house and the welfare of children. Years of civil strife (the Tamil war of separation in the north and east of the island and massive insurrectionary and government violence within the Sinhala population, resulting in a high loss of life, particularly of young men) are evident in the anguish of women at the shrines; they are left with the burden of maintaining their households in often shattering circumstances.

I have selected instances of women's anguish and cursing before the Maligawatta and Modera Bhadrakali shrines. They give a sense not just of the great anxiety that is routinely expressed at the shrines but also the potentially regenerative force of such action.

The Fury of Babynona

Babynona's approach to Suniyam followed a fairly typical pattern. She began by invoking the authority of the Buddha and other cosmic powers through the relatively simple acts of washing the Bo tree and giving flower and light offerings to Buddha, the planets, and the gods. The priest then asked Babynona to hold a coconut on which the priest placed a small square of burning camphor. The coconut had the three germ holes exposed, the fiber which usually covers them having been shaved off. It was a *poison coconut* (*vas pol*), an object that condenses notions of barrenness, infertility, and the obliteration of life. The coconut had been ritually empowered by the priest with this destructive potency and Babynona had bought it from him.

The priest then asked Babynona why she had come. She explained quickly that her landlord had demanded that she and her husband leave within three months. But they had no place to go. The deadline had passed and the landlord had sent his hired thugs to beat Babynona and her husband. "Did you go to the police?" asked the priest. "No," she replied, "the landlord is a friend of the OIC (Officer-in-Charge of Police). He will never help. This is why I have come to Suniyam." The priest asked the landlord's name. He then invoked Suniyam's attention (*kannalavva*) and uttered his curse (*avalada*) on the woman's behalf. The priest's powerful voice boomed and both invocation and curse reverberated around the chamber of the shrine.

I give homage to Isvara and to Rama
Homage to the mighty army of Skanda
Homage to the gem at Vadiga's neck
Homage and gifts to Oddisa.
O God who rules in Sri Lanka
Who carries the Vadiga sword in his right hand
The sword that severed the heads of the Asuras
Who carries the burning pot of fire in his left hand
Look upon this woman.

The landlord (name inserted) has hired thugs.
O God, the thugs have beaten everyone in the house.
This blameless woman cannot go to the police.
The police do not help the poor, they are friends of the landlord.
God look upon this woman. Let her family live in peace.
Break the limbs of the thugs. Cut off their legs. Burn the thugs into ash.
O God who has destroyed the Asuras. Kill the landlord and destroy his thugs.
O God, may you become a future Buddha for carrying out this punishment.

The priest then instructed Babynona to break the coconut, now further infused with the power of his curse, on a stone before the image of Ganesa. She paused for a moment, motionless, and then spoke inaudibly into the coconut. Babynona breathed her anguish into this object of destruction. Lifting the coconut high above her head, she flung it toward the ground. Smashing against the stone, the energy of the priest's curse and Babynona's own suffering anger burst toward the source of her anguish. The action has functional similarity with that of the *tinduva* in the Suniyama and other *kapuma*s. It is a finishing act of judgment.

I asked Babynona to repeat into a tape recorder what she had just whispered, what supplicants call their *dukganavilla,* "suffering striking." Quite possibly she added to and embroidered what she said. But she was still in the heat of her anger, and what she repeated is some indication of the emotional energy and ground of her action.

> O God! Commander of the army that destroyed the Asuras. Grant me a boon. Our landlord has hired thugs. They have beaten me and my whole family. Even my baby girl. Bring honor to your name by punishing these brutal people. Please punish them. I will always worship you. Punish them in three days or after seven days. Break their bones. Smash their heads into seven bits. Cover their bodies in sores. O God, you are the most powerful in the three worlds. O God, this landlord has made himself rich by politics. He beats his own servants. He cares nothing for the people. He has nothing but bad qualities. He is a criminal. He sells pork. He even eats the vehicle on which Suniyam rides. O God! Punish this cruel man. Don't miss this chance to punish this man who harms the people. He worships only money. O God, can you see my poverty? We eat only one meal a day. My children are sick. We have nowhere to live. We are only servants to the rich. We suffer every day. Give us your divine sympathy. Give us life. May you become a Buddha in the future.

A Mother Rejected

Kamalawati had been married to a wealthy furniture merchant. According to the shrine priest, she had been coming to the Suniyam shrine for a number of years and felt isolated and socially demeaned. Her anger had grown toward her adopted son and his wife. The wife, Kamalawati claimed, put on airs in relation to her, the daughter-in-law playing on her Kandyan background and presumed higher-caste status.[18] Kamalawati felt the hostility of her daughter-in-law and even suspected her of using sorcery to kill her husband. Kamalawati blamed the daughter-in-law for influencing her son to take legal action to secure control over her husband's estate. She came to Suniyam's shrine to end her son's marriage, the cause, as she saw it, of her present grief and suffering. Here is the curse she breathed as she broke the coconut on the ground before Suniyam's image.

O God who is soon to achieve Buddhahood. I lived with my husband like a queen. O God, he was as strong as a lion. His death was caused by a *vina*. It was with my help that this woman married my son. She made him kill his father. Her father is a sorcerer (*vinakaraya*). Now they have all the property and riches. I live in the old house, but it is poor. They live in luxury. They have a new Lancer car. O, God, look at my body! I have become thin. My body burns from that woman's *kodivina*. She is the one who brought the court case. They now control the whole business. They are richer than ever. I cannot bear the pain. They give me no respect and say that I am mad. O God, am I mad?

My son was good to me. He treated me well before he married. She has made him ungrateful and turned him against me. O God, burn this woman's face with the fire of your torch. I want to see her dead and to see with my own eyes the ash of her cremation. Burn the marriage.

O God, I have brought you food smelling of perfume. Accept this sweet-smelling rice and make me smile with happiness.

O God, I am unhappy. Bring disputes into their marriage. Make them split apart. Punish them quickly in seven days or in three weeks. O God, you are the most powerful god in Sri Lanka. Heed my plea.

Poverty's Despair

Milinona, a washerwoman, came before the goddess Bhadrakali. She brought an egg in a betel leaf, a common offering to the goddess vital in the striking of the curse (*paligahima*). Milinona suspected sorcery. Her husband had been knocked down in a traffic accident. He was still in the hospital, and the injuries to his legs made it doubtful that he could continue his job as a carter in the market. Moreover, someone had stolen Milinona's valuable possessions, her gold earrings and a small radio. She was distraught, complaining that these were all she had as security, if she should need to borrow money. Milinona was already in debt. A soothsayer told her that a *kodivina* had been made against her and her family, so Milinona came to Bhadrakali to seek the goddess's help. This is what Milinona repeated as her curse as she poised to break the egg as a sacrifice to Kali. She addressed herself to one of the female attendants (*maniyo*s) of the goddess.

> O Kali *maniyo*! You are the most powerful of the seven mothers. I have heard of your great power and how you stopped the storm which flooded the land. I have heard how you protected your husband from the Asura. Punish my enemy who brought the *vina* against me. I cannot feed my children. I cannot send them to school. I know a *kodivina* has been made. My husband's relatives have brought this sorrow.
>
> O Bhadrakali, break the legs of my enemies. I want to see the pig who has caused my suffering hobbling lame. O Fire Kali, burn their lives. Never let them sleep. O Kali, look at me. Help me. O Kali, heal my husband's legs. Make him well to work again. These people are jealous because we are sending our children to school. O *maniyo,* punish these cruel people.

These women are not passive in their anguish before the shrines. They are not frozen in fear or the still foci within an active field of force, as when they are the patient/victim at the center of a Suniyama or *kapuma* or other rite performed by specialists outside the context of the shrines. They express through the priest and within themselves what presses on them and gnaws inside them. This is an externalization of the world that is consuming within, an externalizing or objectifying of a reality that has assumed a malignant shape in relation to the supplicant. In these senses, victims distance and hold before themselves in reflective consciousness the measure of their distress. And then they cut it. This is the import of the anger of both priest and supplicant.

The anger, that of the supplicants especially, is far more than an expression of distress or even of cathartic release, although the notion of catharsis as purgation rather than a release of tension has bearing on this discussion. The anger is powerful as anger. It acts directly on the body of the victim and on the way victims experience themselves as positioned within their life world. Thus, the energy of the anger severs from the victim's body those destructive, or obstructive, qualities that are experienced as adhering to the body, vital to its suffering, and forcing the anguished to the margins of existence. The metaphor of Manikpala in the Suniyama is applicable to the angry action at the shrines. Manikpala is defiled by the conscious action that afflicts her. The cutting of her sorcery, as is the case for all sorcery victims, is integral to the cleansing of her defilement. The cutting is not just the breaking of a destructive relation but the cutting off of something that has established a union within the suffering body. The anger at the shrines, reaching the height of its intensity at that moment when the coconut is poised to be broken, is an expression of distress as defilement. The realized force of the anger, the smashing of the coconut, is the cutting away of the defilement from the body. It is an act that in effect reintegrates the body. Furthermore, it repositions, or reorients, the victim in the world. Like the victim in the *atamagala* of the Suniyama, the supplicant faces or turns back on the world in a move that regrasps and reaffirms an active and reconstitutive relation to a life world in the very energy of its anger. The motional force of the anger at the shrines may be understood as a radical unchaining of consciousness, a breaking out, and an exertion by supplicants of their own intentional being in the world vital to their continuing existence.

Passions of Order and Resistance

The supplicants at the shrines demonstrate an awareness of the wider forces in the field of their social and political life that have bearing on their plight. Indeed, it is through the circumstances of their anguish that they can become acutely aware of and critical of the destructive energies connected with the social and political orders in which they live. The sorcery shrines, rather than the Suniyama rite, can become sites for both the formation and the expression of a *resistant* consciousness.

The resistant potential of the shrines became poignantly apparent at the height of a populist uprising of the Janatha Vimukthi Peramuna (JVP: Popular Liberation Front) against the Sri Lankan government from August 1989 to the early months of 1990 (see Moore 1993; Kapferer 1996). The uprising, which almost toppled the government, caused a dreadful loss of life among the Sinhalese population (current estimates are on the order of 60,000 dead).[19] The scale of the horror and the extent of the death toll, particularly among rural and urban youth, most of whom were probably not directly involved with the JVP, inflicted by government military and paramilitary forces is only now coming to light. The shrines were among the very few places where stricken families could express their plight and assert their own resistance to what was going on.

Thus, Maginona, a woman aged fifty-five, approached the priest at the Suniyam temple in Maligawatta to seek help in finding her seventeen-year-old youngest son. He had been missing for twenty-one days. She had been to a soothsayer (*sastra karaya*) who had told her that her son was in hiding, with twelve others. The soothsayer had assured Maginona that her son would return in fourteen days. But the time had long since passed. There were dead and burning bodies in the streets at the time, grim evidence of army and police action. Bodies were seen floating down the river near which Maginona lived. Maginona was distraught. She suspected that sorcery (*huniyam*) had been sent against her family because of jealousy (*irisiyava*). Indeed, she suspected that neighbors had informed against her sons to the police. Maginona and her husband ran a small shop. Her two eldest sons were employed (one a schoolteacher, the other a bus conductor), and the missing son had just passed his school final exams. Their neighbors were poor, Maginona said. They were jealous of the relative success of her family and were envious of the valuables displayed in her house. Maginona had recently purchased a new television set. She felt that her family was well-off and this was due to the success of her sons. She asked the shrine priest to perform a small rite (*kapuma*) before Suniyam. He did this at midday after closing the doors of the temple so that no other supplicants could witness the action. Maginona declared her suffering in this way at the end of the rite:

> Sadu! Sadu! O Most powerful of gods! Most powerful of kings.
> Listen to me. We were poor but our sons have improved our life.
> Others are jealous. Someone has done a *huniyam*. My
> youngest son has disappeared. I have done my best
> to discover where he is but still no news. I am
> abandoning hope. Grant me a chance to see my son.
> O God, of all my children he is the prince.
> He is loved by everyone. But some Vasavarti Maraya
> has made sorcery against my son. O God,
> he is innocent. He is not a terrorist.
> He sympathizes, but he has done nothing wrong.
> I know my son. O God, I cannot bear the pain.
> O God, kill all those people who have brought sorcery
> against us. We have not made plans to destroy
> anyone. We cannot be accused. Protect my son
> and bring him back.

The human destruction in the wake of the JVP insurrection grew in fury in the latter months of 1989 as government forces gained the upper hand. In October, Premawati came to the same Suniyam shrine. Her twenty-one-year-old son had not come home for over a week. When he disappeared, he had gone with some other youths to an area north of Colombo. Premawati feared that he had been killed. Her neighbors had heard rumors to that effect, and had heard that her son had been burned by either the army or by some government antiterrorist squad. She had been coming to the temple for the past five days. Before she cursed in front of Suniyam, she would wash the sacred Bo tree. The priest had instructed her to come for seven days, and then the following curse, which she uttered as well as the one shouted by the priest, would start to have results.

O God who fought and conquered the Asuras,
Listen to my plea! My son has not come home for
seven days. O God, we have tried our best
to find out what has happened. I have been told that
he has been killed by the special forces. O God, use
your powerful heat (*tejas*) to destroy them!
I still hope that my son is alive. O God, can you
find some way that I can meet him? O God, destroy
those who have killed my son. O God who carries
the pot of fire, burn them, tear them
into pieces, kill them with your sword!
May you live five thousand years!

These kinds of statements were made before the shrines by people who had little other recourse. For many scholars of society, it might be evidence of the pathetic situation of the socially and politically weak, sorcery as a weapon of the weak, which is as powerless as those who must use it. Furthermore, there is the issue that the use of such "irrational" means as appeal to sorcery gods for help and vengeance may actually support the forces of oppression and human destruction. The shrines, some might say, allow the steam of outrage against the crushing force of agents of social and political power to be discharged with little effect and moreover to be dissipated, because it is not directed against the system so much as against particular individuals. Moreover, the fact that the chief patrons of the shrines are frequently powerful members of the bourgeoisie who are connected with controlling and oppressive interests enables the shrines to be seen as "apparatuses of capture" (see Deleuze and Guattari 1988: 424–473; Chapter 8): that is, as institutions for the control of dissent and resistance. I now turn to an examination of these issues.

Discourses of Dominance and Resistance

The shrines (and also the rites) can be seen as sites of class struggle, as some of the cases I have presented indicate (e.g., Babynona). There the urban poor rage against persons and circumstances that express controlling class power. Simultaneously, members of dominant classes or persons who are socially mobile express a consciousness, in their anxieties about the frailty of their own situation, of contemporary class processes and the potential violence that flows in their contradictions. But features of the struggle of class forces, manifested in the suffering and interpersonal conflicts that are aired at the shrines, are contained in sites that are controlled by dominant groups. In other words, those who resist the forces of domination in effect express their grievances by the courtesy of the very interests against whom they rail.

This argument conforms to well-known ruling ideology theses. The sorcery shrines (and especially rites such as the Suniyama) are to be seen as institutions to some degree promoted and encouraged by controlling class interests in order to reproduce their class power. This is worth noting for the reason that it is often members of controlling class fractions who declare openly their disregard for such irrational practices as sorcery. The same persons, however, are major donors to temples renowned for their sorcery practice.

However, there are important criticisms of the ruling ideology or dominant class hegemony position (e.g., Thompson 1978; Abercrombie, Hill, and Turner 1980; Guha and Spivak 1988). Scott (1985: 314–50) extends the critique to his studies of Malay peasantry, and his argument is applicable to the context of the sorcery shrines in Sri Lanka. He argues that subordinated groups are often peripheral to hegemonizing ideologies and do not necessarily internalize the themes stressed by those who command dominant institutions. The persons who are hegemonized are the ruling classes themselves. Indeed, it might be said that the sorcery shrines are counterinternalization. At the shrines supplicants effectively realize the destructive forces contained in the structures of their life world, realize them as polluting and reject them. Moreover, and most relevant for the situation discussed here, the dominant ideology thesis is itself an ideology of domination, for it fails to see that subordinated groups are far from duped by controlling ideas and practices and are able to penetrate them.

The pain of human suffering, as illustrated by much of the anguish at the shrines, is a spur toward a realization of what some of the root problems are. The main orientation of sorcery toward the discovery (and punishment) of faults makes the shrines places for the articulation of protest in a relatively public context. What is screamed out at the sorcery shrines cannot be controlled or easily forbidden.

The shrines can become places (as I think they did during the height of the Sri Lankan government's destruction of its own population) that are vital centers for the expression and formulation of a resistant consciousness fully and angrily aware of major faults in the orders of political society. Families mourning their losses at the shrines angrily questioned the very moral order of the state and its agents. Such questioning is a potential dimension of the image of the god Suniyam to whom the supplicants make their pleas; it is a potential that is immanent in his divided form, his hot destructive side joined to his judgmental, ordering, and protective side. Suniyam is the very ambiguity of power, and he holds before the awareness of supplicants the contradictions and the injustices of power. Such a consciousness, brought to reflective intensity in the passionate context of the shrines, is not dissipated and lost in their space. Rather it is made part of a restored and angry energy of the supplicants which, I suggest, can become integral to other practical action that may indeed topple governments.

But my concern is not to romanticize sorcery as resistance. Those who have authority and power in Sri Lanka, who control the lives of others, engage the force of sorcery to exact revenge, to protect themselves, and indeed, to batter the weak. Nor is it my interest to discover a rationality in the experience of sorcery and the resort to sorcery practice that might satisfy those who see in them only mysticism and superstition.

Sorcery rites and the appeals to the shrines are simply ways in which human beings can address the problematics of their routine and not-so-routine lives and gather their anxieties into a frame that gives them coherence and enables them to renew their lives as participants in the control and generation of their own ongoing existence in-the-world.

The anxieties expressed through sorcery are oriented first and foremost to the world and the fact that individual human being is founded in processes of existence that cannot be reduced to the individual. That is, the experiences brought to shrine and rite manifest dimensions of personal alienation produced by a particular vectoring of forces that focus on supplicants and victims and that can become destructively consubstantial with the victims' very being. If the experiences in rite and shrine are of individuals somehow cast aside from the world, this can be seen as related to both forces in that world and the kind of unity that individuals form with it as a consequence of their own actions and those of others.

Sorcery, Culture, and the Passions

Sorcery beliefs and practices are cultural constructions and representations of the energies of human destruction and renewal. They erupt as the generalized expressions of human agonies and anxieties in the world and the means for overcoming them. These means are the symbolic materializations of the energies whereby human beings recreate themselves and their realities. They do not transcend the world but are grounded within everyday practicalities. Sorcery belief and practice, often highly innovative, emerge as the dynamic of the reinvention or reorigination by human beings both of themselves and of their existential realities on which their continuing existence in all its experiential depth depends.

Sorcery rites and shrines organize the passions and emotions of embodied existence and reveal them as integral to the dynamic of conscious-ness and the formation and reformation of human being-in-the-world. The passions are not just the expressions of existential processes but are vital as the structuring of a particular awareness of persons within their social and political realities and potent in their reorientation to them. Sorcery provokes the passions, not as some kind of culturally inspired attitude, a figuration of the mind that excites fear and anger, but because the cultural constructions of sorcery belief and practice capture the al-ready passionate intensities of lived realities and human beings' urgency for existence in life worlds whose very processes are threatening to exis-tence.

Anthropologists in their culture of relativism insist on the crucial im-port of the cultural categories and social constructions of emotion and emotional meaning (e.g., Lutz 1988; Lutz and Abu-Lughod 1990; Ro-saldo 1980; Lynch 1991). They are critical of the physicalist or psycho-logical perspectives that treat the emotions as things located in the body, which define them in an essentialist, universalist, and unproblematic way, and which fail to see them as the very stuff of social relations, or as the affects which have effect.[20] Broadly, a cognitive view is preferred by rela-tivist anthropologists which ultimately is an extreme Cartesianism of a kind that many anthropologists currently contributing to emotion re-search would appear to reject.[21] My difficulty with such approaches and criticisms is that for all their concern to escape a Western bias, they repro-duce it. Thus, they compartmentalize, dichotomize, and separate out pro-cesses that should be taken together and in relation to each other. The very categories of a Western social science, its divisions into psychology, sociology, anthropology, and so on, determine the way the field of inquiry is carved up and debated. The anthropologists I have cited, although I agree with much of what they say (e.g., their antiessentialism, the impor-tance they give to cultural meanings, etc.), disembody experience and lo-cate it external to the body in social and cultural definitions of the emo-tions. Then, in a parody of Descartes, they make the consciously reflected categories of the nature of experience, here the emotions, the form and content of the experience. In other words, thought determines being and action in the world.[22]

Experience understood by means of cultural categories is already mov-ing toward such reflective apprehension. The emotions—fear, anger, sympathy, and love, for example—are already experienced in their com-ing to reflective awareness. They assume the shape of a thingness, an object penetrating inside from the outside and moving out again, as human beings become aware of themselves through action in-the-world. This inner perception, or acute self-consciousness, is emergent in fearing as an action before it is recognized as fear. The inner perception takes shape in the individual's movement through the world in the process in which a particular awareness of the body is constituted. The victim's body in such movement becomes aware of the body as victim, and furthermore, a body given over to the senses, the body in itself. The victim's senses become objects to the victim, things in themselves, pointing to disturbances in the world of the victim as disturbances of the victim's own organism. Thus, Siyadoris, living his fear in the world, was already experiencing its trembling before he understood it as the trembling of *his* body, significant as a sorcery attack.

My point is that emotional experience is a process that is at once in the world and embodied; it is physical, psychological, and sociological. This is the direction of Sinhalese theory and practice concerning the matter. Merleau-Ponty presents my argument, which the Sinhalese sorcery materials I have presented would appear to support.

> Both universality and the world lie at the core of individuality and the subject, and this will never be understood as long as the world is made into an object. It is understood immediately if the world is the field of our experience, and if we are nothing but a view of the world, for in that case it is seen that the most intimate vibration of our psycho-physical being already announces the world, the quality being the outline of a thing, and the thing the outline of the world. (Merleau-Ponty 1962: 406)

Experience and the emotionality of experience is always more than the cognitive or language categories of its construction. This is self-evident in the contexts of sorcery. In Sinhalese cultural conception and performance, sorcery virtually exceeds its comprehension. It defies classification. The fear, fury, and anger of the supplicants before the sorcery shrines appears as a gathering of experience in language which yet cannot contain it: thus, the poetics of cursing. The sorcery experience, its experiential excess, is brought within the control of language as body and mind are unified in focus, as in the *hatadiya* (see Chapter 5).

The movement to sorcery rite and sorcery shrine is nothing less than that radical upsurge of the human being-in-the-world as a being of sociality of which both Sartre and Merleau-Ponty write so brilliantly. This upsurge, they argue, and the sorcery rites and practices confirm this, is produced in the resistances, ruptures, and threats to existence in the world. The upsurge is the emergence of the individual consciousness aware of itself.

> The tacit cogito, the presence of oneself to oneself, being no less than existence, is anterior to any philosophy, and knows itself only in those extreme situations in which it is under threat: for example, in the dread of death or of another's gaze upon me. The consciousness which conditions language is merely a comprehensive and inarticulate grasp of the world, like that of the infant at its first breath, or of the man about to drown and who is impelled towards life. (Merleau-Ponty 1962: 404)

The pathos of the pleas I have presented and the intense examination of self-experience and the context of experience by sorcery victims manifests the urgency to life. The victims express themselves as the fundamental points of contingency in a world they did not create, which in fact constitutes them in its density, but to which they must establish a new relation. The violence of the shrines is the violence of reorigination as well as rebirth, which is also a major metaphor of the rites.

8

Faces of Power
Sorcery, Society, and the State

SORCERY MANIFESTS the dynamics of power. Most fundamentally sorcery *is* power, power in its totalizing essence. It draws its awful and dreadful force from the fact that it is the energy underlying both creation and destruction. The heat of sorcery, its potencies, is generated in its virtual fusion of contradictory or opposing forces which the practice and idea of sorcery reveals as locked in close relationship with one another. The fusion of forces integral to sorcery constitutes the totalizing power of sorcery.

All that I have described regarding Suniyam and sorcery practices generally among Sinhalese supports my characterization. The primal, primordial presentation of sorcery's power in the myths of sorcery's origin indicates its fusion force. It is a power in which all is potential. The unity of this potential in the power at the root and source of existence is the power that the iconography of sorcery expresses, as does its practice. Suniyam rides a mare, a symbol of the generative energy of *sakti*, and rider and vehicle together signify the fused potency of the male and female principles. Suniyam is represented in the shrines as mediating the heat of destruction with the ordering of justice. These are not so much opposites, in the interpretation I give here, as inseparably joined: the heat of destruction is also the heat of origination which gives rise, as part of its potency, to protective orders.

Suniyam, and I think sorcery more generally among Sinhalese and elsewhere, is raw power, the heat (*tejas*) of the generative power (*bala*) of human beings.[1] Its manifold potential is open. This is its danger and its volatility. It can go in any direction and destroy those who use it. The ambivalent and transgressive dimensions of sorcery are expressions or representations of the extent of its potential spread and of its uncertainty. I have referred to the duality of sorcery and the demon-deities and what might be understood as their ambivalent powers. The heat of their destruction is of a piece with their ordering, protective, and judgmental potency. This signifies a key dimension of their power, which is to convert or transform an abject condition of destructive fragmenting suffering into a reintegrated condition, whole and freed from despair (see Chapters 2 and 7). This dualism of sorcery and of the demon-deities is not the dualism common in some Western interpretations of the good-and-evil, order-and-chaos kind. That is, the destructive and ordering dimensions of Suniyam are not separate principles brought into relation through the mediating body of Suniyam: a dialectical unity of contradiction or of opposites in the sense of a Western political philosophy. Rather, sorcery's power describes destructive and ordering forces, for example, as coextensive, both integral and vital, as dimensions of the other (the power of order is also the power of fragmentation, and the two are inextricably locked as dimensions of power). That they are coextensive and mutually integral and potential is vital to the conversional transformation effected through the power of sorcery. The dualism of Suniyam's representation, as well as those of the other demon-deities, marks the extremes which their transformational powers span. Moreover, the dualist representation at the shrines and the ritual process of sorcery practice is not a mere expression or reflection of the nature of sorcery in the Sri Lankan context. They are dimensions of the urge of human beings to control and direct the very volatility of sorcery's power. Thus, the ambivalent representation of the demon-deities at the shrines is a controlling and directing of their power, defining and orienting the trajectory of power. This is the structure of rite too, most clearly in the Suniyama.

Sorcery is sometimes regarded as dangerous because it is ambiguous and transgressive. Danger, Mary Douglas asserts, is a dimension of the ambiguous and is a property of those forms of life which appear to fall outside the categories of human construction, which defy classification, or cross (transgress) categories. Clearly there is considerable ethnographic support for Douglas's observation, and expansions of her argument are relevant for contexts in Sri Lanka. Sorcery, however, or rather the power that sorcery manifests, is dangerous not because it is ambiguous or transgressive (which it is) but because it is the originary energy, the primordial force of existence itself, the action-power out of which the world in all its constructed actualities is created. This is what the myths of sorcery tell us; moreover, it is a vital message of all their chthonic imagery: the association of the snake of sorcery with the snake at the origin of time

(Maha Kala Naga), the pregnancy dream of Yawudagiri, Suniyam's reaching into the earth to draw the snakes of destruction, and so forth.

The power in sorcery is the power that generates the categories and orders that it also crosses, infringes on, and transgresses. The ambiguity and the transgressive properties of sorcery are secondary dimensions of its extraordinary, generating, all-potentiating force. The power of sorcery is not a product of its ambiguity or capacity to transgress; rather, these are aspects of the more foundational power that is sorcery's heat.

Sometimes in anthropological analyses sorcery is described as immoral and further as being antagonistic to social order, society. Undoubtedly sorcery in Sri Lanka can be an immoral act, but it can also be a moral action. The plaintiffs at the shrines see their action as driven by their own moral sense, by their outrage at personal injustice. They are not necessarily attempting to assuage their guilt or to justify the use of an essentially immoral instrument. The reconstitution of the victims of sorcery in the Suniyama, their regeneration as the vital center of Buddhist morality within which the integrity of community or society can be sustained, is combined with procedures that result in the agonizing destruction of the attacking sorcerer. The power that sorcery condenses is necessarily neither moral nor immoral. Nor is it necessarily ordering or disordering, creative of the social or destructive of it. Sorcery is power as such, without any essential morality. Insofar as it is a force that bears moral or immoral aim or ordering or disordering purpose, this is always relative to the motive and position of the persons who engage it.

Sorcery as a Discourse of Power

I discuss sorcery, its practices and ideas, as a discourse on the nature of power. In other words, sorcery is a cultural recognition of the centrality of power in the everyday worlds of human beings and a recognition that the points from which such power emanates are human beings themselves. Sorcery, in my interpretation of the Sinhalese materials, is specifically the power that human beings exercise. I stress the human nature of sorcery and of the beings of sorcery. The sorcery demon-gods have, at least in part, a human origin, and their birth is frequently traced to events that are part of the temporality of human being. That is, they are born, like the Buddha himself, to the historical world of human beings, with which contemporary human actualities are understood to be continuous. Vasavarti, the energy of sorcery, in the Mahasammata-Manikpala story (see Chapter 3), is brought to life in human beings' creation of their social and political order.

I am not saying that all power is sorcery, but that sorcery ideas and practice accent or point up critical dimensions of the *power of human action,* including the aspects of power exercised by human beings that might not normally be conceived of as sorcery. In other words, sorcery practices trace the magnitude of that most nebulous, intangible, yet most concretely and deeply felt, everywhere materialized yet still elusive force—power.

Sorcery ideas and practice identify power as that embodied force, centered in human being per se, that extends beyond the confines of the body toward that to which the body is oriented. It is a dimension of intentionality, vital in consciousness. This is action, energy, or power in a most general sense. The notions of eye, mouth, and thought evil are a Sinhalese cultural recognition of intentionality and of its destructive, violent possibility. This potential is a function of desire, of an intentionality that is always oriented to objects in the world, to other human beings, and to the general material terms of their existence. Such action or power (intentionality) is also the vital force of social generation, what I call sociality. It constitutes the social will, which also has immanent within it the destruction of sociality, which is equally foundational in being (but ultimately negating being).

The socially creative force of intentional consciousness (action and power), although it originates in the body, is not confined to it. The force of the social breaks out from the boundaries of the body. (In this sense, the sociality of intentionality is not reducible to the individual; rather it is an extension *out from* the individual, sociality only being realized or maintained in such an extension.) The negative potential of action or power is the potential of the same intentional force which destroys as a function of its connecting intentional leap. That is, it attacks or consumes that to which it extends.

The paradox of power, as the energy of human intentionality, is also of course the paradox of sorcery. Sorcery beliefs and practices objectify power as intentional action. They focus on that most intangible, least visible, yet most thoroughly experienced dimension of existence, that force which is the betweenness of relations, the energy that bridges the space between persons and between persons and objects.

What I refer to is the experiential substantiality of social relations and political relations, or what some anthropology might recognize, with Mauss, as the spirit or force in relations. This force not only joins persons, and persons and objects, but is the force that has effect, is the potency of the relation and creates or generates the particular point, project, or meaning of the relation.

The Azande speak of sorcery or witchcraft as the "second spear" (*umbaga*), the force that goes along with other accepted and obvious causes (e.g., the physical fact that the collapsing grain bin actually killed the people seated underneath). The second spear, in the usual interpretation, is the coup de grâce, and Evans-Pritchard (1937:74) notes that the phrase is a hunting metaphor referring to the person that finishes off the animal already brought down by the first spear.[2] Evans-Pritchard says that the Azande use such a metaphor to refer to the other no less lethal social factors that brought, for example, the falling grain bin and its victims into disastrous connection.

I emphasize what is now a classic point and separate it from the rationalist framework within which the observation is often set. The second spear of witchcraft is a recognition by the Azande of the lethal force that is potential in social relationships. They may mistakenly always search for a social explanation, but this is far from mystical or nonempirical, as Evans-Pritchard's evidence affirms. The Azande recognize the energy of social relations, along the lines of Mauss's far-from-mystical and highly empirically oriented notion of the "spirit of the gift."[3]

An equally famous example is Trobriand kula sorcery. Malinowski describes the preparations of the kula voyagers before they land at the island where they will establish trading partnerships. They adorn and otherwise beautify themselves and compose special songs. These songs have the magical capacity to enter the consciousness of their intended partners and to bend their will to make them welcoming and desirous of trade and willing to part with their valuable kula shells. The explicit potency of what the Trobrianders recognize as sorcery is its energy to cross the space between persons who are not yet in a formal relation of kula partnership and to establish the grounds and process of the partnership-to-be. In effect, it not only brings about the relation but is also the vitality of the relation and the force of reciprocity.

Mauss and other anthropologists (following a Durkheimian functionalism) have addressed the Trobriand sorcery in the kula as a sanctioning force. Not to return the gift is to risk the punishment of sorcery. But these anthropologists have insufficiently recognized the conjunction of destructive and generative energy of intentional action and the openness of its potentiality, which sorcery practice at least implicitly recognizes. The kula example reveals sorcery as the potency generative of relations, the force at the heart of social relations and vital, through its destructive potency, to their continuity.

The power that sorcery condenses and underscores is pervasive. This power is simultaneously at the root of the forms of life that human beings inhabit and construct and is the energy of these forms, orders, structures, and processes.

Sinhalese from all walks of life routinely invoke the sorcery gods for assistance in ordinary matters—to avert the risks of a dangerous journey, a business transaction, the outcome of an exam. This is because the gods and practices connected with them condense and intensify the potencies of human agency. In fact, when people at the shrines, for example, insist they are not engaging in sorcery, this may be the case. They do not necessarily have any interest in causing others harm in the common sense of the word *sorcery*. They are simply bringing themselves into close contact with centers where the forces of human agency are at their height.

The mundanity of sorcery and witchcraft is often commented on by anthropologists (at least since Evans-Pritchard's Azande study). This observation is used to distinguish notions of witches and sorcerers present in advanced technological (usually Western) societies from those in "less-developed," more "traditional," and smaller-scale communities. The point is usually that witchcraft and sorcery as imagined in Western situations are regarded as extraordinary, paranormal, and not part of ordinary expectations. This contrast is often used to suggest very different systems of practice and thought and indeed of rationality. The totalization of the contrast is problematic, and this is especially true for Sri Lanka.

Sri Lanka is a contemporary capitalist social and political society and affected by global processes. These processes are refracted in sorcery practice. The anguish at the shrines as well as the performance of more traditional rites are impelled in the agonies and uncertainties of a contemporary social and political world shaped by the contradictions and conflicts of class. Sorcery practice is an available cultural idiom in which personal anxieties can be expressed and acted upon. Sorcery does not necessarily reflect a distinct rationality, that is, an excessive and overdetermining totalizing rationalism—of the kind described for the Azande—that cannot accept the exception or empirically inexplicable events otherwise "understood through concepts like luck or chance."

Furthermore, Sri Lanka has deeply ingrained traditions of a Western rationalist variety (see Gombrich and Obeyesekere 1988). These influence the discourse of contemporary Buddhism in Sri Lanka, as many scholars have discussed with reference to colonial and postcolonial movements of Buddhist reformation. Such Buddhist rationalism is part of contemporary class ideology and is similar to some conventional anthropological views of witchcraft and sorcery. Thus, many Sinhalese, especially the Western-educated and those from politically and economically dominant class fractions or elites, openly disparage sorcery practice. They regard it as an activity of the less-educated and traditionally minded. Nevertheless, persons from the wealthy urban bourgeoisie visit the shrines and hire the services of sorcerers (see Chapter 7). These people express a fascination with the extraordinary and magical properties of sorcery, a fascination that appears similar to that of many of the New Age dabblers in the occult in New York, London, and Sydney. Their irrationalism or discovery of energies or powers yet to be comprehended or tapped beyond those recognized in the rationality of normal technoscientific understanding are often, in my view, the invention of their very constitution within and commitment to the technorationalist contemporary world with which they express their disenchantment.

Thus, Sinhalese sorcery practices and their clientele may be seen as part of a modern contemporary world. Those who appeal to sorcery are brought to practicing it by a diversity of circumstances engaging a variety of rationalities or reasonings. They are not locked in another premodern rationality, the rationality of sorcery or witchcraft of the kind that was overcome in the secularism of the European Enlightenment and the transformation into modernity. It is not the additional factor that human beings ignorant of science and the true relation between cause and effect use to explain their misfortune and suffering.

I have referred to the Zande metaphor of the second spear and Evans-Pritchard's interpretation of its meaning as a finishing off, the additional social factor. The second spear is not merely the coup de grâce, it is the spear, the action that does the killing.[4] The second spear recognizes the primacy of human agency and its social force.

More generally, sorcery practices and beliefs are assertions of human potency. They are declarations of the power of human being and that the potency of other human beings is vital to the life chances of human beings in their life worlds. Sorcery beliefs and practices spring from the awareness (both unconscious and reflected on) that human beings participate in fields of consciousness that are also fields of force. This is neither a mystification nor an irrationality; it is a fact of human existence. That is, far from expressing the difference between distinct historical realities (e.g., the West vis-à-vis the Rest), sorcery beliefs and practices in Sri Lanka and elsewhere manifest the foundational forces engaged in human existence and existential processes everywhere.

Sorcery practice as a pervasive phenomenon in Sri Lanka, engaged in by persons from all walks of life, is influenced by historical and cultural contingencies. For example, forces related to colonialism and resistance to it were refracted in religious and ritual practice. Aspects of belief relevant to sorcery were revitalized in other areas of discourse not immediately relevant to sorcery practice. Sorcery may be seen as part of a discourse of culture relevant in a revitalization of tradition attendant on nationalist expression and resistances.

Sorcery practice (Chapters 2 and 3) is coextensive with other religious and ritual activity. Even in its transmutations, in the emergence of highly innovative forms of sorcery belief and practice, there is a tendency to link it to religious practice that many in Sri Lanka consider antithetical ethically and morally to sorcery.

Human beings work with the cultural materials they have at hand. In their working with such materials in their situated circumstances, human beings are active in maintaining the currency of such practices as sorcery. Through their use of sorcery they develop or transmute it in such a way as to maintain its contextual relevance. This much should be obvious.

However, sorcery is pervasive in Sri Lanka because it is the objectification of power and the condensation of its potentialities. The widespread practice of sorcery among Sinhalese matches the ubiquity of power. The effects and manifestation of power are everywhere in evidence, in positions of authority and control, in poverty and in wealth and in their diverse materialization. There is a potency in social and political position and in things. All this sorcery practice recognizes. Sinhalese sorcery rites attack the materializations of potency and drive at their representation. Sorcerers sometimes make representations of what they wish to destroy. For example, the relation of a husband and wife may be drawn on paper and then burned or otherwise destroyed—a kind of sorcery practice by no means restricted to Sri Lanka. This technique (sympathetic magic) not only directs the sorcerer's venom but is understood as a destructive manipulation of the vital potency of the relation. In one example I witnessed, the sorcerer's aim was to provoke marital arguments leading to divorce and, he hoped, to the decline of the victim's political and economic fortunes, which were based on the harmony of the marriage.

Sorcery practice often attacks the potency of human beings through the objects that are the manifestations or products of human potency, or in which human potency is expressed. Manikpala is a body of creation and the body toward which both Mahasammata and Vasavarti manifest and express their potency. In what can be seen as the obsessive urge of sorcery to get at the guts of power, the very stuff of difference, of self-realization, and of suffering, the sorcerer strives to make it into a thing, to make it manifestly material.

There is a marvelous imaginary to sorcery practice. This is driven partly by the extraordinary diversity of the practical everyday problems it addresses and the value clients place on innovative and hence powerful techniques. The stretch of this imaginary is also excited by the effort to take hold of and control the vital power that is at the heart of the tangible but is itself intangible. I regard the imaginary of sorcery not as something opposed to the actualities of life but as both generated in the circumstances of existence and an attempt to take hold of what these circumstances are. The imaginary of sorcery is not a leap beyond or outside the real but an effort to objectify, materialize, or make symbolically solid the experience that is real in its experiencing but constantly evades the grasp or hides from view.

The aim of the sorcerer to gain control may appear absurd and futile. An objectivist social science argument would declare such practice irrational because the power is in the form and process of social and economic relations. Power is essentialized as a force independent of the structural practices that constitute power and from which power is inseparable. A Marxist analysis might insist that the sorcerer fails to understand the principles of social and political systems as a whole and mislocates the material, gives life to the material and inanimate and spiritualizes it, and gives materiality to the immaterial.

Such social science perspectives, despite assertions to the contrary, do not contradict the nature of sorcery practice as practice. Sorcery examined *in its practice* (i.e., in the fullness of its phenomenalization) does not treat power, at least in Sri Lanka, as a force independent of human being and of the nexus of relations that is the sine qua non of human being. The power at the generative and destructive center of sorcery practice constitutes being and its relations. The radical alienation effected through sorcery, the depth of the experience of alienation that is the condition of fear and terror explored in the previous chapter, is simultaneously a negation of being and the loss of its potency. Power and sociality are inseparable. This is how I would extend an interpretation of the Mahasammata-Manikpala myth. The fury of Vasavarti is the fury of a separation of human being from the relations of social and political existence.

Moreover, sorcery practice is through and through an assertion of the materiality of human existence: an assertion that the power vital in being is no less a material force, and that the materiality of this force is an agency both in the control of an object world and in the power that human beings have over others through both the manipulation and the possession of objects in the world. There is nothing mystical or necessarily fetishistic in what I see as ingrained in sorcery practices among Sinhalese.

Sorcery practices insist on power as the general force and groundedness of human existence. Insofar as they may strike the observer, alien or indigenous, as absurd and futile (one reason for their depiction as irrational), this is because of the ultimate uncontrollability of the forces which are human being and the dynamic of its existence. What may be described as the mania to control, to command power, to harness completely the creative and destructive potencies of existence, to totalize—all of which is certainly one urgency of sorcery—is the absurdity of human being as a whole. It is an impossibility and an anxiety to which sorcery gives vital expression. Such a recognition of the absurdity of human being in relation to power is an interpretational possibility of the sorcery myths. It is the hubris of Queen Yawudagiri's husband in ignoring the cosmic portents that led to the birth of Oddisa/Suniyam, a being virtually beyond control. Mahasammata's inability to cure his queen is a declaration of the limitation of human beings' control of the forces of human existence, of their inability to determine and totalize the energies of human existence.

Of course, Sinhalese sorcery practices also resonate with well-known themes of Buddhist doctrine. Thus, notions of sorcery are relevant to Buddhist concepts concerning the essential suffering of human beings in existence and the dangers of consuming and overbearing attachment to the life world of human beings evident in anger, desire, and greed. The dilemmas and paradoxes of sorcery display the anxieties and inseparable contraries of existence which are at the focus of Buddhist thought and practice. The constructions of Buddhist doctrine and their popularization in Sri Lanka are undoubtedly influential in the framing and development of sorcery practice. However, although the constructions that human beings put on their experience are critical to the communication of their experience, such constructions are always grounded in experience.

The centrality of power, power as a general socially constitutive force, as I describe it in Sinhalese sorcery practice, may be emphasized in the ideological context of a historical culture of Buddhism. Louis Dumont (1980) excludes Buddhist societies from his discussion of Indian hierarchy on the basis (which is highly contested) that power (kings, warriors) is encompassed by the religious (Brahmins) among Hindus, whereas in Buddhist societies, power is valued as being dominant. The constitutive force of power may be expanded in Buddhist contexts where Buddhist ideology places high stress on human agency and the ultimate ordering capacity of human decision and will.

Sinhalese are characterized by some scholars (see Obeyesekere 1981) as placing a premium on relations of authority. Social and political relations are markedly hierarchical in economic class terms and in terms of status, especially in a world where caste identity is significant in the mediating of social and political life. Caste and class together produce social contexts that are riven by division and which create the circumstance for social distance and separation. Mary Douglas (1973) would describe Sri Lanka as a high-grid and high-group society, a world in which there is an intense concern with the classification of social difference and also one in which there is a strong emphasis on group membership and the boundaries between groups. Social-organizationally, in Douglas's terms, Sinhalese realities are precisely those in which sorcery practice is likely to be highly elaborated. In her neo-Durkheimian view, sorcery beliefs develop in social contexts that are authoritarian and tightly ordered. Douglas distinguishes sorcery from witchcraft. She associates witchcraft with more fluid social contexts (low grid or low group) where there is considerable ambiguity and in which witchcraft accusations function to define social relations.

There are other ways in which particular ideological or value processes or social organizational features might account for the character of sorcery belief and practice. However, the kind of power that is at the root of sorcery is the energy of human being toward existence and toward other human beings in existence. This is also the force expressed in witchcraft, which, regardless of anthropologists' attempts at definitional distinctions, is expressive of the same energy.

Nietzsche explored an approach to power which has aspects similar to those of the sorcery practices of the Sinhalese and others. Sorcery or witchcraft practice manifests the power or urgency of human being for the assertion of its being or, in Weberian terms, the need of individuals to assert their will in the context of the existence of others and even against the will of those others. Nietzsche saw clearly the ambiguity in such energy or power of being. He valorized the creative aspects of such energy and despised its destructive potential (*ressentiment*).

There is a moral idealism in Nietzsche's concern to separate the higher from the lower power, perhaps consistent with a European post-Enlightenment. His distinctions bear some similarity to moral assertions surrounding sorcery practice where an effort is made to separate destructive power from creative power. The usual Sinhalese view is that sorcery is the destructive actions of others. One's own sorcery action is reactive. It is not seen as sorcery, or, as in rite and at shrine, it is ultimately oriented to the creative, regenerative dimension of power because it activates the divine aspect of the beings of sorcery. Overall, however, Sinhalese practices in relation to sorcery express the virtual impossibility of the Nietzschean separation of creative from destructive power; indeed they express the ultimate idealism in such a perspective. Creative power, in Buddhist terms, can be achieved only by an orientation and progress toward the transcendental negation of existence; this is a passage to self-extinction rather than self-assertion—the former being a condition for the latter.

Sorcery concentrates on the forces in the realities of human existence, realities that are the creation and construction of human beings, which affect or deny the existence of individual human beings. Sorcery practice is a personal confrontation with the human powers of the world. The enormous powers sorcery addresses and conjures are both an expression of the fragility and vulnerability of individuals before the extraordinary force of human being as a whole and an expansion of the individual human being or a development or extension of the potency of individuals to match and command the direction of forces that are the human world of which the person who engages sorcery is a part. Sorcery as practice manifests the Hydra of power, the manifold shapes of power that human beings confront and that exercise in some way a destructive possibility in relation to them.

The metaphor of the Hydra suggests the potency of human beings in creating the very powers, real or fantasied, that continually rise up to threaten them. Furthermore, this sorcery of power, into which human beings must reach (as Suniyam reached into the earth to draw out the poisonous snakes of destruction) to overcome the barriers presented by the world of power and to protect themselves from it, takes all the possible forms of existence. This could not be otherwise. Sorcery beliefs, ideas, and practices assert the primacy of experience and attend to the problematics of this experience as a function of all its modalities as these are articulated in the world of human action. This factuality of human experience as always an experience in-the-world is the condition for the continual generation, development, and expansion of sorcery practices and beliefs.

The enduring ground of sorcery practice—quite apart from the question of whether or not sorcery is a routine everyday practice in a variety of social worlds—is the fact that the knowledge of human beings about the world is grounded in their immediate and directly felt experience of the world. Sorcery beliefs and practices emerge in this general circumstance of human being and yield intensity to such grounded understanding.

The direction of my discussion is neither to reduce the experience of the forces of power to individual experiences (or to inner psychological structures) nor to understand these individual experiences as so many diverse manifestations of particular forms of wider social and political order. What I aim to demonstrate is that sorcery experiences reflect the dynamics of the worlds that human beings live rather than the form of the order of these worlds. Sorcery experiences are of a dynamic of power that runs through a great many different kinds of social formation or social and political context as these may be empirically described. Although the shape of sorcery practice may reflect the structure of particular socioeconomic orders and the positioning of sorcery practitioners within them, there is no necessary one-to-one correspondence. The type of sorcery does not necessarily reflect the type of social and political order. I stress sorcery as having to do with dynamics and stress that these dynamics extend through a great diversity of social and political forms that are not necessarily historically or geographically continuous. Vastly distinct social and political forms can manifest similar dynamics, not because they are conditioned in such dynamics, but because, for a wide diversity of particular historical and cultural reasons, they produce them (see Deleuze [1968] 1994; Chapter 2). I suggest that the constant reinvention of such dynamics has something to do with the marked resilience of sorcery practice despite enormous social and political changes and discontinuities affecting the circumstances of life. Furthermore, in concentrating on the dynamics of sorcery, and expressly with the dynamic of power, I am concerned to avoid the kind of Durkheimian social correlations that are a feature of certain other, undoubtedly valuable, approaches, such as that of Mary Douglas. In what follows, I shift the focus away from addressing the dynamics of power in the individual experience of sorcery, to sorcery as revealing the dynamics of power in the larger structures that impinge on personal worlds.

I base this approach to the dynamics of power in structures on the work of Deleuze and Guattari (1988), and especially their chapter "Treatise on Nomadology: The War Machine." This is not to use them to authorize what I have to say. Rather, I want to authorize some of their general insights and extend them, through what I believe is revealed in Sinhalese sorcery practices. Deleuze and Guattari cast their analytical net (their "apparatus of capture") over a vast range of concern, ultimately directed to a critique of contemporary capitalism as well as of the philosophical and social science practices in the West which have, even in criticism, been part of the emergence and transformation of capitalism (even the post-structuralism of Deleuze and Guattari and others; see Kapferer 1988a). They are interested in threatening the arrogance of many theories in recent Western history which overlook, or too enthusiastically devalue and dismiss, the wealth of understanding that other human practices at all historical moments may reveal about human action in general. In doing this they draw extensively on anthropological and other ethnographic knowledge and, in many ways, exhibit features in the human practices recorded that deny or are unnecessarily distorted by the rationalist concerns of a post-Enlightenment anthropology. They draw on traditions which are often close to those of the Sinhalese. Perhaps this is why I find considerable resonance with their work in the material I collected. But I think the Sinhalese materials seen through some of their elaborations not only give some additional substance to Deleuze and Guattari's assertions but also expand the import of Sinhalese sorcery practice for a more general discourse on the dynamics of power.

Modalities of Power: War Machine, State, and Sorcery

The dynamics of power that sorcery expresses shares much in its qualities with what Deleuze and Guattari describe as *war machine and state*. For me these terms describe the actual dynamics of a great diversity of structures, not particular kinds of formal organizations on the ground, but rather the dynamics of their process. Thus *war machine* refers to a dynamic not necessarily of organizations for military action, although the dynamics of war machines can be illustrated by actual social and political formations organized for the purpose of waging war. What Deleuze and Guattari, and I, want to show is that the dynamics of the war machine can appear in other modes of social and political action that do not have war as their project. Similarly, *state* refers to a complex of dynamics that are part of formal organizations of government that will be described as states. But the term *state* applies to dynamics of power that can be discovered or repeated in other structures that may not be relevant to state political organization as such.

In taking the war machine and state as distinct modalities of power, there is always a danger of unwarranted and excessive dualism. Deleuze and Guattari, by focusing on war machine and state as dynamics, treat them as interpenetrating. That is, the dynamics of war machine and of state can appear together and in mutual transmutation in one empirically described organizational structure. They are continually interpenetrating modalities of power. Moreover, war machine and state are not metaphors or symbols of power (like objectifications of sorcery) but are the actualizations of the dynamics of power *as dynamics* repeatedly thrown up by diverse assemblages of power (the social structures, relations, organizations of life which human beings inhabit). Rather than models or representations of power, war machine and state are the distinct shapes of power changing, shifting, and transforming in accordance with historical contingency. What constitutes the war machine or the state is vastly different in particular places and times, but their dynamic is enduringly present. The dynamics of war machines and states have always existed in human historical experience. In the antievolutionist position which Deleuze and Guattari espouse (which eschews the view that one kind of dynamic is the prior or inferior modality of the other), the dynamics of war machine and state are continually being realized anew in the emergence of political and economic forms that have no necessary historical antecedent or precursor. This is not to say that they are essential to human experience. They are the inventions of human beings, the (re)creations of human intentional praxis, and are constantly being reinvented.

Power and Sorcery as the Dynamics of Exteriority and Interiority

The war machine is the shape of power as exteriority. This exteriority can become interior to the state, a dynamic of its own inner process, as a consequence of invasion or through acts of appropriation. The myths of sorcery illustrate aspects of Deleuze and Guattari's broad understanding (see also Chapter 3).

The sorcerer stands external to the state, outside the rational order of Mahasammata. But he also becomes interior to the state and to society. Shockingly invasive to the state, he becomes, within Manikpala's womb, the spreading disease of the very interior being of the state. The state and the sorcerer—in Dumezil's terms, jurist/priest and magician/king—demonstrate their singular origin and their mutually creative and destructive tension. The powers of the sorcerer and of the state are complementary. This is clear in the healing work of the sorcerer, whose cure of Manikpala constitutes the restitution of the state. The refounding of the state repeats the separation of the sorcerer from the state—the sorcerer, in the form of violent attacker, is as much the creation of the state as the state is a creation of the sorcerer. This is the meaning of the Vijaya and Kuveni myth.

My earlier discussion of Suniyam, his doubleness and duality, parallels Deleuze and Guattari's notion of the war machine and the state as produced by different (but usually interpenetrating) assemblages of power. The Suniyam of the shrines mediates the destructive ahierarchical demon (war machine) with the hierarchializing, ordering, just, violent power of the god (state). The two modalities of power are coextensive. The demonic aspect is the force of externality, of resistance, of self-assertion, of the subject directed against that which excludes. These forces extend along the line into the god and state aspect, which can be seen as a transmutation of the war machine or an appropriation of it. The god Suniyam alters the modality of power of the war machine, which is independent of the state and also set against it, into the force of state power.

The myths and practices of sorcery may be seen as state-oriented. They value (the myths especially) the notion of the state as a higher, moral, and rational order. The order of the state is the locus of justice. The myths express Buddhist doctrinal themes and a Buddhism closely associated with the state: a state whose power gets its legitimacy in terms of Buddhist virtue. The originary state of Mahasammata is the ideal Buddhist state within which the creative potency of human action finds constitution and direction. The original "historical" Sinhala state, formed by Vijaya, is a non-Buddhist state. It is the formation of this state in Sinhala sorcery traditions to which the suffering of Sinhala kings and people is traced, they suffer Kuveni's curse. One of the many interpretations that may be made of this mythical event is that Vijaya's state is not yet a righteous and just state. Kuveni's curse is legitimate given Vijaya's falsity and his breaking of his marriage vows. The effects of Kuveni's curse, the enduring suffering of humanity, can be overcome only through an orientation to the Buddhist virtues (see Chapter 3).

Despite the value accorded the state in the myths and practice of sorcery, an ambiguity attaches to it. Sorcery is the power of human being that is against the state and the society constituted and protected by it. But alternatively, the state may be interpreted as being against human being and society. This possibility is most evident in Vijaya's story, both in his breaking his marriage vow to Kuveni and in his annihilation of the society of Kuveni's people, the Yakkas. However, in this latter event, Vijaya and his ally Kuveni are the dynamic power of the war machine; both are external to their state and society. Vijaya as war machine is an externality produced by the power of the state—his rejection by society and the state as much as his rejection of them. In effect, Vijaya is the externality of the state process, the state becoming war machine which brings suffering on its subjects. This point could be extended to the Mahasammata myth. The formation of the state brings forth sorcery, a suffering of state and society. The agony of sorcery, a motion to externality, is facilitated by Mahasammata's becoming war machine, his action of moving exterior to the state he creates to overcome the Asuras, although he engages the reason of the state, its weapons of words and not the weapons of arms. I should add here that some exorcists interpret Suniyam (Vasavarti) as the general of Mahasammata's armies—the war machine of the state's creation that turns against the state.

There are aspects of human beings' and society's antagonism toward the state as well as of the state's antagonism to society and human beings in the myths and practices of sorcery. They indicate aspects of what Pierre Clastres discussed in his classic *Society against the State* ([1972] 1989). Deleuze and Guattari develop central parts of Clastres's argument to demonstrate that what they describe as the basis of the separation and distinction of the war machine from the state is in key features of their power assemblages. The contradiction or opposition of the war machine to the state is not a mere negation. That is, the war machine is not a simple inverse of the state in the sense that the war machine is the negative aspect of everything that is positive in the state. The war machine has its own positivity or modality of existence which is not necessarily defined by what its dynamic might contest or oppose.

The negative vision of the systems external to the state, for Clastres, is a view from the position of the state. This view not only sees the state as the most legitimate ordering of power but measures other orderings of power in terms of itself. Thus, Clastres criticizes the work of much political science as well as anthropology, which sees societies without states as on a lower evolutionary rung than state societies. The state, in this perspective, is understood as having achieved a better, although further perfectible, resolution to the problems of power, or the problem of order, than have nonstate systems. The problem of order is interior to the dynamic of the power of the state. It is a state question. In Clastres's perspective, stateless societies are not different resolutions of the problems confronting states. Their organization is against the state. They are not to be defined in terms of an absence or lack of the state: they are not stateless societies so much as societies that actively and positively *deny* the state. Rather than their being a negation of the state, the state is their negation and particularly a negation of the distinctive social process that they engage. Moreover, the violence that societies opposed to the state manifest is not a force of disorder (as perceived from a position interior to the state) but a force of the assertion of the social in the context of the state.

Clastres subverts the Hobbesian stance which sees the state as a necessary monster (Leviathan) for the harmonious functioning of society. The state is the disordering of society. He considers violence as resistance positive. These are aspects of sorcery practice that I have already discussed. The violence of sorcery is an assertion of social being, often against forces connected with economic and political forces articulated through the dynamics of state.

Ultimately Clastres is not so distant from a Hobbesian or anthropological functionalist position (or even a view from within the situation of contemporary states) as might first appear. Hobbes recognized (as did

Weber, this can also be understood as a view constituted from within the state) that the formation of states through a state dynamic involves a loss of individual autonomy and of the capacity of social groups to pursue their interests (although to the disadvantage of others). Clastres simply asserts the value of individual-producing social autonomy over the value of its denial by the state. This is Hobbes's point, but in reverse. Further, there are shades of an anthropological romanticism in Clastres like that of functionalist anthropologists who study stateless, segmentary societies. Thus, Evans-Pritchard's (1940) study of the Nuer can be read, like the work of Clastres, as a primitivist romance of societies without states which sees their egalitarian order as founded in a proud, often violent, assertion of individual autonomy and of the social groups extending from individuals. Contemporary individualism, at the heart of the ideological legitimation of many modern state systems, might be seen as consistent with such arguments and even productive of them (see Dumont 1986; Kapferer 1988a).

Deleuze and Guattari are aware of many of the criticisms that can be made of Clastres. But they recognize the importance of his contribution (and also of the kind of structural-functional anthropology to which he is allied). In particular, they extend the notion that the societies unsatisfactorily called *stateless* constitute a power dynamic entirely distinct from that of states. Deleuze and Guattari develop a major point. The contradiction between the state and the processes external to it—the processes of the war machine—is a contradiction born of forces specific to their externality, to exteriority itself. The war machine is an assemblage of power that is not so much the negative aspects of the state as a particular kind of organization constituted by principles different from those that organize the state.

Deleuze and Guattari's approach emphasizes the *positivity* of the war machine. This does not imply a reversal of value (an aspect of Clastres's approach and of romantic anthropology). Thus, the state is not now the negation of the war machine. Rather, the state and the war machine are two distinct positivities. The violence evident when they interact is produced as a property of two positivities. It is as much or more an emergent property of their coming into conflict or their transmutation within the context of each other.

For example, sorcery is often seen as the negative antisocial aspect of social and political orders. Or conversely, as either the expression of the negative force of political and economic orders—an instance of their breakdown (much functionalist or structural-functionalist anthropology)—or a manifestation of the negation of human beings and their social relations as a function of the properties intrinsic to certain economic and political forces (capitalism in diverse Marxist perspectives). I do not insist that such perspectives are incorrect. They are relevant in specific cases and for understanding particular social and political processes as these relate to sorcery in the Sinhalese contexts that I am discussing. In certain circumstances, they can appear as aspects of what Deleuze and Guattari counterpose as war machine and state.

The difficulty of the functionalist or other positions with respect to sorcery or witchcraft that I address here is that they are highly restricted understandings; this restriction becomes evident when these positions are used to provide a complete or totalized comprehension of processes. Thus the *dysfunction* of economic and political processes is relative to people's position. Elites in contemporary Sri Lanka are not experiencing the same kind of breakdown that peasants and other fractions of a working class are experiencing. As Marxist analyses often indicate, what is disorganization for the downtrodden is often functional for the dominant. Sorcery expresses and manifests processes and problems that differ in relation to the social and economic position of persons and the structure or structuring dynamics involved, which are likely to be diverse. People engage in sorcery rites or attend the shrines for a diversity of problems which are not necessarily manifestations of a single all-encompassing process. However, the key point here is that the violence of sorcery and of the forces that can be interpreted as ranged against it is a function of the conjunction of different processes that have distinct positivities. This does not rule out their being positive or negative reactions to other processes and thus defined in their negativity or positivity by these other processes. However, structuring dynamics (or deconstruction) of sorcery are not to be understood simply by reference to what sorcery appears to contradict or oppose, that is, to processes that are outside of and not integral to the dynamics of sorcery practice.

An implication of the foregoing is that a negative force is not the essential characteristic of the war machine or of sorcery as an aspect of a war machine. Perhaps *war machine* is an unfortunate term, because it indicates that its dynamic is always supreme violence—war—and that this is endemic to its process or to the assemblages of power that manifest it. The war of the war machine, as I interpret Deleuze and Guattari and in my use of the term, is only its potential. It is the directional possibility of the processes that manifest or appropriate it. The war of the war machine emerges when it meets the resistance of the state and is the force of the state when it appropriates or transmutes the dynamic of the war machine to its own ends. In other words, war is not the conditionality of the dynamic of those forces external to the state in some kind of Hobbesian sense. The state, of course, can move toward war as part of its dynamic, as may war machines outside the order circumscribed by the state.

The power of exteriority, that of the war machine, has other dimensions. These may be distinguished from the dynamic of power and the structuring process of the power dynamic of the state, or the force of interiority. Thus, following the image of nomadic segmentary systems (or of the game of Go, as distinct from chess), the war machine is all motion or speed (in the sense developed by Virilio [1977] 1986). It spreads out from particular points, localities, in a horizontal plane, articulating a series of points and linking others as it reaches in new directions. The motion of the war machine is delimiting and unlimited; its force crosses territory, deterritorializes, and breaks down boundaries. The flow of the war machine is nomadic, and Deleuze and Guattari liken its trajectories to a rhizome. It both generates new linkages and moves horizontally along chains of links that are relations. The war machine is ahierarchical, and its internal dynamic of power militates against the formation of centers of power that then start to hierarchialize. The process of change in the war machine is that of metamorphosis. The war machine has the capacity to assume the form of what it overcomes and indeed, as is explicit in my earlier metaphor of the Hydra, to continually take new and often original form.

The assembling power dynamic of the state is constituted altogether differently. This constitution is not an evolution out of the war machine or a transmutation of it. Its characteristics, however, achieve a focus through contrast. The power of the state is hierarchical, and it encompasses a striated space crisscrossed with boundaries and enclosures. It is founded in controlling territory, establishing boundaries, and marking limitations. It is turned in on itself, and its motion is not that of speed but of conservation, and the building of power through conservation. The speed of the nomad, its outward-trajecting force, is present in the horse and in the man-becoming-animal that nomads established with the power of the horse. The motion of the state can be seen as a slowing of this speed, its conservation, and the development of a technology of conservation, the motor rather than the horse.

The state's process of change is one of transformation, and not the metamorphosis of the war machine. That is, the state does not change into the thing that it encounters or overruns, and it does not assume a form appropriate to what it resists. The transformation of the state is a dimension of its hierarchy, its codification of relations and its ordering them into a coherent system. The manner of the transformation is a function of organization that is highly various. The mechanism of transformation depends on organizational factors. The mechanism may be revolution, which changes the organizational form of the state, or rebellion and incessant dynastic struggle, which results in a turnover of the agents of power but maintains the overall organizational-institutional form (cf. Gluckman 1956, cited in Deleuze and Guattari 1988:440).

I will not say much more about the parallels between Deleuze and Guattari's discussion of the dynamics of power as war machine and as state and the figurations of power in the Sinhalese myths and practice of sorcery. The sorcerer traverses space and crosses limitations, and when he encounters boundaries, he clashes with the state; he breaks through them and, in fact, deterritorializes. Part of this deterritorialization is the flattening of space, the leveling of hierarchy.

The ferocity of this flattening deterritorialization could hardly be more dramatically presented than in the story of Suniyam's birth from Yawudagiri and his destruction of the kingdom of his birth. The story of his progress in which he destroys the neighboring kingdoms, cannibalizing their inhabitants, is the flattening and deterritorialization of the war machine in an extremely radical vein (see Chapter 3). Recall that Suniyam comes riding a horse, the speed of the war machine. The terror of Suniyam's approach is symbolized in the clattering of a horse's hooves against stone (see Chapter 5). The metamorphosis of sorcery is recognized in the Mahasammata myth: Suniyam becomes the form of Mahasammata in his invasion of the city-state and in his appearance before Manikpala. Sorcery travels out from a particular point and moves along the lines of relations, rhizomelike. It connects diverse points of experience in an expanding subjective space. This is the dynamic of the sorcery experience—demonstrated by victims as they declare their anguish before the shrines or in the process of diagnosis leading to a Suniyama or *kapuma* rite—wherein victims trace a multiplicity of events that might be connected in their abjection.

It is through a reterritorialization, a reerection of boundaries and limitations marking sedimented layers of horizontal and vertical lines of social and political division and folding—the striating of space; and a reassertion of hierarchialized relations in accordance with the logic of a code—a code in which society is reconstituted through the organizational dynamic of the state—that sorcery is overcome. The antisorcery rites engage these processes as their apparatus of capture, whereby what is moving outside or is external is reincorporated or destroyed. The inner transformational dynamic of their hierarchialization, using an intense codification of substances and relations, operates to transmute the exterior into the terms of the interior.

Sorcery and Its Powers of Capture

In the Suniyama, victims become virtual embodiments of the apparatus of capture of the state, in Dumezil's two senses of magician-king and jurist-priest. They may be seen not only as being in a reconstitutive relation to their communities (see Chapter 5) but also as recomposing (reforming as their power assemblage) the world that has moved outside their control, that is becoming exterior to them and they to it. Suniyamas are frequently performed for persons and households that are economically and politically relatively powerful. These rites do more than reflect power; they extend toward the world of the victim and make the victims agents of their recapture and reformation as a power assemblage, with the victim as its vital (and cosmic) center.

Thus the victim at the center of the Suniyama rite I described (Chapter 5) was experiencing threats to his economic and political fortunes. He was sensing the betrayal of his relatives, allies in his trading activities, and believed that his business was suffering from unfair competition. He had problems in controlling people at the distribution points in the long-distance network of his trucking operation. Aspects of the war machine (kinship alliances, trucking: the connection of points through a flat space external to his immediate social and political world) were integral to his dominant power but acting to subvert it: sorcery. The rite acted as an apparatus of capture, drawing the aspects of the war machine to within the entrepreneur's sphere of control and transmuting them to his interests.

On three separate occasions I recorded the performance of a Suniyama for returning migrants: one of a seaman coming back to his village to settle down after ten years at sea; two of persons who had been laborers in Saudi Arabia. All were returning with wealth that altered the previously impoverished condition of them and their families. They feared the envy and jealousy of their kin and neighbors. In my view, they were projecting as their own fear the dangers that their exteriority threatened to the internal structuring of the worlds of their villages. Their returning wealth suggested a shift in their status relations. (The migrants returning from Saudi Arabia were already planning to build new houses.) In effect, they were the war machines threatening to disrupt, if not flatten, the hierarchies and coded realities they were reentering. They were as much the sorcerers as the ensorcelled. Their Suniyamas may be interpreted as reconstituting them as no longer dangerous. Simultaneously, the rites actively reincorporated them within their village worlds and recomposed the power assemblage of its society, with them and their families repositioned at higher levels in their local political orders.

Similarly, the sorcery shrines are apparatuses of capture. I have commented on their location, at boundaries, at points of conjuncture and transition, and in spaces of social and political turbulence (see Chapters 2 and 3). They are places of articulation between the fragile hierarchical order of the state and the flat (and flattening) spaces of the nomad, of the worlds of the war machine. But they are ultimately oriented to the power of the state and discover their constraining, controlling, and revengeful force in the assemblage of power that is the state.

Those who control and often endow the shrines—often persons of power in local and state apparatuses, wealthy entrepreneurs—may be seen as placing themselves in the position of capture. They identify with and support a center of power that expresses the ordering power of the state. Furthermore, the shrine to which they are powerfully connected is an institution for capture. It attracts those who are in situations of exteriority to central and key forces of power—those who are its victims—and who in many instances may resist, and indeed often express the fury of the resistant: examples are the parents who confront Suniyam with their anguish at the loss of their children in the recent JVP revolt (see Chapter 7). But when the shrines as apparatuses of capture draw them in, the potency of their exteriority is brought within the dynamic power of the state. Paradoxically, the sorcery rites and the shrines, for all the energy of the nomad and of the war machine that is manifest in their context, have a hegemonic function. Thus, the powers of exteriority are converted in the ordering dynamic of the state.

The Dynamics of War Machine and State

The war machine and the state are ever-present modalities of the dynamics of power. In Deleuze and Guattari's sense, they are abstractions of the concrete and are never separate from historical experience. They are somewhat akin to Max Weber's notion of ideal type. However, they are not separated in space and time, nor are they, as in Weber's discussion of Western and Eastern bureaucratic structures, understood as distinct ways of doing similar things (which also carry intimations of superiority and inferiority). They are not polar types at either end of a continuum. The Western and Eastern bureaucratic forms of political organizations are different aspects of the state modality of power. The war machine and the state are not polar types along a continuum of power but exist in every context as simultaneous and distinct dynamics of power with separate orientational trajectories.

Clearly the dynamics of the war machine and the state are emergent in a great and ever-diversifying range of social and political institutions and practices. War machine and state are not totalized characterizations of discrete, bounded actual societies. They are empirically demonstrable within particular ethnographic contexts and as constant processes within historical and contemporary worlds. The war machine and the nomad, as well as the force of the state, can be illustrated with reference to nonstate segmentary tribal systems as described by anthropologists, or to ancient and modern organizations of sovereign nation-states. But they are modalities of the forming of power, modes of power assemblage (i.e., formings of power not restricted to specific social and political organizations or institutions) present in all contexts.

The war machine or nomad and the state describe power *in its dynamic* as this materializes in a diversity of structurating processes on the ground. They are not essential to any particular organization, institution, or relation but are emergent as a potential of their process. Moreover, they are not confined to particular ideological or value arrangements, although such cultural reflections on lived processes may give expression to the dynamics of the war machine and state.

This is the case with the beliefs, myths, and symbolic organization of Sinhalese sorcery practice. Within the changing historical and cultural worlds of the Sinhalese, they are cultural reflections on the dynamics of power, recognitions of power as exteriorizing and interiorizing, as deterritorializing and bounding, and as a flattening and also centralizing, hierarchializing force. Such dynamics and their structurating process are integral to the imaginary of sorcery practice. This imaginary is relevant across different historical moments and in a great variety of different contexts.

It does this because *sorcery is the mirror of power as a dynamic.* This dynamic is in itself at once abstract and concrete. The myths of sorcery and the schemes of ritual practice are frames that can—metamorphose—to any context. Metamorphosis is facilitated by the dynamic of the myths and rites. The practices of sorcery are a general shape of a dynamic that can attach to most processes that human beings encounter. Alternatively, the experiences and exigencies of daily life can be made to fit the dynamic of sorcery myth and rite and are thus set within their motion and trajectory.

The dynamics of power that the myths and rites schematize—those of the war machine and state—were invented at certain times and might be expected to embed aspects of the historical world in which they were invented or the problematics of the situation they addressed. But the dynamics that are their concern are continually being reinvented and reissued in new historical contexts of the life world.

The practice of the Suniyama and the practices of the shrines are different formations, materializations, or objectifications of the dynamics of power and are constituted and reconstituted in differing historical, economic, and political circumstances. The dynamics they express are, however, in general terms very similar.

To look at this the other way, power as a dynamic can have the structurating dimensions of war machine or state or of the aspects of sorcery repeatedly through diverse contexts. The power dynamics of state, as I have described it, is evident in very different concrete circumstances. Archaic states and contemporary nation-states are political formations of very distinct nature and purpose, constructed under entirely different historical, economic, and political circumstances. The archaic state is rarely, if ever, historically continuous with the nation-state. The galactic polities or theater states (Tambiah 1976; Geertz 1980) of South Asia and Southeast Asia are completely distinct from the bureaucratic nation-states of contemporary realities. Nonetheless, they both engage what I call the state dynamics of power. They involve hierarchializing and centralizing forces, they are bounding and limiting, and they usually stress abstract knowledge and the controlling and production of highly coded realities.

The dynamics of the war machine or, indeed, the sorcerer—the power that is constituted exterior to the state, its refusal of territorial limits, its motion along points in flattened space, its antihierarchializing force—these are repeated in very diverse contexts with vastly distinct consequences. Nonetheless, although they are irreducible to each other, they are similar in process.

Suniyam and other demon-deities are described in myths as having to do with trade. As traders they cross boundaries, deterritorialize space, convert things of different value, and in effect operate against the hierarchialization of value. As traders, they express the power of the nomad. These traders are historically discontinuous from the modern capitalist entrepreneur but share a certain dynamic. This correspondence of dynamic is produced in historical action that is formational of contemporary postcolonial, globalizing capitalist actualities. To some extent a contemporary world discovers its own form in the retelling of the myths, as a consequence of the fact that the myths are retold in the contexts shaped by modern processes. Because of this, the dynamic that is already apparent in the myths achieves original significance and a new intensity. This is possibly a factor in the massive deterritorialization that Suniyam's progress describes in the modern retellings of his story (see Gombrich and Obeyesekere 1988: 112–132; Chapter 3). The exteriority of the war machine is dynamic in a multiplicity of large-scale global forces and in microprocesses affecting the routine of life. This is evident in the motions of capitalism, whose power assemblages, international banking organizations (especially the World Bank and the International Monetary Fund), multinationals, industrial complexes (in Sri Lanka, the free trade zones operating to a large extent independently of state regulation), and other processes, including injections of money through international migration and infusion of externally produced consumer commodities, are largely deterritorialized and deterritorializing. They overrun the territorial bounds of the sovereign Sri Lankan state and operate against the sovereign integrity of Sri Lanka—the war machine against the state. Such exterior forces are an element in the exteriorization of groups within the social and political relations controlled and ordered by the agents of the Sri Lankan government and are reacted to as antagonistic to the ordering dynamic of state power. Thus, in recent years community service organizations with foreign funding and other foreign (often development aid) organizations (all described as NGOs, nongovernment organizations) have been subjected to government criticism, inquiries, and regulation—the apparatuses of capture of modern governments.

In these instances, the sorcerer is not so much invented by capitalism as reinvented by its processes. The point is that the dynamics of power that the symbolism of sorcery practice expresses are recreated through diverse historical acts in space and time. The dynamics that sorcery manifests and that Sinhalese routinely use in order to overcome their anxieties are continually being constituted in the social and political worlds of their lives and made integral to experience. Power that is always rooted in the world and takes new forms in the historical processes of the world nonetheless repeats its dynamics. The dynamics are produced through the forces of change and transformations of the world, and these must be the primary concerns of understanding. The dynamic qua dynamic—as modalities of war machine and state—recurs as the concreteness of human experience. It is the concreteness of such dynamics of power that sorcery captures. The relevance of the practice of sorcery in the routine lives of many Sinhalese is maintained because very different forms for the organization of power throw up or repeat the broad dynamics of power that sorcery expresses.

The Sorcery of Power

Power has the shape of sorcery. By this statement I do not mean that sorcery is a representation of power—the direction of much anthropology. Rather, power in various instituted and structuring processes is a representation of the forces in sorcery practice. I have drawn on Deleuze and Guattari in part to make this assertion. Their work is an implicit recognition of this. They draw on ethnographic and other materials—Dumezil and Vernant being the most noteworthy—often with an explicit sorcery reference for developing their insights, frequently in an effort to challenge the authority of Western Enlightenment and post-Enlightenment philosophies and social sciences. When I say that there is a sorcery in the processes of power, or that power has the shape of sorcery, I mean that we can understand power and the processes of power better by taking sorcery seriously.

The Terrorism of Order and Resistance

I turn to a brief consideration of recent events in Sri Lanka, focusing on aspects of a largely nationalist struggle for power in Sri Lanka. The struggle involves war between the Sri Lankan government and Tamil separatists (the Tamil Tigers, or LTTE) and also the violent struggle between the Sri Lankan government and the Sinhala guerrilla insurrectionists of the JVP (Janatha Vimukthi Peramuna: Peoples Liberation Front). These events have been well covered in other sources and I do not attempt to present a sociological analysis of them. But I examine aspects of the sorcery of power that are demonstrated in these struggles.

The war between the Sri Lankan government and Tamils frames and largely conditions a general context of suffering in Sri Lanka. This became a full-scale war after the anti-Tamil riots of August 1983 which swept Colombo and other towns and rural areas. I likened the riots to a gigantic exorcism and also associated their passions with practices of sorcery (Kapferer 1988a). The riots had this character in their violent action, in their dynamic of power. I did not argue that the motivation to exorcism and its dynamic and the motion toward ethnic rioting and destruction were founded in a common cultural cause: a cultural orientation whose logic and meaning had endured untransformed through the centuries. Furthermore, I did not suggest that the cultural ideas and meanings of civilizations long dead were alive and the same as they were then in the structures of action and the psyches of people participating in exorcisms and in ethnic and other forms of human destruction in the Sri Lanka of today. My argument was directed against this kind of essentialist perspective (see Foster 1991).

I drew a distinction between ontology and ideology. My interpretation of ontology was not to be confused with some readings (I think misreadings) of Heidegger, or other positions that imply a fundamental psychology of human being—in the context of Sri Lanka, a mind set that emerged in the dim past and continues through to the present; a psychology that is not only virtually immutable but also conditions personal and collective reactions to different social, economic, and political circumstances. These misreadings of my argument missed my point (e.g., Spencer 1990; Scott 1994; Kemper 1991).[5]

By *ontology* I was referring to the outline of a dynamic identifiable in a diversity of practices. These dynamics of practice (which might be detected in the narrative organization of events in a myth, in the process of eventful action in a rite, or in the motions of power in everyday life) have no essential connection in history or in psychology. The only thing that needs to be the link between diverse practices is their dynamics. This dynamics is generated from very diverse ground separated in space and in time.[6]

A further reason for using *ontology* was to stress the connection between dynamics and persons, to shift away from the sociology that treated human beings as mere pawns in the machinations of structures. I wished to make a further, fairly unexceptionable argument: that human beings constitute or reconstitute the dynamics of their action, the dynamics of structure, from the ground of their experience of their life worlds. They fashion their orientations in existence and through the objectifications or materializations of their experience that they select or manufacture. In effect, they submit themselves to the dynamics of shapes of their own creation. Moreover, in constituting or reconstituting themselves in such dynamics, they generate a particular orientation toward themselves and others and toward the horizons of their experience in their life worlds.

Here the importance of ideology (heterodoxy, reflective discursive practice) comes in. Ideology is for me the overt and relatively coherent organization of reflections on experience. It is produced in practice and is variously regrounded through practice. The production of ideology is the production or construction of meaning or value. There is no necessary sense, meaningful import, direction, project, aim, or purpose in the dynamics qua dynamics of what I call ontological processes. These aims and projects are produced and defined in an ongoing process of ideological or discursive practices. Ideologies not only give meaning to the dynamics of existence but also form an orienting aspect of the way human beings move in their worlds. In specific circumstances, ideologies, or discursive strategies, can forge connections between practices where there were none. They can join previously disjunct sets of activities directed to distinct purposes and can orient the powerful apparatuses of government as well as of those in opposition or resistance.

Thus, in the context of contemporary Sri Lanka, nationalist discourses establish connections between current political practices of ethnicity and practices in the past that used apparently (from the position of the present and its discourse) similar labels of ethnic identity: labels that in the past derived their meaning and direction in entirely different institutional arrangements or assemblages of power (see Kapferer 1996). I specifically discussed the ideological use of ancient and medieval chronicles as part of the ideological construction of contemporary actualities. The meanings of the chronicles were reinvented, and reinvented with the import of the contemporary problematics of the agents of a modern bureaucratic nation-state, and not those of archaic states or galactic polities.

The argument can be extended in another way. The ancient chronicles among other things dealt with the dynamics of power, with what I have described as war machine and state, processes grounded in the actualities of the writers of the chronicles. The problematics of current state ideologues of the Sri Lankan government are entirely different from those of the past. But the dynamics have similar shape. That is, the controlling orders of centralizing bureaucratic organizations were experiencing the threat, for example, of exteriorizing and deterritorializing forces. Thus, Tamil separatist guerrillas were denying the territorial integrity of a Sinhala-controlled Sri Lankan government. Other groups were exteriorizing within the bounds of government control. The liberalizing of the economy after the election of the present controlling party (the United National Party), the opening of the economy to global capitalist forces, and other factors exacerbated crises of social and political control for the government (e.g., increased class agitation, an increase in unrest among the urban and rural poor and the otherwise disadvantaged, such as the Sinhala-educated youth, to be expressed in the reemergence of the JVP).

The processes I discuss above and the processes going on in the chronicles have similar dynamics *as dynamics*. The power assemblages that produced such dynamics obviously cannot be reduced to each other. They are historically disjunct. What modern reinventions of the meaning of the chronicles did as an ideological practice was to invest the past with the sense of the present. Moreover, these reinventions gave contemporary political aims and directions ancient legitimacy. The ideological productions of the agents of state also enabled the similar dynamics of diverse and relatively separate practices in modern contexts (e.g., healing rites, religious worship) to become mutually supportive, or allowed the sense or meaning developed in one context to be extended to a different meaning context. Thus, in some healing rites, the exterior and flattening power of the demonic is sometimes represented as Tamil (see also Tamil as sorcerer in the *vadiga patuna* of the Suniyama in Chapter 5). With the development of a contemporary Sinhala nationalism, such events expanded beyond their immediate practical concern of ending a patient's affliction. The affliction of a patient and household was open to broader interpretational import, a metaphor of exteriority grounded as political actuality and patient reality.

To return to the anti-Tamil riots of 1983, the dynamics of the riots was a popular reaction to what was seen as the growing and threatening exteriority of Tamils. Given that many of the rioters were Sinhalese from poor urban and rural areas (although by no means exclusively), their action might also be seen as a projection of their own exteriorizing experience onto Tamils, often of their own class.

There is a broad similarity here to the sorcery rites, especially at the shrines (see also Kapferer 1988a). The passion of the riots, the intensity of their destructive affect, involves the aspect of the person that is in the subjective, experiential condition of the sorcerer. Affect is the speed of the sorcerer. It crosses open space and spreads out (like the energy of the shattered coconut at the shrines); it is a rhizomic, deterritorializing energy that crashes through the boundaries of limitation.

That the riots and sorcery share a similar dynamic does not mean that the collective political action of the riots is directed through the meaning framework of sorcery. That many Sinhalese engage in sorcery provides no explanation of the riots. But they have a similar dynamics, and the dynamics of sorcery practice highlight certain aspects of the processes of power that help us understand political actions such as the riots.

The dynamics of sorcery expose other aspects of power in contemporary Sri Lanka, such as the power of contemporary nationalism. In Sri Lanka and elsewhere, nationalism is a politics of the local and the subjective. But nationalism seeks the expansion of the local or the extension of the subjective within protective orders, the boundaries of the sovereign nation-state. The energy of nationalism is both war machine and state. The energy of the war machine is an energy of inclusion in the state, and further, it is transmuted as a force of the state. Suniyam is both the energy against the state, which penetrates its boundaries, and indeed breaks them down, or deterritorializes, and also the force of reterritorialization, the establishment of boundaries and the rehierarchialization of order. Suniyam expresses the desire for inclusion and the overcoming of exclusion and marginalization.

Nationalism, as a specific dynamics of power but also a process of a contemporary historical conjuncture, has the form of sorcery. Further, nationalist mythologies and symbols tend to invent or reissue myths and symbols that express the kind of dynamics I have been discussing. Where there are traditions already expressive of the dynamics of power qua dynamics, like chronicles and folk practices, these are likely to be appropriated by a nationalist politics. I believe this is what happened in Sri Lanka. References to events in the chronicles (those of Vijaya and of Prince Dutthagamani, which are symbolic narratives of power as dynamic; see Kapferer 1988a) were made by nationalist ideologues, not only because they constituted glorifications of the past (glorifications denied in colonialism) but also because they expressed a dynamics central to a nationalist project. Nationalists were drawn to the symbolism of the dynamics of power of the chronicles not because the spirit of these chronicles was in their psyche but because they expressed the process of power, its dynamics, in which they were already active. This dynamics was the creation of colonial and postcolonial circumstances but repeated the form of a particular dynamics of power *as dynamics*. The symbolism of a dynamics of power through contemporary nationalism was *reissued* as appropriate to modern political processes and substantialized within the power assemblage of the contemporary nation-state. It is this power assemblage that constituted the armature of the symbolic form of power and gave it particular definition and direction.

The substantialization of the metaphors of the process of power in nationalism (e.g., the identification of symbols of state: Vijaya, Dutthagamani; and of war machine: Kuveni, Tamils; with actual institutions and categories or groups of persons: the Sri Lankan government, Sinhalese, Tamils) gives them an import and a direction, of course, which are produced by the forces that engage them. The metaphors of mythology and rite, for example, which manifest the otherwise intangible dynamics of the process of power, give this dynamics a materiality and are objectified in the actualities of everyday life. Thus, they give further impetus to contemporary political action and facilitate a magnification of its passionate course. The dynamics of individual experience becomes the generalized force of objectified realities. The highly specific and situated experiences of persons are not merely communicated as part of the experience of others (e.g., as in ritual performances; see Kapferer 1983; Chapter 5) but *are constructed* through the materializations and substantializations of nationalist discourse, part of actuality. To put it another way, the virtual realities of ritual and myth are reconstituted as the world of ordinary daily life: nationalism ritualizes the world.[7] This is the sorcery of nationalism's dynamics of power. It achieves something similar to the actual practices of sorcery that materialize the flow of experience and give it a general form (the action of the Suniyama, the rites at shrines).

The major difference, however, is that the directional relation between rite and world is reversed. In actual sorcery practice the potency of the acts is in the reality of the ritual acts as such and extends toward the world. In nationalism, the separation between the reality of rite and the actuality of the everyday world is lost. The world reaches toward rite as the quintessence of its actualities.

The sorcery of power was realized in the political struggle and dreadful human destruction of the JVP insurrection against the Sri Lankan government. The dynamics of the struggle *as dynamics* emerged from within contemporary social and economic processes, those which generated the nationalist energies of ethnic war between the Tamil minority and the Sinhala majority. The dynamics repeated what sorcery materializes. I do not suggest that the repetition of the dynamics flowed out of mythical realities, that they were culturally predetermined. The dynamics were the reinventions of a specific, grounded, political process and, given the appropriate conditions, are repeated elsewhere as present global actualities (Bosnia, Rwanda, Angola, Timor, Yemen, etc.) attest, but in accordance with the specificities of situations.

Following the 1983 riots, the JVP (ostensibly organized on Maoist lines) was incorrectly blamed for the riots and proscribed by the Sri Lankan government. The JVP was very much a party of the youth, frequently from the rural and urban poor. Its force was concentrated in Sinhala areas, especially in the south. The western and southern coastal belt of the island (stretching roughly from Colombo to Hambantota) was a major zone of JVP activity, the region from which the main leadership was drawn and an area renowned for its Sinhala chauvinism and support for the Sinhala nationalist cause. The organization of the JVP was cellular and grassroots. It was based in village relations, and rhizomelike, it spread through ties of kinship, caste, and personal friendship. Proscription intensified these processes and made the JVP more trenchantly the organization of exteriority, the war machine.

The assemblage of power that was (is?) the JVP constituted itself through secrecy, the bonds of interpersonal alliance, and its deterritorializing potency: the radiation of links through a terrain that the JVP regarded as open and across which it attacked the forces that imposed boundaries and limitations. It manifested its potency in the dark, and not in the light of the day.

The agents of the JVP that controlled power in village and in neighborhood made themselves apparent at night. At the height of its operations (between August 1989 and the early months of 1990), when it confronted the Sri Lankan government directly in a bid to wrest total political control, the JVP imposed daytime curfews (as opposed to the nighttime curfews of the government) as an invasive strategy. This was the war machine against the state, smoothing its striated space and attacking the hierarchializing institutions of the government. The JVP declared that persons could not go to work or leave their houses. Indeed, the war machine invaded the citadel of the state: the citizenry of Colombo and Kandy, for example, were seized in the grip of JVP terror.

The violent acts of the JVP insurrection had the instrumentality of the war machine and of sorcery. Agents of the JVP meted out justice. Frequently they presented their justice as a morality of society, of social relations, ignored or subverted by bureaucrats or contravened by other agents of government power. In at least one rural area of my knowledge, a JVP court was set up to hear local grievances, often concerning land claims, which the plaintiffs asserted had been delayed for hearing or unfairly settled in the government courts. Many of those summarily killed by the JVP had a statement of their crimes pinned to their corpses, often of a moral kind. The victim's bodies, made the objects of a social anger as well as the political anger of the JVP, were sometimes terribly mutilated. In such a condition and under threat of death from the JVP, relatives were forced to leave the corpses where they lay for days on end. The outrage on the body was extended to a body of kin, not unlike the act of the sorcerer, whose fragmenting destruction not only destroys a particular human target but radiates destructively through the victim's world, along the lines of kinship and social alliance.

Individuals who were the targets of JVP threats—politicians, bureaucrats, local dignitaries—feared that they were in the process of *destruction by an anonymous other*. Routinely, victims received two warning letters demanding that they change their ways. If they failed to do so, they were killed. The threats knew no social boundaries or limits. They overcame hierarchy. But they were not necessarily destructive, although death was their sanction. They can be seen as potentially constitutive in terms of the expanding, spreading organization of the war machine. The threats had the capacity to establish relations where there had been none; indeed, like the sorcery at the shrines, they made connections and turned another's will by thrusting through the barriers of social order.

The JVP was finally overcome by the military and paramilitary forces of the Sri Lankan government. A feature of its success was its capacity to appropriate aspects of the war machine that it confronted. For ordinary citizens, largely rendered helpless spectators in the space of death created in the struggle, the line separating the killing practices of the JVP from those of government agencies was blurred. A hero of government forces was a high-ranking police officer, Udugampola, who after the JVP massacre of members of his own family—an important aspect of his myth at the time—assumed the form of a virtual demon avenger, destroying all those in his path that he suspected of JVP associations. As the war machine of the JVP sought to take control of the day (war-machine-becoming-state), the military organizations of the government took increasing control of the night (state-becoming-war-machine). The process was one of deterritorialization; villages and other places of suspected JVP association were raided and executions summarily carried out. The course of government violence traveled along the lines of suspicion and betrayal. It also assumed the garb of the sorcerer. The innocent as well as the guilty were caught in the webs of violence of both the government and the JVP; their dynamics of power began to resemble each other's.

Nonetheless, the violence of government agencies was different from that of the JVP. The JVP violence had a highly personal character. It attacked persons in their individual social identities, in the way they were socially and politically articulated into their world. Their prominence was exploded, and the impotence of the world they ordered was revealed. The cruelty of JVP violence was a cruelty that took its shape in relation to the persona of the victim. If anything, the identity of the victim was magnified in the process of the victim's destruction. But the identity of the attacker was relatively anonymous, shadowy and hidden behind a nom de guerre which, although it was used by a particular individual, also stood for a collectivized menace.

The violence of the government forces tended to be different—though undoubtedly it could and did work in the ambiguous space of the sorcerer and disguise its own violence as the violence of the other. The violence of the government, organized through a war machine transmuted as an organ of state, took an ordering, bureaucratic shape (see Kapferer 1994a, 1994b). The bureaucratic shape of the violence was intensified by the anonymity and secrecy of the JVP opposition. Nonetheless, there was a pattern of searching for sites of resistance in terms of abstract taxonomic categories—youth, village, and caste. Although particular persons were targets, the government's apparatus of capture was a net of abstraction which caught its victims through a logic of indicators that presumed association and ties with the JVP. The cruelty of the agents of government violence extended on the same line. A frequent method of destruction was to pile up and burn the bodies of suspects at marginal places (crossroads, at the side of roads) to erase their identities or personas. Otherwise, the victims were buried in anonymous mass graves. In the Suniyama, which engages a dynamics of state power and rebuilds a cosmic order through a logic of abstraction, the sorcerer is made anonymous and destroyed at the boundaries or marginal spaces of society. The victims are made into the deformed and faceless shape of exteriority, a fact of the experience of some of those destroyed. It is such experience, as at the sorcery shrines, that may have motivated the shape of the JVP passionate resistance and the personal particularity of its direction.

None of the patterns of violence that I describe defies a rational understanding. Particular reasons, regardless of ethical sensibilities, can account for aspects of the violence on both sides (of course, there have been manuals for violence throughout history). Many are obvious: the need to hide evidence, the importance of secrecy in resistance, and the utility of terror and its spectacle of death for the (re)assertion of authority and control. The violence of the JVP struggle shows, if anything, how different structures of reasoning can in their dynamic end reason or extend beyond any limits imposed by reason. The dynamic of the war machine rendered incapable of metamorphosing into the ordering dynamic of the state can enter a frenzy of destruction driven to consume and level all the structures and the individuals that are the composing points of structure that rise against it. The power assemblage constituted with the motion of the war machine can begin to consume itself. This is a danger that segmentary societies (like the Nuer) outside the compass of states may implicitly recognize and ritually control.

Perhaps more voracious is the destructive potential of the dynamics of state. In contemporary reality, states have greater access to technologies and other resources of mass destruction. But I stress the destructive potency of their logic of conquest and destruction, especially in the context of the suspension of habeas corpus and other legal rights of citizens (as in Sri Lanka's State of Emergency), when states turn against their own populations. As in much sorcery, the greatest fear and the greatest threat is often the exteriority within one's immediate world rather than that from outside: Vasavarti or Suniyam achieve the height of their destructive potency *within* the womb of state. In this situation, the abstract ordering dynamics of state—in modern contexts, its bureaucratic processes—become its weapon for discovering the points of resistance. Moreover, the abstract or bureaucratic constructions of state become a logic for the *production of victims*—for their creation and invention. What might be called the bureaucratic imaginary of the state may fuel a paranoia of state; it may create a hunger that it must furiously satiate. In this dynamics of abstraction of the state-becoming-war-machine, human beings are resisters by reason of their category membership. They become hostages to a science of indicators and a law of probability. This kind of violence is everywhere visible in global actualities.

Any context where the motion of death is directed through a logic of abstraction has the potentiality for great destruction. But I suggest that the greater potential may be in the state-becoming-war-machine, where the instruments of ordering become the weapons of war. Modern states that use the bureaucratic process as their weapon of war, particularly against their own populations, exhibit extraordinary capacities for human destruction. In Sri Lanka, more Sinhalese (innocents as well as militants) seem to have been killed in the three or four months at the height of the JVP insurrection (more by government forces, I contend, than by the insurrectionists) than in the entire ten years of the Tamil-Sinhala war following the riots of 1983.

Ethnic categorization is widely seen to be at the root of much contemporary human destruction. An additional major factor is a concern to establish the purity of category, especially that of the main perpetrators of ethnic or racial destruction. The Holocaust is the paradigm of such annihilation by categorization. The ethnic cleansing in Bosnia and the horror of Rwanda are repetitions produced by different historical circumstances. But the engine of destruction underpinning these disasters for humanity is the state-become-war-machine, with its sorcery of power, which converts abstract procedures of order (the generative capacity of the bureaucratic imaginary) into a technology for discovering threat and a weapon for war.

The sorcery of power can reach toward metaphors and can invent symbols that unselfconsciously reflect the character of its dynamics. It is out of the process that the idea is grasped or produced. Nationalists in Sri Lanka and participants in other dynamics of power, like the JVP struggle, acting within a diverse and rich cultural field using their dynamics of power, appropriate metaphors already available in other contexts of use and integral to their realities. The meaning of the metaphors was expanded and carried a force produced in other separate contemporaneous contexts, and vice versa. Both the JVP and the agents of government used symbols of their power related to mythical or legendary events in the ancient chronicles, events repeated in popular folklore and vital in local rites. The terror and power were facilitated and intensified because of this. But dynamics of power qua dynamics were already what the cultural metaphors and symbols of the dynamics of power expressed. In other words, the dynamics of power tends toward or discovers its medium of cultural expression. Moreover, the mode of expression is more than this. It unites with the practice in which its process is already implicit and becomes integral to those concrete political practices, extending their directional force. The dynamics of power is the dynamics of sorcery.

9

Thus, Man Is Always a Wizard to Man

THE PHENOMENA OF SORCERY and witchcraft are mirrors to humanity. Above all, they address the problematics of human existence in worlds that human beings make and unmake. For all the fabulation, mystery, and superstition that the word *sorcery* often conjures, especially to those steeped in the rationalism of the contemporary scientific and technological world, sorcery concerns the centrality of human beings in worlds of human creation. This is the primary fact of sorcery, which the often fabulous and terrifying features of its practice both hide and express. In sorcery, human being is in struggle with itself and with the worlds of its own invention.

It has not been my main concern to explain or understand sorcery practices in Sri Lanka in terms of well-tried anthropological approaches or with reference to the problems that guide these approaches. Thus, I have not tried to account for sorcery, for example, as an irrational belief or practice, as an activity that expresses certain patterns of psychosocial order or structure, as a folk explanation for misfortune, as a precursor to scientific knowledge, as a distinct mode of reasoning, or as giving insight into such theological-philosophical issues as the problem of evil. The ethnography presented should assist readers with such interests, but these questions are not the raison d'être for the ethnography or its analysis.

My strategy has been at least partially to suspend such questions and to reduce the degree to which they guide and structure the interpretation of ethnographic materials that broadly fit the anthropological category

298

of sorcery (and of its associated complex of witchcraft and magic). My main reason for this was to allow a little more space for sorcery-related activities to reveal their own problematics. The questions that are frequently asked of sorcery practices have less to do with sorcery per se or how it is manifested in specific contexts than with methodological issues of anthropologists and their rhetoric among themselves and in relation to other disciplines. This has been the case from the beginnings of anthropology as fieldwork, steeped in post-Enlightenment issues and theories, to the more current developments of a postmodernist anthropology.

These debates often reconstitute the practices they address in the terms of the debate. They become practices of the debate, losing their own import and problematic to the concerns of the debates in which they are couched. Sorcery often seems to have suffered this fate, along with numerous other phenomenal categories of anthropological invention, description, and analysis.

Thus, the focus on sorcery as a form of explanation was closely connected to anthropologists' demonstrating their own scientific legitimacy. Sorcery was shaped into an object on which anthropologists could demonstrate their scientific skills. Sorcery was explicitly defined as something distinct from or opposed to science, an irrationality that anthropologists could explain in itself and transcend in their own scientific understanding of the nature of human social existence. Against sorcery, anthropologists could display their credentials as serious scholars, thoroughly familiar with the canons of scientific knowledge. Furthermore, they were able to demonstrate their ability to penetrate the cant of science and reveal its self-delusions as they had exposed sorcery and witchcraft.

Moreover, sorcery was part of the initial definition of anthropological territory: the description of culture or custom (usually non-Western; the sorcery that anthropologists studied was not to be confused with the European variety) and its demystification and translation into general terms. Sorcery and witchcraft exemplified the importance of collecting exotic practices as part of the broader task of verifying general assertions and theories concerning the nature of human kind. Sorcery was also useful for understanding practices in the home worlds of anthropologists, usually Western and bourgeois.

From the beginning, sorcery became shaped to the demands of academic anthropology. More recently, the object sorcery has undergone further metamorphosis. Sorcery, once devalued because the logic of its reasoning was contradictory and inconsistent, has now been revalued on much the same grounds. Furthermore, sorcery is now used to overturn the commitments of its previous anthropological manipulators. It has assumed the image of deconstructionist and postmodernist understanding: antisystematic, transgressive, and subversive. Paradoxically, sorcery has once more been subordinated to debates centered in metropolitan worlds.

The perspectives I have taken on sorcery practice do not stand outside these debates in anthropology. I do not see how they could. Nonetheless, my initial aim has been to turn away from them in an effort to see what sorcery practices themselves may reveal about human action and experience.

Anthropology claims to have a commitment to direct empirical and involved observation. Ideally, statements about the nature of human action must be established on the grounds of what human beings say and do. Anthropologists intend their descriptions to add to a general body of knowledge concerning human beings and to give peoples often ignored a place in establishing this knowledge. Moreover, anthropologists have insisted that the record of such knowledge and practice, one that presents the diversity of human existence, should be the foundation for any theorizing about the meaning or purpose of human activities. This attitude, which is incipiently critical, has sometimes brought anthropologists into fruitful disagreement with those in other disciplines. The broad point of anthropological practice was and is that the proper understanding of human being is in the practices of human beings themselves and in the diversity of these practices in often vastly different cultural and historical contexts. This is the point of anthropological ethnography: to give voice to the actual beliefs and practices of human beings.

The point was to go beyond what scholars in the special conditions of their laboratories, or in their own restricted, isolated and often self enclosed environments may have thought the world was. There was in anthropology a powerful impatience with philosophy, which made pronouncements about the nature of human being with Delphic authority and impenetrability and with an almost mystical claim of direct access to the truth through the properties of its own reasoning. One does not have to agree with the positivism of Durkheim, the materialism of Marx, or the structuralism of Lévi-Strauss (who, if unreflectively, remarks on existentialists blowing clouds of dialectical smoke in their Café du Commerce) to share a disquiet with the facility of some philosophical assertions about the nature of human being and their ready acceptance. This is especially true when philosophical understanding is apparently so often based on self-contemplation and casual experiences of others, and maintains the authority of its own context.

By way of contrast, anthropologists were especially concerned to bring peoples and their visions of human realities that were usually excluded from serious consideration (and frequently the objects of prejudiced popular and informed opinion) into the context of the largely metropolitan intellectual and scientific discussion about human processes. This was important because such discourses had consequence and often death-dealing effects for both the physical existence and the continuity of the ways of life of those peripheral to metropolitan worlds and subjected to their domination.

This book is part of this larger project of anthropological ethnography, which is shared by modernist and postmodernist anthropologists alike, despite their oppositions and the alienating quality of the largely metropolitan abstractions and concerns which subvert, perhaps unavoidably, the aims of anthropological ethnography. These aims are always worth restating.

This ethnography has been designed to present Sinhala sorcery practice as far as possible on its own terms. I have tried to reveal its profundities in relation to an exploration of the way human beings constitute both themselves and their worlds. I have placed these in their social and historical context. On occasion I have used the dynamic of the practices of sorcery to discuss contemporary political and social process in Sri Lanka and elsewhere. I have not reduced such events or processes to sorcery in any causal sense. What I have suggested is that sorcery practice, especially rite, is built around acute pragmatic understanding of the processes of human action. In this book I have tried to take some advantage of sorcery practice to extend a more general understanding of human action.

Furthermore, I have examined sorcery practice in relation to analytical perspectives in anthropology and some philosophy that does have significant influence on anthropological analyses (despite the suspicions of many anthropologists). I have tried to do this so as to give to sorcery practice—especially the ritual practitioners of the major antisorcery rite—authority in the exploration of some perennial and new concerns in anthropology: the gift and reciprocity, the constitutive force of sacrifice, the formation of consciousness, the centrality of the imaginary in the creation and restitution of social realities, and the role of the passions in cognition.

Central to my discussion was sorcery practice as illuminating the processes whereby human beings create themselves and their realities. Anthropologists have observed that sorcery is a representation of the social and of the contradictions and conflicts of social and political realities. This is part of the important way they have demystified it and made it intelligible to those outside the realms of sorcery. But sorcery practices are more than a representation; they are exercises in the construction and destruction of the psychosocial realities that human beings live and share. Their potency as representations results from this.

I concentrated my discussion around the antisorcery rite of the Suniyama. This rite is not so much a reflection or representation of the external realities of everyday life as an archaeology of the dynamics by which human beings routinely make and break the realities that they construct. I described the Suniyama as a virtuality within which the paradoxes and problematics of human intentional consciousness, integral to sociality and social formation are explored. Most significantly, the rite aligns the victim along the fundamental intentional motion of human being (a potency of sorcery and a motion in which all is immanent—the emergence of being and its extinction, the creation of the social and also its destruction). The victim is made to practice the practice of social creation, among other things, on which being in existence is contingent.

This rite and other practices are infused with the heterodox, largely Buddhist, religious influences of the region's history and are embedded in various activities in the Sri Lankan cultural universe. The pragmatic concerns of such rites as the Suniyama resonate with perhaps grander doctrinal themes. They may contribute to an understanding of the import of the abstractions of doctrine. This is one project of such rites, for their practical purpose is the concretization of the abstract.

I want to make it clear, however, that much of what may seem to be existentially removed philosophical abstractions is part of the minutiae of practice. The force of such abstractions is not so much as abstractions, things to reflect on independent of earthly activities, but rather as knowledge practices. In the rites victims are asked to reflect, but the practice is integral to the reflection.

I have tried to demonstrate the contribution that practices connected with sorcery can make to wider anthropological understanding. My aim has been to break the circle of relativism that characterizes so much anthropology. I have brought the knowledge practice of Sinhala exorcists to bear on debates not just in anthropology but in some philosophy relevant to the humanities and human sciences. These practices (taking into account their historical and cultural specifics), offer alternatives to the dualities of mind and body, subject and object, and individual and society that still provide grounds for argument and remain at the heart of many controlling theories.

All this should not obscure what in the end sorcery is primarily about, the crises that human beings must daily confront in personal, social, and political actualities. The kind of extreme suffering to which human beings are subject—in the depth of its existential reach, far more than simply misfortune—is given proportionality in the enormity of its cosmic projections. But the force of sorcery practices is in their constitutive potential, as in the action focused on the shrines. Here human beings can grasp the actuality of their circumstances through the symbolic imaginary of the shrines. In this action they are also reoriented toward the horizons of their worlds and in effect are repotentiated within them.

If there is a closing summary to be made—a contradiction in a book intended to lead to discussion—it is that sorcery is a practical discourse on the dynamics of human-generated social and political realities. Sorcery is founded in the irruption of human consciousness aware of its human condition: of the fact that it is human action and its constructions and formations on which human existence is contingent and that lie at the root of human anxieties. This is expressed in the great Sinhala story of the origin of sorcery, and this story finds echoes in mythic traditions worldwide. Malinowski made this apparent in his accounts of the myths and events of the Trobriand Kula, with which I began the journey of this book. But it has not been my interest to treat such sorcery myths and stories and their practices as specific instances of a single human universal or as illustrations of some kind of Jungian archetype. Sorcery practices do not constitute a unified phenomenon, and they have great differences. Furthermore, they burst the confines of conventional anthropological categories and definitions. The paradoxes and problematics connected with sorcery infuse most areas of human concern and practice, as I hope this book has shown.

Sorcery must be taken seriously. It must neither be addressed as a mad and mysterious mystical tour leading to wonders only dreamed of nor be tamed to the rigors of a solid anthropological common sense that already knows what things are about. Sorcery is a practice that explores the processes of human action and experience with a sense of the wonder of the human being as a creature that not only constitutes the circumstances of its existence through its practice but also fashions and remakes itself. Sorcery practices facilitate an understanding of how these may be achieved, the nature of their paradox, and the dynamics of the social and political worlds that human beings construct. So to complete Sartre's observation with which I began this chapter (and this book):

. . . and the social world is at first magical.

Notes

Chapter One

1. The term *intentionality* has been developed in a variety of phenomenologies. The concept was originally introduced by Brentano ([1874] 1973) and developed by Husserl (1952) and numerous others following him. The notion as I use it does not imply a subject-object separation or any sense of value motivation (or mental attitudes) which is involved in particular applications of the concept (e.g., the early Husserl, and more recently in the approach of Searle 1983; see Dreyfus 1991). My position does not presuppose a subject and then an object. Husserl did not treat subject and object dichotomously but treated them as emergent along a single continuum; the object in one sense developed by Husserl is a continually synthetic product of the motioning of the ego. One extension from Husserl that I apply is to treat the subject and object as emergent simultaneously in the directed motioning (intentionality) of the ego that becomes at once subject and object to itself and to others.

There are many discussions of the concept of intentionality and some of its difficulties. Among the best, in my opinion, is that in the Introductory Lecture by Peter Koestenbaum in the translation of Husserl's *Paris Lectures* (1975). I will develop the concept of intentionality through the ethnography of this book, especially Chapter 3 on. The material presented in Chapter 5 on the ritual events of the *hatadiya* is particularly appropriate, and the analysis in Chapter 6.

2. It was more a rhetorical ploy used by a person concerned with the foundation of the ethnographic importance of the young discipline of anthropology in the midst of more august and established scholarly areas. The dedication of *Argonauts* to Sir James Frazer gathers considerable significance in this context. His famous work *The Golden Bough,* based on the study of texts, continues to be influential in anthropology and other fields. Malinowski effectively made the point that anthropological ethnography could disclose general understandings that might not be retrievable from the texts and, more important, that the study of peoples and practices at a distance from what was imagined to be Western history had as significant a role in the understanding of human beings in general as

the philosophical and theoretical speculations and theories grounded in Western experience. I make this observation to underscore my own position on the critical place of anthropological ethnography.

3. Medea is "the most renowned enchantress through all antiquity . . . . She commands all nature, puts the dragon of Colchis to sleep, makes warriors invulnerable and old men young. She also has the Evil Eye." *The Oxford Classical Dictionary,* 2nd ed. s.v. "Medea."

4. I follow Victor Turner (1964) in not orienting my discussion in terms of an analytic distinction between sorcery and witchcraft.

5. An important distinction between sorcery and witchcraft is developed by Mary Douglas (1966, 1970, 1973), who defines them as a function of the type of social structures in which they are located. Sorcery is the magical form of human action that arises in strongly hierarchical societies with well-defined social boundaries. The Sinhalese context would provide Douglas with excellent material. Witchcraft is that form of magical action that appears in more open and loose-knit societies where the internal boundaries and divisions are less distinct, as in the societies of Central Africa. Her argument is of great interest and certainly has relevance to the arguments I develop in this book. However, in my opinion, it is overly contrastive (even though she applies a scheme sensitive to mix and variation). It is, of course, an unabashed vision from the outside that is more concerned with sorting diverse ethnographic materials into boxes—an effort to tidy up the anthropological house—than with following the details of sorcery practice to see what it reveals about how human beings construct their realities. Sorcery and witchcraft in Douglas's approach are forms of social response to kinds of social structures that she types. She is relatively uninterested in them as forms of knowledge in practice.

6. This possibility was explored most thoroughly by Victor Turner in his various studies. In his development of the "extended-case method" or "social drama" (see Turner 1957; also, Gluckman 1956; Mitchell 1987; Werbner 1989; Kapferer 1987) he pursued some of the deep underlying paradoxes in human action, both of a specific culturally based psychosocial kind and the kind exhibited in a more general way in other cultural and historical situations.

Chapter Two

1. There are indications that he was an enshrined figure in the eighteenth century. Gombrich and Obeyesekere are generally correct, however, that his current great popularity is a phenomenon of this century.

2. Bandaranaike was (is) worshiped as Horagolle Devata Bandara, after the area in which his family has estates. Bandaranaike was also imagined as a *bodhisattva,* a man who had attained the Buddha ideal but refused the ultimate release from suffering and had returned to help his fellow mortals. Soon after his death a political party called Bosat Bandaranayake Peramuna was formed.

3. These can only be rough estimates, and they are inflated or reduced according to the political and social sympathies of the sources of such information.

I have heard both lower and much higher figures. It is likely that the full scale of the human tragedy may never be known.

4. Tanivale Bandara and Rajjaruvo are not only popular sorcery gods but have been achieving growing significance in the present context of Sinhala nationalism. Tanivale is famous for having been a violent defender of Sri Lanka from invasions from South India. Rajjaruvo Bandara's shrine at Morawaka was declared a site of National Heritage in 1991 by the Sri Lankan government. His shrine is located near where it is said that the Sinhala hero King Valagamba took refuge from the invading Colans. One priest said that he is the incarnation of Phussadeva, the champion of Prince Dutthagamani, the hero of the *Mahavamsa,* the fifth century C.E. chronicle of the history of the Sinhala kings. Dutthagamini is famous for restoring the hegemony of Sinhala kings and Buddhism and ending the period of rule of the Tamil king Elara (see Kapferer 1988a). After Elara's death at Dutthagamani's hands, Dutthagamani was attacked by forces led by Elara's nephew Bhalluka. Dutthagamani was then in the process of renouncing violence. Phussadeva protected Dutthagamani and killed Bhalluka.

5. The most dramatic example is the one for Devol Deviyo (Irugal Bandara) located at Sinigama on the south coast. The main shrine where people come to curse (*des devol*) and destroy their enemies is located on a small rock off shore (according to myth, the boat in which Devol arrived at Sri Lanka from India), to which supplicants must be rowed for a small fee. On shore is another shrine for Devol, for the same being changed into an ordering, protective, and purifying figure, accepted among the Sinhala gods.

6. What is sometimes referred to as the cult of the *bandara*s is described by Holt (1991:242) as fast dying out. However, in my experience it seems to be in resurgence, though in a different form, no doubt, than earlier. Most scholars discuss the *bandara*s with reference to the Kandyan traditions. The most useful and extensive discussion of them occurs in Obeyesekere (1984a:285–96). They are described as being associated with the cult of the twelve gods, *dolaha deviyo,* or regional deities linked to the four guardian gods of Sri Lanka (Natha, Vishnu, Kataragama, Pattini). This is also the case in the southern and west coast traditions, although it is also widely asserted among the *adura*s (exorcists) that there are only seven main *bandara*s. These seven (and the actual lists of the *adura*s name far more), I surmise, have strong association with the administrative coastal subdivisions known as the Seven Korales, regions of considerable contestation (violence and migration) affecting Sinhalese especially in the sixteenth, seventeenth, and eighteenth centuries through the periods of the Portuguese, Dutch, and British invasions. Obeyesekere's (1984a) ethnography gives considerable support to the dual demon-deity character of the *bandara*s.

7. I use this term as Sartre (1948) used it to apply to the astonishing moment when human beings leap toward each other and establish the bonds of their relations. He indicates the mutual possessiveness of such intentionality and the transgression of one's own body and that of the other in the motion of intentionality. This is exemplified by Sartre's own oblique reference to events in Henry James's wonderful story "The Turn of the Screw."

8. Stirrat (1992:172–74), in a study of Sinhala Catholics, stresses the importance of a dualistic power in contrast to hierarchical power in the growth in importance of Kataragama and Huniyam. He asserts that a modern postcolonial political structure based on dyadic ties and personal patronage has come into prominence. I partly agree with his argument, but see current developments as more of an extension from colonialism, which, as is well known, encouraged a system of personal patronage even while it ideologically advocated a rational bureaucratic impersonality. Notions of personal patronage are also intrinsic to precolonial politics. I prefer to understand the growth in prominence of such beings as Suniyam and the spread of sorcery shrines as more closely connected to colonial and postcolonial class forces and the development of powerful political elites. These elites, although in a determining relation to the mass of the population, are socially separated from them by processes related to class forces continuing from the colonial period to the present day. There has been some research on the formation of social and political elites in Sri Lanka (Singer 1964; Roberts 1979; Jiggins 1979), but further work is urgently required. Much of the current turmoil in Sri Lanka, especially the ethnic conflicts, as Roberts (1979) has pointed out, has a close bearing on elite politics. The Suniyam shrines are focal centers of power where persons can come into articulation with forces from which they are ordinarily distanced or separated. Here the poor can come and rail at landlords or politicians who affect and control their fate. The shrines are key points of connection in an otherwise disjunct and divided world of social and political action.

9. Grathoff (1970) initially developed the concept of symbolic type to refer to those figures of human interaction that could not be modified through interaction with them. Clowns are examples of symbolic types who furthermore tend to unify contexts of action through their own internal instability of form. In other words, they can continually maintain their type as clown despite the continually changing and disjunct processes in which they are engaged and which they also effect. I applied this concept to the type *demon* in the Sinhala exorcism context (Kapferer 1983). I argued that in the context of rite, demons' internal instability of form was stabilized by making them appear in frozen and fixed masked guise. So appearing, the demons lost their capacity to determine and unify a ritual context or to maintain a terrible relation to a demonically afflicted victim. Suniyam especially, and I think the *bandara*s generally, are internally unstable forms. This accounts for their great potency and their capacity to bring unity to otherwise disjunct and diversifying processes of personal, social, and political experience.

10. *Cuniyam* is also the word used by the Vaddas, the aboriginal population of Sri Lanka, and it is possible that it could have been borrowed from them. The Vaddas are an out-group in Sri Lanka and have suffered discrimination and prejudice from dominant social groups. It is often said or implied that the sorcery and other practices pertaining to demons came into the Sinhala repertoire from the Vaddas, whose ritual practices and concepts share much with Sinhala practice (see Seligmann and Seligmann 1911). Holt (1991) has recently asserted this. He notes an equivalence between the cult of the *bandara*s and that of demons or

yakku and states that the practices associated with such demons "is fast dying out with the fading of traditional Vadda culture" (Holt 1991:242). The observation that practices relating to demons are dying out is not accurate, although the practices are changing radically. The claim that traditions of many kinds are dying out is common among scholars, and reiterated by Holt (1991:242). But it is also true that many practices are constantly being reinvented, though they are very different from what they might have been formerly. But I want to comment on the Vadda role in producing practices related to demons and also *bandaras*. The Vaddas are as much a fantasy as an actual population radically apart from the Sinhalese (see Brow 1978). They symbolize in ritual the chthonic, the originary, the outside, and the dangerous. The notion that demonic practices originate with them accords with their symbolic function. The same point can be made regarding the notion that dangerous forces have a Tamil origin. The belief that practices connected with dangerous demons have an origin among Vadda populations is extremely problematic. Moreover, such constructions may even contribute to the social and political discrimination which has been the lot of the populations defined as Vaddas. This is also a danger in identifying practices as having a Tamil origin.

My overall point is that Sinhalese sorcery practice and many other rites emerge in a cultural and historical region that has numerous sources. What I have emphasized is the symbolic significance of labeling demonic and sorcery practice as Tamil or Vadda. It draws attention to their force as powers of destructive external energy. To underline this observation, in Sinhala exorcist traditions the Vaddas (or *pulindas*) are said to have originated from Kuveni and Vijaya's two children whom Kuveni took with her into exile when Vijaya established the Sinhala state (see Chapter 3).

11. The main source for these definitions is *Winslow's Tamil and English Dictionary* (New Dehli: Asian Educational Services, reprinted 1982). The *Tamil Lexicon* (University of Madras, Madras, reprinted 1982), gives definitions for the following compounds which are of relevance in the context of later discussion, particularly of the Suniyama ritual (see Chapters 4 and 5): *cuniyam-vai,* "to bury articles of witchcraft with a view to injure a person"; *cuniyam-manei,* "bewitched ground"; *cuniyam-ali-tal,* "to be annihilated, ruined, useless, unprofitable"; *cuniyam etu,* "to remove bewitched articles from the ground for averting evil intended, to ward off the evil caused by witchcraft." I am grateful to Saskia Kersenboom at the University of Amsterdam for drawing my attention to these definitions.

Gombrich and Obeyesekere (1988:115–16) discuss Geiger's (1960) claim that the word *huniyam* is derived from the old Sinhala *hu-niyam,* "thread method." They doubt this etymology, stating that if it were Sinhala, then *huniyam* would be *huniyama.* Their comments relate to the derivation of the name of the demon-deity Suniyam. However, the name Suniyama is applied to the ritual that overcomes sorcery, and much of the action of this rite concentrates on the tying and cutting of threads. Gombrich and Obeyesekere also discuss the possible Tamil derivation of the term *huniyam.* They may be correct in their assertion that Tamils could just as easily have borrowed the term from Sinhalese as vice-versa. I note, however, the heavy symbolic implication in Sinhalese practice that sorcery is an external force, a power of the outside. Potent sorcery practice is often conceived of as having been borrowed. If *huniyam* is indeed a term taken from the Tamil, there is some degree of fit with usage.

12. I am grateful to Saskia Kersenboom for this information.

13. These *three poisons* or *evils* are worth further consideration. They indicate that the disruption of body and being is a function of perceptual invasion. The persons with whom one interacts are not simply objects external to the perceiving subject. What is perceived as external is also internal. The means whereby human beings engage with the world and build their consciousness through their extension into it—through sight, hearing, and speech—are also the means through which the world as outside comes inside. I stress this in relation to *hovaha*, which is often translated "poisonous thought." The term is from the Pali *sota*, "ear." It refers to the unsettling of the mind/body through the perceptual capacity of hearing, whereby, for example, the unpleasant things that others say become consubstantial with a person's embodied consciousness. Antisorcery rites (see Chapters 5 and 7) are concerned to restore the integrity of the body by ridding it of the poisons that have invaded it through the major sites of perception.

14. Scott (1994) refers to the art or work of exorcist-sorcerers as *gurukama*. He also applies the term to the healing work of exorcists (*aduras*). The work of exorcists is more typically referred to as *adurukama*. The expression *gurukama* in my experience does not refer to the work of exorcists. It is a minor secret act of sorcery that can be done by anyone. It requires little knowledge and does not demand the kinds of skills that *aduras* possess. Much of Scott's ethnography seems to have come from persons outside the main exorcist or Berava community. He gives very little indication of what his sources are or of the kinds of rites and their context upon which his ethnography is based.

15. *Anavina* is an almost perfect example of what Austin (1962) classed as *performatives* in linguistics: that is, words or utterances that achieve what they declare as a function of their declaration.

16. Wirz (1954:203–6) gives details of *pilluva* of a particularly gruesome kind which, perhaps for obvious reasons, I did not have described to me. Wirz describes the use of the mummified corpse of a child (who had died at the age of three months and was the eldest son of the eldest son of an eldest son) and its revitalization through magical means. The child is then instructed to visit the place of the victim and to destroy the victim or cause some other kind of misfortune. Other kinds of *pilluva* described by Wirz involve using snakes and chickens to attack victims. *Pilluva* is broadly the capacity of the consciousness of the sorcerer to enter the body of another being so that this being becomes the instrument of destructive action. *Pilluva* is the extreme of what I generally describe sorcery as being, the capacity of individual human consciousness to enter into the bodies of others and control their action. The action of the first sorcerer, Vasavarti Maraya, who attacked the queen of Mahasammata, the first world ruler, carries the

sense of *pilluva*. He is transformed into a viper and intrudes into the womb of his victim.

17. Such poisonous creepers are likened to poisonous snakes.

18. This sorcery action is an inversion of the common forms of vow making at shrines to the gods, known generally as *rupeta rupe* (life to life, form to form), whereby supplicants in effect vow to release a life in return for a blessing or help.

19. One sorcerer described a process whereby the heads of a great variety of snakes are boiled in a pot, a mere drop of the resultant brew being enough to cause death. This method is an inversion of the process of making the protective oil paste *nanu* that is used in antisorcery rites and other ritual occasions to cleanse and protect from the dangers of sorcery.

20. The term *hira bandana* is dense with ambiguity. A fundamental sense is that of close, tight, and imprisoning control. The meaning of *marriage* is more secondary and does have a sense of the controlling and restricting aspect of the marital tie. Thus, to be tied to the sorcerer is to be determined, imprisoned, or restricted by the sorcerer's control. There are more explicitly sexual sorcery acts. Thus, one known as the *kalava bandana* is intended to paralyze its victims in the midst of sexual intercourse.

21. The term *kapuma* roughly translates as "cutting"; it is from the Sinhala *kap*, "cut," or *kapanava*, "to cut."

22. *Santi* (Skt.) indicates the positive character of the Suniyama as an antisorcery rite. Eliade notes that it "derives from the root sam, which originally included the meaning of "extinguishing" fire, anger, fever—in the last analysis the heat provoked by demonic powers" (1978:233 n. 26). This description accords very well with the thematic dynamic of the Suniyama rite (see Chapter 5).

23. *Vasa* and *vaha* mean "poison." *Vas* is also used often in the same way, but it also has the sense of destructive force that issues from, for example, protective objects guarding particular domains or spaces.

24. A derogatory term for Portuguese and also the word for gonorrhea.

25. Suniyam is described as a being who knows eighteen languages and has power in eighteen countries. These potencies underline Suniyam as a totalizing force in the worlds of human existence. Lillian, by asserting that she had knowledge of eighteen languages, was declaring that she was the embodiment of the destructive and restorative totalizing forces that Suniyam and also Kali express.

26. Although Suniyam certainly manifests such aspects, as Obeyesekere (1981) explains.

27. The terms *mula*, "original" or "root," and *mulu*, "entirety" or "all-encompassing totality," are used interchangeably and with overlapping sense, although they have distinct etymologies.

28. Deleuze ([1968] 1994:91–92) discusses Marx's notion of absurd or comic repetition as a feature of inauthenticity and an incapacity to metamorphose into something new. In a sense, for Marx, repetition is always absurd because it is out of the historical context of its original appearance. In terms of his more general anti-Hegelian stance, repetition is absurd because an idea formed in the dy-

namic of history is placed in the position of making history rather than being made by it. Deleuze develops the notion of the necessary difference of repetition and indicates that its character or force can be seen in its very originality and not in its defects as compared with its earlier appearance. In other words, Louis Napoleon is absurd by the fact of his historically produced originality.

29. Suniyam is regarded widely among Sinhalese as an extremely hot and dangerous being. People repeatedly told me that it is very dangerous to give him a place or a site to reside in, as in a shrine. If a small shrine is erected to him at one's house, I was told, then it should be well away from the house. It is advisable not to erect a shrine to him at all. To so locate Suniyam is to risk his malign attention, which is all the more risky because he is in effect the force of human action and is always open to being malevolently operated by human beings. I consider that the fact that he condenses extremely volatile human energies is what distinguishes Suniyam from the other deities and distinguishes his shrines. The Suniyam shrines are extremely hot and dangerous places. This is a factor in their marginalization in urban space and is a further aspect of the difference in repetition of the shrines. I also think that this marks out Suniyam as very different from other deities; he is not, as Obeyesekere argues, oriented along the same line of development.

30. Obeyesekere (1984:286–93) has diverse and extensive information about these beings. He makes a number of interesting speculations about their origin and how they fit into patterns of religious change. Obeyesekere (1984: 210–22) discusses the *tunbage* and presents extensive texts relating in particular to Dadimunda. He suggests that Dadimunda rose out of the lowly status of Devata Bandara, one of the *bandara*s. He also has an explanation for why Vahala, the being who becomes entranced, later became identified with Dadimunda. Generally, Obeyesekere's approach is to see the varying forms of particular demon-deities as developing at different times and in a linear historical progression. His argument is important. My own information suggests that the various forms these days are taken as different manifestations of one being and describe an oscillation between demonic and divine attributes.

Chapter Three

1. The spots of the leopard are indicative of the boils that covered King Panduvas's body as a result of Kuveni's curse. The leopard skin is worn by *rsi*s and yogins and indicates the destructive-restorative aspect of the pot and of the ritualists who manipulate it.

2. The canonical versions of these stories have received an in-depth analysis by Tambiah (1976), who relates them to ideologies of Buddhist kingship. He discusses the Buddhist inversions of similar Hindu themes, for example, in Manu. In a later book (Tambiah 1992), he discusses an interpretation of the Mahasammata story and the Oddisa Kumara (Oddi Raja) myth as I first presented them in a preliminary analysis of the Suniyama rite. His criticisms are instructive, although I have some disagreement with them. Our disagreement centered around

the nature of hierarchical transformations in the myths and about whether they reflected the dynamics of power in ancient and medieval states. Generally, I think, we agree that as far as the actual political situations were concerned, the stories constitute ideological discourses and do not represent actual situations. I am interested in the dynamics of power that the myths express but as virtuality (see Deleuze [1968] 1994; Bogue 1989: 61–67) rather than actuality (see also Chapter 8). However, my argument in this chapter is really a departure from earlier themes that I discussed involving transformational processes in hierarchical systems. The analysis is more horizontal than vertical and explores processes that cannot be encompassed within coherent ordered wholes. This is clearly an aspect of the problematics of sorcery that I had not analyzed sufficiently in my earlier discussions (Kapferer 1983, 1988a).

3. This inner light may be indicative of their procreative potential, the "inner light" (*antah-jyoti*) or procreative potential of the Brahman of the Vedas (see Eliade 1978: 243).

4. I have been made intensely aware of this point through my reading of Jadran Mimica's (1988) excellent phenomenological study of number among the Iqwaye of the New Guinea Highlands. Mimica has also enlivened me to aspects of these stories through general discussion that I have had with him.

5. It is certainly possible to expand on the potential value of Mahasammata's restraint in the context of the clearly tantric aspects of the myth, especially in the context of the ritual practice of the Suniyama. The restraint of Mahasammata (and also of the Buddha in the contest with Oddi Raja) is an index of the peak of potency, of power. The love play of Mahasammata and Manikpala without final orgasmic completion (release) attendant on actual penetration is the building of potency to its extreme which is lost in orgasmic release. The metaphors of sexuality and the comments of exorcists to the effect that Mahasammata and Manikpala do not engage in acts of sexual penetration have relevance to concepts of the bodhisattva and of regenerating return that are a clear feature of the Suniyama rite.

6. This name is often interpreted as a corruption of Orissa. This indicates a North Indian origin. However, Wirz suggests a Malabar derivation: "the art of black magic is called '*odi*,' the medicine man '*odiyan*.'" (1954: 33 n. 1). This understanding fits the character of Oddisa, who is regarded by exorcists as a yogin who possesses magical powers and who, in his origin myth, collects the medicines of destruction and of restoration. Other aspects of the myth indicate a South Indian origin. Thus the Vadiga Tamils feature frequently in the myth complexes of late medieval times (see Tambiah 1992: 155). The last kings of Kandy are described as *vadiga*s and were from the South Indian Nayakkar dynasty.

7. In some exorcist traditions, Yawudagiri is regarded as the chief of the seven *giri*s (or *kiri amma,* "milk mothers"). It is said by some *adura*s that she is the daughter of Manikpala and the person for whom the original rite of menstruation was performed.

8. These are sometimes named as the wives of Suniyam.

9. Mangara is important in many ritual traditions in Sri Lanka. In the south

he is regarded as the head of the *gara* demons and mediates between gods and demons (Kapferer 1983).

10. Variants on the story I have repeated here state that Yawudagiri was menstruating (*kilimale*) at the time of her demonic conception, which occurred as she bent down to smell the flower. The energy of sorcery, attracted to her polluting condition, entered through her nostril.

11. Oddisa is often said by *adura*s to be the ritualist who succeeds where others fail. See Chapter 5.

12. The size of Oddisa's mouth may connote that he is a sacrificer who simultaneously consumes and creates. Shulman (1978:102) refers to the Brahmana texts in which demons are said to sacrifice into their own mouths.

13. The figure of the goat in the Oddisa myths of Sri Lanka is associated explicitly by exorcists with insatiable sexuality, a sense which has resonance with similar meaning in other regions of the world.

14. Anthropologists (Southwold 1983; Stirrat 1992; Scott 1994) working on Sinhala materials have argued for distinctions between Buddhist and Christian notions of evil. Other scholars (Ling 1962; Boyd 1973) have noted connections. Doubtless there are numerous differences. These are likely to be especially significant when certain philosophical and social science orientations from the Judeo-Christian tradition are adopted in relation to Sinhala Buddhist orientations to the demonic or evil. For example, Hobbesian or Hegelian perspectives, which are certainly not irrelevant to the theme I have discussed, might encounter difficulties if their Christian foundations went unmarked. Thus, in the myths I have discussed, the ordering power of society, Mahasammata, or the state is integral to society and not necessarily an alien or imposed force, as in a Hobbesian conception (although it could be seen this way if the Vijaya myths, for instance, were made the object of analysis). Mahasammata's ideal state-society might seem to have some affinity with Hegel's notion of the ultimate achievement of an ideal unity or final synthesis. But Mahasammata's ideal state is not the final resolution of the dynamic of the contradictions of existence; this is indicated by Mahasammata's powerlessness before Vasavarti's attack. And there is in the myths no final resolution of the tension between individuality and society, although this often seems to be assumed in relatively romantic communitarian (a kind of heaven on earth) Western social science and political philosophies.

However, to return to anthropological contrasts between Buddhism and Christianity, my view is that they are often not of much value. They present a much too coherent perspective, and anthropologists that want to convey a sensitive understanding of Buddhist practice often radically distort and oversimplify their own Judeo-Christian traditions. The truth is that both Buddhism and Christianity are highly diverse and in practice as well as history have frequently overlapped. In Sri Lanka, Christianity, especially Roman Catholicism, has influenced Sinhala Buddhist practice and vice versa. It seems to me that forms of radical evil—by which I mean beings of totalizing destruction that threaten the ground of existence—are apparent across relatively distinct cosmological conceptions and systems. For example, Mara and Satan share characteristics despite distinctions in their cosmologies. Representations of Satan often depict him as a fragmented unity, a feature of other symbols of destruction: for example, dragons as they are represented in European, Chinese, and Sinhala traditions. Clay images of Suniyam at exorcisms iconographically represent him as death and as the antithesis of fertility and bounteousness. As a fusion of diverse forms, he has the forehead of a bull, the face of a monkey or pig, the ears of a pig, and the feet of a goat.

Chapter Four

1. The potlatch is a ceremonial system of lavish giving and destruction among the peoples of the Northwest Coast of North America. It is of classic importance in anthropological theorizing on the nature of the gift. The potlatch is central in Mauss's discussion of *The Gift* ([1950] 1990). See also Codere 1972; Goldman 1975.

2. Members of these two caste communities often live in adjacent neighborhoods and also intermarry. This indicates not only an equivalence in their caste ranking on the island but also a close association and often cooperation in ritual matters.

3. Devol Deviyo is also understood by *adura*s as being the first exorcist. Certainly his image at his major shrine at Sinigama on the southwestern coast presents him in an exorcist's garb and carrying the cock, the principal sacrificial offering at most demon exorcisms.

4. In the community deity rites, members of the community who are witness to the rite enter into the ritual building that is the key focus of the rites. The building, like the *atamagala* in the Suniyama, becomes a temple alive with the presence of divine cosmic ordering forces and, on some ritual occasions, becomes a devotional shrine that restores those who enter it.

5. This is not to say that it is performed as commonly as other exorcisms. In 1984, in the south of the island where I lived for a year, I was able to see on average one or two Suniyamas a month.

6. Holt (1991: 53–71) has a very useful discussion of the bodhisattva concept in Sri Lanka and its relation to notions of kingship.

7. *Gurunanse* is also the respectful term of address by which master exorcists should be greeted. In the course of performances, the participating exorcists address each other using this term.

8. In exorcist myths, the *vas danda* is said to have been made from the windpipe of the buffalo demon. It is the pipe of the exorcist's authority whereby he controls and summons demons. I have translated the Sinhala as "poison (*vas*) pipe," because this is what the exorcists say it means. The pipe is made from bamboo and it probably derives from the Sanskrit *vamsa*, "bamboo."

9. Although a *maduva* should be built, at least in the ritual tradition on which this description is based, it is not always built. Occasionally a rite is performed on the front verandah of the victim's house or else indoors.

10. There is some similarity between the *atamagala* and a structure known as the *kapala kuduva*, which is erected on the axis of a rice pounder in front of

the demon palace in the other major demon exorcisms (see Kapferer 1983). The *kapala kuduva* is conceived of as a three-tiered structure of the world order and is spun by masked representations of the demons as they enter the performance arena in the closing comic dramas of the exorcisms concerned. The victim does not enter the *kapala kuduva*, however. The *atamagala* might be seen as a transform of the *kapala kuduva*.

11. *Hangala* means "double" or "twin" and usually refers to the cloth that *kapurala*s and *adura*s are robed in during their ceremonies. In this context, *adura*s said that it carried the sense of generative potency.

12. I am unclear on the meaning of *kaksaputa*. Exorcists explain that it refers to a previous birth of the Buddha, when he was born as a merchant. It was at the time of this birth that Buddha had his first confrontation with Devadatta. Another sense is of the bag that Brahmin priests carry over their shoulder. These senses correspond with the contextual meaning, for the patient seated on the mat is in the condition of full consciousness and knowledge.

13. The positioning of Rahu (Dragon's Head) and Ketu (Dragon's Tail) in the *Suniyam purale* and also in the *atamagala* is important. Theoretically, Rahu is located in the central section of the Suniyam *purale* and Ketu in the center section of the *atamagala*. Rahu is conceived by many exorcists as the primordial Suniyam, and this is confirmed in some versions of the *loka uppatiya*. In Hindu mythology (see Dowson 1968: 252–53) Rahu is the great maker of mischief and a figure of terrible vengeance. In disguise he drinks the god's liquid of immortality. He is caught by the Sun and the Moon, and Visnu punishes him by severing his arms and head. Rahu wreaks his vengeance by swallowing the Sun and the Moon. Ketu, the Dragon's Tail, is what Rahu's head was severed from. Ketu is Rahu in the descendant; he is associated with brightness and clearness and, by some exorcists, with Maha Brahma. Exorcists are sometimes quite uncertain about where Rahu and Ketu should be located. Some have positioned Rahu in the central place of the *atamagala*. There is of course an ambiguity. Ketu is made by the severing of Rahu, which is consistent with the acts of cutting throughout the Suniyama rite. The motion of the patient in the *hatadiya* is theoretically a move from Rahu toward Ketu.

14. There is some variation about what events comprise the sixteen *tinduva*s, the number mentioned often exceeds the ideal.

Chapter Five

1. The Duravas have toddy tapping as their traditional caste occupation. Along with other major caste communities along the coast, the Karavas and Salagama, members of the Durava caste, have been important in the development of capitalist and petty capitalist enterprises. They have also been important in nationalist politics and in the promotion of Sinhala cultural traditions. Duravas along with Karavas and Salagamas were part of a long series of migrations from the Kerala region of South India from at least the thirteenth century and possibly

earlier. Many of the ritual traditions of Sri Lanka's coast have their roots deep in South Indian traditions.

2. In Sinhala traditions along the west and south coasts, leprosy *(kusta)* is associated with kingship, and a stone statue outside Weligama, called Kustaraja-gala (the "leprosy king stone"), is said by exorcists to have had the power to heal leprosy or skin diseases generally. There is a noteworthy similarity with the practice in medieval Europe of touching royal statues and royal persons in an effort to cure the skin disease scrofula (see Bloch 1973). Holt (1991:232 n. 2) discusses this statue (which is still an object of worship) in the context of bodhisattva traditions in Sri Lanka.

3. I am unclear as to who the Bagavati demonesses are. They could be the Gara/Giri demons who dwell at waterfalls.

4. There is also a sense that the *kadaturava* deflects the demons' attention from the patient. *Kada* has the meaning in Tamil of "step aside" or "escape" (see Holt 1991:242 n. 4).

5. The myth of Kola Sanniya and the pestilence of Visalamahanuvara is extremely well known among Sinhalese. The best description of this myth is in Obeyesekere 1969. See also Kapferer 1983: 123. There are several myths that relate the birth of Kola Sanniya. The main one concerns his vengeance against the people of Visalamahanuvara. The story expresses a theme common in myths, including the one of the birth of Oddisa (see Chapter 3). The demon is born in the context of the wrongful accusation and punishment of the mother. In Kola Sanniya's case, he is born in the act of the execution of his mother, Kola Sanniya falls from the rent womb of his mother, who is cut in half. Another story of Kola Sanniya's origin links this demon with Suniyam. In my interpretation, Kola Sanniya is the force that causes diseases and destroys the orders of human being, their cities, their communities, and their households. Kola Sanniya as the destructive force of the destruction of the ordered totalities of human beings or of their societies is indicated in his symbolic number eighteen. This number stands for the divisions of human ordering. Suniyam, again in my understanding, is the destructive force of human consciousness and of consciousness destroyed. This is the force of sorcery. Human consciousness is central to the formation of the orders of human societies. This understanding, I think, is implicit in the close connection in the myths between Kola Sanniya and Suniyam. Maha Kola Sanniya and Suniyama are both described as being born from the nostrils of Maha Kala Naga, the great serpent at the beginning of time.

6. The *nuga* (banyan tree) is connected with the planet Saturn (Senasuru). This planet is the most inauspicious one, and Kuveni's connection with Saturn underlines her danger and evil.

7. Barnett (1916: 106) has other versions. The one I have heard at other exorcisms involves Mahi Kantava, the goddess of the earth, who is ordered by Sakra to collect the water for Oddisa.

8. In other performances of the Suniyama, the oil is explicitly referred to as an antidote to the venom of sorcery contained in the fangs of cobras.

9. One myth sometimes sung at a Suniyama tells how Sakra on hearing of

Manikpala's affliction, went to Mount Andungiri to ask Pattini for the cloth that Oddisa needed for the rite. Pattini demanded virgin *(kanya)* threads, so she grew, plucked, and wove the cloth herself. Versions of this myth are also sung during the *gammaduva* ceremonies for Pattini and in the Rata Yakuma exorcism to rid women and their children of the lustful blight of Kalu Kumara (see Obeyesekere 1984a; Kapferer 1983).

10. Obeyesekere (1984a:539) considers the possibility that Catholicism influenced the use of the veil by low-country Buddhists in Sri Lanka. However, he believes Pattini's veil as the symbol of the ideal wife—a far longer tradition in Sri Lanka and South India—is the greater influence. He dismisses the idea that Sinhala women may have borrowed the custom of the veil from Muslim women in Kerala, who wear a similar headdress. Although Obeyesekere is probably right, it is possible that all these different customary and historically founded uses of the veil have interacted and continue to do so, contributing to its multivalent and often contradictory properties, at least in the Suniyama, and thus its symbolic potency.

11. This goddess has different forms (usually seven, Sat Pattini), including her hot and destructive manifestations. At one Buddhist temple in Weligama, on the south coast of Sri Lanka, there are two images of Pattini (and also of Suniyam), one for cursing (her hot form) and the other for blessing (*santi*) or beneficial or protective favors. The goddess combines dangerous, harmful, and inauspicious aspects with auspicious, beneficial, and healing properties. These are inextricably bound together in Pattini's completed and total form and potent being.

12. I was eager to interpret these protuberances as the tails of cocks, but the *adura* I questioned refused to allow such an understanding. I was attracted to the view because Oddisa is a sacrificer, and the cock is the sacrificial animal in Sinhalese exorcism. Occasionally the exorcists wear a *kangul topiya* that has seven locks (cocks' combs? snakes?). This, I am told, is appropriate not to Oddisa but to Devol Deviyo, a magician like Oddisa and with him one of the *tunbage bandara*s. Besides these hats, the dancers also wear a long white sarong cloth (*saluva*) and a length of white cloth (*piruvata*) wound tightly seven times around the midriff.

13. I cannot overstress this point. The most common sorcery-cutting action (*katpuma*) centers around a *preta tattuva*.

14. In many of the ritual texts, Natha is the first to be invoked (Professor Punchi Banda of Peradeniya University, personal communication, 1995). This would therefore seem to be a reorientation in the tradition. In my analysis, I have indicated that his location in the invocation appears to be in accordance with the direction of the process of the rite as a whole.

15. Mihikata is said in some exorcist traditions to have been the person who made the original atamagala yantra. The pots at the entrances to the *atamagala* are also for Mihikata.

16. Boksal is today sometimes identified with Saman, the guardian god (see Obeyesekere 1984a:187). He does have other associations, for example, with the demon Vata Kumara (Barnett 1916:12), a form of Kalu Kumara. Myths of Vata

Kumara tell that his father was a monk in the time of Emperor Asoka, who left the monkhood to become a king known as Boksal (see Kapferer 1983:170). Vata Kumara and Boksal are important figures in the Rata Yakkuma, a rite of healing exclusively for women and their children. The Rata Yakkuma addresses the (re)-generative centrality of women which, of course, is a vital metaphor of the Suniyama. The inclusion of Boksal as a figure to be invoked at the *atamagala* seems to me entirely appropriate. Vibisana is a demonic god, and his main temple is just to the north of Colombo at Kelaniya. He is presented as a brother of Ravana, the demon king of the *Ramayana* (see Obeyesekere 1984a:67). Exorcists say that he is also closely linked to Suniyam, and that he is one of the forms that Suniyam takes.

17. In the main ceremonies to overcome demon attack (*yakkuma, yaktovil*) there are episodes where the *adura* becomes totally inhabited by demonic potency and is entranced. These episodes are distinguished from others where exorcists adopt demon guise—usually in the concluding events of ritual comedy—during which they superficially represent the demonic rather than powerfully live its force (see Kapferer 1993:270–80). I should note that in my earlier ethnography (Kapferer 1983) of demon rites I perhaps did not stress enough the power of the demonic possession but overstressed its constructed and representational aspects.

18. The story of Vessantara relates how King Sanjaya of the Sivis, the father of Vessantara, had a dream foretelling the reunion of Vessantara's family. Soon afterward, Jujaka comes before King Sanjay with Vessantara's children, whom he has enslaved. Sanjaya causes the children to be released by giving Jujaka their ransom in slaves and other possessions. Further acts of reinstating Vessantara and restoring the unity of his family follow. Jujaka, now wealthy because of his exchange of the children, overeats and chokes to death (see Gombrich and Cone 1977:79–86).

19. On the occasion of this performance, a dancer went before the patient and very briefly danced a step and rhythm for Vishnu (Vishnu *saudan*). A dance for the god of the Sun (or Mahasammata?), *suriya saudan,* was performed for the victim's eldest son. Together the dancers performed short dances to a drumroll (*surala*) for the nine planets (*navagraha*) and then went through the audience choosing likely candidates for giving a handsome fee.

20. This is the name of a serpent and could be the name of the cobra that has a gem at its throat. It is possible that the reference could also be to Siva, who wears a cobra as a garland.

21. The snake is not drawn at every Suniyama performance. It should be drawn, I am told, when the patient is in a particularly dangerous astrological period, usually involving Rahu (dragon's head) or Senasuru (Saturn) or their combination. I stress, however, that the seven lotus steps of the *hatadiya* are *always* displayed in the shape of the curved body of the snake.

22. He is described as the uncle or father-in-law of Maha Kala Naga (see Barnett 1916:65). The being of destruction is thus kin to the being of protection, which has some parallel with the popular understanding that Devadatta, a cousin of the Buddha, is Vasavarti Maraya in a former birth, as Mahasammata is a for-

mer birth of Gautama Buddha. In the tradition referred to by Barnett (1916:65), Muchalinda is the cobra that swallowed Sakra's paintbrush. In the tradition of the Suniyama performance described here, it is Maha Kala Naga who swallows the brush.

23. De Silva (1981:51) gives a summary of tantric influence in Sri Lanka. He mentions the introduction of tantric traditions in the ninth century, the Nilapatadarsana and Vajravada schools. Holt (1991:42–45) has an excellent discussion of tantric influences relevant to Sri Lanka. He briefly discusses the Hindu Samkhya school of thought, which had important influence on Hindus and Buddhists. Aspects of the Samkhya tradition are apparent in the performance of the Suniyama and particularly in understanding the positioning of patients in the space of Manikpala and the progression into the *atamagala*.

24. Goudriaan (1985) presents the text of a South Indian Saivite tantric text used in sorcery. It has some parallels with the practice that I describe for the *hatadiya*. This is significant given the association of Suniyam with Siva (Isvara). I speculate that the reversal in the *hatadiya* of the head from its usual positioning in tantra could be an aspect of the anti-Saivite stance of Sinhala Buddhist ritual practice.

25. At other demon exorcisms (in a rite known as the Iramudun Samayama, the gathering time of the midday demon; see Kapferer 1983), the death of the demon Riri Yaka is enacted by an exorcist who climbs a ladder of seven steps to a platform (a funeral pyre?), where he collapses and dies (the demonic essence that has come to inhabit or possess the exorcist leaves). This rite might be seen as expressing the antithesis of the projection of the patient in the *hatadiya,* who proceeds in the direction of life and to a point at the edge of ultimate release from suffering and existence. The implication of Riri Yaka's death in the Iramudun rite is that he is condemned to the agonies and suffering of continuing existence; he is subjected to the full force of the cosmic order but outside the space of the orderings of the human world.

26. After drawing each line, the *adura* places a strip of coconut palm leaf at the spot, miming the placing of a poisonous creeper or root.

27. There is some room for comparison of the process that is set in motion in the *hatadiya* with what is implicit in the myth of Devol Deviyo's encounter with the goddess Pattini; the powers of both are invoked in the Suniyama. The story surrounding the arrival of Devol Deviyo from India into Sri Lanka is popularly known. Obeyesekere (1984a:144, 150–151) describes the main story, in which Pattini throws up seven barriers of fire (in my interpretation, seven destructive aspects of herself as the Seven (Hat) Pattini) to prevent Devol's entry. By means of his own power he is able to cross the seven barriers and, as Obeyesekere argues, is incorporated into the Sinhala pantheon. The crossing of the fires can be understood as similar to my interpretation of the lines of the sorcerer in the Suniyama. That, is the crossing of the barriers is one of (re)incorporation and also of the conversion and subjugation of destructive energy into (re)generative energy. More generally, the victim of sorcery, who is in a hot ensorcelled condi-

tion, moves from a situation metaphorically external to the social world and barred from participating in it to a position internal and central to it. Devol Deviyo's progress can be seen as parallel to the transitional process of the victim in the Suniyama rite.

28. The main vowels of the Sinhala alphabet are also routinely placed at each of the steps.

29. The poem recorded by Nevill which is the closest to the one I document here (which Nevill claimed then was "two or three centuries old") has the paintbrush burning the Naga king's throat. It sprouted from the king's funeral pyre, and thus it is called *dalumura*, "leaf watch." Nevill records further that the branches of the betel grew from different parts of the Naga king's body, and that the one that grew from his hood is called *nagavalli*, "serpent creeper." This is the name exorcists use to refer to the betel placed in the offering lotuses of the *hatadiya*. According to Nevill (1955: 166), this is the name of the betel leaf at the time of the Buddha Kasyapa. Nevill lists a number of beings to whom *dalumura* was ritually offered. Many of these could be regarded as demonic deities of the *bandara* category (see Barnett 1916: 10).

30. The directions and fruits growing from each branch were: (1) east, the leech lime (*kudalu dehi*); (2) southeast, the citron (*nasnaran*); (3) south, the mandarin orange (*jamanaran*); (4) southwest, the orange (*dodan*); (5) west, grapefruit (*mahanaran*); (6) northwest, the orange (*naran*); (7) north, the demon orange (*yakinaran*); (8) northeast, the small green lime used in the cutting of sorcery (*hin dehi*).

31. Nevill records the details of two stories concerning the origin of limes (see also Barnett 1916:51–52). The first is very brief, and there are similar references in Suniyama performances I have attended. According to Nevill's account, eight limes were found beneath seven caskets in the Naga world. Viskam and Valaha journeyed to the Naga world and collected seven of these limes, from which the lime trees on earth were propagated (1955: 343). Nevill presents in greater detail a second myth that has similar themes: A fight broke out between Rahu and the Nagas during which Rahu was bitten. He passed the poison to the Sun and the Moon, and this resulted in a darkening of the world. The *rsis* decided that the spell causing the darkness could be broken by cutting limes. Sakra took a blue gem and wiped his perspiration on it. The gem fell into the Naga world and hit the Naga king on the head. He promptly swallowed it. "Then out of his poison fangs sprang the pulp cells of the lime fruit, its seeds from his teeth, its acidity from his saliva, the fragrance of the fruit from Sakra's sweat, the fruit from Naga's hood." Ananda went to fetch it, but the Naga king gave it up reluctantly, saying that it was *indul* (already used or eaten). The *rsis* threw it into the sea, and it passed through the various oceans (the Blood Sea, the Milk Sea, etc.) and returned to the *rsis*, where the seed of the lime grew into a tree sprouting in four directions. Nine fruits were collected from one branch (the ascending branch), and the spell on the Sun and the Moon was removed (1954, 1: 306). Nevill states that the manuscript of this story was 150 years old at the time he collected it.

32. Exorcists disagree about this. Wirz (1954:20–21) indicates that according to his informants, the one direction from which Mara does not come is the southeast.

33. He sings a few verses of a song, the origin of the *gire* (*gire upata*), which tells that Sakra ordered Visvakarma to forge the cutter. Another verse tells that Oddisa used the cutter as his weapon in the war against the Asuras. My information concerning the cosmic powers located at various parts of the *gire* is the same as recorded by Nevill (1954, 1:97). His account of the making of the *gire* tells how Visvakarma fashioned it from iron mined from Mount Meru. Its left rivet is the Moon, the right rivet the Sun, the Four Guardian Gods are at the handles, and Rahu is the blade.

34. *Aduras* perform a similar rite at the time of childbirth.

35. *Aduras* say that the *aravali kapima* attacks the generative center of the sorcerer and indicate the sexual symbolism of the three limes on a single stem. I believe this makes reference to Siva the brahmanicide, Siva the skull bearer (*kapalika*). In the exorcism traditions I have studied, Riri is a form of Isvara (Siva). Reference to Siva the brahmanicide is made in other exorcisms. In the Suniyama, sorcerers are conceived of as Brahmins, like the healing *rsis* and Oddisa. The invocation of Siva's powers as the brahmanicide appears relevant to this context.

36. Gombrich (1971: 217–26) has an excellent discussion of the notion of *prartana* as a wishing or conscious orientation to the Buddhist release from suffering, or nirvana. He notes that it is against the Buddha's injunction to actively seek or desire nirvana. However, Gombrich says the term expresses an ultimate objective that is not immediately attainable. He notes that involvement of *prartana* to achieve everyday practical ends is part of a general belief in the magical efficacy of the power of religious utterances.

37. There is some agreement between the practice of the *hatadiya* and more abstract Buddhist doctrinal discussion. The power of the *hatadiya* is in the fact that it is volitional action, which as Rahula explains, involves "attention (*manasikara*), will (*chanda*), determination (*adimokka*), confidence (*sadda*), concentration (*samadi*)" (1967:22–23). Such volitional action has karmic effects, that is, it has consequence for one's life's process in this life and in future births.

38. In Suniyama performances the offering packets (*gotu*) generally contain only rice. However, *aduras* in the Weligam *korale* tradition, and in others, specify that different foods should be offered by the patient at each step. Thus, at step 1, milk rice (*kiri bat*) and the seeds of five different cereals; at step 2, boiled rice colored with turmeric (*ranvan bat*); step 3, flower petals for the nine planets; step 4, roasted (*pulutu*) paddy grains (*vi*) and/or five different seed grains; step 5, curd (symbolic of the five flavors of the cow (*pasgorasa*); step 6. treacle (*pani*) from the *kitul* palm; step 7, a mixture of all the preceding offerings. Some *aduras* also add that five different kinds of fruit and five different sweetmeats should be included in the offerings given by the patient. These nutrients and the logic of five relate, of course, to the *mahabutas*, the elements of matter and their derivatives. The utterances surrounding these food offerings indicate their relation to different forces in the cosmic totality, the Buddha, the planets, the Guardian Gods, and

demons. Suniyam in his various aspects is implicated in the offerings at each step. The offerings might be interpreted as indicating his dual aspect and the fact that he embodies the countervailing forces of human existence. *Aduras* say that Suniyam receives both the highest and the lowest categories of food offerings. Thus, he takes the most pure (*pirisindu*) e.g., milk rice, the boiled rice with turmeric, and impure (*apirisindu*) offerings, e.g., fried (*pulutu*) grains and roasted meats of the land and sea (*godadiyamas*). The former are for Suniyam as a protective god and the latter are for Suniyam as an all-consuming demon.

39. This yantra is called the Buvanadipati yantra. This yantra is drawn directly on the ground and is to be distinguished from the Kaksaputa yantra, which is drawn on the mat above it.

40. The ash of brick (*gadol*), lime (*hunu*), crystal (*tirivana*), and cow dung (*goma*). Exorcists say that the ash is bodily essence (*datu*), and I speculate that these four kinds of ash symbolize fundamental body essences. They may also be protective barriers: the moats that Mahasammata built around his cosmic city (see Chapter 3).

41. In the texts, the person involved is the king of Banaras.

42. *Astaka* is a group of eight verses also sung at other auspicious occasions. They are sung as praises for such gods as Vishnu and before the tooth relic (*dalada astaka*).

43. Suniyam/Oddisa is widely understood in the Weligam *korale* traditions to have four wives. At his right are Takari and Makari, and at his left are Kala Raksi and Yama Duti. There is, of course, variation. In the Matara area, Gini Kandi and Mini Kandi are cited rather than Takari and Makari.

44. The character of this event varies between performances. In those I have witnessed, usually where the victim is seriously ill and the household has a history of persistent sorcery attack, a *nicakula tinduva* (outcaste destruction or finishing) may be performed. This rite, as its name might suggest, is seen by exorcists as expressing the particularly loathsome and disgusting nature of sorcery. Non-Berava *aduras* consider it completely beyond any contemplation of performance and state that the Berava exorcists (in the past, virtually social outcastes) are the ritualists who might perform such a rite. A yantra is drawn on the ground in ash, with Sinhala vowels placed at each of the corners. In the center is placed a bull's head, on which are placed three betel leaves and three pinches of salt. A small fire is lit on the skull and a large cooking pot placed on it, in which a variety of grains are roasted. The patient cuts the skull with a machete to the accompaniment of a mantra uttered by the *adura*. Nicakula yantra: In my view, this yantra demonstrates a close association between the demon Suniyam and the demonic aspect of Siva (Isvara).

45. A term that in everyday usage has clear overtones of friendliness and hostility. A person may shout the word at a stranger to catch his attention so as to enter into a relationship with him. In the rite, Oddisa is also addressed as *massina* (cousin), a more respectful form of *machang*, and occasionally with the less hostile term *yaluva* (friend).

46. On some ritual occasions, including Suniyamas and other exorcisms, and

at annual events of worship at Buddhist temples, pots of milk are boiled over (*kiri itiravima*), indicating regeneration. This action might be regarded as a descriptive metaphor for the dynamic of comedy in exorcism and other rites. It is a boiling over of life.

47. Kandiah discusses the term *kaduva,* meaning the negative aspects of the use of the English language. The *kaduva* symbolizes English as indicative of "defeat, subjugation, humiliation and oppression" (1984: 139). Kandiah notes that the use of the term in these senses did not become widespread until after Independence in 1947. The context of nationalism and democratization made Sinhala-speaking peasantry and especially the working classes aware of the role of the English language in the production of inequality and its continuing role, through the educational system, in reproducing an elite and a controlling bourgeoisie who command through their proficiency in English. Kandiah argues that *kaduva* condenses the attitude of the underdog and the bitterness of those who understand that "the sword (of power) is forever destined to remain in someone else's hands" (Kandiah 1984: 139).

48. Black umbrellas are common accoutrements of the ubiquitous bourgeoisie. I note a possible significance in their contrast with more traditional umbrellas usually carried by Buddhist monks. The black umbrella marks the distinction of the religious authority of the Brahmin from that of the monk.

49. Nevill (1955: 350) presents some of the verse relating to a creeper-cutting exorcism. His manuscript, which he estimates is three centuries old, names some of the 108 poisonous vines. He states that each hoop indicates a different creeper.

50. Nevill (1955: 347) presents verses that connect the crown to the Naga king and to Kelaniya, but the context is different. His verses (which he indicates are three centuries old) describe the crown as made from various metals and precious gems and as having been manufactured by the gods. It fell from their possession down to the Nagas living at Kelaniya. The Nagas decided to use its power to curse Mara and to prevent him from injuring the Buddha. Nevill argues for the significance of the historical context of his story, which he thinks derives from its having been constructed when Kelaniya was an independent kingdom. Nevill says that the legend legitimates the Buddhist clergy at Kelaniya as distinct from the other monk fraternities of the Malwatta and Asgiriya chapters in Kandy. Another set of verses that Nevill (1955: 351) records links the crown more directly with the cutting of sorcery, but describes it as being made from nine kinds of leaves. According to Nevill, the crown is a highly charged ambiguous symbol. This aspect is more apparent in the context of its use in the Suniyama performance I describe.

51. The exorcist listed the ten fears and the eighteen diseases, the latter represented by the eighteen *sanni* demons (see Kapferer 1991: 231). The ten fears listed are *bhuta baya* (fear of spirits), *yaksaya baya* (fear of demons), *raksaya baya* (fear of planetary demons), *preta baya* (fear of ghosts), *raja baya* (fear of power), *chora baya* (fear of thieves), *gini baya* (fear of fire), *mara baya* (fear of death), *humbas baya* (fear of anthills and sorcery), *vasangata roga baya* (fear of infectious disease).

52. This creeper is also called *valli*.

53. There is a similar episode in the Kohomba Kankariya (Professor Punchi Banda, personal communication, 1995).

54. There is sound criticism in anthropology of perspectives that attend to *logics* and their implication of internal rational and systematic coherence. Bourdieu states: "Practice has a logic which is not that of the logician. This has to be acknowledged in order to avoid asking of it more logic than it can give, thereby condemning oneself either to wring incoherences out of it or to thrust a forced coherence upon it" (1990: 86). In my view his argument is sound, and I certainly do not write of logics in any rationalist sense. Furthermore, it should be clear that the analysis I have presented here (also Kapferer 1983) is not conceived in textualist terms: the logic of practice as an enactment of the argument contained in a written or memorized work. By *logic* I mean the diverse ways in which human beings through their practices (practices that have various historical influences working on them and are always specific to situations) put their worlds together and generate and continually alter the structures of their contexts and lives. Overall, Bourdieu summarizes very well the phenomenological and deconstructionist traditions that guide my own argument. He states that practical logics defy "logical logic" and are "caught up in 'the matter in hand,' totally present in the present and in the practical functions that it finds there in the form of objective potentialities" (1990: 92). But he then goes on to say that practice "excludes attention to itself (that is, to the past)." This requires some further qualification as Bourdieu goes on to apply this orientation to the practical logic of rite. The Suniyama as I have described it demonstrates that ritual draws attention to its practice. Moreover, the *past* that is invoked in the rite is remade in the present of the rite. The rite is a repetition of the past, but since it is an original repetition, a past that is actualized in the future present (see Deleuze [1968] 1994: 70–128). The past of the rite is not a historical temporality, a past that precedes the present in time, but an originary past that is always present in the actualization of its practice. The creating of such a past is a way in which practice in rite draws attention to itself as practice.

55. Levi-Strauss makes the point that belief is affirmed in practices. He says skepticism is a general human phenomenon and Cartesian notions of radical doubt feature in the worlds of sorcery and shamanism and in contemporary science. Human beings do not believe blindly, and it is through the efficacies of their practical technologies attached to beliefs (of science or sorcery) that human beings become committed to and change their beliefs. I draw attention to this observation of Levi-Strauss to redress a tendency among anthropologists (myself included) occasionally to overlook his stress on practical dynamics and to focus on his intellectualist abstractionism.

56. Heidegger's observations are relevant on the notion that "*techne* is the name not only for the activities and skills of the craftsman, but also for the arts of the mind and the fine arts. *Techne* belongs to bringing-forth, to *poiesis;* it is something poietic" (1977: 13).

57. It should be clear that I wish to avoid the individualist subjectivist tenden-

cies of some social science applications of interpretivist and phenomenological perspectives. People's experience of their worlds is not simply reducible to their perspective on them. The actualities of experience are historical complexities and are the chaotic focus of diverse forces—among them the activities of other human beings in the immediate contexts of experience and activities perhaps more distant but no less immediate, related to global economics, local and foreign wars, ecological shifts, and so forth. The realities of human construction are forged in the force and speed of actualities. These constructions should not be viewed as reflections on actuality but as continually shifting refractions within the chaotic motions of actuality.

58. This kind of position in anthropology sets up conundrums that are largely a problem of anthropological construction. An example concerns the relation between ritual practices and social change and the role of historical forces. If ritual is mainly a symbolic representation of processes external to itself and is entirely a derivative and secondary phenomenon, then it is often difficult to understand the persistence of specific ritual practices. Sometimes this persistence is described as fetishistic, irrational, and an example of the power of tradition. I understand the ritual forms as emerging from the circumstances of lived existence but as in their practice not necessarily attempting to represent these circumstances. The Suniyama does not mirror the circumstances of existence external to itself. It is not a derivative or secondary phenomenon. It is an organization of practices that establishes a more primary relation to the world that surrounds it. The Suniyama is a field of practice for the production of meaning and contains potencies for the creation of meaning. The dynamics of this rite reoriginate victims in the ordinary life world. The potency of the Suniyama is not tied to the historical circumstances that produced it.

59. Handelman's (1990) understanding of ritual has influenced my own approach. In many ways his discussion of ritual as an "event-that-models" has affinities with my discussion of the Suniyama rite. It also has some correspondence with Deleuze's discussion of virtuality, especially his link between his idea of virtuality and models in science. Handelman is concerned to establish the similarities and differences between rites as events that model and the ordinary lived-in world. For him the models of rite are simplified microcosms of the fuzzy and more complex lived-in world. They have considerable autonomy but are organized to operate synechdochically as if they were the whole lived-in world (see Handelman 1990: 27–28). The following statement of Handelman bears comparison with what I said earlier about distinguishing the reality of rite from actuality. "It is vital to stress that a model neither imitates nor reflects any totality of ordered life. This would defeat its principled purpose, by the introduction into the model of the continuously emerging dynamics that make social life finally uncontrollable. Ultimately the model would become the world, and therefore incapable of acting upon the latter" (Handelman 1990:28).

Handelman's perspective is not only extremely useful as he develops it but an exciting attempt to break down the dichotomies prevalent in anthropological views of ritual as antiscience. Handelman sees in ritual modeling procedures similar to those of scientific practice. Their relative success is rooted in similar dynamics. My approach differs from Handelman's mainly in relation to the kind of empirical material with which I am concerned. Handelman is bound to ritual as representation, and the concept of model, however conceived, maintains a stress on representation. Ritual in the understanding I develop of the Suniyama is not representational so much as a descent into the inner dynamics of the way human beings construct, as an ongoing process, their lived realities. The structural formations of lived-in realities are always in flux, always moving in diverse directions and shifting the valencies of their structuration. In rituals like the Suniyama, participants enter into the dynamics of how they are always already constructing the differences and diversities of their social worlds.

Handelman concentrates on the organizational dynamics of rite—what he refers to as their design. His emphasis is basically the same as mine on the dynamics of practice. But he considers the dynamics models of dynamics in the lived-in world. They are still representations and not the practices in themselves. Because the virtuality of the Suniyama is not representational of forms of life external to it, I consider it a virtuality and not a virtual reality, model, or a modeling. The dynamics of the practice are the dynamics involved in the construction of lived realities external to the rite.

60. I have found Richard Coyne's (1993) discussion of virtual reality extremely useful.

Chapter Six

1. In conjunction with a more structuralist perspective, Werbner (1989) systematically extends Turner's scheme to sacrifice and other kinds of rite in Africa and elsewhere.

2. Brian Keenan describes the tortures of his Lebanese confinement with remarkable power and sensitivity. He gives an account of his captors' obsessive interest in information for information's sake and the senseless beatings that accompanied the questioning. In one vivid account, the information is exhausted and the prisoner is shot (Keenan 1992:53). Keenan's account as a whole, the rich detailing of his experiences, has many parallels with what I understand to be the experience of sorcery.

3. Derrida argues that "the symbolic opens and constitutes the order of exchange and of the debt, the law or the order of circulation in which the gift is annulled. It suffices therefore for the other to *perceive the gift* not only to perceive it in the sense in which, one says in French, *on perçoit*, that is, receives, for example, merchandise, payment, or compensation—but to perceive its nature of gift, the meaning or intention.

"The simple identification of the gift seems to destroy it . . . . the simple identification . . . would be nothing other than the process of the destruction of the gift" (Derrida 1992:172).

4. The ideas that gifts have to be forced and are unwillingly accepted and that the system of social relations founded in the gift is fundamentally based in power

are widespread in mythology and in ethnographic literature. Valeri (1985) makes this observation for ancient Hawaii and in the context of Girard's (1977) study of sacrifice, which understands the victim as giving itself willingly to sacrifice. The force or power that impels the gift is often represented as the power of sorcery.

5. This argument for sacrifice is strongly denied by Heesterman (1993) on the basis of ancient Indian materials. In his analysis, sacrifice is inherently ambiguous and unstable. Strangely, however, Heesterman separates the act of sacrifice from ritual. He gives to rite the stabilizing and functional Girardian function.

Chapter Seven

1. Mind-body dualisms are not easily disposed of. This is evident in recent discussions of mind and consciousness in biology and psychology. Thus, as Fodor argues (1983), some approaches in cognitive psychology demonstrate a neo-Cartesianism. Edelman (1994), pursuing a Darwinian evolutionist approach to brain and consciousness and alive to the intentionalist positions of Brentano and Husserl, which make consciousness explicitly a function of the orientation and motion of the body in the world, nonetheless recreates a Cartesianism in a brain/consciousness and body divide. The difficulty in escaping Cartesian dualism, or what Dennett (1991) refers to as the "Cartesian theater" perspective is not merely, I suggest, a function of Western cosmological assumptions grounded in the history of Western philosophical and scientific thought. It may be a distinct historical-ideological formulation of what Husserl (and Heidegger following him) refers to as the "natural attitude" and states is part of the intentionality or thrownness of human beings toward the horizons of their existence as a function of which they become *aware of their existence,* become progressively more conscious beings, and as human beings become interpreting and self-interpreting. That is, it is because human beings emerge in consciousness as a function of their projection toward the world and activities in it—transcend their bodies in the world—that they conceive of the mind and consciousness as something separate from the body and also as capable of transcending the world. By acting in the world, human beings escape the limitations imposed by their physical bodies and therefore come to conceive of their minds as detachable from their bodies.

2. Approximately £10 at current rates of exchange.

3. For the *pita pantiya kapuma,* eight different kinds of grains regarded as unfit for human consumption were collected. These were taken to a grave site where the exorcist lay down, like a corpse, and intoned mantras while the grains were cooked and offered to the ghosts and demons. Simultaneously an egg was cooked in a human cranium. It was explained that the cooking of the grains at the grave site empowered them and filled them with the essence of death, making them attractive to the ghosts and demons concerned. The cooked grains were placed at the doorposts at the entrance to the house and were also placed at the eight cardinal directions around the house. The idea was to draw the ghosts and demons away from the house, which they had inhabited, and with their food

create a boundary, a ring of protection around the house. The exorcist stated that the two main demons who should receive offerings on this occasion were Aivimana and Baihivira. He added that Aivimana is a demon born of a low-caste (*andi*) Muslim.

4. Dufrenne makes the following important criticism of Sartre. "In fact, imagination appears to possess at once the two faces of nature and mind. It belongs to the body to the degree that it animates the modes of implicit knowledge inherited from the experience of presence, while opening up reflection to the degree that it allows us to substitute the perceived for the lived. In this latter role, imagination interrupts the intimacy of presence by introducing not so much an absence as the distance within the presence which constitutes representation, in terms of which the object confronts us at a distance, open to the look or to the judgement" (Dufrenne 1973: 351).

5. My approach to the imagination has been greatly influenced by conversations with Jadran Mimica. He stresses the role of the imagination in the self-creation of human beings as beings-in-the-world. He states: "The fact is that through imagination human beings create themselves both as their own reality and their own illusion. They are not in the world in the mode of merely factual existence. Human beings also live themselves and the world as the continuously changing being of truth and error. Therefore, existence can be that of self-delusion and atrophy. All these modalities of human being-in-the-world are constituted through the activity of imagination" (Mimica 1991:36).

6. Sartre, however, is aware that the imaginary sustains the real. In his argument, this sustaining capacity disappears when confronted with the real—when Peter makes his appearance in the flesh.

7. It is routine in towns and villages for new house owners or residents to hire an exorcist or some other specialist to search out any dangerous charms that may have been planted by previous occupants. The placing of charms and offerings around Siyadoris's house during his *kapuma* is a regular practice in these rites. It is also common after the building of a new house.

8. Obeyesekere (1981) attacks the Durkheimianism of British social anthropology. Although his attack is often well aimed, he tends to overdetermine his victim in a singular mode. A psychoanalytic influence is apparent in much social anthropology (e.g., Fortune, Victor Turner, and even Gluckman). Durkheim's (1915) sociology of religion is founded in a psychology of individual evanescence. His notions of collective representation and group mind have been criticized for psychologism. Obeyesekere's approach, which mingles Freud with Weber, has none of Durkheim's crudity and is of demonstrated insight, though for me it is still too reductionist.

9. The shrines to Kataragama in particular and to gods such as Vibisana are exceptions. Kataragama has major destructive and regenerative qualities. Vibisana has numerous similarities to Suniyam, and according to Gombrich and Obeyesekere (1988), he was probably more involved in sorcery practice until being superseded by others.

10. In folk tradition, Mahasona is the demon form of Jayasena, who according to the fifth century C.E. chronicle the *Mahavamsa,* was one of the ten champions of Prince Dutthagamani. Dutthagamani is the Sinhalese hero who conquered the Tamil king Elara and reestablished Buddhism as the reigning religion.

11. Douglas's (1966) discussion of dirt, pollution, and power has considerable resonance with these aspects of the Suniyam shrines.

12. Wirz (1954:182–84) gives a full account of some of the myths attaching to this demon god. The story begins with King Buvaneka, who ruled at Kurunegala and who took a Muslim woman as his thirteenth wife. Two children were born of the union. When King Buvaneka committed suicide by throwing himself off Kurunegala rock (after his wives had already done so when they had incorrectly been told that Buvaneka had been killed in battle), he was succeeded by his first son, who had adopted Islam. He suppressed Buddhism, and conflict brewed between the Muslim and Buddhist communities. Meanwhile, the second son was brought up by a woman of the washer caste and assumed that caste identity. He was later adopted by another man of higher caste. Bhuvaneka's second son desired to marry the elder of the two daughters of his new protector, but she declined, declaring that she did not wish to marry a man of lower caste. However, her younger sister agreed to marry him. But this created discord between the sisters. To cut a long story short, the elder brother, the Muslim king, along with his wives was killed by his chief minister, who threw them to their deaths off Kurunegala rock. This event resulted in the succession of the much-abused younger brother. When he became king, he had his father-in-law impaled and he also punished the sister who had refused to marry him. He built a shrine for his deceased elder brother, who by then had become a demon deity. Holt (1991:211) also presents a version of this story.

13. Obeyesekere (1982) presents a description of the *punava* and the main texts of the myths surrounding the pot linking it to Kuveni's curse (*dividos*) on Vijaya and his descendants because he broke his vow to her. Obeyesekere also describes some of the sorcery practices associated with the pot and the use of the pot in major rites.

14. A study of the distribution of temples in relation to class and caste is overdue. I attempted a limited survey in Colombo in 1985. Many of the temples were controlled by middle-class members of particular castes, and these temples tended to be organizational centers for the class control of persons from the same caste distributed in a variety of residential areas across the city.

15. But I am not completely certain that this will be so. The outside area of the temple, the space of Bhadrakali's power, is increasingly being captured by Sinhalese. A Buddhist priest has erected a small Buddha *dagaba* outside the gates of the Hindu temple. The temple and its Hindu priests were attacked by Sinhala rioters in 1983. But the temple is maintained as an important place of Hindu worship. The capturing of the outside ground intensifies the general site as one of powerful contradiction and conflict and should contribute to the continuity of the place as a powerful center of sorcery, anguish, and restitution.

16. This was also the case at shrines such as Maligawatta, but in recent years it has begun to operate virtually nonstop. Important shrines like Gatabaruya still operate at restricted times on *kemmura* days, Wednesday and Saturday.

17. An example (very French!) that Kristeva gives is of drinking coffee when the milk has formed a thin skin over the surface which clings to the lips. This evokes a gut feeling of disgust, she says. Of direct relevance to my discussion is an event that Obeyesekere reports: he met a Sinhalese ecstatic who had grown long filthy matted locks of hair which were a sign of her involvement with god Suniyam. Obeyesekere states: "I wrote then in my field notes that I had seen an ugly woman, her teeth stained with betel nut juice and bearing repulsive matted locks" (1981:6). The manner of some of the *maniyo*s at the Modera Bhadrakali shrine is not unlike what Obeyesekere describes, which provoked his initial sense of repulsion.

18. There is an up country–low country opposition in Sri Lanka. Kandy, the capital of the hill country in the Central Province and the site of the last kings of Sri Lanka, is often presented in social and political discourse as the locus of Sinhala cultural tradition, whence the descendants of traditional Sinhalese ruling groups come. This, of course, is hotly disputed in the south, where there are alternative narratives. The caste community from which Kamalawathie comes denies that its status can be set within the terms of the precolonial order of Kandy. It claims a lineage that links to more ancient Sinhalese orders. Such narratives are part of contemporary discourses of Sinhala nationalism and were largely constituted in their present form during British colonial rule. The British favored the Kandyan system and to some extent established the system of indirect rule through their own construction of what the traditional order was, set largely in terms of the Kandyan model. People in the south, who have been particularly active in contemporary Sinhala nationalism and political resistance, are often vociferous in discounting a Kandyan vision of things. This vision tends, among other features, to devalue the status of caste communities such as Kamalawat-thie's.

19. The actual numbers killed will in all likelihood never be fully known, but this figure has been cited frequently in recent months. The actual deaths could be in excess of the number given or considerably less.

20. In *Encounters* (1961), Goffman demonstrated how emotional energy transforms the situations of interaction.

21. Lynch produces a useful survey of approaches to the emotions. I think its overly dismissive stance derives from its relativism, founded in a cultural-categories-of-cognition perspective which no amount of appeal to *deconstruction-ism* will modify adequately. He states: "Cognitivism, as an approach to the study of emotion, has developed into many variations, some of which retain a universalist perspective. One variation of cognitivism, social constructionism, is particularly influential in anthropology. Social constructionism modified by insights from deconstructionism is the theoretical perspective within which most essays in this volume must be understood" (Lynch 1990:8).

22. Csordas (1994) and other contributors to the book he edits make similar points, especially Turner, Jackson, and Jenkins and Valiente.

Chapter Eight

1. The general term *bala(ya)* refers to power, especially that exercised by human beings. Other terms, such as *anuhas* and *sakti* tend to be applied to the powers of deities or divine beings.

2. Evans-Pritchard's observation comes in a section where he asserts that the Azande take into account empirical knowledge of cause and effect and that the "mystical" cause (in Western terms, witchcraft or sorcery) is the process whereby Azande are able to explain "accidents" by reference to the nonarbitrary social and political world. I cite at length his ethnographic reportage of the *second spear* metaphor. "As a matter of fact Zande thought expresses the notion of natural and mystical causation quite clearly by using a hunting metaphor to define their relations. Azande always say of witchcraft that it is the *umbaga* or second spear. When Azande kill game there is a division of meat between the man who first speared the animal and the man who plunged a second spear into it. These two are considered to have killed the beast and the owner of the second spear is called *umbaga*. Hence if a man is killed by an elephant Azande say that the elephant is the first spear and that witchcraft is the second spear and that together they killed the man. If a man spears another in war the slayer is the first spear and witchcraft is the second spear and together they killed him" (Evans-Pritchard 1937: 73–74).

3. I am aware that Mauss's argument about the spirit of the gift and the problem of reciprocity is sometimes criticized for being mystical. I disagree with this particular criticism but also with Mauss's resolution of the problem to which he attends (see Chapter 6).

4. A killing which incidentally is also a regeneration, an act of physical and social replenishment. The division of the killed animal between the person who initially brings down the animal and the hunter who finishes it off has the sense of the gift about it, the gift that generates social relations. Furthermore, this generating gift could be interpreted as occurring in a context of virtual sacrifice—the killing of the hunt among many peoples, certainly throughout much of Africa, often assumes the symbolic form of a sacrifice. The hunter who kills with the second spear is, I suggest, a kind of sacrificer.

5. Kemper (1991) adopts a general argument very similar to mine but is committed to identifying a difference. A discussion of my position in relation to these critics is found in Roberts 1993, 1994.

6. Much of my argument in the whole book is based in my interpretation of Deleuze's argument in *Difference and Repetition* ([1968] 1994). This concerns the nature of difference. Thus the kind of dynamics I have been discussing continually repeats itself in places separated in space and time, always as difference. This is the difference of repetition and not the recurrence of the same. The dynamics qua dynamics emerges under all kinds of historical and social conditions or circumstances. It is a dynamics not essential in human being but continually emer-

gent through the forces of their discursive and historical practice. What I have discussed as sorcery is *not* a unique Sinhala invention but has a dynamics that appears in widely separated contexts of human action, sometimes identified in similar ways as being sorcery. My analysis here, however, is not so restrictive but, as elsewhere in this book, recognizes sorcery as a dynamic of practices that may not be culturally reflected upon in this way. What is seen to be sorcery, of course, is not essentially sorcery.

References

Abercrombie, N., Stephen Hill, and Bryan S. Turner
  1980   *The Dominant Ideology Thesis.* London: Allen & Unwin.
AmaraSingham, Lorna Rhodes
  1973   Kuveni's Revenge: Images of Women in Sinhalese Myth. *Modern Ceylon Studies* 4 (1 and 2): 76–83.
Ames, Michael
  1963   Ideological and Social Change in Ceylon. *Human Organization* 22 (1): 45–53.
Ardener, E. W.
  1971   The New Anthropology and Its Critics. *Man,* n.s., 6: 449–467.
Austin, John
  1962   *How to Do Things with Words.* Oxford: Clarendon Press.
Bachelard, G.
  1969   *The Poetics of Reverie.* Boston: Beacon Press.
Barnett, L. D.
  1916   Alphabetical Guide to Folklore from Ballad Sources. *Indian Antiquary* 29.
Berger, Peter L., and Thomas Luckmann
  1971   *The Social Construction of Reality: A Treatise in the Sociology of Knowledge.* Harmondsworth: Penguin Books.
Bloch, Marc
  1973   *The Royal Touch: Sacred Monarch and Scrofula in England and France,* translated by J. E. Anderson. London: Routledge & Kegan Paul.
Bloch, Maurice
  1992   *Prey into Hunter: The Politics of Religious Experience.* Cambridge: Cambridge University Press.
Bogue, Ronald
  1989   *Deleuze and Guattari.* London: Routledge.

335

Bond, George
  1988   *The Buddhist Revival in Sri Lanka: A Religious Tradition, Reinterpretation, and Response.* Columbia: University of South Carolina Press.
Bourdieu, Pierre
  1977   *Outline of a Theory of Practice,* translated by Richard Nice. Cambridge: Cambridge University Press.
  1990   *The Logic of Practice,* translated by Richard Nice. Stanford: Stanford University Press.
Boyd, J. W.
  1973   Satan and Mara: Christian and Buddhist Symbols of Evil. *Modern Ceylon Studies* 4 (1 and 2): 84–100.
Brentano, F.
  [1874] 1973 *Psychology from an Empirical Standpoint,* translated by L. L. McAlister. London: Routledge & Kegan Paul.
Brow, James
  1978   *Vedda Villages of Anuradhapura: The Historical Anthropology of a Community in Sri Lanka.* Seattle: Washington University Press.
Chandraprema, C. A.
  1991   *Sri Lanka: The Years of Terror. The JVP Insurrection 1987–1989.* Colombo: Lake House Bookshop.
Clastres, Pierre
  [1972] 1989 *Society against the State.* New York: Zone Books.
Clifford, J.
  1988   *The Predicament of Culture: Twentieth Century Ethnography, Literature, and Art.* Cambridge: Harvard University Press.
Clifford, J., and G. Marcus, eds.
  1986   *Writing Culture: The Poetics and Politics of Ethnography.* Berkeley: University of California Press.
Codere, Helen
  1972   *Fighting with Property: A Study of Kwakiutl Potlatching and Warfare 1792–1930.* Seattle: University of Washington Press.
Cohn, Norman
  1961   *In Pursuit of the Millenium: Revolutionary Messianism in Medieval and Reformation Europe and Its Bearing on Modern Totalitarian Movements.* 2d ed. New York: Harper.
  1975   *Europe's Inner Demons: An Inquiry Inspired by the Great Witch Hunt.* London: Chatto: Heinemann for Sussex University Press.
Comaroff, Jean, and John Comaroff
  1991   *Of Revelation and Revolution: Christianity, Colonialism, and Consciousness in South Africa.* Chicago: University of Chicago Press.
Committee for Rational Development
  1983   *The Ethnic Conflict.* Delhi: Navrang Press.
Coyne, Richard
  1994   Heidegger and Virtual Reality: The Implications of Heidegger's Thinking for Computer Representations. *Leonardo* 27 (1): 65–73.

Crick, M.
  1976   *Explorations in Language Meaning: Towards a Semantic Anthropology.* London: Malaby Press.
Csordas, Thomas, ed.
  1994   *Embodiment and Experience: The Existential Ground of Culture and Self.* Cambridge: Cambridge University Press.
Damasio, Antonio R.
  1994   *Descartes' Error: Emotion, Reason, and the Human Brain.* New York: G. P. Putnam's Sons.
Deleuze, Gilles
  [1968] 1994 *Difference and Repetition,* translated by Paul Patton. London: Athlone Press.
Deleuze, Gilles, and Felix Guattari
  1988   *A Thousand Plateaus: Capitalism and Schizophrenia,* translated and foreword by Brian Massumi. London: Athlone Press.
Dennett, Daniel C.
  1991   *Consciousness Explained.* London: Allen Lane. Penguin.
Derrida, Jacques
  1992   *Given Time I: Counterfeit Money,* translated by Peggy Kamuf. Chicago: University of Chicago Press.
De Silva, K. M.
  1981   *A History of Sri Lanka.* London: Hurst.
Detienne, Marcel, and Jean-Pierre Vernant, eds.
  1979   *La cuisine du sacrifice en pays grec.* Paris: Gallimard.
Devereux, George
  1967   *From Anxiety to Method in the Behavioral Sciences.* The Hague: Mouton.
Douglas, Mary
  1966   *Purity and Danger: An Analysis of Concepts of Pollution and Taboo.* London: Routledge & Kegan Paul.
  1970   *Witchcraft: Confessions and Accusations.* London: Tavistock.
  1973   *Natural Symbols: Explorations in Cosmology.* London: Barrie Jenkins.
  1975   *Implicit Meanings: Essays in Anthropology.* London: Routledge & Kegan Paul.
  1991   Witchcraft and Leprosy: Two Strategies of Exclusion. *Man* 26 (3): 723–736.
Dowson, J.
  1968   *Classical Dictionary of Hindu Mythology and Religion, Geography, History, and Literature.* London: Routledge & Kegan Paul.
Dreyfus, Hubert L.
  1991   *Being-in-the-World: A Commentary on Heidegger's Being and Time, Division I.* Cambridge, Mass.: MIT Press.
Dufrenne, Mikel
  1973   *The Phenomenology of Aesthetic Experience.* Evanston, Ill.: Northwestern University Press.

Dumont, Louis
   1980   *Homo Hierarchicus: The Caste System and Its Implications.* Rev. ed. Chicago: University of Chicago Press.
   1986   Marcel Mauss: A Science in Process of Becoming. In *Essays on Individualism: Ideology in Anthropological Perspective,* 183–201. Chicago: University of Chicago Press.
Durkheim, Emile
   1915   *The Elementary Forms of the Religious Life: A Study in Religious Sociology,* translated by J. W. Swain. London: George Allen & Unwin.
Eck, Diana L.
   1985   *Darsan: Seeing the Divine Image in India.* Chambersburg, Pa.: Anima Books.
Edelman, Gerald
   1994   *Bright Air, Brilliant Fire: On the Matter of the Mind.* London: Penguin Books.
Eliade, M.
   1965   *The Myth of the Eternal Return, or, Cosmos and History,* translated from the French by Willard R. Trask. Princeton: Princeton University Press.
   1978   *A History of Religious Ideas,* vols. 1, 2, and 3, translated by Willard R. Trask. Chicago: University of Chicago Press.
   1979   *The Two and the One,* translated by J. M. Cohen. Chicago: University of Chicago Press.
Euripides
   1992   *Medea,* translated by Jeremy Brooks. In *Euripides: Plays One.* London: Methuen Drama.
Evans-Pritchard, E. E.
   1937   *Witchcraft, Oracles, and Magic among the Azande.* Oxford: Clarendon Press.
   1940   *The Nuer.* Oxford: Clarendon Press.
   1956   *Nuer Religion.* Oxford: Clarendon Press.
Favret-Saada, Jeanne
   1977   *Deadly Words: Witchcraft in the Bocage.* Cambridge: Cambridge University Press.
Feyerabend, Paul
   1978   *Against Method.* London: Verso.
Fodor, Jerry A.
   1983   *The Modularity of Mind: An Essay on Faculty Psychology.* Cambridge, Mass.: MIT Press.
Foster, Robert J.
   1991   Making National Cultures in the Global Ecumene. *Annual Reviews in Anthropology* 20: 235–260.
Foucault, Michel
   1993   Dream, Imagination, and Existence, translated by Forrest Williams. In

Dream and Existence, by Michel Foucault and Ludwig Binswanger, edited by Keith Hoeller. Atlantic Highlands, N. J.: Humanities Press.

Frazer, Sir James

1890   *The Golden Bough: A Study in Magic and Religion.* 2 vols. London: Macmillan.

Freud, S.

1991   *Jokes and Their Relation to the Unconscious,* translated from the German by James Strachey. London: Penguin.

Geertz, Clifford

1965   Religion as a Cultural System. In *Anthropological Approaches to the Study of Religion,* edited by M. Banton. Association of Social Anthropologists of the Commonwealth, Monograph 3. London: Tavistock Publications.

1980   *Negara: The Theatre State in Nineteenth Century Bali.* Princeton: Princeton University Press.

Geiger, Wilhelm

1960   *Culture of Ceylon in Medieval Times,* edited by Heinz Bechert. Weisbaden: Otto Harrassowitz.

Gellner, Ernest

1974   *Legitimation of Belief.* Cambridge: Cambridge University Press.

Ginzburg, Carlo

1991   *Ecstasies: Deciphering the Witches' Sabbath.* London: Penguin Books.

Girard, Rene

1977   *Violence and the Sacred,* translated by Patrick Gregory. Baltimore: Johns Hopkins University Press.

Gluckman, Max

1954   *Rituals of Rebellion in South-East Africa.* Manchester: Manchester University Press.

1956   *Custom and Conflict in Africa.* Oxford: Basil Blackwell.

Gluckman, Max, ed.

1972   *The Allocation of Responsibility.* Manchester: Manchester University Press.

Godakumbura, Charles

1955   *Sinhalese Literature.* Colombo: Colombo Apothecaries.

1963   *Kohomba Kankariya.* Colombo: Government Press.

Goffman, Erving

1961   *Encounters: Two Studies in the Sociology of Interaction.* Indianapolis: Bobbs-Merrill.

Goldman, Irving

1975   *The Mouth of Heaven: An Introduction to Kwakiutl Religious Thought.* New York: John Wiley & Sons.

Gombrich, R.

1971   *Precept and Practice: Traditional Buddhism in the Rural Highlands of Ceylon.* Oxford: Clarendon Press.

1988 *Theravada Buddhism: A Social History from Ancient Benares to Modern Colombo.* London: Routledge & Kegan Paul.

Gombrich, R., and Margaret Cone
1977 *The Perfect Generosity of Prince Vessantara.* Oxford: Clarendon Press.

Gombrich, R., and Gananath Obeyesekere
1988 *Buddhism Transformed: Religious Change in Sri Lanka.* Princeton: Princeton University Press.

Gooneratne, Dandris de Silva
1865 On Demonology and Witchcraft in Ceylon. *Journal of the Ceylon Branch of the Royal Asiatic Society* 4: 26–27.

Goudriaan, Teun, trans. and ed.
1985 *The Vinasikahatantra: A Saiva Tantra of the Left Current.* Delhi: Motilal Banarsidass.

Grathoff, R.
1970 *The Structure of Social Inconsistencies: A Contribution to a Unified Theory of Play, Game, and Social Action.* The Hague: Martinus Nijhoff.

Guha, Ranajit, and Gayatri C. Spivak
1988 *Selected Subaltern Studies.* Oxford: Oxford University Press.

Gunawardena, D. C.
1968 *The Flowering Plants of Ceylon: An Etymological and Historical Study.* Colombo: Lake House Investments.

Hall, Harrison
1993 Intentionality and World: Division I of Being and Time. In *The Cambridge Companion to Heidegger,* edited by Charles B. Guignon, 122–140. Cambridge: Cambridge University Press.

Handelman, Don
1990 *Models and Mirrors: Towards an Anthropology of Public Events.* Cambridge: Cambridge University Press.

Handelman, Don, and Bruce Kapferer
1980 Symbolic Types, Mediation, and the Transformation of Ritual Context: Sinhalese Demons and Tewa Clowns. *Semiotica* 30 (1 and 2): 41–71.

Harris, Marvin
1974 *Cows, Pigs, Wars, and Witches: The Riddle of Culture.* New York: Random House.

Harrison, Simon
1993 *The Masks of War: Violence, Ritual, and the Self in Melanesia.* Manchester: Manchester University Press.

Heesterman, J. C.
1993 *The Broken World of Sacrifice: An Essay in Ancient Indian Ritual.* Chicago: University of Chicago Press.

Heidegger, Martin
1962 *Being and Time,* translated by John Macquarrie and Edward Robinson. New York: Harper & Row.

1977 *The Question of Technology and Other Essays,* translated by William Lovitt. New York: Harper & Row.

Heusch, Luc de
  1985 *Sacrifice in Africa: A Structuralist Approach.* Manchester: Manchester University Press.

Hobbes, Thomas
  [1651] 1962 *Leviathan.* London: Collier Macmillan.

Hocart, A. M.
  1927 *Kingship.* Oxford: Clarendon Press.
  1936 *Kings and Councillors.* Cairo: Printing Office.

Holt, John Clifford
  1991 *Buddha in the Crown.* Oxford: Oxford University Press.

Horton, Robin
  1967 African Traditional Thought and Western Science. *Africa* 37 (1 and 2): 50–71 and 155–187.

Hoskins, Janet
  1993 "Violence, Sacrifice, and Divination: Giving and Taking Life in Eastern Indonesia. *American Ethnologist* 20(1): 159–178.

Hubert, H., and Marcel Mauss
  [1899] 1964 *Sacrifice: Its Nature and Function,* translated by W. D. Halls. London: Routledge.

Humphrey, Caroline, and James Laidlaw
  1994 *The Archetypal Actions of Ritual.* Oxford: Clarendon Press.

Husserl, Edmund
  1952 *Ideas,* translated by Boyce Gibson. London: George Allen & Unwin.
  1975 *The Paris Lectures,* 2d ed., translated by Peter Koestenbaum. The Hague: M. Nijhoff.

Jackson, Jean
  1994 Chronic Pain and the Tension between the Body as Subject and Object. In *Embodiment and Experience: The Existential Ground of Culture and Self,* edited by Thomas Csordas, 201–228. Cambridge: Cambridge University Press.

Jenkins, Janis H., and Martha Valiente
  1994 Bodily Transactions of the Passions: El Calor among Salvadoran Women Refugees. In *Embodiment and Experience: The Existential Ground of Culture and Self,* edited by Thomas Csordas, 163–182. Cambridge: Cambridge University Press.

Jiggins, Janice
  1979 *Caste and Family in the Politics of the Sinhalese 1947–1976.* Cambridge: Cambridge University Press.

Kandiah, Thiru
  1984 "Kaduva": Power and the English Language Weapon in Sri Lanka. In *Honouring E. F. C. Ludowyck: Felicitation Essays,* edited by Percy Colin-Thome and Ashley Halpe. Dehiwala: Tisara Prakasakayo.

Kapferer, Bruce

1983 *A Celebration of Demons.* Bloomington: Indiana University Press.

1988a *Legends of People, Myths of State.* Washington, D.C.: Smithsonian Institution Press.

1988b The Anthropologist as Hero. *Critique of Anthropology* 8 (2): 77–104.

1989 Nationalist Ideology and a Comparative Anthropology. *Ethnos* 54: 161–199.

1991 *A Celebration of Demons.* 2d ed. Oxford: Berg; Washington, D.C.: Smithsonian Institution Press.

1993 The Power of the Ludic: Cockfights and Contests in Bali and Sri Lanka. Paper presented to a conference on Ludic, Heidelberg, October 1993. To be published in a volume edited by P. Kopping and Bruce Kapferer, Berg Press, 1996.

1994a Remythologizations of Power and Identity: Nationalism and Violence in Sri Lanka. In *Cultures of Violence,* edited by Kumar Rupesinghe. Tokyo: United Nations University Press.

1994b Nation-States, Nationalism, and Violent Processes. Introduction to *Nationalism and Violence,* edited by Bruce Kapferer. Unpublished manuscript.

1994c Ethnic Nationalism and Discourses on Violence. In *Nationalism and Violence,* edited by Bruce Kapferer. Unpublished manuscript.

1995a From the Edge of Death: Sorcery and the Motion of Consciousness. In *Questions of Consciousness,* edited by Anthony P. Cohen and Nigel Rapport, 134–152. London: Routledge.

1995b Symbolic Practices: Construction and Deconstruction. *Semiotica* 105 (3): 331–341.

1996 Remythologizing Discourses: State and Insurrectionary Violence in Sri Lanka. In *Legitimation of Violence,* edited by D. Apter. London: Macmillan.

Keenan, Brian

1992 *An Evil Cradling.* London: Vintage.

Kemper, Steven

1991 *The Presence of the Past: Chronicles, Politics, and Culture in Sinhala Life.* Ithaca: Cornell University Press.

Kersenboom, Saskia

1995 *Word, Sound, Image: The Life of the Tamil Text.* Oxford: Berg Publishers.

Kersenboom-Story, Saskia

1987 *Nityasumangali: Devadasi Tradition in South India.* Delhi: Motilal Banarsidass.

Knauft, Bruce M.

1985 *Good Company and Violence: Sorcery and Social Action in Lowland New Guinea Society.* Berkeley: University of California Press.

Kristeva, Julia
  1982 *Powers of Horror: An Essay on Abjection.* New York: Columbia University Press.
Levi-Strauss, Claude
  1962 *Le Pensée Sauvage.* Paris: Plon.
  1966 Introduction a l'œuvre de Marcel Mauss. In M. Mauss, *Sociologie et anthropologie.* Paris: Presses Universitaires de France.
  1981 *The Naked Man.* New York: Harper & Row.
  1987 *Introduction to the Work of Marcel Mauss.* London: Routledge & Kegan Paul.
Levy-Bruhl, Lucien
  1923 *Primitive Mentality.* New York: Macmillan.
Lewis, Oscar
  1960 *Tepoztlan: Village in Mexico.* New York: Holt, Rinehart & Winston.
Lienhardt, Godfrey
  1961 *Divinity and Experience.* Oxford: Clarendon Press.
Ling, T. O.
  1962 *Buddhism and the Mythology of Evil.* London: Allen & Unwin.
Loy, David
  1988 *Nonduality: A Study in Comparative Philosophy.* New Haven: Yale University Press.
Luhrmann, T. M.
  1989 *Persuasions of the Witch's Craft: Ritual, Magic and Witchcraft in Present-Day England.* Oxford: Basil Blackwell.
Lutz, C.
  1982 The Domain of Emotion Words in Ifaluk. *American Ethnologist* 9: 113–128.
  1988 *Unnatural Emotions: Everyday Sentiments on a Micronesian Atoll and Their Challenge to Western Theory.* Chicago: University of Chicago Press.
Lutz, C., and L. Abu-Lughod
  1990 *Language and the Politics of Emotion.* Cambridge: Cambridge University Press.
Lynch, O., ed.
  1991 *Divine Passions: The Social Construction of Emotion in India.* Los Angeles: University of California Press.
Mahavamsa
  1934 Translated by Wilhelm Geiger. London: Oxford University Press for Pali Text Society.
Malalgoda, Kitsiri
  1976 *Buddhism in Sinhalese Society 1750–1900.* Berkeley: University of California Press.
Malinowski, Bronislaw
  1922 *Argonauts of the Western Pacific.* London: Routledge & Kegan Paul.

1935   *Coral Gardens and Their Magic.* 2 vols. London: George Allen & Unwin.

1948   *Magic, Science, and Religion and Other Essays.* New York: Doubleday Anchor Books.

Marwick, Max G.

1950   Another Modern Anti-witchcraft Movement in East Central Africa. *Africa* 20: 100–112.

1964   Witchcraft as a Social Strain-Gauge. *Australian Journal of Science* 26: 263–268.

1965   *Sorcery in Its Social Setting: A Study of the Northern Rhodesian Cewa.* Manchester: Manchester University Press.

Mauss, Marcel

1972   *A General Theory of Magic,* translated by Robert Brain. London: Routledge & Kegan Paul.

[1950] 1990 *The Gift: The Form and Reason for Exchange in Archaic Societies,* translated W. D. Halls. London: Routledge.

Merleau-Ponty, Maurice

1962   *Phenomenology of Perception,* translated from the French by Colin Smith. London: Routledge & Kegan Paul.

Mimica, Jadran

1988   *Intimations of Infinity.* Oxford: Berg Press.

1991   The Incest Passions: An Outline of the Logic of Iqwaye Social Organization. Pt. 1. *Oceania* 62 (1): 34–58.

Mitchell, J. C.

1956   *The Yao Village.* Manchester: Manchester University Press.

1987   *Cities, Society, and Social Perception: A Central African Perspective.* Oxford: Clarendon Press.

Moore, Mick

1993   Thoroughly Modern Revolutionaries: The JVP in Sri Lanka. *Modern Asian Studies* 27 (3): 593–642.

Munn, Nancy

1986   *The Fame of Gawa: A Symbolic Study of Value Transformation in a Massim (PNG) Society.* Cambridge: Cambridge University Press.

Muralt, Andre de

1974   *The Idea of Phenomenology: Husserlian Exemplarism.* Evanston, Ill.: Northwestern University Press.

Nash, June

1972   The Devil in Bolivia's Institutionalized Tin Mines. *Science and Society* 36 (2): 221–233.

Nevill, Hugh

1954   *Sinhala Verse,* vols. 1 and 2, edited by P. E. Deraniyagala. Colombo: Ceylon Government.

1955   *Sinhala Verse,* vol. 3, edited by P. E. Deraniyagala. Colombo: Ceylon Government.

Obeyesekere, Gananath

1969 The Ritual Drama of the Sanni Demons: Collective Representations of Disease in Ceylon. *Comparative Studies in Society and History* 11 (2): 174–216.

1975 Sorcery, Premeditated Murder, and the Canalization of Aggression in Sri Lanka. *Ethnology* 14 (1): 1–23.

1981 *Medusa's Hair: An Essay on Personal Symbols and Religious Experience.* Chicago: University of Chicago Press.

1982 The Ritual of the Leopard's Pot: The Puna Yagaya. In *Honouring E. F. C. Ludowyck: Felicitation Essays,* edited by Percy Colin-Thome and Ashley Halpe, 272–313. Dehiwala: Tisara Prakasakayo.

1984a *The Cult of the Goddess Pattini.* Chicago: University of Chicago Press.

1984b The Origins and Institutionalization of Political Violence. In *Sri Lanka in Change and in Crisis,* edited by James Manor. London: CroomHelm.

1990 *The Work of Culture: Symbolic Transformation in Psychoanalysis and Anthropology.* Chicago: University of Chicago Press.

Parkes, Graham, ed.

1987 *Heidegger and Asian Thought.* Honolulu: University of Hawaii Press.

Parkin, David, ed.

1985 *The Anthropology of Evil.* Oxford: Basil Blackwell.

Rahula, Walpola

1967 *What the Buddha Taught.* 2d ed. Bedford, England: Gordon Fraser.

Rappaport, Roy A.

1979 *Ecology, Meaning, and Religion.* Richmond, Calif.: North Atlantic.

Rawson, Philip

1973 *Tantra: The Indian Cult of Ecstasy.* London: Thames and Hudson Books.

Redfield, Robert

1941 *The Folk Culture of Yucatan.* Chicago: University of Chicago Press.

Ricoeur, Paul

1967 *Husserl: An Analysis of His Phenomenology.* Evanston, Ill.: Northwestern University Press.

Roberts, Michael

1982 *Caste Conflict and Elite Formation: The Rise of a Karava Elite in Sri Lanka 1500–1931.* Cambridge: Cambridge University Press.

1993 Nationalism, the Past and the Present: The Case of Sri Lanka. *Ethnic and Racial Studies* 16 (1): 133–166.

1994 *Exploring Confrontation. Sri Lanka: Politics, Culture and History.* Camberwell: Harwood Academic Publishers.

Roberts, Michael, ed.

1979 *Collective Identities, Nationalism, and Protest in Modern Sri Lanka.* Colombo: Marga Publications.

Rosaldo, Michelle Z.
  1980   *Knowledge and Passion: Ilongot Notions of Self and Social Life.* Cambridge: Cambridge University Press.
Rosaldo, Renato
  1989   *Culture and Truth: The Remaking of Social Analysis.* Boston: Beacon Press.
Saez, N.
  1992   Torture: Discourse on Practice. In *Tattoo, Torture, Mutilation, and Adornment,* edited by F. E. Mascia-Lees and Patricia Sharp. Albany: State University of New York Press.
Sahlins, Marshall
  1974   *Stone Age Economics.* London: Tavistock Publications.
  1981   *Historical Metaphors and Mythical Realities: Structure in the Early History of the Sandwich Islands Kingdom.* Ann Arbor: University of Michigan Press.
Sangren, P. Steven
  1988   Authority of Ethnography: "Postmodernism" and the Social Reproduction of Texts. *Current Anthropology* 29 (3): 405–435.
Sarachchandra, E. R.
  1966   *The Folk Drama of Ceylon.* Colombo: Department of Cultural Affairs.
Sardan, Jean-Pierre Olivier de
  1992   Occultism and the Ethnographic "I": The Exoticizing of Magic from Durkheim to "Postmodern" Anthropology. *Critique of Anthropology* 12 (1): 5–25.
Sartre, Jean-Paul
  1948   *The Emotions: Outline of a Theory,* translated from French by B. Frechtman. New York: Philosophical Library.
  1958   *Being and Nothingness,* translated by Hazel E. Barnes. London: Methuen.
  1962   *The Transcendance of the Ego,* translated by Forrest William and Robert Fitzpatrick. New York: Noonday Press.
  1966   *The Psychology of the Imagination.* Secaucus, N. J.: Citadel Press.
  1976   *The Critique of Dialectical Reason,* translated by Alan Sheridan-Smith and edited by Jonathan Ree. London: New Left Books.
Scarry, Elaine
  1985   *The Body in Pain: The Making and Unmaking of the World.* New York: Oxford University Press.
  1994   *Resisting Representations.* New York: Oxford University Press.
Scott, David
  1994   *Formations of Ritual: Colonial and Anthropological Discourses on Sinhala Yaktovil.* Minneapolis: University of Minnesota Press.
Scott, James
  1985   *Weapons of the Weak: Everyday Forms of Peasant Resistance.* New Haven: Yale University Press.

Searle, John R.
  1983   *Intentionality: An Essay in the Philosophy of Mind.* Cambridge: Cambridge University Press.
  1984   *Minds, Brains, and Science.* London: Penguin Books.
Seligmann, C. G., and Brenda Seligmann
  1911   *The Veddas.* Cambridge: Cambridge University Press.
Seneviratne, H. L.
  1978   *Rituals of the Kandyan State.* Cambridge: Cambridge University Press.
Shulman, David Dean
  1978   The Serpent and the Sacrifice: An Anthill Myth from Tiruvarur. *History of Religion* 18: 107–137.
  1985   *The King and the Clown in South Indian Myth and Poetry.* Princeton: Princeton University Press.
Silva, Sauris S. M.
  1970   *Suniyan Santiya.* Colombo: M. D. Gunasena Sons.
Singer, M. R.
  1964   *The Emerging Elite: A Study of Political Leadership in Ceylon.* Cambridge, Mass.: MIT Press.
Southwold, Martin
  1983   *Buddhism in Life.* Manchester: Manchester University Press.
Spencer, Jonathan
  1990   Writing Within: Anthropology, Nationalism, and Culture in Sri Lanka. *Current Anthropology* 31 (3): 283–300.
Spiro, Melford E.
  1967   *Burmese Supernaturalism: A Study of the Explanation and Reduction of Suffering.* Englewood Cliffs, N. J.: Prentice-Hall.
Stirrat, R. L.
  1992   *Power and Religiosity in a Post-Colonial Setting: Sinhala Catholics in Contemporary Sri Lanka.* Cambridge: Cambridge University Press.
Tambiah. S. J.
  1976   *World Conqueror, World Renouncer: A Study of Buddhism and Polity in Thailand against a Historical Background.* Cambridge: Cambridge University Press.
  1979   *A Performative Approach to Ritual.* Radcliffe-Brown Lecture. Oxford: Oxford University Press.
  1985   *Culture, Thought, and Social Action: An Anthropological Perspective.* Cambridge: Harvard University Press.
  1986   *Sri Lanka: Ethnic Fratricide and the Dismantling of Democracy.* Chicago: University of Chicago Press.
  1990   *Magic, Science, Religion, and the Scope of Rationality.* Cambridge: Cambridge University Press.
  1992   *Buddhism Betrayed?* Chicago: University of Chicago Press.

Taussig, Michael T.
  1980 *The Devil and Commodity Fetishism in South America.* Chapel Hill: University of North Carolina Press.
  1987 *Shamanism, Colonialism, and the Wild Man.* Chicago: University of Chicago Press.
Thompson, E. P.
  1978 *The Poverty of Theory and Other Essays.* New York: Monthly Review Press.
Turner, Terence
  1994 Bodies and Anti-bodies: Flesh and Fetish in Contemporary Social Theory. In *Embodiment and Experience: The Existential Ground of Culture and Self,* edited by Thomas Csordas, 27–47. Cambridge: Cambridge University Press.
Turner, Victor W.
  1957 *Schism and Continuity in an African Society.* Manchester: Manchester University Press.
  1964 Witchcraft and Sorcery: Taxonomy versus Dynamics. *Africa* 34: 314–325.
  1967 *The Forest of Symbols: Aspects of Ndembu Ritual.* Ithaca: Cornell University Press.
  1969 *The Ritual Process: Structure and Anti-Structure.* Harmondsworth: Penguin.
Tylor, E. B.
  1889 *Primitive Culture.* New York: Holt.
Valeri, Valerio
  1985 *Kingship and Sacrifice: Ritual and Society in Ancient Hawaii,* translated by Paula Wissing. Chicago: University of Chicago Press.
Van der Veer, Peter
  1988 *Gods on Earth: The Management of a North Indian Pilgrimage Centre.* London: Athlone Press.
Van Gennep, Arnold
  [1909] 1960 *The Rites of Passage,* translated by Monika B. Vizedom and Gabriel L. Caffe. London: Routledge & Kegan Paul.
Vernant, Jean-Pierre
  1981 Le sacrifice, le mythe grec. In *Dictionnaire des mythologies,* edited by Yves Bonnefoy. Paris: Gallimard.
Virilio, Paul
  [1977] 1986 *Speed and Politics: An Essay on Dromology.* New York: Semiotext(e).
Weiner, Annette B.
  1976 *Women of Value, Men of Renown: New Perspectives in Trobriand Exchange.* Austin: University of Texas Press.
  1983 From Words to Objects to Magic: The Boundaries of Social Interaction. *Man* 14: 328–348.

Werbner, Richard P.

1989 *Ritual Passage Sacred Journey: The Process and Organization of Religious Movement*. Washington, D.C.: Smithsonian Institution Press.

Williams, F. E.

1976 *The "Vailala Madness" and Other Essays*, edited by Erik Schwimmer. London: C. Hurst.

Willis, R. G.

1968 "Kamcape: An Anti-sorcery movement in South-West Tanzania. *Africa* 38: 1–15.

Wilson, Bryan R.

1984 *Rationality*. Oxford: Basil Blackwell.

Wilson, Jayaratnam

1988 *The Break-Up of Sri Lanka: The Sinhala-Tamil Conflict*. Honolulu: University of Hawaii Press.

Winch, Peter

1979 Understanding a Primitive Society. In *Rationality*, edited by Bryan R. Wilson. Oxford: Basil Blackwell.

Wirz, Paul

1954 *Exorcism and the Art of Healing in Ceylon*. Leiden: E. J. Brill.

Zimmerman, Michael E.

1993 Heidegger, Buddhism, and Deep Ecology. In *The Cambridge Companion to Heidegger*, edited by Charles Guignon, 240–269. Cambridge: Cambridge University Press.

Zvelebil, Kamil

1973 *The Poets of the Powers*. London: Rider.

Glossary

ābarana—Body ornaments.
aḍavv—Short offering of dance.
adhistāna—Concentrating on achieving the goals of Buddhist virtue.
adimokka—Determination.
ädurā—Exorcist.
ahimsa—Nonviolence.
ailē—Offering troughs or plates made from banana trunks.
akramavat—Disorder.
aluyāma—Morning watch/early morning.
ämbul—Sour.
amma—Mother.
anavina—Sorcery carried out through mantra/yantra or through sound, word, and utterance.
apale—Dangerous planetary period.
äpa-nūl—Threads tied prior to exorcism to protect victim and household from further misfortune.
apirisidu—Impure.
appocci hāmi—Honored father.
äravali käpīma—The ritual of cutting three limes from a single stem at the head, waist, and feet of the patient.
arumōsan—Artificial innovation, modern moves.
aṣṭaka—A group of eight Sanskrit couplets.
aṣṭakarma—The eight actions.
äsvaha—Eye poison.
atamaṅgala/atamagala—Ritual enclosure in the Suniyama, within Mahasammata's palace.
ätul—Internal/inner.
ätul pantiya—Gods of the inside.
äturayā—Patient.

avalada—Curses.
āvēsa—Demonic possession.
avīciya—The hell of ignorance.
avījja—Ignorance.
āyudaya—Weapon.
balaya—Power.
bali tōvil—Rites for the planetary gods and demons.
baliya—An image of Suniyam made from ant-bed clay.
bandara—Demon-deities, also "officials."
bandhana—Ties (of sorcery).
bandinava—To tie (or ensorcell).
Basmāsura—The Ash Demon.
baya—Fear.
Berava—Drummer caste, provide ritual services as soothsayers and healers or
    exorcists.
Bhūmi Dēvi/Būmi Dēvi (Polova Mahi Kāntāva)—Earth goddess.
billa—Sacrificial victim.
bōdhisattva—The past lives of the Buddha or a person who has achieved Bud-
    dhahood who returns selflessly to alleviate the suffering of others.
budu guna—The virtues of the Buddha.
budugē—Shrine to the Buddha.
būmipālu—Ash from a burned corpse or soil from a black ants' nest thrown to
    attack property and to cause ruin to those who inhabit it.
Buvanādhipati—Primordial earth-root yantra.
cakra—Vortex of force, wheel, central point.
cakravarti—World conqueror.
cāmara—Yak-tail whisks.
candragaṇē tīnduva—Reconstitutive judgment which brings forth a brilliant con-
    stellational unity.
chēdana vīdiya—The rite of destroying the demon palace; absolute destructive
    force.
cūniyam—(Tamil) sorcery.
cūniyam-ali-tal (Tamil)—To be annihilated, ruined.
cūniyam-etu (Tamil)—To remove bewitched articles from the ground.
cūniyam-mannei—(Tamil) bewitching ground.
cūniyam-māyam—(Tamil) buried articles of witchcraft.
däkum—An auspicious gaze.
dakunu-paya—Right foot.
dalumura—Betel and areca offering.
dansala—Almshouse to distribute food to the public during Buddhist festivals.
darśana—(Sanskrit) auspicious gaze.
degāta billa—A two-legged animal sacrifice.
dehi—Lime.
dehi käpīma—Lime cutting.
des—Curses.

des devol—Cursing with the power of Devol Deviyo.

deva—God.

dēva lōka—The abode of the gods/heavenly realms.

dēvārūdha—Being entranced by a deity.

dēva saluva—Divine cloth.

dēvatāvā—Demon-deity.

devol maduva—Village community rite for Devol Deviyo.

dhatu—Bodily essences.

diśti—Gaze, glare, eyesight.

dividos—Kuveni's curse on Vijaya.

dodan—Orange (*Citrus aurantium*).

dola duka—Pregnancy craving.

Dolaha Deviyo—Twelve regional deities linked to the four guardian gods.

dola pidēni—Food offerings to the demons.

doratu panīma—Rite of crossing the threshold.

dōśa—Faults.

dukganavilla—"Suffering striking" by supplicants at sorcery shrines.

dukvindinava—Suffering.

dumbul—Burned/roasted taste.

dummala—Powdered tree resin.

Durāva—Toddy-tapper caste.

gaḍol—Brick.

gammaḍuva—Village community rite for Pattini.

ganda—Smell.

garbha—The womb, or germinal center of the world.

gātrākṣara—Open, rather than closed, sounds or letters.

gavva—Sinhalese league, about 3¹/₄ miles.

gedara—House.

geri pas—Earth from a black ants' nest.

gini baya—Fear of fire.

ginijāla—Rings of fire.

ginijāl-polaṅga—Fire viper.

ginivāṭa—Walls of fire.

girē—Areca nut cutter.

gṅati prēta—Ghosts of deceased kin.

godadiyamas—Roasted meats of the land and sea.

gokkola—Decorations made from young coconut leaves.

goma—Cow dung.

goṭu—A small packet (made of jak leaves) for food offerings.

Goyigama—The cultivator/farmer caste.

gu-loriya—Shit truck.

guṇa—Virtues, qualities.

guru—Teacher.

gurukama—A minor, nonspecialist, secretive act of sorcery.

gurunnānse—Master of ceremonies or presiding exorcist.

hadi hūniyam—The "rape" of sorcery experience.

haṅgalā pädura—Rush mat used to cover the *kaksaputa yantra*.

hatadiya—The rite of the seven steps in the Suniyama.

hataravaram deviyo—The four guardian gods of Buddhism and the Sinhalese.

hīn-dehi—Dwarf-lime.

hira bandhana—Tight or marriage bond; custody/jail.

hiragē—Prison/jail.

hisatel—The application of oil to the head.

hita—Mind, consciousness.

hondala—A creeper associated with sorcery (*L. juncus*).

hōvaha—Hearing poisonous words.

huṁbas baya—Anthill fear or fear of sorcery.

hūniyam—Sorcery.

īgaha—The commanding arrow of the exorcist's magical power.

iramudun—Midday period, when the sun is at its zenith.

irdi/iddi—Magical powers.

iripännum—Lines drawn with funerary ash to impede, kill, or block victims.

irisiyāva—Jealousy.

jamanāran—Mandarin orange (*Citrus nobilis*).

jātaka—Accounts of events in the Buddha's previous births.

jīvan—To breathe life into.

kabala—Pot, broiling pot.

kadaturāva—A white cloth used to shield the patient.

kahadiyara—Turmeric water.

Kaksaputa—A Brahmin's woven bag; Buddha's name in a previous birth (as a merchant).

kalavā bandhana—Sorcery to paralyze victims in the midst of sexual intercourse.

Kalu Kumara—The Black Prince, whose main victims are women.

kangul toppiya—Headdress worn by dancers in the Suniyama.

kannalavva—Singing plaints in praise of the gods.

kānsāva—Anxiety.

kanyā nūl—Virgin thread.

kap—Cut.

kapa—World axis.

kapāla kūduva—A three-tiered structure representing the world order, erected on the axis of a rice pounder.

kapālika—Skull bearer.

kapanavā—Cutting.

käpilla—A cutting rite.

käpuma—Antisorcery rite.

käpum vīdiya—Sorcery cutting place.

kapurāla—Shrine priest.

Karāva—Fisher caste.

karavalā—Black-and-white ringed snake.

karma—Action.

kārtikeya—Seven female attendants on Kataragama.

katavaha—Poisonous speech.

kattirikka—Offering stands.

katugasīma—Making wax effigies and sticking thorns into the five vital parts of the body.

kavi—Songs/verses.

kävum—Oil cakes.

keli—Performance.

kemmura—Auspicious days.

kiḷi—Defilement.

kiḷimalē—Menstruating.

kiri—Milk.

kiri amma—Milk mother.

kiri bhat—Milk rice.

kiri-itiravīma—Boiling milk in a pot till it overflows.

kodivina—Malevolent human action.

Kohomba Kankāriya—A cleansing ritual performed in villages in the central highlands.

kondu nāratiya—Spinal column.

kopili—Young green sticks from lime tree?

kōrale—Part of a province.

kramavat—Order/calm.

krema käpuma—Destructive rite.

kūḍalu dehi—Leech lime.

kumba—Pot.

kuṇḍalinī—In the South Indian tradition of Hatha Yoga, the spinal energy flow of micro/macrocosm.

kuṇu pol—Rancid coconut oil.

lakśaṇa—Beauty/beautiful.

lōka—World.

lōka uppattiya—The origin of the world.

mädayāma—Midday period.

maḍu purayā—Ritual assistant, a special officiant in the Suniyama.

maḍu tovil—Exorcisms focused on the village or villages.

maḍuva—Open-sided hut.

magul berē—Ceremonial drum rhythm.

mahā badra kalpa uppattiya—The origin of the world.

mahābhuta—Elemental essences of matter.

Maha-Kala Purusaya—The first human.

Maha Kōla Sanni Yakā—The chief of the *sanni* demons.

mahanāran—Giant grapefruit (*Citrus decumana*).

maha tē—The great refreshment break.

mahēśakya—A great deity.

mal asna—flower bed/altar.

mal-bulat taṭṭuva—Offering basket with objects used to cleanse and cool the patient.

malavara dōśa—Puberty illness.

māḷigāva—Palace.

māmā—Mother's brother.

manasa—Mind, consciousness.

manasikāra—Attention.

mānel—Blue water lily *(Nymphaea stellata)*.

māṇiyō—Female attendants to demonic or sorcery gods.

mantra—Potent prescribed organizations of sound and word.

māpilā—Bloodsucking snake.

massinā—Cross-cousin; brother-in-law.

mätirīma—To utter mantras.

māyā—Illusion.

māyama—Midnight watch.

mēse—Table.

minī alu—Ash from a burned corpse/funerary ash.

mōksa—Release.

mōlgaha—Rice pounder.

moṭṭakkiḷi—Shawl.

moṭṭākku (Tamil)—Veil.

mukha bandhana—Sorcery to control speech or strike a victim dumb.

mul/mula—Root, originary.

muḷu—Entire, whole.

nāga—Snake.

nāgavalli—Betel vine.

näkatśāstra—Astrologer.

namaskāraya—Salutation to the Buddha.

nānu—Protective oil paste used in antisorcery and other rites.

nānu-mura—Oil-anointing ceremony?

nāran—Species of orange *(Citrus reticulata)*.

nasnāran—Wild lime, citron.

navagraha—The nine planets.

navaguna väla—Necklace with the nine qualities.

navakuru—The letters of the nine planets.

nayanāyudaya—The eye weapon.

nētra pinkama—Eye-painting ceremony on Buddha statues.

nīcakula tīnduva—The low caste or outcaste judgment.

nirvāṇa/nibbana—Release from existence/nothingness.

nūl—Thread.

Olī—Dancer caste; perform ritual services as soothsayers and healers?

otunna—Crown.

paccavadam—Red cummerbund worn by sorcerers.

pahan-päla—A small shrine for the Buddha and Guardian Deities.

pahantira—Oil wicks.
paligahīma—Vengeful cursing.
pambayā—Effigy of the sorcerer.
paṇa-nāti—Lifeless.
pañca—Five.
pañca mahābhuta—The five elemental essences of all matter.
pañca varṇa—Five colors.
pañcōpacāra—The offering of flowers, food, incense, light, and betel.
pandaṃ—Torches, flares.
paṇduru—Coin offerings.
päṅgiri—Sour smell/citrus.
päṅgiri kōtu atta—Lime branches.
päṇi—Treacle from the *kitul* palm.
pāramitā—The glorious deeds/spiritual reflections of events in the Buddha's previous births.
paramparāva—Lineage.
paramgi—Foreigner.
pasgōrasa—Five flavors of the cow.
pätali giniam—Burning copper foil shaped like a human to cause furious and maddening fever.
pätīma—Active wishing for the goals of Buddhist virtue.
pēna—Fortune-tellers.
piḷikul—Loathsome.
piḷiveḷa—Ordering.
pilluva—Sending an animal as an instrument of destruction.
pin—Meritorious action.
pirisa—Following.
pirisidu—Pure.
pirit—Protective rites.
pirivara—Retinue.
piruvata—A length of white cloth worn by exorcists.
pita—External.
pita pantiya—Gods of the outside.
polgediya—Coconut.
poloṅg telissā—Jumping viper.
poḷova—Earth.
pōruva—Bridal bower.
prāṇākṣara—Life-giving letters.
prārtanā—Active wishing. See *pätīma*.
prayōga—Practical experience.
prēta bandhana—Sorcery binding ghosts (of dead relatives) to a house.
prēta baya—Fear of ghosts.
prēta taṭṭuva—Offering basket for ghosts.
puda—Offerings.
puhul tīnduva—The ash pumpkin judgment.

puḷuṭu—Roasted grains.
pūnanūla—Sacred thread.
pūnāva—Seven-spouted pot used for cursing; also known as the "leopard pot."
punkalas—Pots with areca flowers used in rites.
puruṣa—Cosmic man.
rāja baya—Fear of power.
rājakāriya—Caste-based services performed for the king.
rākṣayā—Planetary demon.
rākṣaya baya—Fear of planetary demons.
ranvan bat—Turmeric rice.
rasa—Taste.
ratgal—Red rock.
rat-nil piliyena—Canopy of red and blue cloth
ṛṣi—Sage; holy man.
rūpa—Form.
rūpeta-rūpe—Vow made to the gods to give form for form, life for life.
śabda—Sound.
śabda pūjā—The offering of sound.
sädapalu—The matted hair of Visvakarma.
saddha—Confidence.
śakti—Potency; female principle.
sakvala—Cosmic entirety.
Salāgama—Cinnamon-peeler caste.
salita vanava—Condition of heightened excitement.
saluva—Shawl.
samādhi—Contemplation, concentration.
sambrāni—Incense.
sāmi—Shrine priest, holy man.
sändāyāma—The evening watch.
sandhisthāna—Main periods or junctures.
sandun—Incense; sandalwood.
sanni kalukumara pilluva—Sorcery with the potency of the demon of erotic and lustful obsession in his disease form.
śānti karma—Major antisorcery rites.
śantiya—See *śānti karma.*
ṣāstra kārayā—Soothsayer.
ṣāstra kāri—Female soothsayer.
satta/satya—Truth.
satyākriyā—Achieving knowledge or realizing the truth.
saudaṅ—Drumming rhythm.
set kavi—Songs and verses that protect and cool.
sīma—Ritual boundary.
sīma midula—Ritually bounded space?
sirasapāda—From head to foot.
sita pinavanava—To soothe the mind.

soḷos tīnduva—Sixteen corrective acts, sentencing or judgments.
sota (Pali)—Ear.
sparśa—Touch/feeling.
sūniyam käpakirīma—The main invocation rites which start the Suniyama.
sūniyam-kārayā—Sorcery expert.
Sūniyam puralē—Suniyam's death space.
sūnya—Void.
surala—Drumroll.
sūriya—The sun.
susumnā—Spinal column.
suvaṅda—Fragrant.
täṁbili—King coconut.
taṇhā—Desire.
taṭṭuva/taṭuva—Offering basket.
tējas—Heat.
tel—Oil.
tiṁbol—A tree with toxic fruit and thorns.
tīnduva—Sentence, judgment.
tirivāṇa/tiruvāṇa—Crystals.
tovil—Exorcism.
tovil gedara—Exorcism house.
tunbāge baṇdāras—"Officials"/demon-deities of the three divisions.
tun dōṣa—The three body humors.
ukkurassa/ugurassa—A fruit that parches the throat (*Flacourtia ramontchi*).
unā—Fever.
uturudiga—Northerly direction.
vā/vāyu—The wind element.
vacana—speech
väddas—The aboriginal population of Sri Lanka.
vaḍiga paṭuna—The farce of the Brahmins in the Suniyama.
vaha—Poison.
väl pännum—Planting poisonous creepers in the way of victims to kill, impede, or block their activities.
välvalalu—The rite of cutting the bonds of sorcery in the Suniyama.
varam—Authority from the Buddha to control demons.
varṇa—Colors.
vasa—Poison.
vasaṁgata rōga baya—Fear of infectious diseases.
vas daṇda—The demon or poison pipe.
vas dos—The evils, poisons, misfortunes arising from the action of others.
vas kavi—Cursing verses of the sorcerer.
vaṭṭiya—Basket.
vēdanā—Pain, sensation.
vedarāla—Village physician in the *ayurveda* tradition.
velaṁba—Mare.

Velaṅda—Trader caste.

vēramba vataya—Typhoon.

vī—Paddy grains.

vīdi-upata—Origin of the demon palace.

vīdiya—Demon palace in exorcisms.

vidurasna—The diamond seat.

vihāra—Buddhist temple.

vilakku—Lighted tapers.

vina—The action of bringing disaster or suffering to others.

vina karayō—Sorcery expert. *See* sūniyam-kārayā.

vina kirīma—Immoral sorcery action.

visipas gäba—Twenty-five places for offerings.

yāgapati—Sacrificer.

yāgaya—Sacrifice.

yahanāva—Bed.

yak berē—Long, cylindrical drum.

yakināran—Demon lemon (*Atlantia zeylanica*).

yakku—Demons.

yakśa senādhipati—General of the demon army.

yak tovil—Demon exorcisms.

yakuma—Ceremonies to overcome demon attack.

yak-vīdiya—The main building of ritual orientation in exorcism.

yantra—Powerful diagrams.

yodun—The distance of four *gavva*s or sixteen miles.

Index

Abercrombie, N., 25
Abu-Lughod, L., 258
adura. See exorcists
AmaraSingham, L., 63
Ames, M., 90
anavina, 38, 310 n. 15
anger: reextension to world, 238, 252; as purgation, 252
apparatus of capture, 255, 283; government inquiries as, 286; shrines as, 283; Suniyama as, 281–82
aravali kapima, 148–49
Ardener, E., 18
atamagala (atamangala), 84, 90, 92, 117, 118, 125, 188, 198, 205–6, 213, 216; destruction of, 173–74; and house, 136; and *kapala kuduva* 315 n. 10; site of nonviolence, 213; structure of, 98–99; yantra, 99, 100
aturaya. See patient
Azande sorcery, 1, 3, 237, 265, 266, 267, 323 n. 2

Bachelard, G., 231
bali tovil, 88
bandara gods, 32–33, 51–52, 58, 59; duality of, 32, 58; and nationalism, 305 n. 4; regional variation, 305 n. 5; as symbolic types, 308 n.9; *tunbage,* 312 n. 30
Bandaranaike, S.W.R.D., 29; as divinity, 306 n. 2

Barnett, L. D., 80, 317 n. 7, 318 n. 16
Bereva, 90, 107; Suniyama practice, 88–89, 91, 103. *See also* exorcists
Bhadrakali, 33, 49, 51
Bloch, Marc, 317 n. 2
Bloch, Maurice, 25 ,187, 188, 208; rebounding violence, 216; and ritual violence, 210–19
bodhisattva, 92, 206
body: generation of consciousness, meaning, 166, 177; gift of, 200; and mental projection, 119–20; and mind unity, 223; perceptual, 2, 157–59, 227–28, 258–60; and power, 264; rebirth from, 169–70
Bond, G., 90
Bourdieu, P., 20, 136, 177, 203; on practice, 325 n. 14
Boyd, J. W., 314 n. 14
Brentano, F., 305
Brow, James, 309 n. 10

cakra, 142–43
chedana vidiya, 121, 198; as total act of sorcery cutting, 177
Clastres, P. 277–78
Clifford, J., 11
Codere, H., 315 n. 1
Cohn, N., 17
Comaroff, Jean, 11
Comaroff, John, 11

comedy: and consciousness, 161–67; in
dance, 122–23; power and, 164
consciousness, 222–25; as action, activity,
44, 168, 170; chained, 168, 231–32;
and objectification in comedy, 161–
67; focus of, 149–51; and fullness of
Being, 152, 259–60; and healing, 119;
as in-the-world, 224; perception
against, 226–28, 230; and sight, 157–
58; and sorcery, 44, 163, 165, 171,
175, 184, 267; speech and, 161, 162,
164
Coyne, R., 327 n. 60
Crick, M., 18–19
curses, 242, 246–47, 248, 251; of Kuveni,
35, 41, 63–65, 312 n. 2
—events of: Babynona, 249–50, 255;
Kamalawati, 250–51; Milinona, 251–2;
Maginona, 253–54; Premawati, 254–5

dakum (Skt. *darsana*), 128–30
Damasio, Antonio R., 222–23
dance: of *aduras*, 121–23; dress, 120–21;
of Guardian Gods, 125–30; sexuality
of, 122
De Heusch, L., 187, 189, 200, 211
Deleuze, G., 25, 180, 255; difference and
repetition, 57, 273, 311 n. 28; war machine and state, 273–87
Derrida, J., 203, 204, 205, 206
De Silva, K. M., 64, 320 n. 23
deterritorialization, 281, 285–86; anti-
Tamil riots as, 290, 291; by JVP, 292–
94; moral, 217; by Oddisa, 79–80; pilgrimage as, 217
Detienne, Marcel, 189, 211
Devadatta, 192
Devereux, G., 15
Devol Deviyo, 51, 58, 83, 115, 243, 307
n. 5
devol maduva, 83
disti, 111, 112
dividos, 35
doratu panima, 134–35
Douglas, M., 19, 20–21, 123, 237, 262;
grid/group, 271; on witchcraft and sorcery, 306 n. 5
dream, 2; of death, 235; as demonstrating
embodiment of consciousness, 232; and

imagination, 231, 232; sorcery, 227,
229, 232
Dreyfus, H. L., 305
Dufrenne, M., 231
Dumont, Louis, 11, 203, 273
Durkheim, Emile, 9, 10, 187, 188, 215,
216, 222, 237
Dutthagamani, Prince, 51, 168, 291, 307
n. 4

emotion: as cognition, 258; exorcist view
of, 223–24
ethnic conflict, ethnicity, 29, 164, 287,
289–92, 296; as sacrificial crisis, 217
Evans-Pritchard, E. E., 3, 9, 12, 13, 14,
19, 190, 237, 265, 278
evil: sorcery as, 314 n. 14; three poisons
or evils, 310 n. 13
Euripides, 6
exorcists, 47, 96, 107; distinct practice of,
48, 53–55; as ritual embodiment of
Oddisa/Suniyam, 137–38; as Suniyama
experts, 87–88, 91

Favret-Saada, Jeanne, 194
fear: and anxiety, 235–38; closure of,
232–33, 236; imaginary of, 226–28; paralysis of, 236; types of, 324 n. 51
feud, and sorcery, 41
Feyerabend, P., 10
Foucault, M., 232
Frazer, James, 9, 10, 211, 305 n. 2

Gale Bandara, 32, 51
gammaduva, 83, 129
gaze, 128–30, 157, 166, 227, 245
Geiger, W., 209 n. 11
Geertz, C., 26, 180, 285
Gellner, E., 10
ghosts. See *preta*
gift: constraint of, 202; and cosmic differentiation, 200–201; destruction of interest in, 199–200, 204, 205; givenness,
spirit of, 199, 203, 205, 265; madness
of, 206; temporality of, 201, 202; yield
of, 204
Girard, René, 94; sacrifice and violence,
210–19
gire (areca cutter), origin of, 322 n. 33

Gluckman, Max, 16, 19, 213, 225, 281
Godakumbura, Charles, 31, 63
Goldman, I., 315 n. 1
Gombrich, Richard, 18, 27, 36, 45, 52, 57, 74, 90, 92, 136, 266, 286
Grathoff, R., 308 n. 9
Goudriaan, T., 320 n. 24
Guardian Gods, 122; invocation, 108; dance of, 125–30
Guattari, Felix, 180; war machine and state, 273–87
Guha, Ranajit, 256

habitus, 237; *atamagala* as, 136; of gift, 200
Hall, Harrison, 196
Handelman, Don, 35, 178, on ritual modeling, 326 n. 59
Harris, M., 17
Harrison, S., 209
hatadiya, 87, 92, 103, 111, 113, 130; and Buddhist doctrine, 322 n. 37; and gift, 203–4; as intentionality, 195–97; rites of, 131–56; and offerings, 322 n. 38; and Sinhala letters, 144; and tantra, 320 n. 24
Hatha Yoga, 142
Heidegger, Martin, 177, 195, 196, 198, 205
Hobbes, Thomas, 203, 212, 222, 278, 279
Hocart, A. M., 213
Holt, J. C., 64, 307 n. 6, 308 n. 10, 317 n. 2, 320 n. 23
Horton, R., 25, 225
Hoskins, J., 211
Humphrey, C., 178
huniyam, 27, 45; derivation of, 36–37, 308 n. 10, 309 n 11. *See also* Suniyam
Husserl, Edmund, 4, 195–96, 197, 226; on intentionality, 305 n. 1

idea: embedded in practice, 107, 198; nondualism of Ideal/Real, 66
ideology, and ontology, 288–89
imaginary: as constitutive, 197, 234, 329 n. 5; dynamics of, 229–33; and fear generation, 227, 236; Sartre on, 231–32; of sorcery, 268–69

IMF (International Monetary Fund), 29; as war machine, 286
Indra. *See* Sakra
intentionality: Azande witchcraft as, 1, 12; defined, 4–5, 33 n. 7, 194–95, 252–53; and gift, 200–201; *kula* as, 5, 265; *hatadiya* and, 149–56, 195–97; paradox of, 264; power as, 264; snake as, 140–41; and sociality, 73; transformational moment of, 152–53, 157; Transgressive force of, 78–79; Vasavarti as destructive force of, 73
iri, 140, 217; symbolism of, 143, 320 n. 27
Isvara, 135. *See also* Siva

Jiggins, J., 308 n. 8
Jujaka, 136, 138, 319 n. 18
JVP (Janatha Vimukthi Peramuna), 29, 289; organization of, 292–93; rebellion, 29–30, 215, 253–55, 287, 292–97; becoming-state, 294; as war machine, 293–94

Kabalava shrine, 39
kahadiyara, origin of, 116
kaksaputa yantraya, 99, 316 n. 12
Kali, 111. *See also* Bhadrakali
Kalu Yaka, 223
Kandiah, Thiru, on *kaduva*, 324 n. 47
Kapferer, Bruce, 11, 18, 29, 32, 44, 64, 80, 83, 104, 122, 123, 125, 201, 212, 214, 215, 248, 253, 278, 287, 289, 291, 294
kapuma, 88, 228, 237, 248, 252; *pita pantiya kapuma*, 328 n. 3; and Suniyama, 94–95
kapurala, deity priest, 47, 246–47; as embodying potency, 48–50, 52
Kataragama, 45, 49, 51, 125, 126; dance of, 128
Kemper, Steven, 288
Kersenboom, Saskia, xv, xvii, 142, 143
kingship, alienation of, 31
Knauft, Bruce, 16
kodivina: definition, 36; derivation, 37–38
Koestenbaum, P., 305
Kohomba Kankariya, 31

Kristeva, Julia, 247
kula, 3–6, 7, 265
Kuveni, 6, 41, 308 n. 10; curse of, 63–64, 65; historical import, 64–65; myth of, 31, 35, 63, 64, 276; songs of, 115; as war machine, 276

Laidlaw, James, 178
Lévi-Strauss, Claude, 178, 187, 203, 206, 300
Lewis, Oscar, 16
Lienhardt, G., 190
Loka Uppattiya, 67–69; analysis of, 69–74
Loy, David, 205

magicality, 2, 33; of gift, 203, 307 n. 7
Maha Brahma, 90, 142, 153
Maha Kala Naga, 263, 319 n. 22; and lotus steps, 142; and Oddisa, 79, 147–48
Mahasammata, King, 40, 83, 99, 104, 188; becoming-war machine, 276; and Hegel, 314 n. 14; myth of, 67–69; myth in history, 63, 65; myth relation to Vijaya/Kuveni, 65–66; and potent love, 313 n. 5; and power of Vasavarti, 72, 263, 268
Mahasammata palace, 66, 84, 86, 90, 112, 194; destruction of, 86, 173–74, 199; making of, 97–98; as temple, 156
Mahasona, 380 n. 10; as Suniyam army commander, 241
Malalgoda, K., 90
Malaraja Bandara, 58
Mangara, 313 n. 9
Malinowski, B., 3, 4, 5, 8, 12, 265, 303
Manikpala, Queen, 61, 81, 83, 99, 104, 153, 268; myth, 67–69; myth analysis, 70–74; and *mottakkili,* 117; song of, 133–34; sorcery victim as, 113, 116
Marcus, G., 11
Marwick, Max, 16, 17
Marx, Karl, 57, 203, 300
Mauss, Marcel, 3, 10, 198, 211, 264; on gift, 24–25, 187, 203, 265; sacred/profane, 187–188, 215; on sacrifice, 186–89
maya, 231
Medea, 6, 306 n. 3

Merleau-Ponty, Maurice, 177; and knowing body, 259–60
Mihikata (Polova Mahi Kantava, Bumi Devi), 132, 134, 153
mimetic desire, 211
Mimica, Jadran, 209, 313 n. 4; on imagination, 329 n. 5
mind: body balance and, 120, 222; and body dualism, 222–23, 328 n. 1; irreducible to body, 222–24. *See also* consciousness
Mitchell, J. C., 16
Moore, M., 253
mottakkili, 116–18, 172, 174; in Pattini rite, 116, 174
myth, as open to meaning, nonrepresentational, 62
Munn, N., 4, 8

nanumura, 114–16; origin of, 115; as sorcery antidote, 171–72, 311 n. 19
Nash, J., 21
Natha, 45, 125, 126, 318 n. 14; dance of, 128; significance of, 126–27
nationalism: regionalism and, 331 n. 18; ritualization and, 292; sacrificial violence and, 210–19; and sorcery gods, 307 n. 4; and Suniyama, 91, 92; as war machine and state, 290–91
Nevill, Hugh, 64, 87; on crown origin, 324 n. 5; on *dalumura,* 321 n. 29; on Rahu myth, 321 n. 31
nicakula tinduva, 323 n. 44
Nietzsche, F., 57; and *ressentiment,* 271
nomad, nomadology. *See* war machine
nonviolence, 213, 215; of Suniyama, 191, 209–10; of Suniyama victim, 208–9

Obeyesekere, Gananath, 15, 18, 27, 29, 43, 45, 52, 74, 83, 90, 92, 104, 109, 116, 169, 266, 286; on *bandara* gods, 32, 307 n. 6, 312 n. 30; on Devol Deviyo, 320 n. 27; on *huniyam* derivation, 36; on *mottakkili,* 117; and rise of Suniyam, 57–58
obscenity, as nonambiguous, 123
Oddi Kumara. *See* Oddisa
Oddi Raja. *See* Oddisa
Oddisa, 31, 61, 69, 74, 78–80, 132–49

passim, 153, 207; dancers as, 120–24, 128; derivation of, 313 n. 6; as first exorcist, 88, 113; and Maha Kela Naga, 79, 147–48; myth, 31, 74–77; ritual metamorphosis into Suniyam, 121, 155, 172; as sacrificer, 318 n. 12; song of, 155; as Suniyam god, 58; as tantra master, 142; turban, 117; in *vadiga patuna,* 158, 165; as war machine, 281

Panduvas, King, 63, 64, 66
Parkes, Graham, 205
Parkin, D., 18
patient, in Suniyama: entry to *atamagala,* 153–54; as Mahasammata, 171; as Manikpala, 113, 117; orientation and seating of, 112, 149–50, 196; as sacrificer, 174–76; potency within *atamagala,* 205–6
Pattini, 32, 45, 49, 51, 83, 104, 124, 169; and Devol Deviyo, 320 n. 27; forms of, 318 n. 11; and *mottakkili,* 116–17, 317 n. 9, 318 n. 10
perception, sorcery and, 44, 310 n. 13
Phussadeva, 307 n. 4
pilluva, 38, 118, 310 n. 16
power: ambiguity of, 28, 34, 262–63, 264; Buddhist emphasis on, 270–71; dynamics of, 34–35, 78–79, 273–82; Hydra of, 272; knowledge and, 89–92; intangibility of, 269, 270; metaphors of, 31, 35, 78; sorcery as primordial, 262; Suniyam as secular, 28, 33; of victim, 192–93, 206
practice, 289, 302; logic of, 325 n. 54; and meaning, 177; originating force of, 178, 179; Suniyama as structure of, 176–77, 198
preta, 109, 110–11; removal of, 123–24
puhul tinduva, 174–75
punava, 63–64

Rahu, 70, 316 n. 13, 319 n. 21, 321 n. 31
Rahula, Walpola, 322 n. 37
rajakariya, 64
Rajjaruvo Bandara, 32, 51, 243, 307 n. 4
Rappaport, Roy, 178
Rawson, P., 197

Redfield, Robert, 16
relativism, 11, 12, 302
repetition: as continual ritual origination, 178; as differentiation, 57, 286, 311 n. 28
reterritorialization, 281–82, 291
Ricoeur, P., 196
riots, anti-Tamil, 18, 29, 290; exorcism metaphor of, 287–89, 290
Riri Yaka, 104, 227
ritual: as determinate and nonrepresentational, 179–80; dualist, triadic models of, 188; as logic of practice, 323 n. 54; virtuality of, 180
Roberts, M., 64, 90, 308 n. 8
Rosaldo, R., 11
Rosaldo, Shelley, 258

Sacrifice: in *atamagala,* 152, 154; exorcist sacrificer into sacrificial victim, 138, 174–76; of hare, 146–47; and intentionality, 191–98; and nationalism, 214–18; Oddisa as sacrificer, 79, 314 n. 12; scapegoat in, 211, 212, 213, 218; theories of, 187–90; as total act, 189–90; violence and, 175, 190–91, 210–20
Saez, N., 193
Sahlins, Marshall, 203, 204, 213
Sakra, 111, 119
sakti, 112, 261
Saman, 125, 126; dance of, 128
Sandakindiru Jataka, 153
Sanni Yaka (Maha Kola Sanniya), 79, 80, 109–10, 114, 119; and Oddisa, 317 n. 5
Sarachchandra, E. R., 31
Sardan, J-P., 9
Sangren, P. S., 11
Sartre, Jean-Paul, 2, 196, 231–33; on magicality, 307 n. 7
Sasa Jataka, 146–47
sastra karaya, 47, 50, 228, 253; biography of, 48–50; case of, 30; practice of, 48–49, 53–54, 55; state, becoming-war machine, 294–97; as bounding power, 280
Scarry, E., 192–93
Scott, David, 288, 310 n. 14, 314 n. 14
Scott, James, 256

Searle, John, 198
Seligmann, C. G., 308 n. 10
Seneviratne, H. L., 114
Silva, S., 91
Singer, M. R., 308 n. 8
sirasapada, 118, 119, 120
situational analysis, xiv–xv, 19–20
Siva (Isvara), 11, 112, 118, 135, 319 n. 20
sociality, 1, 185, 186; and consciousness, 161–62, 188, 194, 259–60; of *kula,* 5, 6; and power, 269; reciprocity as, 203
society, as copy, 197
solos tinduva, 104
song: of Betel origin, 146–47; Buddha qualities in, 151–52; corrective, instructional import of, 114–15; healing properties of, 119; of Kuveni, 115; of lime origin, 147–48; of Manikpala/Mahasammata love, 133–34; of Oddisa/Suniyam, 134; sorcery symptoms in, 145–46, 151–52
sorcery: anthropology and, 8–21, 299–300; amorality of, 80; bond of, 311 n. 20; and class forces, 249, 255–57, 266–67; as closed and open belief, 234; divination of, 228; fear and, 235–38; and feud, 41; imaginary of, 268–69; immorality of, 45, 46, 175–76, 263; origin of, 67–69; paralysis, 167–68; and torture, 192–94; types of, 38–39, 143, 145, 268; as war machine, 285, 286, 290
sorcery shrines: as apparatus of capture, 255, 283; chthonic nature of, 241, 242; disgust in, 242–43, 247, 331 n. 17; marginality of, 239
—locations of: Bhadrakali (Modera), 244, 245, 248, 330 n. 15; Rajjaruvo Bandara (Gatabaruya, Morawaka), 243; Devol Deviyo (Sinigama), 243; Suniyama (Kabalava), 240; Suniyam (Lunava, Moratuwa), 241, 242; Suniyam (Dematagoda, Maligawatta), 240–41, 242, 248, 253–54; Gale Bandara (Kurunegala), 242–43, 330 n. 12
sorcery victims, 106–7, 201–2, 282–83; Simon, 41–42; Kumudu, 42–43; Premawati, 43, 45; Siyadoris, 226–35, 236, 237; Jeanette, 236; Nandawati, 236–37

Southwold, M., 314 n. 14
Spencer, Jonathan, 288
state, becoming-war machine, 294–95
Stirrat, R. L., 308 n. 8
Suniyam: as *bandara* category, 32, 58–59; colonial emergence of, 28; duality of, 27, 34, 262, 275; image, 27, 31, 103, 173; metamorphosis of, 281; and modern state, 33–35, 308 n. 8; Mulu, 52, 58; potencies of, 28, 30–31, 33–34; shrines of, 51–52, 57, 312 n. 29; urban formation of, 57–60; as war machine, 265–66
Suniyama rite; and Buddhist revitalization, 90, 91, 93; as corrective rite, 114–15; decision for, 94–96, 106; *hatadiya* rites in, 131–56; and intentionality, 187; and *kapuma,* 94; nonviolence of, 186, 209, 215; performance preparation and layout, 96–104; potlatch, total prestation, 86, 199–206; region of, 87–88; and social class, 91–92, 130, 282
—watches: evening, 108–25; midnight, 131–56; morning, 156–71; midday, 171–77
—Suniyam Purale, 100, 110, 111, 112; yantra of, 101
symbolic types, 35, 308 n. 9

Tambiah, S. J., 8, 9, 285; on medieval kingship, 312 n. 2
Tamil Tigers (LTTE), 43, 287, 289
Tanivale Bandara, 32, 51, 307 n. 4
tantra, 142–43, 197, 313 n. 5, 319 n. 23
Taussig, M., xiv, 13, 21
terror: dynamics of, 287; as spectacle, 294–95
Thompson, E. P., 256
tunbage gods, 58, 312 n. 30
Turner, V. W., 8, 16, 19, 118, 188, 211
Tylor, E. B., 10

Vadda, and sorcery, 308–9 n. 10
vadiga patuna, 156, 157, 158–67, 198, 212, 290
Valeri, V., 187, 211, 213
valvalalu tinduva, 167–71, 198, 202; as rebirth, 170, 183; self-closure of, 233

Van Gennep, A., 188, 211
Van der Veer, P., 217
Vasavarti Maraya, 40, 99, 192, 208, 225, 229, 238, 263; destructive intentionality of, 73, 121, 133, 153, 192; as Mahasammata, 281; myth, 68–69
Vata Kumara, 318 n. 16
Vessamuni, 122, 125–26
Vernant, J-P., 189, 211
Vessantara, Prince, 119, 136–37, 204
Vijaya, Prince, 41; historical effects on use, 64–65; myth, 31, 35, 63, 64, 168, 276, 291; song of, 115; as war machine, 276
violence: bureaucratic, 294, 296; as differentiation, 207–8; metaphors of, 289, 291, 296–97; as rupture, 140, 190–91, 208–9; sacrifice and, 190–91; of war machine/state, 293–95
Virilio, P., 280
virtuality: and computer virtual reality, 181; ritual as, 179, 180

Vishnu, 45, 69, 80, 125, 126, 137; dance of, 127–28; song for, 127

war machine: dynamics of, 273–76; JVP as, 292–94; metamorphosis of, 280; missionization, pilgrimage as, 217; Oddisa as, 79, 281
Weiner, A., 4
Williams, F. E., 17
Willis, R., 17
Wilson, B., 14
Wilson, J., 29
Winch, P., 13
Wirz, P., 74, 80, 104, 125, 141, 310 n. 16, 322 n. 32, 330 n. 12
World Bank, 29; as war machine, 286

Yasawati, 244
Yawudagiri, Queen, 75–76, 77, 169, 229, 263

Zvelebil, Kamil, 142